Tribunal Practice and Procedure

Kandace Bond Wileman

Rochelle Ivri

Liz Nastasi

Deborah Pressman

emond ▪ Toronto, Canada ▪ 2018

Emond Montgomery Publications Limited
60 Shaftesbury Avenue
Toronto ON M4T 1A3
http://www.emond.ca/highered

Printed in Canada.

We acknowledge the financial support of the Government of Canada. Canada

Vice president, publishing: Anthony Rezek
Publisher: Lindsay Sutherland
Director, development and production: Kelly Dickson
Developmental editor: Darryl Kamo
Production supervisor: Laura Bast
Copy editor: Dawn Hunter
Permissions editor: Alison Lloyd-Baker
Typesetter: Kathy Kaulbach
Proofreader: Judy Hemming
Indexer: Michael Bunn
Cover image: Sergye Nivens/Shutterstock

Library and Archives Canada Cataloguing in Publication

Bond Wileman, Kandace, author
Tribunal practice and procedure / Kandace Bond Wileman, Rochelle Ivri, Liz Nastasi, Deborah Pressman.

Includes index.
ISBN 978-1-77255-249-2 (softcover)

1. Administrative procedure—Ontario—Handbooks, manuals, etc. 2. Administrative courts—Ontario—Handbooks, manuals, etc. 3. Handbooks and manuals. I. Ivri, Rochelle, author II. Nastasi, Liz, author III. Pressman, Deborah, author IV. Title.

KEO891.B55 2018 342.713'0664 C2017-907315-X
KF5417.B55 2018

I, wholeheartedly and with extreme gratitude, dedicate this book to my family. Without their support and sacrifice, it simply could not have been written. To my husband, Luke, and three sons, two of whom were born during this writing process, thank you for your understanding and love.

—KBW

I would like to dedicate this book to my heavenly Father and to my family. Without them, I would not have been able to fulfill this undertaking. Your words and actions of support are immensely appreciated. To my husband, Eldean, and our four children, thank you for your love, encouragement, understanding, and, most of all, your hugs.

—RI

To Alex, Bella, and Alanna.

—LN

To Rachel (Yaya) Kishinevski, my mother.

—DP

BRIEF CONTENTS

Detailed Contents vii
Preface xv
Acknowledgments xix
About the Authors xxi

1 Understanding the Tribunal Landscape 1
2 Human Rights Tribunal of Ontario 27
3 Ontario Landlord and Tenant Board 49
4 Social Benefits Tribunal 69
5 Criminal Injuries Compensation Board 99
6 Local Planning Appeal Tribunal 115
7 Assessment Review Board 135
8 The Licence Appeal Tribunal and Automobile Accident Benefits Service 157
9 Ontario Labour Relations Board 189
10 Workplace Safety and Insurance Board/Workplace Safety and Insurance Appeal Tribunal 229
11 Law Society Tribunal 255
12 Canadian Human Rights Tribunal 277
13 Social Security Tribunal 295
14 Immigration and Refugee Board 317

Glossary 349
Index 359
Credits 369

DETAILED CONTENTS

Brief Contents v
Detailed Contents vii
Preface xv
Acknowledgments xix
About the Authors xxi

1 Understanding the Tribunal Landscape

Overview and History 2
Ontario 7
- Clusters: The New Approach 7
- Independence and Accountability in Non-Clustered Tribunals 11
- Transparency Concerns in Ontario Tribunals 13
- Statutory Powers Procedure Act 13
- Appointments 15
- The Adjudicator's Role 15

Federal 17
- Federal Governance and Accountability 18
- Appointments 18

Conclusion 19
Case Law 20
Key Legislation 24
Key Terms 25
Review Questions 25

2 Human Rights Tribunal of Ontario

Overview and History 28
Legislation and Regulations 34
Application Process 37
Hearing Process 40
- Mediation 40
- Preliminary Hearings 41

Decisions, Reconsideration, and Appeals 42

Case Law 44
Key Legislation 46
Key Terms 47
Review Questions 47
Scenario 48

3 Ontario Landlord and Tenant Board

Overview and History 50
Legislation and Regulations 52
Application Process 53
Hearing Process 61
Decisions, Reconsideration/Review, Enforcement, and Appeals 62
Case Law 64
Key Legislation 66
Key Terms 67
Review Questions 67
Scenario 68

4 Social Benefits Tribunal

Overview and History 70
Legislation and Regulations 70
- Ontario Works Act, 1997 and Regulations 70
- Ontario Disability Support Program Act, 1997 and Regulations 71

Tranchemontagne 73
Rules of Procedure and Practice Directions 76
Application Process 78
- Ontario Works 78
- Ontario Disability Support Program 78

Overpayments 79
Director's Decisions, Internal Reviews, and Appeals to the Tribunal 79
Hearing Process 80
- Written Submissions 82
- Oral Hearings 82

Decisions, Reconsiderations, and Appeals 83
- Forms 83

Case Law 91
Key Legislation 96
Key Terms 97
Review Questions 97
Scenarios 98

5 Criminal Injuries Compensation Board

Overview and History 100
Legislation and Regulations 100
Application Process 104
Hearing Process 105
Decisions, Reconsiderations, and Appeals 106
Other Notable Rules of Procedure 106
Case Law 107
Key Legislation 111
Key Terms 112
Review Questions 112
Scenarios 113

6 Local Planning Appeal Tribunal

History and Overview 116
Legislation and Regulations 120
Application Process 123
Expropriation Matters 126
Hearing Process 127
Decisions, Reconsideration, and Appeals 129
Case Law 130
Key Legislation 132
Key Terms 133
Review Questions 133
Scenario 134

7 Assessment Review Board

Overview and History 136
Legislation and Regulations 137
Application Process 142
Assessment Appeals 143
Tax Appeals 143
Hearing Process 145
General Proceedings 145
Summary Proceedings 146
Adjournments and Mandatory Meetings 146
Streaming 147
Settlement Conferences 148
Mediation 149

Decisions, Reconsiderations, and Appeals 150
Case Law 151
Key Legislation 152
Key Terms 154
Review Questions 155
Scenarios 156

8 The Licence Appeal Tribunal and Automobile Accident Benefits Service

Overview 158
  Licence Appeal Tribunal General 158
LAT AABS 158
  What Types of Benefits Are Available? 159
Legislation 161
  The Insurance Act 161
  The SABS—Statutory Accident Benefits Schedule 161
  LAT Common Rules of Practice and Procedure 162
Superintendent's and Commissioner's Guidelines—Auto Insurance SABs 163
Decisions and Case Law 163
The AABS Dispute Resolution Process 164
  Filing an AABS Application 164
  Two-Year Limitation Period 164
  Filing an AABS Response 166
  Preliminary Issues 166
  The Case Conference 167
  Disclosure 169
  How Do I Ask for an Adjournment? (Rule 16) 170
  Withdrawing an Application 170
  What Is a Motion? 171
  The Hearing 171
  Expert Witnesses 174
  Costs 175
  After the Hearing 176
  Orders 176
  After the Decision: What If My Client Did Not Get the Remedy He or She Was Seeking at the Hearing? 176
Case Law 179
  Limitation Periods 179
  Limitation Defences and Section 7 of the LAT Act 179
  Technical Non-Compliance 180
  Section 55 Defences 180

Definition of "Insured Person" 181
Exclusion Defences 181
Repayment 181
The Minor Injury Guideline 181
Chronic Pain and the Minor Injury Guideline 182
IRB Disability Test—Post 104 weeks 182
NEB Disability Test 183
Reasonable and Necessary Test 183
Interest 184
Section 10 Ontario Regulation 664 184
Key Legislation 185
Key Terms 186
Review Questions 186
Scenario 1 187
Scenario 2 188
Scenario 3 188

9 Ontario Labour Relations Board

Overview and History 190
Legislation and Regulations 193
Application Process 198
Hearing Process 201
Decisions, Reconsiderations, Appeals 203
Case Law 204
Key Legislation 207
Key Terms 208
Review Questions 208
Scenarios 209

10 Workplace Safety and Insurance Board/Workplace Safety and Insurance Appeal Tribunal

Overview and History 230
Authority and Jurisdiction of the WSIB 231
Who Is Covered Under the WSIA? 231
Administration and Adjudication by WSIB 232
Appealing a WSIB Decision 233

The Workplace Safety and Insurance Appeals Tribunal 234
Legislation, Regulations, and Other Sources Relevant to WSIB and WSIAT 235
The Right to Sue 235
The Legislative Frameworks and Recent Amendment 236
Relevant Sources 236
Disputes at WSIB and WSIAT 237
Appearing Before the Workplace Safety and Insurance Appeals Tribunal 241
Starting the Appeal 241
Confirmation of Appeal 241
Mediation 242
Pre-Hearing 243
Hearing 243
Expert Evidence 244
Decisions, Reconsideration, and Judicial Review 244
Decisions 244
Reconsideration 244
Judicial Review 246
Case Law 247
Key Legislation 251
Key Terms 252
Review Questions 252
Scenario 1 253
Scenario 2 253
Scenario 3 253

11 Law Society Tribunal

Overview and History 256
Legislation and Regulations 258
The Hearing Division 259
The Appeal Division 260
Application Process: Hearing Division 265
Hearing Process: Hearing Division 267
Decisions, Reconsiderations, and Appeals 270
Case Law 273
Key Legislation 274
Key Terms 275
Review Questions 275
Scenarios 276

12 Canadian Human Rights Tribunal

Overview and History 278
Legislation and Regulations 280
Initiating an Application 283
Mediation/Mediation-Adjudication 284
The Hearing Process 286
Decision, Reconsideration, and Appeals 287
Case Law 288
Key Legislation 291
Key Terms 292
Review Questions 292
Scenario 293

13 Social Security Tribunal

Overview and History 296
Legislation and Regulations 300
Application Process 305
Decisions and Appeals 310
Case Law 311
Key Legislation 314
Key Terms 315
Review Questions 315
Scenarios 316

14 Immigration and Refugee Board

Overview and History 318
Legislation and Regulations 320
Initiating an Application 324
  Immigration Division 324
  Refugee Protection Division 327
Hearing Process 330
  Immigration Division 330
  Refugee Protection Division 333
Decisions 334
  Admissibility Hearings 334
  Detention Reviews 334
  Refugee Protection Division 334

Appeals 335
  Immigration Appeal Division 335
  Refugee Appeal Division 337
  Federal Court 340
Case Law 342
Key Legislation 344
Key Terms 345
Review Questions 345
Scenarios 346

Glossary 349
Index 359
Credits 369

PREFACE

We are thrilled that you have chosen *Tribunal Practice and Procedure* as a resource for your learning. This text is not only the first edition but also the first of its kind to be available to the current population of teachers, students, and new practitioners. Our team is excited about advancing the teaching of tribunal practice, filling the void in learning resources, and equipping you with the materials that will help you navigate and succeed in your course and in your early practice.

After you have read the introduction, each chapter will then give you an in-depth look into a specific tribunal, covering its history, applicable legislation, procedural rules, hearing and appeal processes, and key cases. Additional tools at the end of each chapter, including case scenarios and review questions, will further your learning. At the time of writing, all cases and legislation was current. Please check the text's website for any updates at www.emond.ca/tribunal.

To our student audience, we hope that you enjoy your course and embrace this text as a hands-on guide to the tribunals that you are most likely to encounter in your practice. To our teaching audience, we trust that this resource will provide you with dynamic material to meet your students' needs as you equip them for life in practice. To our professional audience, we hope that this resource serves as a practical, on-the-go guide to assist you in your practice.

Chapter 1 introduces to the tribunal landscape. It lays the framework for understanding why tribunals were created and covers such topics as the appointment of tribunal members, key rules of practice for paralegals, tribunal clusters, independence and accountability, the *Statutory Powers Procedure Act*, and the distinctions between provincial or territorial and federal jurisdictions.

Chapter 2 covers the Human Rights Tribunal of Ontario and introduces the evolution of human rights in Ontario. Readers gain a firm understanding of the Ontario *Human Rights Code*, prohibited grounds, and prohibited areas of discrimination. Along with learning about the initiating, hearing, and appeal processes, readers are introduced to cases that are important to human rights law in Ontario. Notably, a review of *OHRC v Ontario (Community Safety and Correctional Services)* is included, which provides guidance on the use of segregation in Ontario detention centres as it relates to mental health.

Chapter 3 discusses Ontario's Landlord and Tenant Board. In addition to providing historical context for the landlord and tenant law in Ontario, this chapter takes a broad view of the entire process before the board. Charts outlining the notice type, notice periods, termination dates, and fees are provided for ease of reference.

Chapter 4 focuses on the Social Benefits Tribunal, walking readers through both the Ontario Works and Ontario Disability Support Program regimes, which underpin this tribunal's jurisdiction. A focused study of the *Tranchemontagne* case, a precedent-setting decision that highlights the intricacies of the appeal processes, is included.

The often overlooked Criminal Injuries Compensation Board is highlighted in Chapter 5. It is one of the eight tribunals that make up the Social Justice Tribunals Ontario cluster. Key cases, such as *Pitters* and *Sweet* are discussed in the wider context of the book.

Chapter 6 begins with a historical framework for one of Ontario's newest tribunals, the Local Planning Appeal Tribunal (LPAT). The LPAT was created in 2018 to replace the Ontario Municipal Board (OMB) and its work relates to everyday life in many ways. This chapter will increase readers' awareness of those ways. Readers are provided with information regarding process and procedure before the LPAT, and case law from the OMB is provided to enhance learning and understanding.

Chapter 7 covers the Assessment Review Board (ARB), which is a part of the Environmental Land Tribunals Ontario cluster. The ARB operates with more complexity than some of the other tribunals discussed in this text. Readers gain a greater understanding of the property tax assessment process, identify the legislation that empowers the ARB, and learn how the Rules of Practice and Procedure streamline hearings into different types of appeals and hearing processes.

Chapter 8 focuses on the Licence Appeal Tribunal—specifically disputes under the Statutory Accident Benefits Schedule (SABS). These disputes were previously under the jurisdiction of the Financial Services Commission of Ontario. As of April 1, 2016, the Licence Appeal Tribunal assumed responsibility for accident benefits disputes under the SABS. This chapter sets out the key practices, procedure, and case law to assist readers in appearing before the tribunal.

The Ontario Labour Relations Board (OLRB) and its effective functioning pattern as a tribunal with deep historical roots is the focus of Chapter 9. Numerous changes to its structure and legislative regime over its many years of existence have matured the OLRB into a high-functioning board.

Chapter 10 covers workplace safety and insurance in Ontario, commonly referred to as "workers' compensation," and disputes under the *Workplace Safety and Insurance Act, 1997* (WSIA) before the Workplace and Insurance Board (WSIB) and Workplace Safety and Insurance Appeals Tribunal (WSIAT). The chapter sets out the key benefits available to injured workers and the legislation, procedures, and case law that will assist paralegals appearing before the tribunal.

Chapter 11 discusses the practices of the Law Society Tribunal (LST), which hears professional regulation matters pertaining to lawyers and paralegals in Ontario. The LST, though created by the Law Society of Ontario (LSO), is independent from it. In addition to revealing the legislative framework and rules that govern the hearing process, this chapter looks at the types of proceedings before the LSO.

Chapter 12 is about the Canadian Human Rights Tribunal (CHRT) and is the first of three chapters that discuss federal tribunals. The chapter provides insight into what distinguishes the CHRT from its provincial or territorial counterparts and identifies the jurisdiction of the CHRT and federal prohibited grounds of discrimination. This chapter discusses Jordan's Principle and the 2016 CHRT decision relating to the discriminatory child welfare practices of the federal government in Canada's Indigenous communities.

Chapter 13 highlights one prominent federal tribunal, the Social Security Tribunal, that has undergone recent restructuring. It discusses the birth of the tribunal, including some early challenges and plans for development. Distinctions between the different divisions and sections are covered.

Chapter 14 is a robust chapter that covers all four tribunals under the Immigration and Refugee Board (IRB). Immigration is a popular area of practice, and this chapter clarifies the scope of practice for paralegals. It also provides a discussion of the *Singh* case and explains how the IRB came to be. The jurisdiction of the board, the refugee determination process, and the grounds of inadmissibility are laid out. Additionally, this chapter discusses *Brown v Canada*, a 2017 decision related to the constitutionality of the current immigration detention scheme.

ACKNOWLEDGMENTS

The authors and publisher would like to thank the reviewers of the text: Barbara Moyle, Fleming College; Kent Peel, Seneca College; Tamra Alexander, Algonquin College; Jasteena Dhillon, Humber College; and Emma Sims, Fanshawe College.

From Kandace
I wish to express a huge thanks to Lindsay Sutherland, who united us all and kept us on track throughout this process. Special thanks also to Darryl Kamo, Dawn Hunter, and Laura Bast for your editorial and production skills, which helped propel this project into its final version. This entire work could not have been completed without the commitment and passion of my co-authors Rochelle Ivri, Deborah Pressman, and Liz Nastasi, whose countless hours of work have helped make this textbook a top-quality resource. I want to thank all of my colleagues at Durham College, who have given their utmost support and encouragement. Finally, I can't give enough gratitude to the family and friends who have walked with me throughout this process, cheering me on and propelling me forward.

From Rochelle
I would like to thank Lindsay Sutherland, who provided such wonderful compassion and support during a very difficult time and who kept us all on course to produce an awesome and much-needed resource. I would be remiss to not also sincerely thank Darryl Kamo, Dawn Hunter, and Laura Bast who worked patiently and tirelessly to bring this project come to fruition. To my co-authors, Kandace, Deborah, and Liz, I cannot thank you enough for being on this journey with me. We have done something amazing and I am truly grateful to have been a part of it! I want to also send sincere thanks to my colleagues and students at Mohawk College whose support, enthusiasm, and encouragement through this entire process has not gone unnoticed. Last, but certainly not the least, I would like to express my heartfelt gratitude to my family and friends who were literally the wind beneath my wings. Thank you for keeping me focused, encouraged, and steadfast.

From Deborah
Thank you to Stephanie Abrahams for her help with Chapter 10.

ABOUT THE AUTHORS

Kandace Bond Wileman

Kandace Bond Wileman (BA Hons, LLB) is a professor with the School of Justice and Emergency Services at Durham College, where she teaches tribunal practice and procedure, legal research and writing, introduction to the Canadian legal system, contracts, and torts. Before teaching, Kandace practised poverty law at legal clinics in Ontario and acted as review counsel for a student legal clinic established at Durham College, the first of its kind in the province. Kandace obtained her undergraduate degree in political science and history (double major) from York University. She studied law both abroad (University of Leicester, UK) and at home in Ontario (University of Windsor). Kandace's passions are advocating for the underdog, the advancement of mental health awareness, and Canadian legal history and constitutional studies.

Rochelle Ivri

Rochelle Ivri (BA Hons) is a Canadian citizenship judge and paralegal professor with the McKeil School of Business at Mohawk College where she teaches administrative law, tribunal practice and procedure, residential and landlord tenant law, and alternative dispute resolution. Rochelle is a paralegal and immigration consultant licensed with the Law Society of Ontario and the Immigration Consultants of Canada Regulatory Council (ICCRC). She is also a former member of the Discipline, Appeal, and Review Committee of the ICCRC and spent eight years on the Council of the College of Midwives of Ontario. Before teaching, Rochelle worked with the federal courts and Immigration and Refugee Board, and coordinated a restorative justice diversion program for the Ministry of the Attorney General. Rochelle received an undergraduate degree in criminology (with a minor in forensic anthropology) from the University of Windsor and a postgraduate certificate in alternative dispute resolution from York University. Rochelle enjoys spending time with her family and is passionate about the Charter and human rights law.

Liz Nastasi

Liz Nastasi (LLB), a graduate of Osgoode Hall Law School called to the Ontario Bar in 1996, is a lawyer, a dispute resolution practitioner, and an educator. Currently, she is counsel with the Ministry of the Attorney General at the Safety Licensing Appeals and Standards Tribunal Ontario (AABS-LAT). Previously, she was an arbitrator and the senior arbitrator with the Financial Services Commission of Ontario (FSCO) in the litigation group of the legal services branch, where she adjudicated more than 1000 disputes. Liz was a mediator with the Ontario Human Rights Commission, legal counsel with the Human Rights Tribunal of Ontario, and a volunteer mediator in the criminal courts. She is a dedicated trainer, teacher, and coach who has worked as a dispute resolution educator with York University and delivered administrative law courses at Osgoode's professional development LLM programs. Liz has taught courses in the paralegal program at George Brown College since 2010 and recently created Osgoode's first online program to help prepare foreign-trained lawyers for their certification exam. Liz's other past employment highlights include family and insurance law and time as a policy advisor at the Ministry of Housing. Her work as an immigration consultant in Korea left her with impressive karaoke skills and a love for all things spicy.

Deborah Pressman

Deborah Pressman (BA, LLB, LLM) is a lawyer, a mediator, an adjudicator, an innovative legal educator, and a consultant. She is currently counsel with the Ministry of the Attorney General, providing legal, policy, and strategic support to executive chairpersons, adjudicators, senior managers, and staff at the tribunals of the Safety, Licensing Appeals, and Standards Tribunals Ontario cluster. Previously, she was the director's delegate in the appeals unit at the Financial Services Commission of Ontario (FSCO), having begun there as a mediator in 2004, then as a senior policy analyst, and as an arbitrator, adjudicating disputes arising from Ontario's no fault accident benefits scheme. Deborah leads various training and teaching initiatives, including teaching in the paralegal program at George Brown College, being a professor of administrative law in the master's program at Osgoode Hall, acting as a lead instructor for the Certificate in Adjudication, developing remote learning courses for Osgoode and Emond Publishing, training tribunal members, and speaking on topics such mediation, ODR, active adjudication, and clear decision writing. Deborah completed her undergraduate degree in political science at York University, studied law at Osgoode Hall, was called to the bar in 2002, and acquired her LLM degree in alternative dispute resolution in 2005. When she's not working, she spends time with family and friends and a terrier named Gilly.

CHAPTER 1

Understanding the Tribunal Landscape

Overview and History 2

Ontario 7

Clusters: The New Approach 7

Independence and Accountability in Non-Clustered Tribunals 11

Transparency Concerns in Ontario Tribunals 13

Statutory Powers Procedure Act 13

Appointments 15

The Adjudicator's Role 15

Federal 17

Federal Governance and Accountability 18

Appointments 18

Conclusion 19

Case Law 20

Key Terms 25

Review Questions 25

Overview and History

So, you want to practise before a **tribunal**. Or maybe you think you do. Or perhaps you are unsure but are taking a course that requires you to understand a bit more about appearing before tribunals. Whatever has brought you to this place, we will shed some light for you on tribunal practice, both in Ontario and federally.

In the context of an old judicial system in Ontario (borrowed from the English tradition), tribunals are the new kid on the block. Granted, tribunals in Ontario have been in existence for some time, with the Ontario Municipal Board dating back to 1906.[1] But the use of tribunals as a means of rendering greater access to justice for Ontarians really exploded in the last few decades of the 20th century.

You may be asking, What is a tribunal? Perhaps you've heard the term in relation to some well-known tribunals in Ontario, such as the Human Rights Tribunal of Ontario. Perhaps you realize that they have something to do with determining legal disputes. Essentially, they are mini courts. Tribunals function in many different areas, such as assisting with municipal land planning, settling landlord and tenant disputes, or awarding compensation to individuals who have suffered an injury as the result of a violent act. Tribunals are like mini courts because they have a trier of fact (like a judge), typically called an adjudicator or a tribunal member, who makes a determination based on arguments from (usually) two opposing parties. Adjudicators are governed by the legislation that empowers them to act, which means they can do only what the enabling legislation for that tribunal gives them jurisdiction over. Certain tribunals have more than one adjudicator assigned to a case or hearing, and these are referred to as panels. Two or three panel members may be assigned to a case. Tribunals are unlike courts in that the hearings are typically not held in formal courtrooms; rather, tribunal hearings can be held in boardrooms, hotel rooms, community centres, or government offices. For this reason, along with a few others (less strict rules of evidence, increased self-representation, shorter time frames), tribunals are seen as a less rigid approach to justice and as more user-friendly.

The basic concept behind tribunals is to give individuals greater, more efficient, and more effective access to justice. Tribunal procedures can eliminate the months, and even years, people can spend in litigation. Many tribunals provide in-and-out service within a year of filing an application; a few, much

tribunal a quasi-judicial body with limited jurisdiction that determines questions of fact or law

1 Then called the Office of the Provincial Municipal Auditor; see Ontario Municipal Board, "About the OMB" (2017), online: <http://elto.gov.on.ca/omb/about-the-omb>.

less time than that; and a few, a bit more. In addition, applicants can self-represent, thereby eliminating the cost of hiring a representative for a legal proceeding. Arguably, self-representation has become more complicated in the years following the big tribunal boom in Ontario, but it is nevertheless an easier system to navigate for individuals without legal training than is the traditional court system. A recent initiative called Steps to Justice CLEO (Community Legal Education Ontario) hopes to provide greater access to justice and to empower individuals as they experience the legal system in Ontario. The program is accessed predominantly through <http://stepstojustice.ca>, which provides hands-on tools for Ontarians dealing with legal disputes in housing, employment, social assistance, and consumer law matters, among other issues. Central to our discussion in this text, the website offers guidance in matters before the Landlord and Tenant Board, the Human Rights Tribunal of Ontario, and the Social Benefits Tribunal. Forms, checklists, and even online chats are available for users to equip and prepare them for the legal road ahead. Steps to Justice has been supported by a number of partners, one being Social Justice Tribunals Ontario.

Tribunals should be staffed with adjudicative experts in the field, thereby increasing their quality of care (more discussion on appointments to come!). Individuals have enjoyed greater access to justice since tribunals entered the judicial landscape. Of course, the landscape is not perfect, but there is much to be gained by embracing tribunal practice.

The user-friendly approach to justice that tribunals offer should not translate into less procedural or legislative awareness for practitioners. Indeed, the atmosphere is more relaxed than a court-room setting, but as a representative, your reputation is just as much at stake, and your client's interests are just as integral. Therefore, you must be familiar with the procedural rules of the tribunal that you appear before, and you must be equally well-prepared with the legal knowledge required for your case. Professional responsibility should never be sacrificed, regardless of setting.

Because you are a licensee of the **Law Society of Ontario** (LSO), professional responsibility and ethics play a fundamental role in your career. Indeed, the **Rules of Conduct**[2] that apply to paralegals in Ontario are an underpinning of your entire legal practice. How you go about representing your client is birthed from your inner passion and knowledge about a particular legal subject matter. But your ethical boundaries will also set the stage for how representation

Law Society of Ontario the licensing and regulatory body in Ontario for lawyers and paralegals

Rules of Conduct mandatory ethical guidelines for licensed paralegals in Ontario

---

2 See Law Society of Ontario, *Paralegal Rules of Conduct* (1 October 2014; amendments current to 28 September 2017), online: <http://www.lsuc.on.ca/paralegal-conduct-rules>.

will play out. Ethical boundaries, including morals and values, are subjective. However, the Rules of Conduct as established by the LSO apply to all paralegal licensees, regardless of where your personal ethics lie. The Rules of Conduct establish many parameters for client representation, including the duty that you owe to your client, professionalism, and advocacy. Some key rules are listed below:

> 2.01(1) A paralegal has a duty to provide legal services and discharge all responsibilities to clients, tribunals, the public and other members of the legal professions honourably and with integrity.
>
> 2.01(3) A paralegal shall be courteous and civil, and shall act in good faith with all persons with whom he or she has dealings in the course of his or her practice.
>
> 3.01(1) A paralegal shall perform any services undertaken on a client's behalf to the standard of a competent paralegal.
>
> 3.01(2) A paralegal is required to recognize a task for which the paralegal lacks competence and the disservice that would be done to the client by undertaking that task. A paralegal shall not undertake a matter without being competent to handle it or being able to become competent without undue delay or expense to the client.
>
> 3.01(4) For the purposes of this rule, a competent paralegal is one who has and applies the relevant knowledge, skills, and attributes appropriate to each matter undertaken on behalf of a client including,
>
> (a) knowing general legal principles and procedures and the substantive law and procedures for the legal services that the paralegal provides;
>
> (b) investigating facts, identifying issues, ascertaining client objectives, considering possible options, and developing and advising clients on appropriate courses of action;
>
> (c) implementing, as each matter requires, the chosen course of action through the application of appropriate skills, including,
>
> (i) legal research,
> (ii) analysis,
> (iii) application of the law to the relevant facts,
> (iv) writing and drafting,
> (v) negotiation,
> (vi) alternative dispute resolution,
> (vii) advocacy, and
> (viii) problem-solving;
>
> (d) representing the client in a conscientious, diligent, and cost-effective manner;
>
> (e) communicating with the client at all relevant stages of a matter in a timely and effective manner;

(f) answering reasonable client requests in a timely and effective manner;

(g) ensuring that all applicable deadlines are met;

(h) managing one's practice effectively;

(i) applying intellectual capacity, judgment, and deliberation to all functions;

(j) pursuing appropriate training and development to maintain and enhance knowledge and skills;

(k) adapting to changing requirements, standards, techniques and practices; and

(l) complying in letter and in spirit with all requirements pursuant to the Law Society Act.

3.02(1) A paralegal has a duty to provide courteous, thorough and prompt service to clients. The quality of service required of a paralegal is service that is competent, timely, conscientious, diligent, efficient and civil.

3.02(2) A paralegal shall be honest and candid when advising clients.

3.02(3) A paralegal shall not undertake or provide advice with respect to a matter that is outside his or her permissible scope of practice.

3.03(1) A paralegal shall, at all times, hold in strict confidence all information concerning the business and affairs of a client acquired in the course of their professional relationship and shall not disclose any such information unless:

(a) expressly or impliedly authorized by the client;

(b) required by law or by order of a tribunal of competent jurisdiction to do so;

(c) required to provide the information to the Law Society; or

(d) otherwise permitted by this rule.

4.01(1) When acting as an advocate, the paralegal shall represent the client resolutely and honourably within the limits of the law while, at the same time, treating the tribunal and other licensees with candour, fairness, courtesy and respect.

4.02(2) This rule applies to appearances and proceedings before all tribunals in which the paralegal may appear.

4.02(5) When acting as an advocate, the paralegal shall not,

(a) abuse the process of the tribunal by instituting or prosecuting proceedings which, although legal in themselves, are clearly motivated by malice on the part of the client and are brought solely for the purpose of injuring the other party;

(b) knowingly assist or permit the client to do anything that the paralegal considers to be dishonest or dishonourable;

(c) knowingly attempt to deceive a tribunal or influence the course of justice by offering false evidence, misstating facts or law, presenting or relying upon a false or deceptive affidavit, suppressing what ought to be disclosed, or otherwise assisting in any deception, crime or illegal conduct;

(d) deliberately refrain from informing the tribunal of any binding authority that the paralegal considers to be directly on point and that has not been mentioned by an opponent;

(e) appear before a judicial officer when the paralegal, a partner of the paralegal, a paralegal employed by the paralegal firm or the client has a business or personal relationship with the officer that gives rise to, or might reasonably appear to give rise to, pressure, influence or inducement affecting the impartiality of the officer, unless all parties consent and it is in the interests of justice;

(f) knowingly assert as true, a fact when its truth cannot reasonably be supported by the evidence or as a matter of which notice may be taken by the tribunal;

(g) make suggestions to a witness recklessly or knowing them to be false;

(h) endeavour or allow anyone else to endeavour, directly or indirectly, to influence the decision or action of the tribunal or any of its officials in any case or matter by any means other than open persuasion as an advocate;

(i) knowingly misstate the contents of a document, the testimony of a witness, the substance of an argument or the provisions of a statute or like authority;

(j) knowingly permit a witness or party to be presented in a false or misleading way or to impersonate another;

(k) knowingly misrepresent the client's position in the litigation or the issues to be determined in the litigation;

(l) needlessly abuse, hector, harass or inconvenience a witness;

(m) improperly dissuade a witness from giving evidence or suggest that a witness be absent;

(n) when representing a complainant or potential complainant, attempt to gain a benefit for the complainant by threatening the laying of a criminal charge or by offering to seek or to procure the withdrawal of a criminal charge;

(o) needlessly inconvenience a witness; and

(p) appear before a court or tribunal while under the influence of alcohol or a drug.

6.01(1) A paralegal shall encourage public respect for, and try to improve, the administration of justice.

6.01(2) A paralegal shall take care not to weaken or destroy public confidence in legal institutions or authorities by making irresponsible allegations or comments particularly when commenting on judges or members of a tribunal.

> 7.01(2) A paralegal shall agree to reasonable requests concerning trial dates, adjournments, waiver of procedural formalities and similar matters that do not prejudice the rights of the client.

Of course, you will become more familiar with the Rules of Conduct as you continue in your studies and prepare for your licensing exam. And you will be well versed in them by the time you practise. But don't wait until then to get to know the rules that apply to you as a practitioner. As a student of legal studies, and future legal representative (perhaps current, if you are doing summer or placement work), you should understand the field that you are entering now; so pick up a copy of the Rules of Conduct to read. Rules that govern your ethics play a big role in this career path, and you should try to emulate the expected behaviour of a licensee while you are en route to that goal.

Ontario

Clusters: The New Approach

At the turn of the 21st century, Ontario toyed with the idea of restructuring the tribunal landscape and proposed a "super-tribunal" in the labour area.[3] Not long after the proposal, the plan was scrapped because of a lack of support.[4] In another more successful attempt to address further concerns about serving parties, the Ontario government recently introduced a new structure of tribunal clustering. Ushered in by the *Adjudicative Tribunals Accountability, Governance and Appointments Act, 2009* (ATAGAA),[5] the idea behind the scheme was to create even greater efficiency between like-minded tribunals (of sorts).

Independence

With the advent of this new scheme came concern for tribunal independence.[6] **Judicial independence** is a cornerstone of our democracy and common law legal system, and it remains one of our constitutional doctrines. Judicial independence enshrines the main aspects of security of tenure, financial security, and administrative independence.[7] The Supreme Court of Canada has stated that the principle of judicial independence is reflected in the *Canadian*

judicial independence a cornerstone of the Canadian judicial system that ensures security of tenure, financial security, and administrative independence

3 Ron Ellis, "Super Provincial Tribunals: A Radical Remedy for Canada's Rights Tribunals" (2002) 15 Can J Admin L & Prac 15.

4 *Ibid.*

5 SO 2009, c 33, Schedule 5.

6 The Ontario Bar Association (Report), "Adjudicative Tribunals Accountability, Governance and Appointments Act, 2009: Cause for Concern—The Tribunal Independence Issue" (2011) 24 Can J Admin L & Prac 225.

Charter of Rights and Freedoms[8] at section 11(d), and the *Constitution Act*,[9] sections 96-100, as well as the preamble:[10]

> Judicial independence consists essentially in the freedom "to render decisions based solely on the requirements of the law and justice" .... It requires that the judiciary be left free to act without improper "interference from any other entity" ... — i.e., that the executive and legislative branches of government not "impinge on the essential 'authority and function' ... of the court."[11]

Closely aligned to this central notion of judicial independence is tribunal independence, and the Ontario Bar Association (OBA) was quick to react to concerns stemming from the ATAGAA. The Ontario Bar Association is an independent body and the provincial chapter of the Canadian Bar Association (CBA). It is made up of voluntary membership by lawyers, judges, and students. The OBA and the CBA jointly offer professional development opportunities for paralegals and lawyers, and seek to advocate for the legal profession and facilitate law reform.[12] The OBA was not silent in its concern for the impact that the ATAGAA scheme might have on tribunal independence:

> while it is to be admired for its progressive provisions concerning the appointment and re-appointment of tribunal members, and for its creation of a number of instruments of public accountability for tribunals, it is also noteworthy for its disturbingly pervasive provisions that guarantee each line-ministry's control of "its" tribunals. These provisions cannot be reconciled with the rule-of-law principle of judicial independence and to see them now formally embedded in the Province's laws is deeply concerning.[13]

And further,

> The new Act is formally about governance and accountability of tribunals. However, since it addresses the governance and accountability of adjudicative tribunals only, it is, most importantly, about justice. And, from a justice perspective, it seems to this Association that this legislation's repudiation of

---

7 Lori Hausegger, Matthew Henninger & Troy Riddell, *Canadian Courts: Law, Politics, and Process* (Toronto: Oxford University Press, 2009) ch 6.

8 Part I of the *Constitution Act*, 1982, being Schedule B to the *Canada Act 1982* (UK), 1982, c 11.

9 *Constitution Act*, 1867 (UK), 30 & 31 Vict, c 3, reprinted in RSC 1985, Appendix II, No 5.

10 *British Columbia v Imperial Tobacco Canada Ltd*, 2005 SCC 49, [2005] 2 SCR 473.

11 *Ibid* at 45.

12 Ontario Bar Association, "Who We Are" (2017), online: <https://www.oba.org/About-US>.

13 *Supra* note 6 at preface.

> the rule-of-law principle of judicial institutional independence must not go unnoticed or unremarked.[14]

The OBA's report specifically cited concern with the ATAGAA's placement of significant control of tribunals in the hands of the overseeing minister, thus fettering the independence of the tribunal body: "Of course, adjudicative tribunals are not courts, but their principal assignment is the exercise of judicial, adjudicative functions, and the law requiring them to be independent and impartial is clear."[15] In particular, concerns were raised over the amount of ministerial control pertaining to budget control, planning and reporting, complaints procedure, and members code of conduct,[16] to name a few. Further concerns about independence were raised in that the ATAGAA's power that enabled the minister to invoke a performance review of a tribunal at any time under the supervision of any appointee, at the minister's discretion.[17] Among listing other omissions and recommendations, the report concludes with an ominous statement that the ATAGAA leaves plenty to be desired as a long-term plan for administrative justice in Ontario.[18]

The first tribunal cluster appeared in 2010 and was made up of five "linked" tribunals: Assessment Review Board, Board of Negotiation, Conservation Review Board, Environmental Review Tribunal, and Ontario Municipal Board. This monster was given the name of Environmental Land Tribunals Ontario (ELTO).[19] The ELTO cluster transformed in April 2018, and its composition is now reflective of the following boards and tribunals: Local Planning Appeal Tribunal (formerly the OMB), Mining and Lands Tribunal, Assessment Review Board, Board of Negotiation, Conservation Review Board, Environmental Review Tribunal. Another cluster of tribunals, known as the Safety Licensing Appeals and Standards Tribunals Ontario was created, joining the individual bodies of Animal Care Review Board, Fire Safety Commission, Licence Appeal Tribunal, Ontario Civilian Police Commission, and Ontario Parole Board.[20] And still a third cluster to hit Ontario was Social Justice Tribunals Ontario (SJTO) in 2011. This cluster of eight was formed by the Human Rights Tribunal of Ontario, Child and Family Services Review Board, Custody Review Board, Social Benefits Tribunal, Landlord and Tenant Board, Criminal Injuries Compensation Board, and the Ontario Special Education

---

14 *Ibid* at preface.

15 *Ibid* at para 2.

16 *Ibid* at para 3.

17 *Ibid* at para 8.

18 *Ibid* at preface.

19 Environmental Land Tribunals Ontario, "About ELTO" (2017), online: <http://elto.gov.on.ca/about-elto/>.

20 Safety Licensing Appeals and Standards Tribunal Ontario, "Homepage" (2018), online: <http://www.slasto.gov.on.ca/en/Pages/default.aspx>.

Tribunals.[21] Aside from the OBA's concerns with the original ATAGAA, the clustering efforts to date have been touted by other parties as the start of modernization success, with certain improvement in the administrative justice realm.[22] The cluster landscape has yet to hit the federal tribunal structure.

Independence in decision making is addressed by the SJTO in its mandate, mission, and values as available online.[23] This cluster pays heed to the importance of independence by ensuring that "SJTO and its constituent tribunals must be, and be seen to be, impartial and independent in their decision making functions," and "Our decisions will be based on the evidence and the applicable law, and will be supported by clear, concise and coherent reasons."[24] Similarly, the ELTO provides assurances around the same: "ELTO and its constituent tribunals must be, and be seen to be, neutral, unbiased and independent from improper influence."[25]

Accountability

Efficiency and independence are not the only pillars of serving the public. Accountability is a key feature as well. Accountability is also reflected in the clustering plan, as evidenced by the title of the legislation: *Adjudicative Tribunals Accountability, Governance and Appointments Act*. And one doesn't have to read far into the Act to find further reference to accountability. The purpose of the Act, as stated in section 1, is to "ensure that adjudicative tribunals are accountable, transparent and efficient in their operations while remaining independent in their decision-making." In fact, the term "accountability" appears no less than 31 times throughout the entire piece of legislation, in reference to various matters, including public accountability documents[26] and the requirement of tribunal ethics policies,[27] including the review and governance of such documents,[28] and member accountability.[29] The ELTO and the SJTO each have policies in place that align with the legislative requirements

21 Social Justice Tribunals Ontario, "Welcome to SJTO" (2015), online: <http://www.sjto.gov.on.ca/en>.

22 Michael Gottheil & Doug Ewart, "Lessons from ELTO: The Potential of Ontario's Clustering Model to Advance Administrative Justice" (2011) 24 Can J Admin L & Prac 161.

23 Social Justice Tribunals Ontario, "Mandate, Mission, Values" (2015), online: <http://www.sjto.gov.on.ca/en/mandate-mission-values>.

24 *Ibid.*

25 Environmental Land Tribunals Ontario, "Mandate, Mission, and Values" (2017), online: <http://elto.gov.on.ca/about-elto/mandate-mission-values>.

26 ATAGAA, ss 3-6, 8-10.

27 ATAGAA, s 6.

28 ATAGAA, s 11.

29 ATAGAA, s 7.

for such accountability measures. The SJTO includes a code of conduct for members of all of the constituent tribunals, which operates as "an important element of the accountability framework."[30] Members of SJTO tribunals are required to sign this code of conduct, which includes some key topics, such as impartiality, confidentiality, integrity, expertise and competence, collegiality, quality, timeliness, accessibility, and outside public interests. Also available on the SJTO website are the ethics plan[31] and conflict of interest rules.[32] Annual reports, business plans, memorandums of understanding, and service standards are all also publicly available online.[33] The ELTO offers similar online public viewing of these documents.[34]

Note that each of these components is required by the ATAGAA,[35] and equally with the regulations made under the Act, which provide greater specific requirements for the following: contents of ethics plans,[36] accountability document deadlines,[37] and contents of business plans.[38]

Independence and Accountability in Non-Clustered Tribunals

Independence and accountability, among other key tribunal values, obviously apply to "non-clustered" tribunals as well. These tribunals are governed by the requirements in the legislation, the overseeing ministry, and the pressing need for public satisfaction in creating and instituting such policies. The levels of transparency in their internal processes vary. For example, the Ontario Labour Relations Board provides online annual statements[39] and a host of accountability documents, such as a member accountability framework, an ethics plan, and a service standards policy.[40] The Financial Services Commission of

---

30 Social Justice Tribunals Ontario, "Code of Conduct" (August 2017), online: <http://www.sjto.gov.on.ca/documents/sjto/Code%20of%20Conduct.html>.

31 Social Justice Tribunals Ontario, "Ethics Plan" (August 2017), online: <http://www.sjto.gov.on.ca/documents/sjto/Ethics%20Plan.html>.

32 Social Justice Tribunals Ontario, "Conflict of Interest Rules" (23 July 2015), online: <http://www.sjto.gov.on.ca/documents/sjto/Conflict%20of%20Interest%20Rules.html>.

33 Social Justice Tribunals Ontario, "Reports, Plans and Standards" (2015), online: <http://www.sjto.gov.on.ca/en/reports-plans-standards>.

34 Environmental and Land Tribunals Ontario, "Accountability Documents" (2017), online: <http://elto.gov.on.ca/about-elto/accountability-documents>.

35 ATAGAA, ss 3-7, 11-13.

36 O Reg 91/11.

37 O Reg 90/11.

38 O Reg 89/11.

39 Ontario Labour Relations Board, "Publications" (2017), online: <http://www.olrb.gov.on.ca/english/Public.htm>.

Ontario provides online documents pertaining to a memorandum of understanding[41] and various other accountability documents,[42] as well as accessibility standards.[43]

To further the accountability oversight, the Ontario Ombudsman plays a key role in investigating complaints from individuals about Ontario tribunals. The Ombudsman's role is clearly defined as investigating when individuals feel they were treated unfairly by a tribunal. The power to review a tribunal's process comes from both legislation and case law, which allows the Ombudsman to make recommendations to a tribunal. Specifically, the Ombudsman can consider whether

- the decision of the tribunal is authorized by the legislation,
- the decision is based on the evidence that was before the tribunal,
- the process the tribunal followed was fair and relevant and the material issues have been addressed,
- adequate reasons have been provided for the decision, and
- whether there are any underlying systemic issues related to the decision that the Ombudsman should look at.

Ombudsman staff will try to work with administrative tribunals to resolve complaints when possible and appropriate.[44]

The legislative powers of the Ombudsman in this respect flow from the *Ombudsman Act*.[45] Various cases have also discussed this power.[46]

---

40 Ontario Labour Relations Board, "Member Accountability Framework" (February 2012), online: <http://www.olrb.gov.on.ca/english/MEMBER%20ACCOUNTABILITY.pdf>; Ontario Labour Relations Board, "Ethics Plan" (January 2013), online: <http://www.olrb.gov.on.ca/english/ETHICS%20PLAN.pdf>; Ontario Labour Relations Board, "Service Standards Policies" (December 2016), online: <http://www.olrb.gov.on.ca/english/SERVICE%20STANDARD%20POLICIES.pdf>.

41 Financial Services Commission of Ontario, "About FSCO" (7 July 2017), online: <http://www.fsco.gov.on.ca/en/About/Pages/default.aspx>.

42 *Ibid.*

43 Financial Services Commission of Ontario, "Accessibility Standards For Customer Service" (13 September 2016), online: <http://www.fsco.gov.on.ca/en/about/Pages/accessibility.aspx>.

44 Ontario Ombudsman, "Make a Complaint: Administrative Tribunals" (2017), online: <https://ombudsman.on.ca/Make-a-Complaint/Administrative-Tribunals.aspx#Authority>.

45 RSO 1990, c O.6.

46 *Ontario (Ombudsman) v Ontario (Health Disciplines Board)* (1979), 26 OR (2d) 105, 104 DLR (3d) 597; *Ontario (Ombudsman) v Ontario (Labour Relations Board)* (1986), 58 OR (2d) 225, 44 DLR (4th) 312; *Ontario (Ombudsman) v Ontario (Board of Radiological Technicians)* (1990), 72 OR (2d) 632, 68 DLR (4th) 311.

Transparency Concerns in Ontario Tribunals

In February 2017, the *Toronto Star* upped the ante when it launched a legal suit in attempts to demystify what it calls "blanket secrecy" in the Ontario tribunal system.[47] The editorial piece criticizes tribunals for lack of access to records, which it correctly states as being central to the principle of openness that is a hallmark of judicial proceedings. The *Statutory Powers Procedure Act* requires that tribunals in Ontario hold open hearings (there are exceptions written into enabling pieces of legislation for some tribunals), and while this editorial recognizes the ability of journalists to attend those hearings, it argues that the public "right to know" is impaired by inaccessible tribunal records that flow from these open proceedings. In the lead-up to the legal challenge, the *Star* tested nine Ontario tribunals. The findings were widely diverse. The Environmental Review Tribunal and the Ontario Energy Board came out as top performers. The processes at the Ontario Workplace Safety and Insurance Appeals Tribunal and the Ontario Civilian Police Commission proved to be more difficult, with access to basic records denied (although access was later granted by the Police Commission). Sometimes, the record-accessing process can begin through filing a freedom of information request, but it can be lengthy, costly, and even still, denied.[48]

The legal challenge was launched with a Notice of Application filed at the Superior Court of Justice on February 6, 2017.[49] The *Toronto Star* is seeking a number of declarations by the court: (a) that the *Freedom of Information and Protection of Privacy Act*[50] is unconstitutional and an infringement on section 2(b) of the *Canadian Charter of Rights and Freedom*, and of no force or effects; (b) that the "open court" principle applies to tribunal practices and proceedings; (c) that restrictions to tribunal records should only be allowed in accordance with established common law tests; and (d) other grounds that the court sees fit.[51]

Statutory Powers Procedure Act

A central piece of legislation in Ontario that governs tribunal procedure is the *Statutory Powers Procedure Act* (SPPA).[52] The SPPA was originally enacted in 1971 but has undergone numerous changes since then, with the most recent

47 "Star Launches Legal Challenge to End Secrecy in Ontario Tribunals," Editorial, *Toronto Star* (7 February 2017), online: <https://www.thestar.com/news/canada/2017/02/07/star-launches-legal-challenge-to-end-secrecy-in-ontario-tribunals.html>.

48 *Ibid.*

49 *Ibid.*

50 RSO 1990, c F.31.

51 *Supra* note 47.

52 RSO 1990, c S.22.

amendment in 2015.[53] The Act's birth followed the McRuer Report[54] after a police scandal left a gaping need for administrative reform.[55] The SPPA's purposefulness has been questioned over the years;[56] nevertheless, it has offered important basic procedural requirements that govern the Ontario tribunal setting. At its core is the purpose of ensuring "the just, most expeditious and cost-effective determination of every proceeding on its merits."[57] Some features of the SPPA include the empowerment of tribunals to make their own rules[58] and specifically offers guidance with respect to

- creating alternative dispute mechanisms (s 4.8);
- allowing for written or electronic hearings, in addition to or in conjunction with oral hearings (ss 5.1, 5.2, and 5.2.1);
- awarding costs (s 17.1), which is rarely used;[59]
- providing opportunity for parties to examine witnesses (s 10.1);
- determining the admissibility and inadmissibility of evidence (s 15; here, note that the strict rules of evidence are relaxed for administrative tribunal matters and that the SPPA allows for the inclusion of hearsay evidence);
- protecting the rights of witnesses to representation (s 11);
- summoning witnesses (s 12);
- referring a case to Divisional Court for a contempt hearing (s 13); and
- creating rules to review its own decisions (s 21.2).

In addition, the SPPA mandates that tribunals

- provide "reasonable notice of hearings" to parties (s 6),
- hold public hearings (with specified exceptions; s 9),
- protect witnesses against self-incrimination (s 14),
- provide written reasons for a decision (s 17), and
- create a record of proceeding for each matter (s 20).

---

53 The amendment, found in the *Protection of Public Participation Act*, 2015, SO 2015, c 23, s 5, pertains to written cost submissions.

54 Internet Archive, *Report of the Royal Commission on an Inquiry into Civil Rights in Ontario* (1968), online: <https://archive.org/stream/royalcommissioni01onta/royalcommissioni01onta_djvu.txt>.

55 Hudson Janisch, "Something Old, Something New" (2010) 23 Can J Admin L & Prac 219.

56 David J Mullan, "Willis v McRuer: A Long-Overdue Replay with the Possibility of a Penalty Shoot-Out" (2005) 55 U Toronto LJ 535.

57 SPPA, s 2.

58 SPPA, s 25.1.

59 Robert A Centa & Denise Cooney, "Trends in Costs Awards Before Administrative Tribunals" (2014) 27 Can J Admin L & Prac 259.

Section 32 of the SPPA also explicitly states its own prevalence when found in conflict with another act (unless expressly stated in another act or regulation). In addition to the groundwork laid in the SPPA, each tribunal has its own piece(s) of enabling legislation, which works in conjunction with the SPPA. These separate pieces of legislation will be addressed in each of the specific tribunal chapters throughout this text.

Appointments

Now that we have an idea about where tribunals came from and how they are organized, it would be useful to know how adjudicators are appointed.

The ATAGAA and its regulation[60] outlines a process for tribunal appointments that is competitive and merit-based, taking into consideration "experience, knowledge or training" and aptitude for both "impartial adjudication" and application of "alternative adjudicative practices."[61] However, the merit-based approach as recommended in section 14 of the Act need not apply in circumstances of re-appointment, cross-appointment, or the appointing of a previous candidate, or for other reasons.[62] The process must also be made public, and any appointment or re-appointment must be recommended by the chair,[63] although the requirement for the Chair to approve re-appointments may be waived.[64] In Ontario, tribunal position openings and appointments are posted on the Public Appointments Secretariat website.[65]

The Adjudicator's Role

Once appointed to a tribunal, adjudicators (or tribunal members) obviously play a key role in the resolution of the dispute and the manner in which access to justice truly plays out. Adjudicators should be fair, impartial, patient, respectful, and efficient, all the while equipped with good organization, training, leadership, writing, and listening skills (to name just a few). Other key indicators of a good adjudicator are avoiding conflicts of interest, being on time for hearings, writing understandable decisions backed with solid reasons, and knowing their place in the hearing. On this final point, typically, adjudicators are assumed to take a passive role in our adversarial system of justice. In an adversarial system of justice, two parties present their cases to an independent trier of fact (adjudicator), who evaluates the evidence and makes a decision on the matter, predominantly based on what has been presented to

60 O Reg 88/11

61 ATAGAA, s 14.

62 *Ibid.*

63 *Ibid.*

64 *Ibid.*

65 Public Appointments Secretariat, "Welcome to the Public Appointments Secretariat Web Site!" (7 July 2015), online: <https://www.pas.gov.on.ca/scripts/en/Home.asp>.

the trier of fact. Typically, this means a less active role for the adjudicator in hearings. However, it is becoming more commonplace for adjudicators to take more active roles in the hearing room. This role is usually taken when there are self-represented parties who stand to benefit from additional guidance around the procedure and process of the tribunal.

> The comparatively relaxed rules of procedure of many tribunals, combined with increasing numbers of self-represented participants in proceedings before them, have made tribunals ripe grounds for the adoption of active adjudication—that is, methods of adjudication that see the decision-maker take on a more interventionist role in proceedings than the traditional model of a passive judge.[66]

The line of appropriateness in active adjudication can become blurred as tribunal members become increasingly comfortable in the role or, in particular, when tribunal policies pave the way for an active role by the adjudicator. For example, the Social Benefits Tribunal Rules of Procedure empower the tribunal to question witnesses;[67] this is typically a role left to the parties' representatives through direct and cross examinations, although certainly adjudicators and judges alike have for some time interceded to question for clarification. Likewise, the Ontario Municipal Board is vested with the power through summons to examine witnesses for inquiries.[68] And the *Human Rights Code* takes this approach one step further by empowering the Human Rights Tribunal of Ontario to conduct direct or cross-examination of witnesses in a hearing.[69]

The quotation above is taken from an article ("Sketching the Boundaries") that outlines the boundaries of active adjudication and points to the distinctions between where active adjudication may be more (intervening in questioning to focus issues) or less (professional disciplinary matters).[70] One example from the article highlights a Divisional Court decision[71] on appeal from the Landlord and Tenant Board, where the court found the adjudicator, while taking an active role in questioning witnesses, was respectful to both parties, giving "due concern to the procedural rights of both" and ensuring

---

66 Brian Gover & Pam Hrick, "Sketching the Boundaries: Active Adjudication As a Means of Enhancing Fairness in Tribunal Proceedings" in *The Six-Minute Administrative Lawyer* 2017 (Toronto: Law Society of Ontario, 2017) at 3-1.

67 Social Justice Tribunals Ontario, "Social Benefits Tribunal: Rules and Practice Directions" (2015), r 1.5(i), online: <http://www.sjto.gov.on.ca/sbt/rules-of-procedure>.

68 *Ontario Municipal Board Act*, RSO 1990, c O.28, s 53(c).

69 RSO 1990, c H.19, s 43(3)(c).

70 Gover & Hrick, *supra* note 66 at 3-5.

71 *Paul v Wollen*, 2015 ONSC 1458.

"both sides had the opportunity to give evidence and test the evidence of the other party."[72]

The conclusion of the article offers general guidelines for appropriate active adjudication, including asking open-ended questions, not those typical of cross-examination; intervening at the end of a witness's testimony and for clarification; fairly questioning all parties' witnesses; seeking consent from the parties to engage in active adjudication; and ensuring parties understand the expected hearing procedure.[73]

Federal

The distinction between federal and provincial tribunals exists because of the structure of our government and constitution. As you are likely aware from previous courses and readings, our *Constitution Act* creates a federal government that is empowered to legislate over specific matters as a result of section 91. Conversely, our provincial governments have jurisdiction over matters of a "local and private nature," as outlined in section 92. For example, the federal government legislates over Employment Insurance, and, consequently, a federal tribunal governs legal issues arising out of that program, known as the Social Security Tribunal. In the same way, the provincial governments have jurisdiction over landlord and tenant matters, hence the Ontario Landlord and Tenant Board. Of course, some tribunals appear to be in both realms, such as the Canadian Human Rights Tribunal and the Human Rights Tribunal of Ontario. These are separate entities and exist in both jurisdictions because both the federal and the provincial governments can legislate over these matters to the extent that a matter falls within their jurisdiction. For example, the Canadian Human Rights Tribunal is the place to go if you feel that you have been discriminated against at work and at your employer is a federal agency (e.g., Canada Post). However, if your employer is not a federal agency (e.g., the local barber shop where you are employed), then you would pursue your discrimination matter before the Human Rights Tribunal of Ontario. Understanding the difference in jurisdiction as a result of sections 91 and 92 of the *Constitution Act* are key to grasping the federal and provincial tribunal divide. However, even with these jurisdictional differences, there is essentially no difference in how tribunals operate or how you should prepare strictly based on the provincial/federal distinctions. Each tribunal, whether federal or provincial, can have very different operating structures and result in different approaches to preparation for the practitioner.

72 *Ibid* at 6.

73 Gover & Hrick, *supra* note 66 at 3-12, 3-13.

Federal Governance and Accountability

Federally, some measure of tribunal independence and accountability is enabled by the *Administrative Tribunals Support Service of Canada Act*.[74] This Act creates its namesake, the Administrative Tribunals Support Service of Canada, and establishes the office of the chief administrator, whose role is to support federal administrative tribunals in their duties and functions. Independence of tribunals is recognized in the confirmation of responsibilities of each tribunal's chairperson. The service supports eleven federal tribunals, some of which you will read about later in this book. Two of those federal tribunals, the Canadian Human Rights Tribunal and the Social Security Tribunal, provide for some measure of accountability within their internal structure. This is evidenced by the documents available on their respective websites. For example, the Social Security Tribunal provides a code of conduct for members and service standards. The Canadian Human Rights Tribunal (CHRT) website is less forthcoming with similar information; however, a contact is provided for the offices of the CHRT.

Appointments

Federal tribunal appointments are handled through the **Governor-in-Council**. Essentially this means that the power lies with the Governor General of Canada but through the advice of the federal cabinet. Each federal tribunal has an appointment process that is outlined in its enabling legislation. For example, the Canadian Human Rights Tribunal, which is governed by the *Canadian Human Rights Act* (CHRA)[75] has 15 members to be appointed through the Governor-in-Council.[76] Similarly, the Immigration and Refugee Board takes its appointment process through the *Immigration and Refugee Protection Act*.[77] Available openings and appointments for federal tribunals are made public on the Government of Canada website, on the Federal Organizations page.[78]

Governor-in-Council the Governor General acting on the advice of the federal cabinet members

74 SC 2014, c 20.

75 RSC 1985, c H-6.

76 CHRA, s 48.1.

77 SC 2001 c 27, s 153(1).

78 Government of Canada, "Governor in Council Appointments" (22 May 2015), online: <https://www.appointments-nominations.gc.ca/prsnt.asp?menu=2&page=gicIntro&lang=eng>.

The Auditor General investigated the appointment process of various federal agencies, and specifically the Immigration and Refugee Board (IRB) in 2009 and in 2016, and furnished a report[79] about the federal tribunal appointment process. This report cited concerns with candidate criteria and reference checking, as well as a lack of performance-based insights during the appointment process.[80] In response to recommendations made to the House of Commons, and despite a plan proposed by the Standing Committee on Public Accounts (for guidance and transparency in the appointment process, among other things), the Public Appointments Committee was never created because of a 2012 budget claw-back.[81] The most recent audit considered 24 tribunals, with a specific focus on 4, the IRB being one of those.[82] The report concluded that there was still a lack of transparency about the tribunal appointment process.[83]

Conclusion

Now that you have had a taste of the tribunal landscape, the following chapters will guide you through the more intricate procedures of some key tribunals, both federally and in Ontario. The focus of the remaining chapters is on those tribunals that dominate paralegal practice. Each chapter will offer relevant case law, as well as scenarios and review questions based on the content. As you step into the tribunal realm, you will find many colleagues (and perhaps some challenging foes!) navigating the same tribunal path with you; some will be paralegals and some will be lawyers. The uniting factor is that all will be licensees of the Law Society of Ontario, with some exceptions. The *Law Society Act*[84] and By-Law 4[85] of the Law Society of Ontario allow for exceptions to representation without a licence, some of those being a law student, a paralegal student, or a family member or friend who acts without payment. Hopefully, as a student, you will have the chance for entry-level representation through a placement or volunteer opportunity, while working under the supervision of a licensee. To help you prepare, start navigating the chapters that lie ahead!

---

79 Office of the Auditor General of Canada, *Report 3—The Governor in Council Appointment Process in Administrative Tribunals* (Ottawa: Office of the Auditor General of Canada, 2016), online: <http://www.oag-bvg.gc.ca/internet/English/parl_oag_201602_03_e_41247.html>.

80 *Ibid*, s 3.4.

81 *Ibid*, ss 3.5-3.7.

82 *Ibid*, s 3.

83 *Ibid*, ss 3.13 and 3.29-3.30.

84 RSO 1990, c L.8.

85 Law Society of Ontario, By-Law 4—Licensing (amendments current to 23 February 2017), online: <https://www.lsuc.on.ca/uploadedFiles/By-Law-4-Licensing-01-15-18.pdf>.

Case Law

Clustering is essentially a non-issue in case law to date. The following decisions have to a minimal extent touched upon clustering.

Concerned Citizens Committee of Tyendinaga and Environs v Ontario (Ministry of the Environment and Climate Change), [2017] OERTD No 35

This was a motion before the Environmental Review Tribunal to review a Costs Dismissal Order in a previous related decision. The Mohawks of the Bay of Quinte (MQB) were seeking the motion to review the Costs Dismissal Order that dismissed their claim for costs against Waste Management of Canada Corporation (WM). After the main hearing in the matter, MQB brought an application for costs of $445,037.19 against WM for unreasonable behaviour. The costs they sought were to cover legal expenses and expert evidence.[86] MQB requested that a panel be appointed, pursuant to the Rules of Practice, to hold a hearing to review the Costs Dismissal Order.[87] MQB believed that the approach used by the panel in dismissing the application for costs was contradictory to other similar decisions arising out of the Ontario Municipal Board, a related tribunal under the cluster of Environment and Land Tribunals Ontario. Furthermore, MQB stated that rules of natural justice should uphold a like-minded approach between the Environmental Review Tribunal and the Ontario Municipal Board in their approaches to applications for cost.[88] Similar procedural rules around costs between the two tribunals and their relationship in the same cluster is not sufficient to give a legal basis for the two to be harmonized.[89] Ultimately, MQB's motion was dismissed.[90]

Grand River Conservation Authority v Ontario (Minister of Transportation), [2010] OMBD No 326

This decision stemmed from the Ontario Municipal Board (OMB), in which Grand River Conservation Authority made a request for compensation from the Ministry of Transportation, pursuant to section 26 of the *Expropriations Act*.[91] Among the issues to be determined around compensation "are the highest and best use of the lands, with the Claimant claiming valuation based upon commercial highest and best uses valuation, and the Crown at agricultural zoning and conservation use valuation."[92] Central to Grand River's arguments around compensation was the use of an expert witness, LJ Simmons. The

86 *Concerned Citizens Committee of Tyendinaga and Environs v Ontario (Ministry of the Environment and Climate Change)*, [2017] OERTD No 35 at 4.

87 *Ibid* at 5.

88 *Ibid* at 19.

89 *Ibid* at 96.

90 *Ibid* at 119.

91 *Expropriations Act*, RSO 1990, c E.26.

92 *Grand River Conservation Authority v Ontario (Minister of Transportation)*, [2010] OMBD No 326 at 1.

Crown brought a motion to block Simmons as a witness based on a reasonable apprehension of bias because of Simmons's role as a board member on the Board of Negotiation (BON) and the legislative structural changes that had clustered the BON with the OMB under the Environmental Land Tribunals Ontario.

> Based upon allegations of close professional, structural and communication linkages between the BON and the OMB, the Crown argues a reasonable apprehension on bias arises such that the testimony of Simmons would not result in an impartial decision by the OMB. It is the position of the Crown, based upon annual public reports to the Attorney General and the Legislature, that the OMB and BON share administrative space and staff, that both Boards have the same Chair, and that both Boards are linked in budgeting. The Crown's position is that both Boards deal with the same subject matter—compensation claims under the Ontario Expropriations Act—and that Members of both Boards may commingle.[93]

The OMB found a central link between the two boards based on a uniting process under the *Expropriations Act*.[94] Though Simmons had no involvement with the case while carrying out his duties at the BON, his involvement as witness before the OMB could lead to a reasonable apprehension of bias.[95] The Crown's motion was allowed and Simmons was barred from testifying.[96]

Landlord and Tenant Board (Re), [2011] OIPC No 133

This is a decision from the Ontario Information and Privacy Commissioner ordering the Landlord and Tenant Board (LTB) to release a report (Order PO-3002). The appellant, who had previously received weekly reports from the LTB about upcoming hearings, was told he was no longer able to do so because of the new electronic database used as a result of clustering. The new case management system was a feature of the Social Justice Tribunals cluster and did not allow for the same weekly report to be generated.[97] The LTB offered to manually generate the report for a fee of $16,349, with 50% payment upfront. The appellant disagreed and filed an appeal with the Information and Privacy Commissioner.[98] The issue is "whether the Board can charge the proposed fee for recreating a previously existing reporting function, as a consequence of adopting a new case management system." The LTB's fee choice was based on

---

93 *Ibid* at 4.
94 *Ibid* at 31.
95 *Ibid* at 32.
96 *Ibid* at 36.
97 Order PO-3002; *Landlord and Tenant Board*, [2011] OIPC No 133 at 2.
98 Ibid at 3-4.

an Ontario Court of Appeal decision, also pertaining to records release but in the context of Toronto Police Services (TPS).[99] The Privacy Commissioner distinguished the facts of this case from the TPS decision but also highlighted the discussion centred on the importance of public access to records.[100] The order required the LTB to remove the fee and provide the records, stating that it should take a "proactive approach to access and should build access directly into new systems as they are developed"[101] and that by failing to do so, particularly where there is a history of access to records, the LTB has breached important access principles.[102]

The following cases highlight tribunal independence, efficiency, and accountability.

Ontario Hydro, [1997] OLRD No 3578

Ontario Hydro is an Ontario Labour Relations Board decision centred on an allegation of bias and impartiality against the adjudicator. The applicants to an unfair labour practice complaint requested the board member recuse himself for what appeared to be a reasonable apprehension of bias because of his adjudication with other similar related matters.[103] The board member dismissed the applicants request on the basis that he was not bias, did not show any bias, or could not point to any objective reasonable apprehension of bias on his part.[104] In his reasons, the member differentiated between independence of the tribunal and impartiality of a member. The former is the "institutional structure on adjudicative freedom" and the latter is the "characteristics of attitudes of the individual adjudicator."[105] While both are inextricably linked to the justice system and the duty of fairness,[106] and the focus of this decision is on impartiality of the adjudicator, the reasons offer guidance on the concept of tribunal independence.

> To summarize, the "independence" of a tribunal refers to its status and freedom to make decisions free from the influence or interference of the government, whether it be by the influence or interference of the persons who appoint tribunal members or otherwise, or that of others.[107]

---

99 *Toronto Police Services Board v Information and Privacy Commissioner*, 2009 ONCA 20.

100 Order PO-3002, *supra* note 97 at 9-10.

101 *Ibid* at 11.

102 *Ibid* at 12.

103 *Ontario Hydro*, [1997] OLRD No 3578 at 3.

104 *Ibid* at 12.

105 *Ibid* at 37.

106 *Ibid*.

107 *Ibid* at 39.

Stepanova v Ontario (Human Rights Tribunal), 2017 ONSC 2386

Stepanova is a complex decision with many facets; ultimately, this brief reflection discusses only the tribunal's focus on accountability. The Divisional Court is considering this judicial review of a Human Rights Tribunal of Ontario decision, which dismissed Stepanova's complaint citing discrimination against the City of Windsor and the Ministry of Community and Social Services through the results of an unfavourable Social Benefit's Tribunal decision. Among a discussion of many factors, including standard of review,[108] judicial immunity,[109] and reasonable accommodation of disability,[110] the court considered Stepanova's request for anonymization of the proceedings and the tribunal member's order against the request.

> The "open court" principle is a cornerstone of accountability for decision-making tribunals and courts. Publication of legal decisions is but one way in which the court system is open. It is true that there is greater scope for the protection of the vulnerable through sealing orders or anonymity orders, a development that is reflected in the HRTO's general approach to this issue. But it remains the general principle that the open court principle trumps desires for anonymity, and to overcome this general principle, a litigant must do more than make bald assertions about potential risks for them if their names are published.[111]

Decision No 650/98I, 1998 CanLII 15958, [1998] OWSIATD No 990

In this Ontario Workplace Safety and Insurance Appeals Tribunal decision, the issue raised pertains to the consolidation of similar matters into one hearing. A widow was appealing a decision about a Non-Economic Loss (NEL) award, and her representative found a very similar case that was also under appeal. The representative requested that the matters be consolidated into one hearing or, at the very least, be heard one immediately after the other by the same panel: "from the perspective of Tribunal efficiency, it made sense for both cases to go forward at the same time and to be decided in a consistent manner."[112] The employer of the widow's deceased husband did not agree with the consolidation of appeals for confidentiality reasons and because the other employer was not participating. The tribunal considered its own powers under enabling legislation, as well as those provided in the *Statutory Powers Procedure Act*, the latter of which gives specific power to combine proceedings involving "the same or similar questions of fact, law or policy."[113] Because of

---

108 *Stepanova v Ontario (Human Rights Tribunal)*, 2017 ONSC 2386 at 19.

109 *Ibid* at 20.

110 *Ibid* at 33.

111 *Ibid* at 36.

112 *Decision No 650/98I*, [1998] OWSIATD No 990 at 19.

113 *Ibid* at 25, citing SPPA, s 9.1(1).

the concerns around fairness and reasoning that suggested the cases were not similar enough to benefit from a consolidation, the tribunal determined that "arguments of timeliness and efficiency" were outweighed, and the matters would not be consolidated.[114] However, consecutive hearings were appropriate:

> Nor is it uncommon for the Tribunal to "batch" similar issue cases (for consecutive consideration) as a means of increasing efficiency and facilitating consistency. In our view, these are reasonable and proper aims. Administrative tribunals, in general, face increased caseloads and might be expected to be undertaking reasonable ways of increasing efficiency in order better to serve the parties and to hear appeals in a timely manner.[115]

Based on this reasoning, the two appeals were scheduled to be heard consecutively by the same panel.[116]

KEY LEGISLATION

Adjudicative Tribunals Accountability, Governance and Appointments Act, 2009
- Adjudicative Tribunals and Clusters, O Reg 126/10
- Appointment to Adjudicative Tribunals, O Reg 88/11
- Business Plan—Contents, O Reg 89/11
- Deadlines re Accountability Documents, O Reg 90/11
- Ethics Plan—Contents, O Reg 91/11

Law Society of Ontario Paralegal Rules of Conduct

Statutory Powers Procedure Act

114 *Ibid* at 29.

115 *Ibid* at 31.

116 *Ibid* at 35.

KEY TERMS

Governor-in-Council, 18
judicial independence, 7
Law Society of Ontario, 3
Rules of Conduct, 3
tribunal, 2

REVIEW QUESTIONS

1. How does the Steps to Justice program enhance access to justice?
2. Tribunals are often viewed as being more efficient and relaxed than the standard court room. How does this translate into your practice as a paralegal before tribunals?
3. Choose one of the rules of conduct highlighted in this chapter and explain, in your own words, what it will mean for you as a practitioner.
4. What was the purpose of the *Adjudicative Tribunals Accountability, Governance and Appointments Act, 2009?*
5. Why is independence of a tribunal important?
6. Why is tribunal accountability important?
7. What is the significance of the *Statutory Powers Procedure Act* in Ontario?
8. What powers does the Ombudsman have when investigating a complaint about a tribunal?
9. What is the Administrative Tribunals Support Service of Canada?
10. How are federal tribunal appointments made?

CHAPTER 2

Human Rights Tribunal of Ontario

Overview and History 28

Legislation and Regulations 34

Application Process 37

Hearing Process 40

Mediation 40

Preliminary Hearings 41

Decisions, Reconsideration, and Appeals 42

Case Law 44

Key Terms 47

Review Questions 47

Scenario 48

The ownership of no lot on plan 269 and no part of the low-water beach aforesaid shall be transferred by sale, inheritance, gift or otherwise, nor rented, licensed to or occupied by any person wholly or partly of negro, Asiatic, coloured or Semitic blood, nor to any person less than four generations removed from that part of Europe lying south of latitude 55 degrees and east of longitude 15 degrees east. Relationship, however slight, to any class forbidden as aforesaid shall be deemed sufficient to prevent transfer to or occupancy by such persons of northern and western European descent, other than Jews. Such restrictions, however, shall not apply to bona fide domestic servants of actual occupants during the period of such occupancy. The land and premises herein described shall never be sold, assigned, transferred, leased, rented or in any manner whatsoever alienated to and shall never be occupied or used in any manner whatsoever by any person of the Jewish, Hebrew, Semitic, negro or coloured race or blood, it being the intention and purpose of the Grantor, to restrict the ownership, use, occupation and enjoyment of the said recreational development, including the lands and premises herein described to persons of the white or Caucasian race not excluded by this clause. No building shall be erected on these premises except by a person who is a white Gentile, nor by any limited company whose shareholders are not entirely Gentile.

—Dominique Clément 2014 (excerpt from a restrictive covenant that was signed by residents in an ontario neighbourhood in 1951)[1]

Overview and History

The Human Rights Tribunal of Ontario (HRTO) was established in 1962 under the Ontario *Human Rights Code* (the Code).[2] The role of the HRTO is to adjudicate matters and provide remedy to those who have faced **discrimination** or **harassment** in connection with the 5 social areas and 17 **prohibited grounds** identified in the Code. As a paralegal, you will be assisting and supporting clients through very difficult situations. Most hearings before the HRTO are related to discrimination in employment, with over 70 percent of cases falling under that social area.[3] A further 25 percent of matters are associated with discrimination in relation to goods, services, and facilities.[4] Additionally, matters related to discrimination because of a **disability** are commonly heard before the HRTO, with over 50 percent of its hearings associated with this discriminatory ground.[5] Other common grounds are **reprisal** for making a complaint (over 20 percent), **race** (20 percent), and **sex**,

1 Dominique Clément, *Equality Deferred: Sex Discrimination and British Columbia's Human Rights State, 1953-84* (Vancouver: UBC Press/Osgoode Society for Canadian Legal History, 2014), online: <http://historyofrights.ca/history/human-rights-law/>.

2 RSO 1990, c H.19.

3 Social Justice Tribunals Ontario, "2015-2016 Annual Report" (2016), online: <http://www.sjto.gov.on.ca/documents/sjto/2015-16%20Annual%20Report.html#hrto6>.

4 *Ibid.*

5 *Ibid.*

pregnancy, and **sexual harassment** (20 percent).[6] It is common for applications to claim more than one discriminatory ground, so percentages will add to more than 100 percent. You should familiarize yourself with legislation relating to the social area and/or **discriminatory ground** that your client presents to you in order to provide effective and knowledgeable representation.

The journey that led to the creation of the HRTO and the corresponding Ontario Human Rights Commission (OHRC) followed a long and arduous path. In the early 1900s, the social climate in Ontario was problematic for marginalized individuals and groups. Discrimination based on **country of origin**, race, **gender**, religion, and **sexual orientation** was rampant. As illustrated in the quotation that opens this chapter, many discriminatory practices were considered normal and condoned by society. Legislation did not exist to provide protection for, and recourse to, anyone who was adversely affected by discriminatory practices. Without legislative protection and provisions, those who faced discrimination had no recourse in the courts even if there was a finding that a particular practice or process was discriminatory.

At that time, the courts upheld prevailing societal beliefs and **stereotypes** and offered no protection or remedy for those facing discrimination who had the courage and resources to pursue matters through the courts.[7] The first example of legislative protection in Ontario was an amendment to insurance laws in 1932 to address racial and religious discrimination in the insurance assessment process. This was the only protection in Ontario until the 1940s, when Ontario enacted the *Racial Discrimination Act, 1944* (RDA)[8] and amended the regulations of the *Community Halls Act*[9] in 1944. The RDA was intended to prohibit signs and publications from expressing racial or religious discrimination, and the *Community Halls Act* included a regulation that prohibited discriminatory practices in halls that received public funds.

The RDA faced intense opposition when it was introduced, and both the *Globe and Mail* and the *Financial Post* condemned the Act as an unnecessary intrusion in business.[10] Those who opposed the legislation saw it as "special treatment" for one group over another rather than recognizing the necessity for the legislation in order to achieve equity. At the time, Ontario was a hostile environment for visible minorities, and discrimination in employment was routine. It was common to screen persons out of the employment consideration process if their names or physical features identified them as unsuitable, and, if they granted an interview, employers routinely asked about race, nationality, religion, and place of birth. It was also commonplace to see

---

6 *Ibid.*

7 An example of this, despite being a Quebec case, is *Christie v The York Corporation*, [1940] SCR 139, 1939 CanLII 39.

8 SO 1944, c 51.

9 RSO 1927, c 247.

10 *Supra* note 1.

discrimination subjecting another person to differential treatment by either imposing a burden on them or denying them a privilege, benefit, or opportunity enjoyed by others because of their characteristics*

harassment "engaging in a course of comments or actions that are known, or ought reasonably to be known, to be unwelcome. It can involve words or actions that are known or should be known to be offensive, embarrassing, humiliating, demeaning or unwelcome."†

prohibited or discriminatory grounds personal characteristics outlined in the Ontario *Human Rights Code* upon which discrimination is prohibited

disability (1) a medical condition that a person has; from this perspective, disability covers a broad range and degree of conditions, some visible and some not visible; (2) a problem that occurs when people's environments are not designed to suit their abilities

reprisal actions or threats that are intended to retaliate against an individual who has exercised his or her rights under the Code or has refused to violate someone else's rights under the Code

race "There is no such thing as race—instead, it is a 'social construct.' This means that society forms ideas of race based on geographic, historical, political, economic, social and cultural factors, as well as physical traits, even though none of these can legitimately be used to classify groups of people."‡

sex a person's biological characteristics; discrimination under this Code ground is closely related to gender and includes pregnancy and breastfeeding

sexual harassment similar to harassment, sexual harassment is any conduct or commentary that is unwanted or unwelcome. Sexual harassment comes in many forms and can include:

- "sexual solicitation and advances (your teacher asks for sex in exchange for a passing grade)
- "a poisoned environment (pornographic images in the workplace)
- "gender-based harassment (targeting someone for not following sex-role stereotypes)
- "violence (if inappropriate sexual behaviour is not dealt with, it may move to more serious forms, including sexual assault and other violence)."§

---

* Ontario Human Rights Commission, "Appendix 1: Glossary of Human Rights Terms," online: <http://www.ohrc.on.ca/en/teaching-human-rights-ontario-guide-ontario-schools/appendix-1-glossary-human-rights-terms>.

† Ontario Human Rights Commission, "Appendix 1: Glossary of Human Rights Terms," online: <http://www.ohrc.on.ca/en/teaching-human-rights-ontario-guide-ontario-schools/appendix-1-glossary-human-rights-terms>.

‡ Ontario Human Rights Commission, "Appendix 1: Glossary of Human Rights Terms," online: <http://www.ohrc.on.ca/en/teaching-human-rights-ontario-guide-ontario-schools/appendix-1-glossary-human-rights-terms>.

§ Ontario Human Rights Commission, "Policy on Preventing Sexual and Gender-Based Harassment" (May 2013), online: <http://www.ohrc.on.ca/en/policy-preventing-sexual-and-gender-based-harassment-0>.

country or place of origin country or region a person is from

gender societally attributed characteristics of masculinity and femininity

sexual orientation sexual orientation is a personal characteristic that traverses the range of human sexuality; distinct from gender identity

stereotypes incorrect assumptions about an individual or members of a group that are often based on misconceptions and false information

restrictive covenants that would ban religious and racially diverse individuals from purchasing property and cemetery plots.[11] Religious and visible minorities were frequently refused service in restaurants and were blatantly deemed unwelcome in other public establishments.

Despite the opposition and prevailing thoughts of the day, the RDA was passed and established the first framework for those facing discrimination to seek recourse through the courts. The Act was not perfect by any means and had a neutral effect on the discrimination that was experienced by many at the time. In the 1950s, Ontario introduced amendments to the *Labour Relations Act, 1950*[12] that included protections against discrimination based on race and creed. Ontario also introduced the *Fair Employment Practices Act* (FEPA)[13] in 1951 to further address discrimination in employment.

Interestingly, legislation up until this point did not address gender discrimination at all. Discriminatory practices affecting women in the workplace and generally in society were also entrenched and deemed acceptable. Legislation related to pay equity was not introduced until 1951 when Ontario enacted the *Female Employee's Fair Remuneration Act* (FEFRA).[14] This Act, however, was largely symbolic and not enforced for fear of retaliation for making a complaint.

The *Fair Accommodation Practices Act* (FAPA)[15] was enacted in 1954 to address discrimination in public places on race, ethnic, and religious grounds. It was amended in 1961 to include prohibitions on discrimination related to rental apartments with more than six units.[16] Discrimination, however, was difficult to prove, and many advocates and advocate organizations fought tirelessly for real and tangible change to enact more effective legislation.

In 1958 Ontario created the Anti-Discrimination Commission, which operated under the jurisdiction of the *Ontario Anti-Discrimination Commission Act* (OADCA).[17] The commission comprised three members whose role

11 *Supra* note 1.

12 SO 1950, c 34.

13 SO 1951, c 24.

14 SO 1951, c 26.

15 SO 1954, c 28.

16 Ontario Human Rights Commission, "Human Rights: The Historical Context" in *Teaching Human Rights in Ontario: A Guide for Ontario Schools* (Toronto: OHRC, 2013) appendix 2, online: <http://www.ohrc.on.ca/en/book/export/html/10949>.

17 SO 1966, c 270.

was to advise and make recommendations to the minister about the administration of the FEPA, the FEFRA, and the FAPA.[18] The commission was also responsible for developing and conducting educational programs for the public about the existence of anti-discriminatory legislation and for promoting the elimination of discrimination. In 1961, the Act was amended to change the name of the commission to the Ontario Human Rights Commission.[19]

The Code was enacted in 1962, making Ontario the first Canadian province to introduce comprehensive anti-discrimination legislation. One of the key influences on Ontario's Code was the United Nations' *Universal Declaration of Human Rights*, which outlined key fundamental principles of fair and equal treatment for all. The Code also incorporated existing Ontario anti-discrimination legislation under one statute for ease of reference and efficiency. At its inception, the commission was responsible for enforcing the Code. Complaints came to commission staff who investigated the legitimacy of the complaint and made a referral to a human rights officer to mediate the matter if it was deemed legitimate. If the mediation was unsuccessful, the issue was referred to the Board of Inquiry, which was an independent panel appointed by the Ministry of Labour to make a determination on the matter. In 2002, the government introduced *Bill 179, Government Efficiency Act*, which changed the name of the Board of Inquiry to the Human Rights Tribunal of Ontario.[20]

Originally, the prohibited grounds of discrimination included religion, race, and **ethnicity**, and discrimination in accommodation, employment, and services. As societal norms and awareness increased, the grounds were expanded to include age (with the enactment of the *Ontario Age Discrimination Act* in 1966)[21] and gender discrimination in employment (with the inception of the Ontario *Women's Equal Employment Opportunity Act* of 1970).[22] Discrimination against differently abled individuals was not prohibited until the 1980s, and sexual orientation was added as a prohibited ground in the late 1990s. In 1982, the Code was amended to acknowledge the existence of **systemic discrimination** and to recognize the adverse and disproportionately negative effect that it has on marginalized groups.

Most recently, gender identity and gender expression were added to the Code, and in late 2017 Bill 164, the *Human Rights Code Amendment Act* was introduced. If successful, Bill 164 "would amend the Human Rights Code (Code) to include social condition, police records, genetic characteristics and immigration status as prohibited grounds of discrimination."[23] The addition

18 *Ibid.*

19 *Supra* note 16.

20 Legislative Assembly of Ontario, *Bill 179: Government Efficiency Act, 2002*, online: <http://www.ontla.on.ca/web/bills/bills_detail.do?locale=en&BillID=1047&isCurrent=false&ParlSessionID=37%3A3>.

21 SO 1966, c 3.

22 SO 1970, c 33.

23 Ontario Human Rights Commission, "OHRC Supports Bill to Improve *Human Rights Code*" (5 October 2017), online: <http://www.ohrc.on.ca/en/news_centre/ohrc-supports-bill-improve-human-rights-code>.

of genetic characteristics would also align the Ontario Code with the federal legislation, the *Canadian Human Rights Act.*

The Ontario Human Rights Commission remained responsible for the enforcement of the Code and acted as the gatekeeper and investigator for complaints until 2008 when Bill 107 was enforced. Significant reforms to Ontario's human rights system included:

- Changing the role of the Ontario Human Rights Commission to not have carriage of individual human rights complaints, focusing instead on working on systemic or root causes of discrimination;
- Having people make complaints—called applications—directly to the Human Rights Tribunal of Ontario;
- Creating a new organization—the Human Rights Legal Support Centre—to provide legal advice to people making complaints.[24]

Even though complainants now go directly to the tribunal, the commission has the right to be informed of all applications before the tribunal and receives copies of all applications and responses. It also has the right to intervene in HRTO matters either on request to the board or on consent of the applicant. Additionally, the commission can bring its own applications before the tribunal if it believes that move is in the public interest.

The tribunal is composed of 60 adjudicators who are referred to as either vice-chairs[25] (full-time adjudicators) or members[26] (who work on a part-time basis). One member is appointed as the associate chair,[27] is responsible for pro-

ethnic origin/ethnicity sharing a distinctive cultural and historical tradition; often connected to race, place of origin, ancestry, religion, or creed

systemic discrimination "patterns of behaviour, policies or practices that are part of the social or administrative structures of an organization, and which create or perpetuate a position of relative disadvantage for groups identified under the Human Rights Code"*

* Ontario Human Rights Commission, "Appendix 1: Glossary of Human Rights Terms" (2017), online: <http://www.ohrc.on.ca/en/teaching-human-rights-ontario-guide-ontario-schools/appendix-1-glossary-human-rights-terms>.

24 *Supra* note 16.

25 Social Justice Tribunals Ontario, "Vice-Chair Position Description" (August 2017), online: <http://www.sjto.gov.on.ca/documents/sjto/Vice-Chair%20Position%20Description%20EN.html>.

26 Social Justice Tribunals Ontario, "Member Position Description" (August 2017), online: <http://www.sjto.gov.on.ca/documents/sjto/Member%20Position%20Description%20EN.html>.

27 Social Justice Tribunals Ontario, "Associate Chair Position Description" (August 2017), online: <http://www.sjto.gov.on.ca/documents/sjto/Associate%20Chair%20Position%20Description%20EN.html>.

viding leadership to the members on the [illegible] ıd sits on the executive committee of the Socia[illegible] ΓTO). Given that the tribunal receives over 3,0[illegible] ıunal must keep a large roster of adjudicator[illegible] in a timely manner.

Legislation and Regulatio[illegible]

The HRTO (originally the Board of Inquir[illegible] ves its jurisdiction through the Ontario *Huma*[illegible] ri-bunals in the SJTO cluster. The Ontario *Hu*[illegible] a-si-constitutional, and all legislation and re[illegible] be compliant with it. The Code identifies sever[illegible] upon which discrimination and harassment are prohibited:

- race,
- **colour**,
- **ancestry**,
- **place of origin,**
- **citizenship**,
- **ethnic origin**,
- **family status**,
- **marital status** (including single status),
- age,
- disability,
- **creed**,
- sex (including sexual harassment, pregnancy, and breastfeeding),
- sexual orientation,
- **gender identity**,
- **gender expression**,
- receipt of public assistance (applies only to claims about housing), and
- record of offences (applies only to claims about employment and to criminal convictions for which the person has received a pardon).[28]

Additionally, the Code prohibits discrimination in the following social areas:

- accommodation (housing) (s 2),
- contracts (s 3),
- employment (s 5),
- goods, services, and facilities (s 1), and
- membership in unions, trades, or professional associations (s 6).

---

28 Social Justice Tribunals Ontario, "Human Rights Tribunal of Ontario: What We Do" (2015), online: <http://www.sjto.gov.on.ca/hrto/what-we-do/>.

For an application to be considered, differential treatment must have occurred in one of the five social areas identified in the Code and have a nexus to one or more of the grounds outlined in the Code. The Code also includes Regulation 290/98, which provides guidance to landlords that can assist them in selecting residential tenants without violating the Code. Familiarize yourself with how each of these prohibited grounds and related social areas are defined to ensure that you are providing proper legal advice and advocacy.[29] Section 12 of the Code also prohibits discrimination based on being associated with, in a relationship with, or dealing with someone who can be identified by one of the prohibited grounds. Section 8 of the Code also provides protection against reprisal (e.g., punishment or retaliation) or threat of reprisal because of someone exercising his or her right to file a complaint, refusing to

colour the hue of a person's skin; associated with race

ancestry family descent or genealogy

citizenship membership in a state or nation

family status according to the OHRC, "the status of being in a parent and child relationship. This can also mean a parent and child 'type' of relationship, embracing a range of circumstances without blood or adoptive ties but with similar relationships of care, responsibility and commitment"

marital status section 10 of the Code defines marital status as "the status of being married, single, widowed, divorced or separated and includes the status of living with a person in a conjugal relationship outside marriage," including both same-sex and opposite sex relationships

creed a set of beliefs or aims that guides one's actions; sometimes connected to religion or faith

gender expression the external attributes, behaviour, appearance, dress, etc., by which people express themselves and through which others perceive those people's gender*

gender identity a person's conscious sense of maleness and/or femaleness; this sense of self is separate and distinct from biological sex†

* Ontario Human Rights Commission, "Appendix B: Glossary for Understanding Gender Identity and Gender Expression" (14 April 2014), online: <http://www.ohrc.on.ca/en/policy-preventing-discrimination-because-gender-identity-and-gender-expression/appendix-b-glossary-understanding-gender-identity-and-expression>.

† Ontario Human Rights Commission, "Appendix B: Glossary for Understanding Gender Identity and Gender Expression" (14 April 2014), online: <http://www.ohrc.on.ca/en/policy-preventing-discrimination-because-gender-identity-and-gender-expression/appendix-b-glossary-understanding-gender-identity-and-expression>.

29 Section 10 of the Code provides definitions, online: <https://www.ontario.ca/laws/statute/90h19>.

discriminate against someone, or for participating in a proceeding before the tribunal. Finally, the Code also provides protection against sexual solicitation or advances by a person who is in authority or in a position to grant or deny a benefit. It is also prohibited for someone to face reprisal or a threat of reprisal for rejecting sexual harassment (s 7).

Also noteworthy is the fact that in some circumstances outlined in section 11 of the Code, an **exemption** allows for a discriminatory practice if it is reasonable and bona fide (i.e., having different monetary tiers of life insurance premiums based on age, or determining a prospective tenant is not suitable based on gender because that person will be sharing accommodations with the landlord). Familiarizing yourself with the exemptions is essential in order to ask appropriate questions and to advise or advocate effectively.

The HRTO provides Rules of Procedure (the Rules)[30] that are a combination of the SJTO Common Rules and rules that are particular to the work of the tribunal. The rules set out the procedures to provide effective representation before the HRTO. They provide guidance related to such things as initiating proceedings, servicing and filing documents, providing disclosure, and holding mediations and expedited hearings. You must be familiar and up-to-date with the Rules, as failure to follow them can result in detrimental consequences for your client. The HRTO also publishes Practice Directions[31] that assist practitioners and lay people in understanding the Rules. The Practice Directions support the Rules by providing advice regarding the tribunal's expectations and how to properly proceed with matters before the tribunal. It is imperative to review and become familiar with the HRTO's Practice Directions; these often provide more in-depth information regarding the application of the Rules, and they are the easiest and most accessible way for the tribunal to communicate with legal representatives and advocates.

Finally, the *Statutory Powers and Procedures Act* is the overarching framework which every tribunal references to ensure compliance when determining their rules.

exemption not bound to fulfill an obligation or a requirement that others must observe

30 Social Justice Tribunals Ontario, "Human Rights Tribunal of Ontario: Rules of Procedure" (24 October 2017), online: <http://www.sjto.gov.on.ca/documents/hrto/Practice%20Directions/HRTO%20Rules%20of%20Procedure.html/>.

31 Social Justice Tribunals Ontario, "Practice Directions" (2015), online: <http://www.sjto.gov.on.ca/hrto/rules-and-practice-directions>.

Application Process

To initiate a proceeding before the HRTO, you must use Form 1[32] in accordance with Rule 6 of the Rules of Procedure, which is a lengthy, comprehensive form. No fee is required to initiate a proceeding before the HRTO, which ensures accessibility for the most vulnerable and marginalized in society to seek recourse for discrimination. Supporting documentation must be listed on the application, but it is not necessary to attach it to the application, unless the form expressly asks for a document (e.g., a copy of the statement of claim). Including a list of witnesses that have knowledge of the issues outlined in the application is advisable. The list remains confidential but provides the adjudicator with an understanding of how many witnesses may be participating and whether individuals may be able to corroborate the allegations made by either party. Applications must be filed within one year of the incident that precipitated the complaint or, if there were a series of events, within one year after the last incident.[33] If that time limit has expired, you can request on the form an extension of time to file your application.[34] Generally, this request will be granted if the tribunal believes that the delay was in good faith and has not significantly prejudiced the rights of the other parties.[35]

Pursuant to Rule 7, the tribunal also allows for applications to be filed with a request to defer consideration. This situation occurs when other means are used to resolve an issue, but you would still like to have the option of pursuing the matter before the tribunal. For example, if your client has filed a grievance in accordance with his or her collective bargaining agreement and would like to see if the matter can be resolved in that forum, he or she would still need to file that grievance within the one-year time limit and request a deferral from the tribunal to see the grievance through. The applicant has 60 days to commence proceedings before the HRTO (after requesting a deferral) once the other matter has concluded.[36] The tribunal will not deal with issues that have been resolved in another forum. In our example, any issues dealt with by the union grievance would not be heard by the tribunal. The tribunal itself (often at the request of the respondent) may dismiss all or part of the application if it has been dealt with elsewhere. In addition to monetary compensation, the HRTO allows for non-monetary remedies and for remedies that are in the public interest. It is also one of the few tribunals, if not the only one, that

---

32 Social Justice Tribunals Ontario, "Human Rights Tribunal of Ontario: Forms and Filing" (2015), online: <http://www.sjto.gov.on.ca/hrto/forms-filing>.

33 The Code, ss 34(1)(a), 34(1)(b).

34 Question 7(d) on Form 1.

35 The Code, s 34(2).

36 Social Justice Tribunals Ontario, "Human Rights Tribunal of Ontario: Rules of Procedure—Rule 7, Application with Request to Defer Consideration" at para 7.5 (24 October 2017), online: <http://www.sjto.gov.on.ca/documents/hrto/Practice%20 Directions/HRTO%20Rules%20of%20Procedure.html#7>.

allows for compensation and restitution for injury to dignity, feelings, and self-respect.[37]

When initiating an application:

- identify the nexus grounds upon which the application is based, since there can be more than one. Intersectionality is very common in human rights matters;
- include any supplemental forms that may correspond with the social area ground upon which you are filing (Forms 1A through to 1E). The links for Forms 1A through to 1E are in the Applicant's Guide under question 6;[38]
- think carefully about who is named as a respondent, as this can result in delays;[39]
- refer to the Practice Direction to assist in naming appropriate respondents;[40]
- if you are applying on someone else's behalf, ensure that you have included the form that allows you to do so (Forms 4A, 4B, or 27); [41]
- when thinking about remedies, be forward-looking and consider requesting remedies that promote prevention and anti-discriminatory practice; and
- clearly identify the remedies that you are seeking and what you would like the tribunal to do.

Once an application is filed, the HRTO will serve the named respondents and any other affected persons on your behalf. They will also mail a letter to the applicants indicating the file number and detailing the next steps in the process.

Upon receiving the application with the appropriate file number from the HRTO, they have 35 days to send a response to the tribunal using Form 2. Failure to respond indicates to the tribunal that there has been an acceptance of the allegations and proceedings can commence in absentia. In this case, an adverse finding and an order can be made against the respondent without notice. It is also important to calculate time correctly so that no deadlines are missed.

---

37 The Code, ss 46.1(1), (2).

38 Human Rights Tribunal of Ontario, "Applicant's Guide to Filing an Application with the HRTO," online: <http://www.sjto.gov.on.ca/documents/hrto/Guides/Applicants%20Guide.html#3>.

39 Human Rights Tribunal of Ontario, "Before You File an Application" (2015), online: <http://www.sjto.gov.on.ca/hrto/application-and-hearing-process/#step2>.

40 Social Justice Tribunals Ontario, "Human Rights Tribunal of Ontario: Practice Direction on Naming Respondents" (April 2014), online: <http://www.sjto.gov.on.ca/documents/hrto/Practice%20Directions/Naming%20Respondents.html>.

41 *Supra* note 32.

The response should consider and indicate:

- if the applicant disclosed information about the issues relating to the human rights concern;
- if there is a complaints process in place within the organization, if applicable;
- whether an investigation took place and what the respondents did to address the issue(s);
- whether there are human rights, anti-harassment, or anti-discrimination policies in place to address the concerns;
- if there are applicable exemptions outlined in the Code;
- if there are additional persons affected or additional respondents that the tribunal should be aware of;
- what allegations the respondent does and does not agree with; and
- whether mediation will be attempted.

The HRTO allows requests for an early dismissal without filing a full and proper response (question 6). If the request does not fall within one of the following allowable exemptions, a complete response must be filed:

1. if the civil courts are already dealing with the same matter;
2. if the parties have settled the claim and the applicant has signed a full and final release;
3. if there is a claim that the issues outlined in the application fall within federal jurisdiction (or *ultra vires* to the HRTO); and
4. if the applicant made a complaint to the Ontario Human Rights Commission about the same matter before June 30, 2008 (which is the date when the OHRC stopped receiving complaints under the Code) (Form 2).

If a request is made for early dismissal, enclose the corresponding documents with the response to substantiate the request (i.e., a signed release or statement of claim). It is also possible to request a dismissal under section 45.1 of the Code but, again, a full response is required (question 7).

If the HRTO indicates that your response is incomplete, if you missed something, or if you asked for an early dismissal and did not fill in the form completely, a full and proper response must be filed within 20 days of receiving the incomplete documents from the tribunal.

In the final step of the initiating process, the applicant to file a reply (Form 3) with new arguments arising from the respondent's submissions. Those submissions must be served on the responding parties and submitted to the tribunal within 21 days. The tribunal requires a paper copy and an electronic copy (or second unbound paper copy of any bound document) of all documents submitted for filing.

The Human Rights Legal Support Centre (HRLSC) is an agency funded by the Government of Ontario to provide legal services to those who have faced discrimination as defined by the Code. Its services include assistance with filing an application, and it may represent applicants at mediations and hearings before the HRTO. On average, the HRLSC provides representation at 20 percent of mediations and a little over 5 percent of hearings.[42] Although the HRLSC is not a resource for legal representatives (it exists solely to assist unrepresented parties), its website is an excellent source of information and resources to deepen your competency.

Hearing Process

Mediation

When both parties indicate on Forms 1 and 2 that they are open to mediation, the tribunal will send a notice of mediation indicating the date, time, and location of the mediation. Sometimes, on review of the application and responding documents, the tribunal will deem a matter appropriate for mediation even when the parties have not indicated an interest. The tribunal provides a guide on mediation that can familiarize the parties with the process and help them prepare accordingly.[43] The parties will each have to sign a confidentiality agreement, and if the matter is successfully resolved, a Form 25 confirmation of settlement must be filed to conclude the matter. The actual minutes of settlement are not filed with the tribunal for confidentiality reasons. For high-profile cases, it is common to see a redacted or public version of minutes of settlement published by either the HRTO or the HRLSC because of the public interest nature of the matter.[44]

The parties also have the option of requesting that the tribunal issue a consent order (s 45.9(2)). The terms in the consent order are a matter of public record. If settlement was not achieved at mediation, the parties can attempt to mediate matters on the day of hearing, which is discussed below under Hearing/Case Resolution Conference. This happens quite often. Most matters before the HRTO result in settlement.

42 Social Justice Tribunals Ontario, "2015-2016 Annual Report: Statistics" (2016), online: <http://www.sjto.gov.on.ca/documents/sjto/2015-16%20Annual%20Report.html#hrto7>.

43 Human Rights Tribunal of Ontario, "A Guide to Mediation at the Human Rights Tribunal of Ontario," online: <http://www.sjto.gov.on.ca/documents/hrto/Guides/Guide%20to%20Mediation.pdf>.

44 One example is in the public minutes of settlement in the *Grant v York Region District School Board* matter. This was a very high-profile case that resulted in admissions by the board that it failed to respond appropriately to incidents of anti-Black racism. Ontario Human Rights Legal Support Centre, "Minutes of Settlement for Public Distribution: *Grant v York Region District School Board*," online: <http://www.hrlsc.on.ca/sites/default/files/docs/en/Media/2017-05-17%20Grant%20v%20YRDSB%20Backgrounder%20Website%20English%20version.pdf>.

If one of the parties has been non-compliant with the terms of settlement, the harmed party has six months from the date of contravention to file an application for contravention of a settlement (Form 18).

Preliminary Hearings

Upon reviewing the file, the HRTO may schedule a preliminary hearing to gain clarity on any jurisdictional issue or if it believes another proceeding may have already taken place respecting the substance of the application. Generally, in a preliminary hearing the adjudicator will require the parties to make submissions and possibly present evidence before determining how the matter will proceed.

Another type of preliminary hearing is a summary hearing. The tribunal may order the parties to attend a summary hearing if it appears that the application (or a part of it) has no reasonable prospect of succeeding. The respondent can also serve and file a request for summary hearing using Form 26 after a completed response (Form 2) has been filed. A copy of the practice direction on summary hearing requests[45] must accompany the request when served on the applicant, and a statement of delivery must accompany the request when filing with the tribunal. The applicant has 14 days to serve and file a response to request for order (form 11), with proof of service accompanying the document on filing with the tribunal (Form 23). Shortly after receipt, the tribunal will issue a case assessment direction that will detail which issues will be dealt with at the summary hearing, along with the nature and timing of reciprocal disclosure of necessary documents. The parties will receive a notice of summary hearing detailing its date, time, and location. Following the hearing, the adjudicator will issue written directions on how, or if, the matter will proceed.

Hearing/Case Resolution Conference

Matters before the HRTO are heard by one adjudicator who is the sole decision-maker. If a matter proceeds to a hearing, the HRTO will send a notice of hearing detailing the time, date, format, and location of the hearing. Reciprocal disclosure of documents must be completed within 21 days of receipt of the notice of hearing with a Form 23 filed with the tribunal. Lists of witnesses and copies of documents that will used at the hearing must be served and filed at least 45 days before the hearing (rr 16, 17). It is common to have multiple days set aside for hearings.

45 Social Justice Tribunals Ontario, "Human Rights Tribunal of Ontario: Practice Direction on Summary Hearing Requests" (May 2013), online: <http://www.sjto.gov.on.ca/documents/hrto/Practice%20Directions/Summary%20Hearing%20Requests.html>.

Procedurally, the HRTO use a **mediation-adjudication** framework (commonly referred to as "med-adj") (r 15A). At the commencement of the hearing, the adjudicator asks the parties if they would like to pursue mediation. If the parties agree, the adjudicator then takes on the role of mediator and helps the parties to resolve the issue. If settlement is unsuccessful, the adjudicator returns to the role of decision-maker and hears the case on its merits. It is common for matters to be held *in camera* (i.e., behind closed doors and not open to the public) because of the sensitive nature of the matters before the tribunal. Upon completion of the hearing, the adjudicator will likely reserve the decision. Matters before the HRTO can be very complex, and it is common to have decisions reserved so that the adjudicator can contemplate the evidence and make a sound finding.

Decisions, Reconsideration, and Appeals

Most matters that result in hearing are reserved because of the length, volume of documentation, and complexity of the matters. If your hearing lasts three days or less, you should receive your final decision within three months. If your hearing lasts longer than three days, you should receive your final decision within six months.[46] All decisions are a matter of public record and are available on the Canadian Legal Information Institute's website (CanLII). When you receive the decision, make sure to read it for any discrepancies. If any aspect of the decision is unclear, seek clarifications. Pursuant to Rule 25, parties have 30 days to request an amendment of typographical errors. Remedies awarded by the HRTO generally fall into three categories:

1. monetary compensation (money),
2. a non-monetary award (human rights training for the respondent's employees, building an accessible entrance), or
3. an order to promote future compliance with the Code (develop human rights policies, training).[47]

mediation-adjudication the framework that the HRTO uses for its hearings. Rule 15A provides guidance for mediation-adjudication: when all parties sign the mediation/adjudication agreement, the tribunal member conducting the hearing may also act as a mediator to resolve the issues. If mediation fails, the parties continue through to the hearing with the same tribunal member as adjudicator.

46 Social Justice Tribunals Ontario, "Human Rights Tribunal of Ontario: Decision," 2015, online: <http://www.sjto.gov.on.ca/hrto/application-and-hearing-process/#step8>.

47 *Ibid.*

The Rules provide for the ability to request a reconsideration of the tribunal's decision. Rule 26 indicates that reconsideration is discretionary and a request for reconsideration (Form 20) must be filed within 30 days of the date of decision. The request must include:

- the reason(s) for the request,
- the basis upon which the request is made,
- written submissions, and
- the remedy or relief sought.[48]

If required, a response (Form 21) must contain full written submissions in support of the responding position. Reconsideration requests are heard by the associate chair who makes a determination based on the submissions. According to Rule 26.5, reconsideration requests will only be granted if the tribunal is satisfied that:

> a. there are new facts or evidence that could potentially be determinative of the case and that could not reasonably have been obtained earlier; or
>
> b. the party seeking reconsideration was entitled to but, through no fault of its own, did not receive notice of the proceeding or a hearing; or
>
> c. the decision or order which is the subject of the reconsideration request is in conflict with established jurisprudence or Tribunal procedure and the proposed reconsideration involves a matter of general or public importance; or
>
> d. other factors exist that, in the opinion of the Tribunal, outweigh the public interest in the finality of Tribunal decisions.[49]

If the parties are unsatisfied with a decision made by the tribunal, they can pursue an application for judicial review at the Divisional Court of the Ontario Superior Court. The review is outside the paralegal scope of practice and requires a referral to a lawyer specializing in administrative law.

If one party is non-compliant with the terms of the tribunal's order, the first step is to write a letter requesting the outstanding remedy and providing an appropriate date for compliance. If the monetary amount is $25,000 or less, the order can be filed with the Small Claims Court. A further request for a writ of seizure and sale for personal property or for land must be made for property and assets to be seized to recover the debt.

---

48 Social Justice Tribunals Ontario, "Human Rights Tribunal of Ontario: Rules of Procedure—Rule 26.3, Practice Direction on Reconsideration" (24 October 2017), online: <http://www.sjto.gov.on.ca/documents/hrto/Practice%20Directions/HRTO%20Rules%20of%20Procedure.html#26>.

49 Social Justice Tribunals Ontario, "Human Rights Tribunal of Ontario: Rules of Procedure—Rule 26, Request for Reconsideration" (24 October 2017), online: <http://www.sjto.gov.on.ca/documents/hrto/Practice%20Directions/HRTO%20Rules%20of%20Procedure.html#26>.

Monetary amounts over $25,000 indicate matters that should be pursued in the Superior Court of Justice. Writs and garnishment of wages are available at this level.[50] Monetary amounts over $25,000 are outside the paralegal scope of practice and must be initiated and pursued by a lawyer.

Case Law

Peel Law Association v Pieters, 2013 ONCA 396

This important Court of Appeal matter involves racial discrimination. Mr Pieters, a lawyer, along with a colleague, Mr Noble, and an articling student used the lawyer's lounge while attending to a matter at the Brampton courthouse. Mr Pieters and his colleagues are Black males. Additionally, Mr Pieters and the articling student wore their hair in locs. According to the Peel Law Association's policy, only lawyers and law students may use the lounge, robing room, and library, and it is the role of the librarian to enforce the policy.

Other people were in the lounge along with Mr Pieters and his colleagues, yet the librarian asked only Mr Pieters, Mr Noble, and the articling student for identification.

After the matter was heard, the tribunal found that a *prima facie* case of discrimination had been established. The matter was appealed to the Divisional Court, which quashed the decision of the tribunal. On appeal, the decision of the tribunal was reinstated and $30,000 in costs awarded.

This case is significant because it provides guidance on the complexities of establishing a case under the racial discrimination ground.

Dabic v Windsor Police Service, 2010 HRTO 1994

Although this case was unsuccessful before the tribunal, it provides guidance on the purpose and scope of summary hearings before the HRTO. Dabic was the first case to apply and discuss the two part test:

1. whether, assuming the truthfulness of all the allegations, the application has no reasonable prospect of success; and
2. whether, on a balance of probabilities, there is a reasonable prospect that the applicant can prove that their Code rights were violated.

Ontario Human Rights Comm v Simpsons-Sears, [1985] 2 SCR 536, 1985 CanLII 18

This Supreme Court decision dealt with issues surrounding creed, adverse effect discrimination, and duty of the employer to accommodate to the point

50 Human Rights Legal Support Centre, "Enforcing Your Tribunal Order or Settlement," online: <http://www.hrlsc.on.ca/en/publications-resources/information-sheets-guides/enforcing-your-tribunal-order-or-settlement>.

short of undue hardship. Mrs O'Malley was a full-time employee of Sears for seven years before she converted to thee Seventh Day Adventist faith. As part of the expression of her faith, she observed the Sabbath day from sundown on Friday until sundown on Saturday and could no longer work during this time. Her employer was not accommodating and eventually offered her part-time employment. When she took the matter to the Board of Inquiry, it determined that there was not a case of intentional discrimination and dismissed the complaint. The Divisional Court and the Court of Appeal upheld the decision of the board. The Supreme Court held that this was a case of adverse effect discrimination and that the employer had a duty to accommodate to the point of undue hardship:

> An employment rule, honestly made for sound economic and business reasons and equally applicable to all to whom it is intended to apply, may nevertheless be discriminatory if it affects a person or persons differently from others to whom it is intended to apply. The intent to discriminate is not a governing factor in construing human rights legislation aimed at eliminating discrimination. Rather, it is the result or effect of the alleged discriminatory action that is significant.
>
> In a case of adverse effect discrimination, the employer has a duty to take reasonable steps to accommodate short of undue hardship in the operation of the employer's business.

OHRC v Ontario (Community Safety and Correctional Services), 2018 HRTO 60

This decision is an HRTO consent order resulting from years of advocacy on the part of the OHRC to enact the public interest provisions of the 2013 settlement agreement in *Jahn v MCSCS*.[51] Ms Jahn filed a complaint with the HRTO due to her long-term placement in segregation at the Ottawa Carlton Detention Centre as a result of her mental health disabilities and gender. The full historical context is outlined on the OHRC website.[52] In January 2018 the minister of community safety and correctional services agreed to a number of undertakings to address the concerns of discriminatory treatment of individuals with mental health disabilities with the Ontario correctional service, namely:

> The Order requires Ontario to:
>
> - Achieve operational compliance with the original *Jahn* public interest remedies (including mental health screening, access to mental health services, and prohibiting segregation barring undue hardship for people with mental illness)
> - Undertake a series of compliance reviews

51 2013 HRTO 169.

52 Ontario Human Rights Commission, "Segregation and Mental Health in Ontario's Prisons: Jahn v Ministry of Community Safety and Correctional Services" (2018), online: <http://www.ohrc.on.ca/en/segregation-and-mental-health-ontario%E2%80%99s-prisons-jahn-v-ministry-community-safety-and-correctional>.

- Use a baseline definition of segregation for the purposes of meeting its ongoing *Jahn* obligations, as well as its additional obligations under the new settlement; segregation will be understood to include at least all circumstances where prisoners are physically isolated and confined to a cell for 22 hours or more per day
- Track segregation placements based on conditions of confinement
- Develop a plan for tracking segregation-like placements, called "restrictive confinement" placements, based on conditions of confinement
- Develop and fully implement a system for accurately identifying prisoners with mental health disabilities, using alerts that are verified by mental health professionals
- Formalize timelines for:
  - Mental health screening—96 hours after admission
  - Mental health reassessment—at least every six months
  - Referrals—within 24 hours of completing the screening
  - Putting treatment plans in place after appointments with doctors—within 48 hours of the appointment with the assessing physician or psychiatrist
- Collect human rights data to provide annual public reporting on the use of both segregation and restrictive confinement. The data will be disaggregated by sex/gender and mental health disability, and released in a way that allows for meaningful analysis of how segregation and restrictive confinement are used on and affect individuals based on mental health disability and sex/gender
- Retain an independent expert to assist with implementing the settlement, and an independent reviewer to publicly report on Ontario's compliance with the terms of the settlement.[53]

The OHRC will monitor the provinces implementation of the provisions noted above to ensure that they are completed in a timely and effective manner. This is a very significant case that will help to address concerns involving persons with mental health disabilities who are facing confinement.

KEY LEGISLATION

Human Rights Code

Business Practices Permissible to Landlords in Selecting Prospective Tenants for Residential Accommodation, O Reg 290/98

Statutory Powers Procedure Act

53 *Ibid.*

KEY TERMS

ancestry, 35
citizenship, 35
colour, 35
country or place of origin, 31
creed, 35
disability, 30
discrimination, 30
ethnic origin/ethnicity, 33
exemption, 36
family status, 35
gender, 31
gender expression, 35
gender identity, 35
harassment, 30
marital status, 35
mediation-adjudication, 42
prohibited or discriminatory grounds, 30
race, 30
reprisal, 30
sex, 30
sexual harassment, 30
sexual orientation, 31
stereotypes, 31
systemic discrimination, 33

REVIEW QUESTIONS

1. What is the name of the enabling legislation that created the HRTO and the OHRC?
2. In Ontario, discrimination is prohibited in five social areas. What are they?
3. List and briefly describe 8 of the 17 prohibited grounds of discrimination.
4. What major international document influenced the creation of the Code?
5. What framework does the HRTO use in its hearing process?
6. What is the name of the agency that provides legal advice to lay litigants?
7. Name and give examples of the three categories of remedies that the tribunal issues.
8. What must a request for reconsideration include?
9. In what year did the Board of Inquiry become the Human Rights Tribunal of Ontario?
10. You have faced an incident of discrimination and you are contemplating filing an application with the tribunal. How long do you have to file an application?

SCENARIO

Jane is 17 years old, is estranged from her parents, and needs a permanent place to live. She is currently a ward of the local Children's Aid Society. Jane works and is in her final year of high school. She also receives monetary support from the government because of her status as a ward of the province. At the beginning of April, Jane made a phone call in the morning in response to an ad she saw on Kijiji looking for a female tenant to rent an entire apartment. Mary, the building superintendent, answered the call. Jane inquired about the apartment and asked if it was still available. Mary let her know that the rent would be $600 per month with utilities included. They had a cordial, although brief, conversation over the phone during which Jane disclosed that she works and goes to school but could easily pay the rent. Mary invited Jane to come to see the apartment as it was still available. They arranged for a viewing in the afternoon that same day.

Jane arrived at the building at the agreed upon time and saw Mary standing in the lobby on the other side of the locked entrance. Jane knew it was her because Mary had indicated on the phone that she would be wearing a red sweater. Jane motioned for Mary to open the door, but Mary refused. Someone else came along and opened the door, and as Jane entered Mary made a comment about "rude young people." Jane approached Mary and introduced herself as the prospective tenant for the vacant apartment. Mary looked shocked, and then she told Jane that unfortunately the apartment was no longer available. Jane reminded Mary that they had just spoken a few hours earlier, but Mary was insistent that the apartment was now rented by someone else, and Jane would have to look elsewhere. Jane left feeling very disappointed and frustrated, as she had had a difficult time finding somewhere to live. Does Jane have any options?

CHAPTER 3

Ontario Landlord and Tenant Board

Overview and History 50
Legislation and Regulations 52
Application Process 53
Hearing Process 61
Decisions, Reconsideration/Review, Enforcement, and Appeals 62
Case Law 64
Key Terms 67
Review Questions 67
Scenario 68

Overview and History

The Landlord and Tenant Board (LTB) was created on January 31, 2007 and is one of eight tribunals under the Social Justice Tribunals Ontario umbrella. It is enabled by the *Residential Tenancies Act, 2006* (RTA)[1] and to resolve disputes between landlords and tenants and disputes arising from eviction applications filed by non-profit housing co-operatives. The LTB also provides information to both landlords and tenants about their rights and responsibilities under the Act.

The first piece of legislation regarding the resolution of residential tenancies issues, Part IV of the *Landlord and Tenant Act*,[2] came into force on January 1, 1970. It was the result of recommendations from the Ontario Law Reform Commission report of 1968.[3] The recommendations of additional reports in 1972, 1974, and 1976 resulted in further amendments to the Act. Disputes between landlords and tenants related to the Act were resolved by the County Courts from 1970 until 1984, when the County Court merged with the Superior Court of Justice. From 1984 until 1998, judges of the Ontario Court (General Division) heard **landlord** and **tenant** matters.

Rent regulation and the need for **rent control** were long-standing issues in Ontario and worsened after the Second World War when many veterans returned home and required housing. The first piece of legislation that attempted to address these issues was the *National Housing Act, 1944*;[4] however, it was repealed less than ten years after it was enacted.

A new legislative structure to deal with rent control did not come into effect until 1975 when the *Residential Premises Rent Review Act*[5] was established.

landlord an individual or a corporation that owns real estate and, in turn, leases use of the owned premises to another entity (individual or corporation) for a specified term

tenant an individual or a corporation that possesses real estate for a set term under a lease that stipulates the amount of rent to be paid for the term

rent control legislation and regulations that govern residential rents and provides a price ceiling on residential rents in Ontario

---

1 SO 2006, c 17.

2 RSO 1970, c 236.

3 Ontario Law Reform Commission, *Report on Landlord and Tenant Law* (Toronto: Ministry of the Attorney General, 1976), online: <http://digitalcommons.osgoode.yorku.ca/library_olrc/96/>.

4 "Housing" (1945) 60:3 Mon Labor Rev 585, online: <http://www.jstor.org/stable/41817782>; and Jean Dupuis, *Federal Housing Policy: An Historical Perspective* (Ottawa: Library of Parliament, 2013), online: <https://lop.parl.ca/Content/LOP/ResearchPublicationsArchive/bp1000/prb0255-e.asp>.

5 SO 1975, c 12.

The Residential Premises Rent Review Board, enabled under the Act, dealt with rent control issues[6] until 1987, when the *Residential Rent Regulation Act*[7] came into force and the Ministry of Housing became the responsible decision-making body. At one time, the Rent Review Hearings Board also made decisions about these matters, but this role was returned to the Ministry in 1992 with the enactment of the *Rent Control Act, 1992*.[8]

Landlord and tenant law and rent control law were decided by separate entities until the enactment of the *Tenant Protection Act, 1997* (TPA),[9] which consolidated landlord tenant law and rent control law under one legislative framework. This Act maintained certain provisions in Part IV of the preceding *Landlord and Tenant Act* but repealed the dispute resolution process outlined in the Act and repealed the *Rent Control Act*. With the repeal of the dispute resolution process of the Act, decision-making responsibilities of the courts were transferred to a newly created quasi-judicial body called the Ontario Rental Housing Tribunal (ORHT) in 1998.[10] The ORHT's purpose was to decide cases related to both landlord and tenant applications and rent control applications.

Tenants felt that the TPA was biased against them by denying them procedural fairness in relation to evictions and the right to be heard. This dissatisfaction culminated in a complaint to the Ontario Ombudsman on behalf of the Advocacy Centre for Tenants Ontario and the Legal Clinics Housing Issues Committee requesting an investigation under the *Ombudsman Act*.[11] Additionally, the Ontario Human Rights Commission completed various discrimination consultations in the early 2000s, and it found many instances of housing discrimination.[12] Some of those concerns would be addressed by reforming the legislation. The RTA was enacted on January 30, 2007 to address many of the concerns over fairness and to strengthen protections for tenants. The RTA also created a new quasi-judicial tribunal referred to as the Landlord and Tenant Board.

---

6 Peter Russell, *Federalism and the Charter: Leading Constitutional Decisions* (Montreal: McGill-Queen's Press, 1989) at 240, 241, online: <https://books.google.ca/books?id=AKigyfekmYsC&pg=PA236&redir_esc=y#v=onepage&q&f=false>.

7 SO 1986, c 63.

8 SO 1992, c 11 [repealed].

9 SO 1997, c 24 [repealed].

10 Ontario Human Rights Commission, "The Rental Housing Landscape in Ontario: Access to Affordable Rental Housing," online: <http://www.ohrc.on.ca/en/human-rights-and-rental-housing-ontario-background-paper/rental-housing-landscape-ontario>.

11 RSO 1990, c O.6; Katherine Laird, *Submission to the Ombudsman Ontario: Concerning the Failure of the Tenant Protection Act and the Rules and Procedures of the Ontario Human Rights Tribunal to meet Ombudsman Fairness Standards* (Toronto: Advocacy Centre for Tenants Ontario, 2002), online: <https://web.archive.org/web/20030429081316/http://dawn.thot.net:80/docs/ombudsman_final.pdf>.

12 *Ibid.*

Legislation and Regulations

As outlined above, the RTA is the enabling legislation of the LTB. In May 2017, the province amended the Act by enacting the *Rental Fairness Act, 2017* (RFA)[13] as part of the Ontario Fair Housing Plan. The RFA strengthened requirements related to rent control to include all rental units and increased tenant protections.[14] The legislative framework for the Landlord and Tenant Board also includes the Regulations that provide further guidance regarding procedure. O Reg 516/06 is the regulation that provides information regarding reductions in rent and above-guideline rent increases. It also provides additional general guidelines, information regarding the LTB's administration and powers, and a schedule regarding useful life of work done or things purchased. O Reg 517/06 provides information relating to maintenance standards, and O Reg 394/10 provides guidance regarding suite meters and the apportionment of utility costs.

Generally, matters related to landlord and tenant issues that involve discriminatory grounds fall under the purview of the Ontario *Human Rights Code* (Code), and individuals must file an application with the Human Rights Tribunal of Ontario to seek relief.[15] That being said, the Code provides guidance in O Reg 290/98 on permissible business practices for landlords in selecting prospective rental tenants. The LTB is also required to provide accommodations related to Code grounds in its provision of services and in facilities. Additionally, adjudicators are required to ensure that they are interpreting the Act in light of the Code as it is quasi-constitutional in nature and must also consider and apply the Code when necessary.[16]

The LTB also provides rules[17] in accordance with the minimum standards set by the *Statutory Powers Procedures Act* (SPPA).[18] The rules set out the procedures to provide effective representation before the LTB. They provide

---

13 SO 2017 c 13.

14 Ministry of Finance, "Backgrounder: Ontario's Fair Housing Plan" (20 April 2017), online: <https://news.ontario.ca/mof/en/2017/04/ontarios-fair-housing-plan.html>.

15 Social Justice Tribunals Ontario, Landlord and Tenant Board, "Human Rights: Interpretation Guideline 17" (15 October 2009), online: <http://www.sjto.gov.on.ca/documents/ltb/Interpretation%20Guidelines/17%20-%20Human%20Rights.html>.

16 *Ibid.*

17 Social Justice Tribunals Ontario, Landlord and Tenant Board, "The Landlord and Tenant Board's Rules of Practice" (16 January 2017), online: <http://www.sjto.gov.on.ca/documents/ltb/Rules/LTB%20Rules%20of%20Practice.html>.

18 RSO 1990, c S.22.

guidance related to such things as the initiating of proceedings, service and filing of documents, amendments, adjournments, and mediations, and so on. It is important to be familiar and up-to-date with the rules, as failure to follow them can be detrimental to your client. The LTB publishes practice directions[19] that help practitioners and laypeople understand the rules. They support the rules by providing advice about the tribunal's expectations.

As an additional resource, the LTB provides interpretation guidelines,[20] which are **non-binding** explanations of the how the LTB may interpret the RTA and the Regulations. Note that some adjudicators may not agree with all guidelines and may render decisions contrary to what is outlined in the interpretation guidelines.

The SPPA is the overarching framework that all tribunals reference and ensure compliance with when determining their rules.

Application Process

To initiate a proceeding before the LTB, you should be familiar with the LTB forms, what they are for, and the fees associated with each type of application. If you are representing a landlord, you will be required to serve tenants with a notice that outlines the issue and the time period within which the tenant can address the issue. Tenants are encouraged to detail their concerns to their landlord in writing and to provide reasonable timelines to resolve the issue. Tenants may have to provide some notices, depending on the type of matter. Section 191 of the RTA and Rule 5 provide information regarding methods of service that are acceptable to the LTB. Table 3.1 outlines each type of notice, the purpose, and the notice period or date of termination that must be provided to the other side.[21]

non-binding materials or case law that the decision-maker is not required to follow; items are persuasive but no requirement to abide by them

19 Social Justice Tribunals Ontario, Landlord and Tenant Board, "Rules, Practice Directions and Guidelines" (2015), online: <http://www.sjto.gov.on.ca/ltb/rules-practice-directions-guidelines/>.

20 *Ibid.*

21 Social Justice Tribunals Ontario, Landlord and Tenant Board, "Forms" (2015), online: <http://www.sjto.gov.on.ca/ltb/forms/>.

TABLE 3.1 Notices, Notice Periods, and Termination Dates for Landlord Tenant Matters

	Notice Type	Purpose	Notice Period/ Termination Date
Notices for Landlords	N1	Notice of Rent Increase	90 days • at least 12 months have passed since last increase
	N2	Notice of Rent Increase (Unit Partially Exempt)	90 days
	N3	Notice to Increase the Rent and/or Charge for Care Services and Meals	90 days • at least 12 months have passed since last increase
	N4	Notice to End Your Tenancy Early for Non-payment	**1st breach** Monthly: 14 days Daily/Weekly: 7 days
	N5	Notice to End Your Tenancy for Interfering with Others, Damage, or Overcrowding	**1st breach** 20 days Interfering (small landlord): 10 days **2nd breach** 14 days Interfering (small landlord): not applicable
	N6	Notice to End Your Tenancy for Illegal Acts or Misrepresentation	**1st breach** 20 days Illegal act (drugs): 10 days **2nd breach** 14 days Illegal act (drugs): not applicable
	N7	Notice to End Tenancy for Causing Serious Problems in the Rental Unit or Residential Complex	**1st breach** 10 days

	Notice Type	Purpose	Notice Period/ Termination Date
	N8	Notice to End Your Tenancy at the End of the Term	60 days: Monthly 28 days: Daily/Weekly
	N10	Agreement to Increase Rent Above the Guidelines	As agreed upon by the parties
	N12	Notice to End Your Tenancy because the Landlord, a Purchaser, or a Family Member Requires the Rental Unit	60 days
	N13	Notice to End Your Tenancy because the Landlord wants to Demolish the Rental Unit, Repair It, or Convert It to Another Use	120 days (1 year if a mobile home park or land lease community and you own the mobile home or the land lease home) • termination date must be the last day of the rental period (i.e., end of the month)
	N14	Landlord's Notice to the Spouse of the Tenant Who Vacated the Rental Unit	Served within 45 days of spouse leaving Spouse has 15 days to respond • does not apply to situations with three or less units
Notices for Tenants	N9	Tenant's Notice to End the Tenancy	60 days
	N11	Agreement to End the Tenancy	As agreed upon by the parties
	N15	Tenant's Notice to End My Tenancy Because of Fear of Sexual or Domestic Violence and Abuse	28 days • does not have to be the last day of a rental period or of a fixed-term lease

It is essential to be aware of **notice periods** and the **computation of time** (i.e., how the LTB counts days) to schedule your time correctly and provide effective representation before the LTB. Section 193 of the RTA and Rule 4 of the LTB rules of practice outline how time is calculated. Generally, "the time between two events is computed by excluding the day on which the first event occurs and including the day on which the second event occurs."[22] Any errors with regard to notice periods and termination dates may result in the notice being nullified. Section 185 of the RTA and Rule 8 specify the factors and errors that may result in an invalidation of your notice. If you have incorrectly served notice or have missed an important date, create a new notice and serve the revised document on the other parties. If you need to shorten or extend time limits, section 190 of the RTA, section 56 of O Reg 516/06, and Rule 15 can provide guidance on the extension or abridgment of time. Some time limits can be amended while others cannot.

The notice must outline the possibility of remedying the situation (if applicable) and provide clear details on what is required to remedy it. Note in Table 3.1 that reference is made to the first versus the second breach. You must become well versed in which infractions provide an opportunity to remedy (i.e., overcrowding) and which do not (i.e., illegal activity related to drug offences). It is also important to understand that, in some circumstances, a second breach within six months will result in automatic eviction (with notice served on the other side) without an opportunity to remedy. The six-month rule is in keeping with section 81 of the RTA. Essentially, section 81 provides that

> an order of the Board that evicts someone expires within 6 months of the date [of] the order unless it is filed with the appropriate Court Enforcement Office before that time. This expiration provision applies notwithstanding any appeal proceeding that may be initiated in a court of competent jurisdiction. Once an eviction order expires, there is no authority to renew it, nor will the landlord be able to apply again for the same remedy for the same time period.[23]

notice period the timeframe within which a landlord or tenant is required to provide an opportunity to remedy or resolve an issue

computation of time the act of computing, counting, or numbering for the purpose of serving legal documents, providing notification to parties, or filing documents with the tribunal; errors may lead to the legal action being invalidated

22 Social Justice Tribunals Ontario, Landlord and Tenant Board, "The Landlord and Tenant Board's Rules of Practice: Rule 4.1" (16 January 2017), online: <http://www.sjto.gov.on.ca/documents/ltb/Rules/LTB%20Rules%20of%20Practice.html#r4>.

23 Social Justice Tribunals Ontario, Landlord and Tenant Board, "Procedural Issues Regarding Eviction Applications: Interpretation Guideline 10" (31 January 2007), online: <http://www.sjto.gov.on.ca/documents/ltb/Interpretation%20Guidelines/10%20-%20Procedural%20Issues%20Regarding%20Eviction%20Applications.html>.

You should serve a notice for each infraction—and as soon as possible—to avoid compounding issues and to mitigate any delays in obtaining the relief that you are seeking.

After the notice period or **termination date** associated with the issue has expired, you will have to file the appropriate application and pay the corresponding fee to initiate a proceeding at the LTB. In accordance with section 29(2) of the RTA, tenants have a one year from the time of the breach to file an application.[24] Table 3.2 details each type of application, the purpose, and the fees associated with initiating an application.[25] Familiarity with the Act, Regulations, and rules is imperative for ensuring that you know the requirements for which your client is responsible (i.e., on becoming aware of an unauthorized tenant, a landlord has 60 days to file an A2 application). Missed deadlines can result in additional costs or a missed opportunity to seek the relief that your client wants.

TABLE 3.2 Applications and Fees for Landlord Tenant Matters

	Application Type	Purpose	Fees
Landlord Applications	L1	Application to Evict for Non-payment of Rent and to Collect Rent the Tenant Owes	$190 $175 if e-filed
	L2	Application to End a Tenancy and to Evict a Tenant	$190 $175 if e-filed
	L3	Application to End a Tenancy—Tenant Gave Notice or Agreed to Terminate the Tenancy	$190
	L4	Application to End a Tenancy—Tenant Failed to Meet Conditions of a Settlement or Order	No charge

termination date an expiration date; the date on which a leasing agreement is no longer active

24 Social Justice Tribunals Ontario, Landlord and Tenant Board, "Tenant Rights: Interpretation Guideline 6" (1 September 2017), online: <http://www.sjto.gov.on.ca/documents/ltb/Interpretation%20Guidelines/06%20-%20Tenants%20Rights.html>.

25 Social Justice Tribunals Ontario, Landlord and Tenant Board, "Filing and Fees" (2015), online: <http://www.sjto.gov.on.ca/ltb/filing-and-fees/>.

	Application Type	Purpose	Fees
	L5	Application for an Above-Guideline Increase	$220 for first 10 units and $10 for each additional unit to a maximum of $1,000
	L6	Application for Renewal of a Provincial Work Order	$190
	L7	Application to Transfer a Care Home Tenant	$190
	L8	Application Because the Tenant Changed the Locks	$190
	L9	Application to Collect Rent the Tenant Owes	$190
Tenant Applications	T1	Application for a Rebate	$50 for first application and $5 each additional unit up to a maximum of $450
	T2	Application About Tenant Rights	$50 $45 if e-filed and $5 each additional unit up to a maximum of $450
	T3	Application for Rent Reduction	$50 for first application and $5 each additional unit up to a maximum of $450
	T4	Landlord Did Not Comply with an Agreement to Increase Rent Above the Guideline	$50 for first application and $5 each additional unit up to a maximum of $450
	T5	Landlord Gave a Notice of Termination in Bad Faith	$50 and $5 each additional unit up to a maximum of $450

	Application Type	Purpose	Fees
	T6	Application About Maintenance	$50 $45 if e-filed and $5 each additional unit up to a maximum of $450
	T7	Application About Suite Meters	$50 for first application and $5 each additional unit up to a maximum of $450
	A1	Application About Whether the Act Applies	$50
	A2	Application About a Sublet or an Assignment	$50 if filed by tenant $190 if filed by landlord
	A4	Application to Vary the Amount of a Rent Reduction	$50 if filed by tenant $190 if filed by landlord

As noted above, the LTB allows for L1, L2, T2, and T6 applications to be filed via e-filing and provides discounted fees for these. According to section 192(1) of the RTA and Rule 6, an application can be filed at one of the LTB's regional offices or at a Service Ontario Centre that accepts documents on behalf of the LTB. Appendix A to the rules lists all the Service Ontario Centres where documents can be filed. The LTB will then issue a Notice of Hearing (hearings are normally booked three to six weeks in advance). Generally, if you attend in person at a regional office, the LTB will issue your Notice of Hearing as you wait. LTB staff will inform you if they are unable to do so and provide you with an order to serve documents that will outline what needs to be served on the other parties. If you filed your document at a Service Ontario Centre, your Notice of Hearing will be sent in the mail. Bulk filers (those who file a significant number of applications at once) will be emailed their Notices of Hearing.[26]

26 Social Justice Tribunals Ontario, Landlord and Tenant Board, "LTB Bulk Application Information Sheet" (3 January 2017), online: <http://www.sjto.gov.on.ca/documents/ltb/Other%20Forms/Bulk%20Application%20Info%20Sheet.pdf>.

In accordance with Rule 10.1, the LTB will serve your Notice of Hearing along with the application and any motions or requests. The LTB will not serve any documents, photos, or other evidence that you intend to use at the hearing.[27] You must do this yourself. It is good practice to provide the other party with disclosure and documentation to support the allegations being made. Be mindful that the adjudicator will be making findings of fact, and this task will be made easier with supporting documentation and evidence.

In some situations the LTB will not serve the Notice of Hearing and application on your behalf. Rule 10.2 outlines circumstances when the LTB may ask you to serve the other parties yourself (i.e., applications for above guideline rent increases).

Before filing, proofread your document to ensure that you have properly calculated monies owing, computed dates appropriately, and included copies of notices served along with proof of service. This extra step will save you from potential headaches later.

Both parties (especially when represented) are encouraged to discuss possible remedies and solutions to the outstanding issue. This process is eased by reciprocal disclosure. Rule 19 provides guidance regarding disclosure. In addition to documentary evidence, parties may exchange information that will be disclosed via witnesses (will-say statements) to promote settlement. Some matters may require expert witnesses and generally involve reports and findings that become a part of the evidence before the tribunal. Expert reports must be filed ten days before the hearing or as soon as possible.

The LTB also provides mediation to parties to assist them in resolving their disputes. Mediation is a free service that is generally provided on the day of the hearing, but you can contact the LTB before the hearing date to set up a mediation hearing.[28] If parties are able to settle, they avoid having to have a hearing, and the **terms of settlement** (the mediation outcomes) are converted into an order of the LTB. One benefit of mediation is that you can attempt to resolve additional issues that may not have been detailed on the application, with meaningful results. If the parties are unable to settle, their matter goes back in the hearing queue and will be heard by an adjudicator that same day (time permitting).

terms of settlement the details of an agreement made between parties by way of negotiation or mediation

27 Social Justice Tribunals Ontario, Landlord and Tenant Board, "Step 3: Application and Hearing Process" (2015), online: <http://www.sjto.gov.on.ca/ltb/application-and-hearing-process/#step3>.

28 Social Justice Tribunals Ontario, Landlord and Tenant Board, "Step 4: Mediation and the Hearing" (2015), online: <http://www.sjto.gov.on.ca/ltb/application-and-hearing-process/#step4>.

Hearing Process

LTB is a very busy tribunal. Staff mediators and duty counsel, supplied by Legal Aid Ontario, are available onsite to assist those who require assistance. Most hearings before the LTB are oral hearings. Some are very informal (e.g., when dealing with lay litigants on a non-payment of rent matter), and others are more formal. The expectation is that licensed and trained legal professionals will increase the efficiencies of the tribunal by being prepared; by being well-versed in legislation, rules, and procedure; and by being capable advocates. If a matter goes to hearing, the process can be very similar to other tribunals.[29] In control of the hearing is the adjudicator. Each party (the applicant side and the respondent side) must make their arguments to the adjudicator who will make findings of fact and determine credibility.

The adjudicator will ask the applicant to proceed first, and the applicant will begin with the examination-in-chief, followed by cross-examinations and finishing with re-examination, if necessary. After re-examination, adjudicators commonly ask questions and seeks clarification from the parties. When finished, the adjudicator will ask if there are any questions arising from the adjudicator's questions in order to provide an opportunity to address any issues that arose during the questioning. This process is repeated until the applicant's case is completed. Once the applicant has stated his or her case, the respondent has an opportunity to conduct examination-in-chief, be subject to cross-examination, and be given an opportunity for re-examination. Once again, the adjudicator may question the respondent to clarify the evidence presented and ask the parties if they would like to re-examine as a result of the questioning. This process is also repeated until the respondent has finished presenting his or her case.

At this stage, the applicant has an opportunity to reply and to call reply evidence to answer any new evidence from the respondent's case. Following reply, the parties will be asked to provide closing submissions, beginning with the applicant. At this stage, you would introduce case law supporting your position and the remedies you are seeking. Be mindful that decisions from the Divisional Court and Court of Appeal are binding on the LTB while decisions of the LTB are persuasive. Thus, when possible, use case law that would be binding on the tribunal. The respondent then has an opportunity to provide closing submissions, and there is a final opportunity for the applicant to provide reply submissions. The matter is then deemed complete.

---

29 Social Justice Tribunals Ontario, Landlord and Tenant Board, *Your Hearing Day* [video] (2015), online: <http://www.videodelivery.gov.on.ca/player/download.php?file=http://www.media.gov.on.ca/3c23399b4c9c3360/en/pages/text.html>.

Some things to consider at the LTB:

1. The LTB is a high-volume tribunal. While contested matters are provided with a hearing, many cases are scheduled each day, so your time before the board is limited. Typically, the LTB will not set aside a half day or full day for your matter. Be clear, concise, and thorough, and get to point (i.e., what is the relief you are seeking and why? What documentation do you have to support the relief you are seeking?).
2. It is worthwhile to observe the LTB in your jurisdiction or where you conduct business to become familiar with how things differ in various jurisdictions (i.e., Hamilton's LTB sits on Tuesdays and Thursdays each week, whereas in areas in Northern Ontario, hearings are held in a hotel space once per month).

Decisions, Reconsideration/Review, Enforcement, and Appeals

Upon conclusion of the submissions, the adjudicator will either reserve his or her decision or render a decision on the spot. Make sure you accurately write down the decision and its associated terms and conditions so that you can properly communicate the findings to your client and have a record for yourself. If the decision is reserved, the adjudicator will tell you how long it will take to receive your decision in the mail. Generally, the board issues orders within a few days of the hearing. You may also request to pick up the order if that is more convenient. For additional convenience, the LTB has an online process that allows you to check online to see if the decision is available.[30] In most cases, the LTB issues orders outlining terms and conditions that the parties were unable to resolve (e.g., termination dates, amount of outstanding rent, or amount of **abatement** owed). In some cases, however, the matters are more complex, and the LTB will issue reasons along with the decision to demonstrate that the adjudicator has weighed all the evidence fairly and objectively (i.e., determining who may be at fault for damage, or determining that the LTB has jurisdiction over a matter). If you would like reasons for your decision, you must request them either at the hearing or within 30 days of the issuance of the order.

abatement a reduction in the amount of rent due awarded by the Landlord and Tenant Board when landlords fail to fulfill their maintenance obligations

30 Social Justice Tribunals Ontario, Landlord and Tenant Board, "Check File Status" (2015), online: <http://www.sjto.gov.on.ca/ltb/check-file-status/>

Sections 209(1) and 210(1) of the RTA indicate that the decisions of the LTB are final and binding and are only appealable on questions of law.[31] When you are in receipt of the decision, make sure to read it for any discrepancies between it and what transpired during the hearing. If an aspect of the decision is unclear, seek direction for any clarifications you require. If upon review, you identify clerical errors, section 21.1 of the SPPA gives the LTB authority to amend such errors, and you would request to amend an order as identified in Rule 28.[32]

If you identify serious errors in the order, you have 30 days to request a review of it pursuant to Rule 29, which states the following:

> The LTB has the discretion to review a final order where the order contains a serious error or a party was not reasonably able to participate in the proceeding. In making a decision to review, the LTB considers the public interest in preserving the finality of its decisions together with the opportunity to correct a serious error without the need to appeal or seek judicial review.[33]

This process has two stages: a preliminary review conducted by a vice-chair or senior member of the tribunal and then a review hearing. If the preliminary review is not successful, the matter is not referred on to a review hearing.

Parties also have the right to seek an appeal to Divisional Court within 30 days from the date the LTB issued the order.[34] The Divisional Court is a branch of the Superior Court that hears matters on appeal from Ontario boards and tribunals.[35] The appeal is governed by the *Rules of Civil Procedure*[36] found in the *Courts of Justice Act*.[37]

Appeals of this nature are outside of the scope of practice for paralegals. It is not advisable to mention anything about the appeal process, with the exception that the parties have the right to appeal and have the option of obtaining the services of a lawyer or representing themselves in the proceeding. As a matter of interest, "when an appeal of an order is filed with the Divisional

31 Social Justice Tribunals Ontario, Landlord and Tenant Board, "Reviewing an Order: Interpretation Guideline 8" (15 July 2016), online: <http://www.sjto.gov.on.ca/documents/ltb/Interpretation%20Guidelines/08%20-%20Review%20of%20an%20Order.html>.

32 Social Justice Tribunals Ontario, Landlord and Tenant Board, "Amending an Order: Interpretation Guideline 15" (31 January 2007), online: <http://www.sjto.gov.on.ca/documents/ltb/Interpretation%20Guidelines/15%20-%20Amending%20an%20Order.html>.

33 *Supra* note 31.

34 <https://www.attorneygeneral.jus.gov.on.ca/english/courts/divisional/Guide_to_Appeals_in_Divisional_Court_EN.html>. Guide to Appeals in Divisional Court

35 Social Justice Tribunals Ontario, Landlord and Tenant Board, "Challenging or Correcting an Order" (31 January 2007), online: <http://www.sjto.gov.on.ca/ltb/application-and-hearing-process/#step6>.

36 RRO 1990, Reg 194.

37 RSO 1990, c C.43

Court, the order is automatically **stayed**, and cannot be enforced unless the Divisional Court or the LTB lifts (or removes) the stay at the request of a party."[38] After hearing the appeal, the Divisional Court has the ability to affirm, amend, replace, or rescind the order. The court also has the ability to remit the matter back to the LTB with its opinion.[39]

Assuming you find no errors, and you want to enforce the terms of the order, it is recommended that you request the relief you have been ordered to receive in writing to the other party. Pursuant to section 184(1) of the RTA, you should also file one of the certified copies of the order with the registrar of the Superior Court of Justice in the area where the other party resides. You must notify the LTB that you have done so within ten days of filing the order. The other certified copy should be filed with the sheriff's office (Court Enforcement Office) in any jurisdiction where the other party holds assets. The sheriff is required to enforce the order as if it were an order of the court. By registering the order with the **registrar** and the **sheriff**, you can use Rule 60 of the *Rules of Civil Procedure* to obtain relief. It is common to obtain a **Writ of Possession** to obtain remedy.

Case Law

Toronto Community Housing Corporation v Allan Vlahovich, 2010 ONSC 1686

In this case, the tenant, Mr. Vlahovich was facing eviction for rental arrears (rent owing) and also made a tenant claim. The LTB awarded Mr. Vlahovich a rent abatement that resulted in $74.50 of arrears owing. Once the arrears were paid, Mr. Vlahovich was able to have the eviction notice voided. The decisions of the LTB were appealed to the Divisional Court on the grounds that the rent abatement was granted for a period outside the one-year limit provided for in section 29(2) of the RTA. The appeal was successful. The court held that

> in light of the one year limitation period in s. 29 (2), the Board can only make a determination that a landlord has breached an obligation under

stay the stopping of an action or a proceeding

registrar an officer of the court who is responsible for the registry or register of the Ontario courts

sheriff the person who manages and transports court prisoners and serves and enforces orders that have been filed with the court

Writ of Possession a writ of execution used to enforce a judgment to recover property; this authorizes the sheriff to enter premises and give possession back to the landlord when there has been a finding against a tenant

38 *Supra* note 36.

39 RTA, s 210(4)(a)(b).

> s. 20 (1) during the one year period before the making of the application. Accordingly, the remedy that may be granted may only be granted in relation to breaches during that one year period.

This case establishes that any claims for maintenance and rent abatements must be made within the one-year period as set out in section 29(2) of the RTA.

Pajelle Investments Ltd v Herbold, [1976] 2 SCR 520

This is a long-standing Supreme Court of Canada case that sets out the right to make tenant claims with regard to maintenance. It also gives guidance with respect to the duty of landlords to maintain not only the unit being occupied but the common areas and amenities as well.

In this case, the tenants rented an apartment and were assured that the premises were air conditioned and that they would also have use of additional amenities like a sauna and indoor swimming pool. Sometime after occupying the unit, the tenants were no longer provided with air conditioning or use of the sauna or swimming pool. The building itself was also in a bad state of repair. The landlord indicated no intention of fixing any of the amenities as fixing them would mean considerable cost. The court held that

> goods and services include not only walls and ceilings but adequate heat, light, and ventilation, serviceable plumbing facilities, secure windows and doors, proper sanitation and maintenance, the rights guaranteed to the tenant...If the duty of the landlord is not fulfilled the tenant has the right to seek relief.

The court went on to indicate that rent abatements should be granted for a lack of maintenance that falls outside of what would be reasonable to have something repaired:

> A Court should only in the most exceptional cases grant an abatement for rent because of failure to provide common facilities and services during a short period required for necessary repairs and renovations. However where there are important and long continuing delays in providing the facilities which it is the responsibility of the landlord to provide these should be compensated by an abatement of rental.

Onyskiw v CJM Property Management Ltd, 2016 ONCA 477

The tenants in this case made an application for rent abatement as a result of the inconvenience of being without an elevator for 96 days in one year. Many of the tenants were seniors and this caused great difficulty for them. The LTB held that the tenants were not entitled to a rent abatement because of the efforts and considerable cost borne by the landlord to replace the elevator in a timely fashion. Circumstances beyond the landlord's control also affected timeliness (i.e., a province-wide elevator technician strike). The LTB used the reasonableness standard of review to make its determination. The matter was appealed on the basis that the tenants felt that correctness was the appropriate standard of review.

The Court of Appeal upheld the decision of the LTB and reiterated that reasonableness was the appropriate standard of review regarding section 20 of the RTA.

This case provides good guidance on determining the appropriate standard of review and illustrates how the court determines whether or not a landlord has met the maintenance obligations.

Walmer Developments v Wolch, 67 OR (3d) 246, 230 DLR (4th) 372

This is a very important decision that deals with the responsibility of a Board of Inquiry (in this case the Ontario Rental Housing Tribunal) in applying section 17 of the *Human Rights Code* (HRC) with respect to its decision-making and use of discretion. In this case, the tenant had schizophrenia and experienced some unfortunate episodes of yelling and disruption of others when she was not on her medication. The landlord issued two notices of eviction and the LTB proceeded on the second eviction notice without giving the tenant an opportunity to remedy. This in and of itself was problematic, but the ORHT also failed to apply section 17 of the HRC when determining whether they would apply discretion under section 84 of the *Tenant Protection Act* (now section 83 relief under the RTA). The court held that this failure was very problematic:

> a board of inquiry under the Code or a court, it is bound to comply with s. 17 in full in its decision-making and in particular when exercising its discretion under s. 84 of the Tenant Protection Act, 1997 as to whether it would be unfair to the landlord not to evict a person suffering from a disability. The ORHT must consider whether any disruption in the enjoyment of other tenants may be sufficiently alleviated by a reasonable accommodation of the disabled tenant without undue hardship to the landlord.

This decision speaks to the duty of the LTB to conduct an analysis to ensure compliance with section 17 of the HRC especially in circumstances where there is an ability to exercise discretion.

KEY LEGISLATION

Ombudsman Act
- General Rules, RRO 1990, Reg 865
- Local Boards, O Reg 114/15

Rental Fairness Act, 2017

Residential Tenancies Act, 2006
- General, O Reg 516/06
- Maintenance Standards, O Reg 517/06
- Suite Meters and Apportionment of Utility Costs, O Reg 394/10

Statutory Powers Procedures Act
- Forms, O Reg 116/95

KEY TERMS

abatement, 62
computation of time, 56
landlord, 50
non-binding, 53
notice period, 56
registrar, 64
rent control, 50
tenant, 50
termination date, 57
terms of settlement, 60
sheriff, 64
stay, 64
Writ of Possession, 64

REVIEW QUESTIONS

1. What is the purpose of the Landlord and Tenant Board?
2. What are the main pieces of legislation that provide the Landlord and Tenant Board with jurisdiction and scope?
3. What is rent control?
4. How do you initiate a proceeding before the Landlord and Tenant Board?
5. What role does mediation play at the Landlord and Tenant Board?
6. What effect does the *Rental Fairness Act, 2017,* have?
7. Where would you appeal a decision of the LTB?
8. What happens if someone has an issue with a landlord (or prospective landlord) that is related to the denial of human rights?
9. What should you do if you require written reasons resulting from a hearing before the LTB?
10. What effect does an appeal have on Landlord and Tenant Board decisions?

SCENARIO

Marita inherited a three-bedroom, two-car garage home when her aunt died in 2016. She was content where she lived and decided to renovate and rent out the home for additional income. Marita spent $15,000 to update the kitchen and bathrooms, and paint the home throughout. On June 1, Marita signed a rental agreement with Sven and his partner, Sasha, to rent the house. They seemed like nice, respectable people who had good jobs. Sven and Sasha paid first and last month's rent for a total of $3,000 (utilities extra). Shortly after moving into the home, Sven bought a pet goat to help maintain the backyard by eating the grass. It was summer and the goat stayed outside. Over a few more months, Sven also brought home a few rabbits, some quail, chickens, a dog, and a cat. The rabbits, quail, and chickens also lived in the backyard. Marita expressed her concerns about the number of animals living on the premises but was assured that the yard and home would be kept clean. As the weather got colder, Sven moved the animals into the garage as neither he nor Sasha drove a car.

On January 15, there was a blackout caused by a snowstorm. Marita stopped by the home to provide flashlights, a backup generator, and water. Upon arrival, there was no one home but Marita saw a goat in the living room, and the remainder of the animals in the kitchen and bathroom. Animal urine and feces were everywhere and the house was in a state of disrepair. Horrified, Marita contacts you for legal advice. What are your recommendations?

CHAPTER 4

Social Benefits Tribunal

Overview and History 70

Legislation and Regulations 70

Ontario Works Act, 1997 and Regulations 70

Ontario Disability Support Program Act, 1997 and Regulations 71

Tranchemontagne 73

Rules of Procedure and Practice Directions 76

Application Process 78

Ontario Works 78

Ontario Disability Support Program 78

Overpayments 79

Director's Decisions, Internal Reviews, and Appeals to the Tribunal 79

Hearing Process 80

Written Submissions 82

Oral Hearings 82

Decisions, Reconsiderations, and Appeals 83

Forms 83

Case Law 91

Key Terms 97

Review Questions 97

Scenarios 98

Overview and History

The Social Benefits Tribunal (SBT) hears appeals stemming from the *Ontario Works Act, 1997* (OWA)[1] and the *Ontario Disability Support Program Act, 1997* (ODSPA).[2] The SBT was created in accordance with the OWA,[3] but its hearings predominantly stem from the denials of disability claims under the ODSPA. The SBT was created when its enabling legislation created a new welfare scheme in Ontario known as Ontario Works (OW). Simultaneously, the Ontario Disability Support Program (ODSP), a benefit program offering financial assistance to Ontarians with disabilities, was legislated. The SBT hears appeals from individuals who have been denied, cut from, or suspended from OW or ODSP, or from individuals who owe an overpayment to either program. The SBT has a chairperson, one or more vice-chairs, and multiple tribunal members.[4]

OW is administered through the municipalities in Ontario[5] under the power of the director, who is appointed under the OWA and whose powers include the delivery and oversight of OW in its entirety.[6] The director also oversees the administration of the ODSP.[7]

Legislation and Regulations

The OWA and ODSPA are the key pieces of legislation governing the SBT, in conjunction with legislative requirements in the *Statutory Powers Procedure Act* (SPPA).[8] The SPPA is discussed in the Chapter 1 and specifically does not apply to OW and ODSP internal reviews or interim assistance.[9]

Ontario Works Act, 1997 and Regulations

The OWA sets out its purpose in section 1, which clearly outlines both a social agenda and an accountability requirement in subsections (a) through (d). The social agenda is highlighted in the statute's aim to provide financial assistance to Ontarians "most in need" (ss 1(a) and (d)) and to "effectively" serve people requiring assistance (s 1(c)). Accountability to taxpayers is evident in the sections that impose employment searching obligations and promote "individual responsibility" and "self-reliance" (ss 1(a) and (d)).

---

1 SO 1997, c 25, Schedule A.
2 SO 1997, c 25, Schedule B.
3 OWA, s 60.
4 OWA, ss 61(1), 62(1).
5 OWA, ss 37, 38; and O Reg 136/98.
6 OWA, ss 47, 48.
7 OWA, ss 37, 38.
8 RSO 1990, c S.22.
9 OWA, ss 27(4), 30(3); and ODSPA, ss 22(4), 25(3).

Eligibility for financial assistance is determined through section 7(3) of the OWA and requires residency in Ontario, budget and asset limits,[10] information disclosure,[11] and cooperation with all of the above by all dependants.[12] There are exceptions to the Ontario residency rule: some of these include incarcerated persons,[13] persons subject to a removal or deportation order,[14] certain classes of students enrolled in full-time study at a postsecondary institution,[15] or, more generally, persons under 18 years of age.[16] Eligibility may also require additional undertakings, such as job-searching.[17] Just as dependants of an applicant are required to abide by the eligibility factors, they are also able to receive benefits[18] along with the applicant, as members of a **benefit unit.**[19] Emergency assistance and temporary assistance are also made possible under the OWA.[20] Employment assistance is part of the financial assistance piece of this program and may include help finding a job or similar activities.[21]

Four regulations exist pursuant to the OWA.[22] The main regulation, known as the General Regulation, outlines key aspects of OW.[23] This General Regulation is central to understanding the OWA, SBT jurisdiction, and SBT process because it gives additional insight to the sections outlined in the statute. Other regulations created under the OWA are O Reg 564/05 (Prescribed Policy Statements), O Reg 136/98 (Designation of Geographic Areas and Delivery Agents), and O Reg 135/98 (Administration and Cost Sharing).

Ontario Disability Support Program Act, 1997 and Regulations

Like the OWA, the ODSPA sets out its purpose at the beginning: to create income and employment supports; however, this Act is aimed at assisting persons with disabilities in Ontario (section 1(a)). The purpose also outlines the

benefit unit a person and all dependants on behalf of whom the person receives or applies for income support

10 O Reg 134/98, ss 38-39, 48-54.1.
11 *Ibid*, ss 14, 20.1.
12 OWA, s 7(3); and O Reg 134/98, s 4.
13 O Reg 134/98, s 8(a).
14 *Ibid*, s 6(1)1.
15 *Ibid*, s 9.
16 *Ibid*, s 10.
17 OWA, s 7(4).
18 OWA, s 8.
19 OWA, s 2.
20 OWA, ss 9, 10.
21 OWA, ss 3-4; and O Reg 134/98, ss 3, 25-31.
22 OWA, s 74.
23 O Reg 134/98.

same accountability to taxpayers as in the OWA (section 1(d)). Financial assistance under the ODSPA is available to persons with disabilities as per section 4(1) of the Act, which outlines specific requirements for being found eligible:

> 4(1) A person is a person with a disability for the purposes of this Part if,
> (a) the person has a substantial physical or mental impairment that is continuous or recurrent and expected to last one year or more;
> (b) the direct and cumulative effect of the impairment on the person's ability to attend to his or her personal care, function in the community and function in a workplace, results in a substantial restriction in one or more of these activities of daily living; and
> (c) the impairment and its likely duration and the restriction in the person's activities of daily living have been verified by a person with the prescribed qualifications.

Of course, an eligible individual must also meet financial (income and asset)[24] and information[25] requirements and must be a resident of Ontario[26] to receive assistance. Similarly to those for OW, dependants of the applicant/recipient are subject to eligibility requirements[27] and are made ineligible through certain factors.[28] Recipients may also be found ineligible because of a failure to pursue other resources.[29]

Section 5(2) of the ODSPA originally included additional requirements that were a barrier to eligibility. That section has since been made inoperable by the courts after a lengthy court battle that started as a standard ODSP application. Section 5(2) states that

> A person is not eligible for income support if,
> (a) the person is dependent on or addicted to alcohol, a drug or some other chemically active substance;
> (b) the alcohol, drug or other substance has not been authorized by prescription as provided for in the regulations; and
> (c) the only substantial restriction in activities of daily living is attributable to the use or cessation of use of the alcohol, drug or other substance at the time of determining or reviewing eligibility.

---

24 *Ibid*, s 5(1)(c); and O Reg 222/98, ss 27, 28.
25 ODSPA, s 5(1)(d); and O Reg 222/98, ss 12, 14(2).
26 ODSPA, s 5(1)(b).
27 ODSPA, s 5(1)(e); and O Reg 222/98, ss 3-4, 6.
28 O Reg 222/98, ss 7-9.
29 *Ibid*, s 11.

Essentially, this created a barrier to ODSP for individuals who suffered from a drug, alcohol, or other substance addiction and suffered substantial impairments and restrictions in their daily living as a result thereof, unless this addiction existed alongside another substantially impairing condition. Individuals could not get ODSP based on addiction alone, even if their impairments and restrictions met the test in section 4(1). For example, if Joe's application for ODSP listed "addiction to oxycontin" as the condition, and all other boxes on the application verifying the resulting impairments, restrictions in daily living, and duration of the condition were satisfactorily completed, he would still be denied ODSP on the basis of section 5(2) alone. However, if Joe's application for ODSP listed two conditions, one being "addiction to oxycontin" and the second being "degenerative disc disease," and both conditions were fully verified with resulting impairments, restrictions in daily living, and duration, then he would stand a good chance of being accepted for ODSP.

This legislative provision came under review in a case known as *Tranchemontagne.*

Tranchemontagne

In 1999, two applications were made to the ODSP based on addiction alone. One was made by Norman Werbeski, and the other was made by Robert Tranchemontagne. At the SBT, both appellants argued that section 5(2) was a violation of their human rights under Ontario's *Human Rights Code* (Code),[30] on the grounds of disability. Disability under the Code had not previously been interpreted to include alcoholism, but both appellants felt that it was a reasonable extension of the definition. Both applications were based on alcoholism, and in 2001 both were denied by the SBT on the basis of section 5(2), even though the SBT found them both to have substantial impairments and restrictions because of their alcoholism.[31] The SBT deferred jurisdiction on the human rights arguments.

Werbeski appealed the SBT decision to the Divisional Court, and the judgment of the court was delivered on March 25, 2003 (one day after it was heard, which is remarkable!).[32] Tranchemontagne's appeal was joined with Werbeski's, and as such this decision applied to both appellants. The appeals were based on the SBT failing to recognize the paramountcy of the Code over the ODSPA. Specifically, the appellants argued that section 1 and section 47(2) of the Code trumped section 5(2) of the ODSPA and sought a declaration that the Code should override the section 5(2) bar on alcoholism as a condition eligible

30 RSO 1990, c H.19.

31 *Tranchemontagne v Ontario (Director, Disability Support Program)*, 2006 SCC 14 at 5-6.

32 *Werbeski v Ontario (Disability Support Program)*, [2003] OJ No 1409.

for ODSP. (Section 1 of the Code outlines the rights of Ontarians to receive services free from discrimination on a number of grounds, one of those grounds being disability. Section 47(2) of the Code states the primacy of the Code over other pieces of legislation, unless there is a legislative statement to the contrary.)

The Divisional Court found that the SBT was restricted by its enabling legislation, and although the SBT was required to apply the Code in interpreting its enabling legislation, it could not apply the Code in way that would override its enabling legislation or jurisdiction (as per previous case law).[33] Furthermore, the court found that the SBT did not have the expertise to determine such a jurisdictional matter, although the court indicated that the apparent conflict must be addressed by a court with competent expertise and jurisdiction to do so.[34] The court denied the appeal.[35]

Werbeski and Tranchemontagne, unsatisfied, appealed the Divisional Court decision to the Ontario Court of Appeal. In a decision dated September 16, 2004 this court also denied their appeal.[36] The appeal was based on the Divisional Court's erroneous decision not to recognize the SBT's jurisdiction to acknowledge the paramountcy of the Code.[37] Specifically, the issue before the Court of Appeal was whether the Divisional Court was wrong to find that the SBT does not have jurisdiction to order that section 5(2) is contrary to the Code.[38] The judgment delivered by Weller J on behalf of the court concluded that the SBT did have jurisdiction to determine if section 5(2) offends the Code on the basis that the SBT was a tribunal capable of determining questions of law and that the enabling legislation did not specifically exclude the SBT from doing so.[39] However, because of practical considerations, the court also determined that the Human Rights Tribunal was a more appropriate venue to determine this legal issue.[40] For the latter reason, the appeal was dismissed.[41]

Once again, the appellants refused to give up, and they appealed the Ontario Court of Appeal decision to the Supreme Court of Canada.[42] The issue on appeal raised the following question: "Is the Social Benefits Tribunal ('SBT'), a provincially created statutory tribunal, obligated to follow provincial human rights legislation in rendering its decisions?"[43] The Supreme Court of

---

33 *Ibid* at para 3.

34 *Ibid* at paras 4, 6.

35 *Ibid* at para 8.

36 *Tranchemontagne v Director of the Ontario Disability Support Program of the Ministry of Community Family and Children's Services* (2004), 72 OR (3d) 457.

37 *Ibid* at 3.

38 *Ibid* at 3.

39 *Ibid* at 4-5, 52-53, 58-59.

40 *Ibid* at 6-7, 61, 69.

41 *Ibid* at 70.

42 *Tranchemontagne v Ontario (Director, Disability Support Program)*, *supra* note 31.

43 *Ibid* at 1.

Canada found that the SBT did have jurisdiction to consider the Code,[44] that it could not decline to consider Code issues when raised,[45] and that it was the best venue to determine the issue.[46] The appeal was allowed, and the Supreme Court ordered that the matter be sent back to the SBT for a determination on the merits of the applicants' cases while mandating that it determine the human rights arguments.[47]

Once again, the appellants found their applications for ODSP before the SBT. It was 2006, and a significant amount of time (seven years!) had passed since their original applications had been filed for assistance. In a decision dated November 30, 2006, and after days of hearing evidence, the SBT concluded that both Werbeski and Tranchemontagne were disabled according to section 4(1) of the ODSPA and that section 5(2) constituted discrimination in accordance with the Code.[48] The director appealed the decision to the Divisional Court on an error of law, with a number of complicated issues on appeal that focused on the evidence presented before the SBT and the correct application of the test to determine inconsistency in the Code.[49] Ultimately, the Divisional Court dismissed the director's appeal, upholding the SBT's decision in favour of Werbeski and Tranchemontagne. The court's decision was based on the following determinations: the SBT did not err in considering the respondent's witness evidence,[50] and the SBT applied the correct test to determine Code violations, including contextual factors,[51] and to identify the correct comparator groups.[52]

The case was not done yet. The director appealed the 2009 Divisional Court decision to the Ontario Court of Appeal, which was the final stop.[53] The director's appeal once again advanced complicated questions of law based on errors in the Divisional Court's reasoning in considering the correct application of the test to determine a Code violation and in the court's upholding of the SBT's approach to the expert evidence supplied by Werbeski and Tranchemontagne.[54] The Ontario Court of Appeal denied the director's appeal, although it did not accept the test put forth by the Divisional Court[55] and found that there had been a questionable application of the evidence.[56]

44 *Ibid* at 40-42.
45 *Ibid* at 46.
46 *Ibid* at 48-52.
47 *Ibid* at 53.
48 *Ontario (Director, Disability Support Program) v Tranchemontagne* (2009), 95 OR (3d) 327 at 21-25.
49 *Ibid* at 26.
50 *Ibid* at 52.
51 *Ibid* at 94, 123.
52 *Ibid* at 116.
53 *Ontario (Director, Disability Support Program) v Tranchemontagne*, 2010 ONCA 593.
54 *Ibid* at 9-11.
55 *Ibid* at 12, 127.
56 *Ibid* at 13, 143.

The result was that section 5(2) of the ODSPA, though still part the Act, is of no force or effect, as it was found to discriminate unfairly against individuals disabled through alcoholism. Since the final 2010 Ontario Court of Appeal decision, application to ODSP for assistance can be made based on substance abuse or addiction alone, provided they satisfy the requirements in section 4(1) of the ODSPA. This decision also affected the determination of "disability" under the Code in other jurisdictions, such as before the Human Rights Tribunal of Ontario,[57] in Ontario Labour Arbitration Awards,[58] and in criminal matters.[59] In addition, it has been considered in other decisions as a basis for interpretation.[60]

Sadly, Werbeski did not live to see the matter resolved.[61]

In addition to the legislative provisions outlined above, the ODSPA has five regulations,[62] with the General Regulation being most important.[63] Like the OW General Regulation, the importance of the ODSP General Regulation lies in its depth and detail. It provides greater clarity on subject matter raised in the legislation; for example both the legislation and this General Regulation are required to understand the requirements of a Notice of Decision and the appeal process. The other regulations outline specifics around employment supports,[64] assistance for children with severe disabilities,[65] administration and cost sharing,[66] and prescribed policy statements,[67] and while important to these specific topics, they do not cover as broad areas as the General Regulation does.

Rules of Procedure and Practice Directions

SBT procedure is primarily governed by its internal rules and practice directions. The SBT rules of procedure are divided into two parts: the Social Justice Tribunals Ontario (SJTO) Common Rules and the SBT Rules of Procedure.[68]

---

57 See *Carter v Chrysler Canada Inc*, 2017 HRTO 168; and *Appleton v Artisan Co-operative Homes Inc*, [2016] OHRTD No 1709.

58 See *Ontario Nurses' Assn v Sunnybrook Health Sciences Centre (Discharge Grievance)*, [2016] OLAA No 361; and *Toronto District School Board v Ontario Secondary School Teachers' Federation District 12 (Accommodation Grievance)*, [2015] OLAA No 301.

59 *R v Jewett* (2010), 9 MVR (6th) 306.

60 See *Hendershott v Ontario (Ministry of Community and Social Services)*, 2011 HRTO 482; *Hay v Ontario Provincial Police*, 2012 HRTO 2316; Decision No 681/10, [2012] OWSIATD No 1025; *Andrews v Canada (Indian and Northern Affairs)*, 2013 CHRT 21; and *Riche v Treasury Board (Department of National Defence)*, 2013 CRTFP 35.

61 *Ontario (Director, Disability Support Program) v Tranchemontagne*, *supra* note 53 at para 17.

62 ODSPA, s 55.

63 O Reg 134/98.

64 O Reg 223/98.

65 O Reg 224/98.

66 O Reg 225/98.

67 O Reg 562/05.

68 Social Justice Tribunals Ontario, Social Benefits Tribunal, "Rules of Procedure" (1 July 2018), online: <http://www.sjto.gov.on.ca/documents/sbt/SBT%20Rules%20Parts%201%20&%202%20EN.html>.

Ten different practice directions[69] also guide the SBT and parties on topics such as litigation guardians,[70] reconsideration requests,[71] and recording proceedings.[72]

The SJTO Common Rules apply to all tribunals in the SJTO cluster (see Chapter 1 for more details on clustering). The purpose of the Common Rules is to allow for a cohesive set of binding practices among the tribunals in the cluster, but they have been part of the SBT's structure only since October 2013. The SBT Rules of Procedure have been in effect since January 2016. As per the preamble to the Rules of Procedure, the two parts should be read together. This means that when faced with an issue covered in either set of rules, parties and members are obliged to consider both sets of rules in the interpretation of the issue raised.

The SJTO Common Rules advance the ideals of fairness and an expeditious resolution of matters. They promote a liberal and purposive interpretation for the "fair, just and expeditious resolution of disputes," while promoting effective party participation and proportionality between the outcomes and issues.[73] The rules also mandate courtesy, respect, and good faith by participants in the tribunal process,[74] which clearly establish boundaries for self-represented litigants while simultaneously echoing the requirements of licensed counsel as set out through rules of conduct.[75] Tribunal powers are also touched upon, specifically with respect to innate ability to exercise its own powers[76] or to waive or vary any of the applicable rules,[77] or even to dismiss a vexatious matter for abuse of process.[78] Such powers, and others, are also outlined in the SBT Rules of Procedure at 1.4 and 1.5.

Other topics in the SBT Rules of Procedure are noted throughout this chapter.

---

69 Social Justice Tribunals Ontario, Social Benefits Tribunal, "Rules and Practice Directions" (2015), online: <http://www.sjto.gov.on.ca/sbt/rules-of-procedure/>.

70 Social Justice Tribunals Ontario, Social Benefits Tribunal, "Practice Direction on Litigation Guardians before the Social Justice Tribunals Ontario" (1 October 2013), online: <http://www.sjto.gov.on.ca/documents/sjto/Practice%20Directions/Litigation%20Guardians%20before%20SJTO.html>.

71 Social Justice Tribunals Ontario, Social Benefits Tribunal, "Practice Direction on Reconsideration Requests" (2015), online: <http://www.sjto.gov.on.ca/documents/sbt/Reconsideration%20Requests.html>.

72 Social Justice Tribunals Ontario, Social Benefits Tribunal, "Practice Direction on Recording Proceedings" (2015), online: <http://www.sjto.gov.on.ca/documents/sbt/Recording%20Proceedings.html>.

73 *Supra* note 68, r A3.1.

74 *Ibid*, r A7.1.

75 Law Society of Ontario, *Paralegal Professional Conduct Guidelines* (1 October 2014; amendments current to 28 September 2017), online: <http://www.lsuc.on.ca/paralegal-conduct-guidelines>; and Law Society of Ontario, *Paralegal Rules of Conduct* (1 October 2014; amendments current to 28 September 2017), online: <http://www.lsuc.on.ca/paralegal-conduct-rules>.

76 *Supra* note 68, r A4.1.

77 *Ibid*, r A4.2.

78 *Ibid*, rr A8.1, A8.2.

Application Process

Individuals apply to the SBT by completing an appeal form and submitting it to the tribunal if their application for OW or ODSP had been denied, if their OW or ODSP had been cancelled or suspended, or if an overpayment had been rendered against them. Practitioners must understand the entire process of applying for OW and ODSP, including the lead-up to this appeal.

Ontario Works

Applications for OW are enabled through section 15 of the OWA. The General Regulation for Ontario Works provides greater insight into the application process.[79] The standard procedure is for an individual to go to a local office, meet with a caseworker, and take a financial eligibility test. Decisions about eligibility are usually made within a day or two, and the applicant is informed immediately. The amount of monthly assistance is determined by the regulations.[80] Typically, a single person on OW receives approximately $706 per month, inclusive of basic needs and shelter allowances.[81]

Ontario Disability Support Program

Applications for ODSP assistance are made under section 10(1) of the ODSPA but are further referred to in section 14 of the General Regulation for ODSP.[82] Applications for ODSP must be completed by a medical professional.[83] An optional personal statement portion may be completed by the applicant. ODSP eligibility determinations take significantly longer than for OW eligibility because local offices must wait to receive the disability determination package back from the medical practitioner, which can take up to 90 days. The amount of monthly assistance awarded, if the person is found eligible, is determined by the regulations.[84] Typically, a single person on ODSP receives approximately $1128.00 per month, inclusive of basic needs and shelter allowances.[85] ODSP also enables recipients to work and offers employment supports,[86] as well as a scheme for treatment of earnings.[87]

---

79 O Reg 134/98, ss 16-20.

80 *Ibid*, ss 40-47.2.

81 *Ibid*, ss 41(1)1, 42(2)2.

82 O Reg 222/98, ss 14-16.

83 ODPSA, s 4(1)(c); and O Reg 222/98, s 46.

84 O Reg 222/98, ss 29-37.

85 *Ibid*, ss 30(1)1, 31(2); and O Reg 223/98, ss 30, 31.

86 ODSPA, ss 32-36.

87 O Reg 222/98, ss 38-40.

Overpayments

If recipients receive more assistance than they are entitled to, an **overpayment** may be rendered against them, which means they must pay the money back.[88] Overpayments can be collected through a reduction in the amount of monthly financial assistance,[89] through a court order for recovery,[90] or through recovery from other programs,[91] as well as a debt owing to the Crown.[92]

A recipient will receive a written notice of overpayment under section 21(1) of the OWA or section 16 of the ODSPA that will list the amount of the debt and any information necessary. After a notice of overpayment is received, the recipient may launch an internal review of the decision[93] and then proceed to an appeal at the SBT.[94] A decision of the SBT that upholds the overpayment is final and enforceable against the appellant.[95]

Director's Decisions, Internal Reviews, and Appeals to the Tribunal

Decisions concerning overpayments, suspensions, and denials must be given to the affected individual and contain information about appeal rights, which begin with an internal review.[96] Internal review requests must be made within 30 days of the date of the decision,[97] and the director will allow or deny the request.[98] Often, the internal review decision will uphold the director's original decision. The applicant or recipient may then appeal to the SBT[99] but

overpayment money paid to a recipient that is in excess of the correct amount the person should have received, thus creating a debt to the Crown

---

88 OWA, s 19; ODSPA, s 14; and O Reg 222/98, ss 51, 52.

89 OWA, s 20(1); O Reg 134/98, s 62-64; ODSPA, ss 14(4), 15.

90 OWA, s 22.

91 ODSPA, s 14(3); and OWA, s 19(3).

92 OWA, s 22.1; and ODSPA, s 14(2.1)(4).

93 OWA, s 27; and ODSPA, s 22(1).

94 OWA, s 26(1); and ODSPA, s 21(1).

95 OWA, s 21(3).

96 OWA, ss 24, 26; O Reg 134/98, s 67; ODSPA, s 19; and O Reg 222/98, s 56.

97 OWA, s 27 (3); O Reg 134/98, ss 69, 70; ODSPA, s 22(3); O Reg 222/98, s 58; and Social Justice Tribunals Ontario, Social Benefits Tribunal, "Social Benefits Tribunal: Rules of Procedure for Appeals to the Social Benefits Tribunal" (1 January 2016), r 2.1, online: <http://www.sjto.gov.on.ca/documents/sbt/SBT%20Rules%20Parts%201%20&%202%20EN.html#rule2>.

98 O Reg 134/98, s 71; and O Reg 222/98, ss 59, 60.

99 OWA, s 28; and *supra* note 68, rr 2.3, 2.5.

only if the original decision pertained to the "eligibility for or the amount of basic financial assistance"[100] for OW or to "eligibility for or the amount of income support, assistance ... or extended health benefits"[101] for ODSP.

Some decisions cannot be appealed, including the denial of discretionary assistance[102] (i.e., a recipient's request for moving costs) or a decision related to emergency assistance.[103] Appeals must be made within 30 days from the date of the internal review decision, although the SBT may grant an extension.[104] Appeals to the SBT must be made on the tribunal-approved appeal form.[105] See Form 1 under the Forms heading later in this chapter. Appeals are denied if the appellant fails to file within the limitation period or fails to attend the hearing, whether in person or by other means (e.g., phone or teleconference).[106] This appeal process is essentially the application process at the SBT.

Hearing Process

Once an appeal has been filed with the SBT, a notice of hearing will be sent from the tribunal to the parties within 60 days, and with at least 30 days' notice of the pending date.[107] The SPPA has specific requirements for what must be included in a written notice of hearing.[108] The SPPA standards are reflected in the requirements that are laid out in the OWA General Regulation, which requires:

> The notice of hearing shall set out,
>
> (a) in the case of an oral hearing, the place, date and time of the hearing; or
>
> (b) in the case of a paper hearing, the dates by which the parties are required to provide their written submissions and documentary evidence to the Tribunal.[109]
>
> Hearings are held across the province,[110] usually at community centres or hotels.

---

100 OWA, s 26(1).

101 ODSPA, s 21(1).

102 ODSPA, s 21(2); and O Reg 134/98, ss 59, 68; see also O Reg 222/98, s 57.

103 OWA, s 26(2); and ODSPA, s 21(2).

104 OWA, ss 28(1), (2); O Reg 134/98, s 72; ODSPA, s 23(1); O Reg 222/98, s 61; and Social Justice Tribunals Ontario, *supra* note 97, rr 3.1, 3.3.

105 *Supra* note 68, r 3.2.

106 OWA, s 34(1).

107 O Reg 134/98, s 74(1), (3); and O Reg 222/98, s 63.

108 SPPA, ss 6(3)-(5).

109 O Reg 134/98, s 74(2).

110 *Ibid*, s 65; and *supra* note 68, r 7.5.

Although the appellant may feel odd showing up at a local library boardroom for a hearing, this approach reduces expenses (by avoiding bricks-and-mortar costs) and promotes greater access to justice (by limiting appellants' need to travel). The OWA and the SBT Rules of Procedure also provide for written hearings, specifically where all parties agree.[111]

SBT now provides the option of video conferencing.[112] This pilot project in conjunction with the Rexdale Community Legal Clinic (Rexdale), which hosts the conferencing option, is testing how effective and efficient video conferencing is. Rexdale has identified some early benefits of the pilot project as increased scheduling efficiencies and cost savings for the SBT, reduced travel time and costs for representatives and appellants, decreased stress for appellants, and greater overall convenience.[113] Rexdale also highlights some innate challenges concerning security, privacy, integrity, budget, training, and communication, as well as challenges specific to the self-represented appellant.[114]

Despite the provisions of the SPPA,[115] all SBT hearings are closed to the public.[116] On appeal, the burden of proof lies with the appellant.[117]

The OWA promotes fairness in decision-making through its mandate that members

> (a) shall not have taken part in any investigation or consideration of the subject-matter of the hearing before the hearing; and
>
> (b) shall not communicate directly or indirectly in relation to the subject-matter of the hearing with a person except upon notice to and opportunity for all parties to participate.[118]

The exception, of course, is the tribunal's legal adviser, from whom members can seek legal advice.[119] Tribunal members are also required to take notes at the hearing.[120] Typically, only one member presides over a hearing; however, the OWA allows for more than one member to be appointed to sit in a hearing, with one as the presiding member.[121]

---

111 OWA, s 65; O Reg 134/98, s 83; and *supra* note 68, rr 7.7-7.10.

112 E Ann McRae, "Video Conferencing as an Option at the Social Benefits Tribunal: Completely unscientific analysis of the issues faced in the pilot project at the Rexdale Hub, 2015-2016" in *Designing the Infrastructure of Tribunals: The Six-Minute Administrative Lawyer 2017* (Toronto: Law Society of Ontario, 2017) at 6C-1.

113 *Ibid.*

114 *Ibid.*

115 SPPA, s 9.

116 OWA, s 66(1); and *supra* note 68, r 7.1.

117 OWA, s 28(11); and ODSPA, s 23(10).

118 OWA, s 66(2).

119 OWA, s 66(3).

120 O Reg 134/98, s 76(4).

121 *Ibid*, s 64.

Written Submissions

Any documents that a party wants to use at the hearing are subject to disclosure requirements.[122] For matters arising out of the OWA, the appellant must provide disclosure at least 20 days before the hearing, and the administrator, at least 10 days before the hearing.[123] The same timelines apply for matters arising out of the ODSPA,[124] except for medical evidence in disability determination appeals, where the timeline for new evidence is at least 30 days before the hearing.[125] Written disclosure timelines are also addressed in the SBT Rules of Procedure, Rules 4 and 5.9 to 5.11.

Oral Hearings

Oral hearings before the SBT follow an **adversarial** hearing approach. Hearings usually begin with the tribunal member introducing himself or herself and then explaining the procedure that will be followed. Typically, SBT hearings last one to two hours. After the introductory comments have been made, the member will proceed by asking if any preliminary issues need to be addressed. Preliminary issues may be a request for further disclosure from the other side or an adjournment for grounds that were not previously obvious (in other words, you should not leave an adjournment request to the day of the hearing if you knew that it was required before then).

After preliminary matters have been dealt with, or if there were no preliminary issues, then the member will invite the appellant (the individual appealing the decision of the director) to begin presenting of his or her case.[126] Usually, the appellant's legal representative directly examines the appellant. If the party is unrepresented, the member will likely question the appellant. After the direct examination, if the director's representative is present (known as the case presenting officer), that person will cross-examine the appellant and call upon any of the director's witnesses (usually there are none). A representative of the director need not be present to proceed with the hearing; in the representative's absence, the tribunal relies upon the written submissions of the director (previously provided).[127]

adversarial two parties arguing their case before an independent trier of fact

122 OWA, s 28(10); and ODSPA, s 23(9).

123 O Reg 134/98, s 76(2)(a)(b).

124 *Ibid*, s 65(2)(a)(b).

125 *Ibid*, s 64(1)(b).

126 O Reg 134/98, s 76(1).

127 OWA, s 28(8)(9); and ODSPA, s 23(7)(8).

After all parties have presented their cases, the tribunal may ask if anything further needs to be addressed or may request closing statements, though they are rare and may be reserved for more complicated matters. At this point, the member will close the hearing and will reserve his or her decision.

Decisions, Reconsiderations, and Appeals

The decision is mailed to the parties within 60 days, per legislative requirements,[128] although it is typically sent sooner. The SBT has the power to deny the appeal, grant the appeal in full or in part, or refer it back to the administrator.[129] Reasons must be given for the decision.[130] Either party may request a **reconsideration** of the SBT's decision. In a reconsideration request, the requesting asks the tribunal to take a second look at its decision. Reconsideration requests must be made within 30 days of receiving the hearing decision.[131] Further rules concerning reconsideration requests are found in both the SBT Rules of Procedure[132] and the practice direction on reconsideration requests.[133] Appeals from SBT decisions can be made to the Divisional Court on questions of law[134] within 30 days of receiving the decision.[135] The Divisional Court may deny the appeal, grant the appeal in full or part, or refer the matter back to the tribunal.[136]

Forms

The SBT Rules of Procedure refer to a number of forms. The Appeal Form (Form 1) and the Application for Reconsideration (Form 2) are just two examples. These forms have been reproduced here.

reconsideration a request to the tribunal to review the decision

128 O Reg 134/98, s 78(1); and O Reg 222/98, s 67(1).
129 OWA, s 31(1); and ODSPA, s 26(1).
130 OWA, s 31(2); and ODSPA, s 26(2).
131 O Reg 134/98 at 79(1); and O Reg 222/98, s 68.
132 *Supra* note 68, r 15.
133 *Supra* note 71.
134 OWA, s 36(1); ODSPA, s 31(1); and *supra* note 68, r 16.1.
135 O Reg 134/98, s 81; ODSPA7, s 70; and *supra* note 68, r 16.1.
136 OWA, s 36(5); and ODSPA, s 31(5).

FORM 1 Instructions for Filing an Appeal

Social Justice Tribunals Ontario
Providing fair and accessible justice
Social Benefits Tribunal

Instructions for Filing an Appeal: Form 1

1. Before you can appeal to the SBT you must request an internal review by the Ontario Disability Support Program (ODSP) or Ontario Works (OW) office that made the decision. The SBT does not decide internal reviews. You must file your appeal with the SBT within 30 days of receiving the internal review decision. If you are late filing you need to explain why. The SBT will decide whether to allow a late appeal.

2. Attach copies of the following to this form:
   i) the original **Notice of Decision** from the OW or ODSP office
   ii) your **request for an internal review** from the OW or ODSP office
   iii) the **internal review decision** (if you received one).

3. The SBT does not have the authority to review all social assistance decisions. If we can't hear your appeal, we will send you a letter with the reasons why.

4. If you are experiencing financial hardship while you wait for your appeal to be decided you can ask the SBT for interim assistance by completing Part 4 of this form. Interim assistance is financial help while waiting for your appeal to be decided. If the SBT decides you are eligible for interim assistance, you will be notified in writing. If you lose your appeal, your interim assistance will be assessed as an overpayment and you will have to pay it back.

   Note: The SBT does not issue cheques. Your local ODSP or OW office will pay the interim assistance.

5. If you do not attend your hearing and don't provide a reasonable explanation for your absence, your appeal will be denied and you will not be allowed to appeal a subsequent decision on the same issue for two years. For more information, visit our website at www.sjto.ca/sbt or phone the SBT at one of the numbers below:

   Tel: 416-326-0978
   Toll-free: 1-800-753-3895
   TTY: Call the Bell Relay Service at 1-800-855-0511

Social Benefits Tribunal • 655 Bay Street, 14th Floor, Toronto, Ontario M7A 2A3 • Fax 416-326-5135

Social Justice Tribunals Ontario
Providing fair and accessible justice
Social Benefits Tribunal

Appeal
FORM 1

File Number: [| | | | - | | | | |]
(Office use only)

Part 1: General Information

Appellant's Name:				Appellant's date of birth:	
Address:				Unit Number:	PO Box:
Municipality (City, town):	Province:	Postal Code:	Telephone 1:	Telephone 2:	

Which office made the decision you are appealing?

◯ Ontario Works office
◯ Disability Adjudication Unit
◯ Ontario Disability Support Program office

Member / Case ID:	
Office name:	
Office address:	
Case worker's name:	
Case worker's telephone:	

Part 2: Internal Review Information

If you did not request an internal review, you may not appeal to the SBT.

What is the date of your original Notice of Decision? [| / | / | | |]
dd/mm/yyyy

When did you make your request for an internal review? [| / | / | | |]
dd/mm/yyyy

Did you receive an internal review decision? ◯ Yes ◯ No

Part 3: Your Appeal

Why are you appealing? Check **all** the boxes that apply to you.

☐ I was refused assistance.
☐ My assistance has been reduced.
☐ I have an overpayment.
☐ The amount of my assistance is wrong.
☐ My assistance has been cancelled.
☐ My assistance is on hold.
☐ They say I am not disabled.
☐ They say I am no longer disabled, as a result of a medical review.

Explain what you disagree with in the original decision and why. Use the space below and attach additional pages if necessary.

In what language would you like your hearing? ◯ English ◯ French

Will you need any of the following services at the hearing?

☐ Interpreter:

Language

Dialect

☐ Sign language interpreter

Physical or other accommodation to participate in the hearing. Please specify.

Signature:

Name:	
Signature:	Date:

Collecting Personal Information: The Social Benefits Tribunal (SBT) collects the personal information requested on this form under the *Ontario Works Act*, 1997 or the *Ontario Disability Support Program Act*, 1997. It will be used for the purpose of conducting the appeal and will be shared with the parties. If you have any questions, contact the FIPPA representative at the SBT at 1-800-753-3895.

v. 01/10/2016

This completes the appeal section.

If you are experiencing financial hardship, complete Part 4 Application for Interim Assistance.

Social Benefits Tribunal • 655 Bay Street, 14th Floor, Toronto, Ontario M7A 2A3 • Fax 416-326-5135

Page 2 of 4

Part 4: Application for Interim Assistance

Describe your household. How many people, including yourself, are you applying on behalf of?

Adults ☐ Children ☐

Check the box beside those sentences that best describe your situation.

☐ I am looking for work.
☐ I am in an employment assistance program.
☐ I am attending school.
☐ Full-time ☐ Part-time ☐ High School ☐ College ☐ University ☐ Other
☐ I am under 18 and cannot live at home.
☐ I am working, but earn less than the Ontario Works entitlement.
☐ Other

Are you receiving any money at all? ○ Yes ○ No

If you live with your spouse, is he/she receiving any money? ○ Yes ○ No

If you or your spouse are receiving money, provide details of your household income below. Include the amount you receive, when you last received it and how often you receive this income.

Type of Income	Amount	Date Last Received (dd/mm/yyyy)	Weekly, Monthly or Other (Specify)
Example: Income A	**$100.00**	**01/06/2011**	**Monthly**
Earnings from a job			
Vacation pay			
Ontario Works (OW)			
Ontario Disability Support Program (ODSP)			
Workplace Safety & Insurance Benefits (WSIB)			
Employment Insurance			
Canada Pension Plan			
Disability insurance (other than CPP, WSIB)			
Support payments			
Trust fund income			
Ontario Student Assistance Plan (OSAP)			
Rental/boarder income			
Borrowed money			
Foreign pension			
Self-employment earnings			
Other 1			
Other 2			

Will you be receiving any money next month that you have not already listed? ○ Yes ○ No

What type? ☐ Amount: ☐

Provide the details below of the value of the assets you or any member of your household have.	
Bank accounts (personal and business)	
Stocks, bonds, GICs	
RSPs	
Land and property other than your home	
Other	
How much money do you pay each month for:	
Rent	
Mortgage	
Property taxes	
Room and board	
Heat	
Electricity	
Water	
Food	
Other	

Are you behind in any of your payments or unable to pay these expenses?

◯ Yes ◯ No What expenses have you been late paying or unable to pay?

Have you received an eviction notice or notice your electricity or other service will be shut off?

◯ Yes ◯ No Provide details:

Below, provide any additional information that you feel the tribunal should know regarding your financial circumstances.

Name:	
Signature:	Date:

Collecting Personal Information: The Social Benefits Tribunal (SBT) collects the personal information requested on this form under the *Ontario Works Act*, 1997 or the *Ontario Disability Support Program Act*, 1997. It will be used for the purpose of conducting the appeal and will be shared with the parties. If you have any questions, contact the FIPPA representative at the SBT at 1-800-753-3895.

Social Benefits Tribunal • 655 Bay Street, 14th Floor, Toronto, Ontario M7A 2A3 • Fax 416-326-5135 Page 4 of 4

FORM 2 Application for Reconsideration

Social Justice Tribunals Ontario
Providing fair and accessible justice
Social Benefits Tribunal

Application for Reconsideration
FORM 2

About an Application for Reconsideration

Use this application to ask the Social Benefits Tribunal (SBT) to reconsider a decision made on an appeal. You have 30 days from the time you receive your decision to ask for a reconsideration by submitting this application form. The SBT will review your application, determine if a new hearing should be held and send you a letter with that decision within 60 days.

You must send a copy of this Application for Reconsideration to the other parties to the original appeal decision. Other parties may file a response to this application within 15 days of receiving a copy. The Practice Direction on Reconsideration Requests explains the process in more detail.

Part 1: Information about the appeal

Are you the appellant or the respondent? ○ Appellant ○ Respondent

The file number on the appeal decision is: ☐☐☐☐ - ☐☐☐☐☐

The date of the appeal decision is: ☐☐ / ☐☐ / ☐☐☐☐
dd/mm/yyyy

Part 2: Information about the appellant

Appellant's name:				Appellant's date of birth:	
Address:				Unit Number:	PO Box:
Municipality (City, town):	Province:	Postal Code:	Telephone 1:	Telephone 2:	

Part 3: Information about the respondent

The respondent is:

○ Ontario Works office
○ Disability Adjudication Unit
○ Ontario Disability Support Program office

Office name:			Name of contact at the office:
Address:			
Municipality (City, town):	Province:	Postal Code:	Telephone:

Part 4: Reasons for your request for reconsideration

Why should the SBT grant your request for a reconsideration hearing? Please give your reasons below.

The SBT may reconsider if it appears:

- there is a legal or jurisdictional error
- there was procedural unfairness
- there are new facts that were not available at the time of the hearing which could change the decision

Attach more sheets if necessary.

Part 5: Notice of service

Were there other parties to the original hearing other than the appellant and respondent?

○ No ○ Yes Names: ______________________

I have served a copy of this application on the other parties by:

○ Regular post to the last known address

○ Delivering it personally

○ Sending a fax

Part 6: Signature

Name:	
Signature:	Date:

Collecting Personal Information: The Social Benefits Tribunal (SBT) collects the personal information requested on this form under the *Ontario Works Act*, 1997. It will be used to decide whether to grant a reconsideration and will become part of the SBT file. If you have any questions, contact the FIPPA representative at the SBT at 1-800-753-3895.

v. 01/10/2016

Case Law

A number of significant decisions stem from the SBT. The *Tranchemontagne* decision was one. Some other notable decisions are outlined briefly here.

Ontario (Director, Ontario Disability Support Program) v Gallier, [2000] OJ No 4542 (QL) (Div Ct)

Gallier is a 2000 decision from the Divisional Court that contemplates the SBT decision to find Gallier "a person with a disability" in accordance with section 4(1) of the ODSPA, stemming from an appeal by the director. The Divisional Court applied the standard of correctness in the appeal and considered "whether the Tribunal was 'correct' in its interpretation of the legislation."[137] The court dismissed the appeal[138] on the following findings:

- There must be verification of the disability, in accordance with section 4(1), including "the circumstances of the impairment, its duration and its effect on the applicant"; however, not every detail requires verification in this sense, and some details may be provided by the appellant in testimony.[139]
- The SBT can consider the appellant "in the context of her own situation" and in consideration of "the person": "The test is not whether any person with these impairments and restrictions met the criteria, but whether this person met the criteria."[140]

Consideration of the person requires the tribunal to conduct an objective inquiry into who this person is that appears before it: What are her limitations? What is her age? What is her work history? Can she likely retrain or be re-educated? This type of inquiry allows for a greater understanding of the individual in the grand scheme of life and whether her situation is well aligned with the purposes of the ODSPA. This case was critical to the development of ODSP law in creating a holistic approach to interpretation, rather than a strict reading of legislation.

Gray v Ontario (Disability Support Program, Director) (2002), 59 OR (3d) 364, 212 DLR (4th) 353 (CA)

Gray is a 2002 decision from the Ontario Court of Appeal that considered, in part, the reasoning in *Gallier*. It stems from an application for ODSP by Cassie Gray, which was denied by the director and by the SBT and the Divisional

137 *Ontario (Director, Ontario Disability Support Program) v Gallier*, [2000] OJ No 4542 (QL) at para 6 (Div Ct).

138 *Ibid* at 14.

139 *Ibid* at 7-8.

140 *Ibid* at 12.

Court. Following the Divisional Court decision, Gray appealed to the Ontario Court of Appeal.[141] Her application was based on the conditions of low abdominal pain, menstrual headaches, and migraines, and while there were restrictions provided on the application as well as through the appellant's testimony, the SBT found insufficient medical evidence to show that she was disabled according to section 4(1) of the ODSPA, as she was able to cope on a day-to-day basis.[142] On appeal, the Divisional Court focused on the activities of daily living interpretation and also found that Gray did not meet the criteria in section 4(1).[143]

The Ontario Court of Appeal disagreed with the lower court's reasoning and referred to the dissenting opinion of that court, which considered *Gallier* (consideration of "the person"); the remedial nature of the legislation (to be interpreted "broadly and liberally");[144] that ambiguity in the interpretation of the legislation (being for social welfare) should be interpreted in the applicant's favour;[145] and that there is a legislative requirement to give sufficient reasons supported by findings of fact.[146] Failing to give reasons in accordance with the legislative requirements, specifically section 67(3) of the Regulations, amounts to an error of law, as does focusing on the incorrect question of whether the applicant could cope on a day-to-day basis (and not just about substantial restrictions in activities of daily living). As such, the matter was sent back to the tribunal for determination but with a strong suggestion from the Court of Appeal that it be returned to the SBT "with the direction that this court is satisfied that the appellant is "a person with a disability within s. 4(1) of the Ontario Disability Support Program Act."[147]

Crane v Ontario (Director, Disability Support Program) (2005), 83 OR 3d 321, 278 DLR 4th 374 (CA)

Crane is a 2005 decision of the Ontario Court of Appeal affirming the decision from the Divisional Court (ultimately ordering a new hearing[148]), although disagreeing with part of the reasoning.[149] *Crane* has been considered in numerous other cases.[150] The respondent, April Crane, was denied ODSP for

141 *Gray v Ontario (Disability Support Program, Director)*, 59 OR (3d) 364, 212 DLR (4th) 353 at 1.

142 *Ibid* at 3.

143 *Ibid* at 6.

144 *Ibid* at 7-9.

145 *Ibid* at 10.

146 *Ibid* at 23-24.

147 *Ibid* at 27.

148 *Crane v Ontario (Director, Disability Support Program)* (2005), 83 OR (3d) 321 (CA) at 38.

149 *Crane v Director of the Ontario Disability Support*, 2005 CanLII 21115, 75 OR (3d) 282 (Div Ct).

150 See some recent cases: *Graham v Ontario (Director, Disability Support Program)*, 2015 ONSC 5791; *Ferris v Ontario (Director, Disability Support Program)*, 2014 ONSC 6151.

failing to meet the requirements in section 4(1), which she appealed to the Divisional Court. The Divisional Court allowed her appeal and a new tribunal hearing was ordered.[151] The director appealed the Divisional Court decision to the Ontario Court of Appeal, with the issues before the appeal court being the interpretation of "person with a disability" in section 4(1) of the ODSPA and "substantial physical or mental impairment" in section 4(1)(a), as well as whether there was a significant factual error amounting to a "palpable and overriding error."[152] Crane's application was based on the conditions of "fibromyalgia, asthma, anxiety/depression, headaches," with fibromyalgia being the "principal condition" on which her application was based.[153] She was working a couple of days per week at a convenience store.[154]

The Ontario Court of Appeal's decision summarized the SBT's denial of Crane's appeal on the basis that her "impairments did not have substantial impact on lifestyle," claiming there has to first be a substantial impairment, and then the direct and cumulative effect of the impairment has to be substantial restriction in activities of daily living.[155] Ultimately, the Court of Appeal dissected the section 4(1) test, finding that subsections (a) and (b) cannot be merged and must be considered separately (an error made by Divisional Court in its reasoning); however, there may be overlapping evidence in the consideration of the individual sections:[156]

> In summary, s. 4(1) of the ODSPA presents three questions—substantial impairment, substantial restriction in certain activities, and verification. These are separate questions that require separate analysis and answers. The onus is on the claimant to establish all three factors. Accordingly, if the Tribunal concludes that the claimant has failed to establish one of the factors, it need not deal with the other factors. Finally, in some cases (but not all) there can be an overlap in the evidence relevant to the factors in paras. (a) and (b) of s. 4(1). That is because although the concept of impairment is anchored in medicine, the determination of whether an impairment is substantial will require consideration of the whole person, including a person's ability to function in the domains of personal care, community and workplace.[157]

The "consideration of the whole person" was an important interpretive aspect stemming from this case. The court echoed the same sentiment earlier in the decision: "the inquiry would have to go beyond simple medical description and take account of the whole person, including some of her activities."[158]

---

151 *Supra* note 149.

152 *Ibid* at paras 2-3.

153 *Crane v Ontario (Director, Disabiltiy Support Program), supra* note 148 at para 7.

154 *Ibid.*

155 *Ibid* at paras 9-10.

156 *Ibid* at para 20.

157 *Ibid* at para 25.

158 *Ibid* at para 20.

Jennings v Ontario (Minister of Social Services), 2015 ONSC 6689

Jennings is a 2015 decision from the Divisional Court based on an assessed overpayment. Darrell Jennings appealed a decision by the director to cancel his ODSP support and render an overpayment of $25,712.30 because of failing to declare income and not meeting the eligibility requirement for income and assets. His appeal was denied by the SBT, so he appealed to the Divisional Court. The court found that there was a misapprehension of the evidence at the SBT, based on an inaccurate finding of wilful failure to disclose information,[159] and that this constituted an error of law.[160] Furthermore, the court starkly reprimanded both the tribunal and the director in their approach to finding the recipient responsible for overpayment, stating in the judgment:

> I prefer to see the Tribunal's findings reflecting a tunnel vision based on its fundamental misunderstanding of the nature of a legal partnership, a misunderstanding apparently encouraged by the Director's representative.[161]

Surdivall v Director (Ontario Disability Support Program), 2014 ONCA 240

Surdivall is a 2014 decision from the Ontario Court of Appeal also dealing with an issue of overpayment. At issue was the discretionary power of both the director and the SBT in altering or forgiving an overpayment amount rendered against a recipient.[162] The appeal arose from an overpayment that was ordered against Glynn Surdivall, a recipient of ODSP until he reached the age of 65.[163] In a notice from the director, Surdivall was found to owe $3,050 (made from an innocent reporting error) and was ordered to pay the full amount. Surdivall appealed the overpayment to the SBT, where it found that the overpayment decision was correct, but the SBT cut the total amount to $1525, with a repayment rate of $10 per month.[164] The director appealed the SBT's decision to Divisional Court, where the judgment stated neither the director nor the SBT had the authority to forgive an overpayment debt.[165] The Ontario Court of Appeal disagreed with the finding of the lower court. On the issue of the director's discretion, the Court of Appeal considered the powers and duties of the director under the ODSPA, specifically sections 38(a)-(g); the purpose of the legislation, found at sections 1(a)-(d); and the recovery of overpayment sections, found at sections 14(1), (2.1), (4), and (5).[166] Interpretation of the term

159 2015 ONSC 6689 at 2, 3, 59, 60, 66-74.

160 *Ibid* at 41 ("However, where a tribunal completely misapprehends the evidence or completely fails to take relevant and important evidence into account, this constitutes an error of law," *Shooters Sports Bar v Alcohol and Gaming Commission* (2008), 238 OAC 9, 2008 CanLII 25052 (Div Ct) at para 38).

161 *Ibid* at 4; see also at 64.

162 *Surdivall v Director (Ontario Disability Support Program)*, 2014 ONCA 240 at 2-3.

163 *Ibid* at 4.

164 *Ibid* at 5.

165 *Ontario (Disability Support Program) v Surdivall*, 2012 ONSC 1851 at 19.

166 *Supra* note 162 at 22-34.

"may be recovered" resulted in a conclusion that the director has "broad discretion,"[167] including discretion not to recover part or all of an overpayment.[168] The Court of Appeal also noted that flexibility is required in the collection of overpayments, particularly where overpayments result from innocent mistakes.[169] Finally, the court discussed at length the overall objective of the ODSPA as lending support for its interpretation.[170] On the issue of the SBT's discretion, the court considered the SBT's powers on appeal, found in the ODSPA sections 21(1) and 26(1), and the limited authority in section 29(3), which disallows the tribunal from making any decision that the director was not authorized to make, from which the court implied a positive discretion on the tribunal to be granted the authority to make any decision that director could make[171] and that the SBT should have authority to exercise discretion when faced with an appeal from a discretionary decision, unless expressly granted otherwise in the legislation.[172] Ultimately, the Court of Appeal found:

> [T]he Director has discretion to forego recovery of part or all of an overpayment. As the Director has this discretion, so too did the tribunal have discretion to order that the Director collect only half of the overpayment Surdivall received. I would allow the appeal and reinstate the Tribunal's decision.[173]

Rea v Administrator (2005), 79 OR (3d) 583 (CA)

Rea is a 2005 decision from the Ontario Court of Appeal dealing with a cancellation of OW assistance for failure to provide information about change of circumstances. The director cancelled Rea's OW for failing to comply with the information requirements in section 7 of the OWA. Rea agreed that she failed to comply with these requirements but argued that because of O Reg 134/98, specifically sections 14 and 35, her payments should have been terminated, but her dependant daughter's payments should not have been terminated.[174] Rea argued that the two sections are related, but the Ontario Court of Appeal disagreed with this interpretation.[175] Section 14 places an obligation on the director to find a recipient ineligible for failure to provide information and does not provide an exception for dependants.[176] Section 35 seems to contradict this, stating that if assistance is cancelled and there is a dependant, then the

167 *Ibid* at 30.
168 *Ibid* at 22-34.
169 *Ibid* at 37.
170 *Ibid* at 35-45.
171 *Ibid* at 72.
172 *Ibid* at 74.
173 *Ibid* at 212.
174 *Rea v Administrator* (2005), 79 OR (3d) 583 at 1-2.
175 *Ibid* at 6.
176 *Ibid* at 4.

assistance should be reduced according to the amount of benefit that the person who failed to comply is entitled to.[177] Ultimately, the Court of Appeal disagreed that the two sections are related, finding that section 14 deals with foundational information that is required for initial and ongoing assistance, while section 35 refers to the calculation of entitlement.[178] Both sections must be read with the entirety of the Act in mind, specifically section 7, which outlines ineligibility factors and is central to the entire scheme; reading otherwise would undermine the purpose of the Act.[179]

KEY LEGISLATION

Ontario Disability Support Program Act, 1997 and Regulations
- Administration and Cost Sharing, O Reg 225/98
- Assistance for Children with Severe Disabilities, O Reg 224/98
- Employment Supports, O Reg 223/98
- General, O Reg 222/98
- Prescribed Policy Statements, O Reg 562/05

Ontario Works Act, 1997 and Regulations
- Administration and Cost Sharing, O Reg 135/98
- Designation of Geographic Areas and Delivery Agents, O Reg 136/98
- General, O Reg 134/98
- Prescribed Policy Statements, O Reg 564/05

Statutory Powers Procedure Act

177 *Ibid.*

178 *Ibid* at 7.

179 *Ibid* at 8-9.

KEY TERMS

adversarial, 82

benefit unit, 71

overpayment, 79

reconsideration, 83

REVIEW QUESTIONS

1. What are the two pieces of legislation from which appeals are made to the Social Benefits Tribunal? Name and briefly explain the differences between the two.
2. What other piece of legislation is central to the Social Benefits Tribunal's decision making, and why is this?
3. What larger organization does the Social Benefits Tribunal belong to, and how does this impact it's functioning?
4. Name two types of appeals that the Social Benefits Tribunal will consider, from either piece of legislation in question 1.
5. Why are the regulations important to understanding and interpreting the Acts?
6. What is the significance of the *Tranchemontagne* decision?
7. If you had to request an internal review of a decision from the Director under the *Ontario Disability Support Program Act*, what authorities would you rely on?
8. If a new client approached you about an appeal form that he submitted to the Social Benefits Tribunal and you discovered that an internal review had not been completed, how would you advise this client? What authorities would you rely on?
9. After the Social Benefits Tribunal makes a decision following a hearing, if either party disagrees, what options might they pursue? State your authorities for your answer.
10. What information is required to appear on a notice of hearing, as per the OWA?

SCENARIOS

1. **OWA Denial:** Joshua Insame applied for Ontario Works assistance on February 13, 2016 at the local OW office. Upon disclosing all information that the caseworker requested about his financial affairs (including bank statements and infrequent earnings from a temporary landscaping position) and personal information (address, phone number, health card information), Joshua was found ineligible for OW on the basis that he failed to provide his dependant's health card information and proof of school enrolment. Joshua requested an internal review of the decision, which was upheld. He now wonders if he is out of options or if he can take the denial of his application to the next step. What do you advise? Include references to the statutory or policy authorities that you rely on.
2. **ODSP Denial:** Peter Garvett applied for ODSP based on numerous medical conditions, including sciatica, anxiety/depression, migraines, and diabetes. Peter's application was denied. He requested an internal review, which upheld the original decision. Peter sent in his appeal form to the SBT but has now come to you for assistance with his appeal. What are your next steps, and how would you advise Peter concerning SBT procedure before the hearing? Include references to statutory or policy authorities that you rely on.
3. **OWA Overpayment:** Leah Hanball started receiving OW in January 2016. In March 2017, she received a notice from the director stating that she has been overpaid for a few months because of an administrative error. The notice letter stated that she was required to pay back the full amount of the overpayment and that a portion of the overpayment would be deducted from her ongoing monthly assistance. Leah is concerned about the monthly deductions as she is barely able to scrape enough money together each month for food and rent. She comes to you in May 2017 for advice. What would you tell Leah about how the law affects her in this situation? Include references to statutory or policy authorities that you rely upon.

CHAPTER 5

Criminal Injuries Compensation Board

Overview and History 100

Legislation and Regulations 100

Application Process 104

Hearing Process 105

Decisions, Reconsiderations, and Appeals 106

Other Notable Rules of Procedure 106

Case Law 107

Key Terms 112

Review Questions 112

Scenarios 113

Overview and History

The Criminal Injuries Compensation Board (CICB) is one of the lesser known tribunals in Ontario. The CICB came into existence in 1971 under the *Compensation for Victims of Crime Act* (CVCA).[1] It is one of the eight tribunals in the cluster known as Social Justice Tribunals Ontario (SJTO), as discussed in Chapter 1. Before the CICB, a compensation scheme was available to Ontarians in accordance with the *Law Enforcement Compensation Act*.[2] The CICB provides compensation to individuals who have suffered loss as the result of a violent crime, as well as the families of deceased victims of violent crimes.

Legislation and Regulations

The CVCA is the empowering statute behind the CICB. Section 5 of the CVCA is a crucial part of the compensation scheme provided for under the Act and outlines what injuries are compensable (in other words, who can claim for what):

> Where any *person is injured or killed* by any *act or omission* in *Ontario* of any other person occurring in or resulting from,
>
> (a) the *commission of a crime of violence* constituting an offence against the *Criminal Code* (Canada), including poisoning, arson, criminal negligence and an offence under section 86 of that Act but not including an offence involving the use or operation of a motor vehicle other than assault by means of a motor vehicle;
>
> (b) *lawfully arresting or attempting to arrest* an offender or suspected offender for an offence against a person other than the applicant or his or her dependant or against such person's property, or assisting a peace officer in executing his or her law enforcement duties; or
>
> (c) *preventing or attempting to prevent the commission of an offence or suspected* offence against a person other than the applicant or his or her dependant or against such person's property,
>
> the Board, on application therefor, may make an order that it, in its discretion exercised in accordance with this Act, considers proper for the payment of compensation to,
>
> (d) the *victim*;
>
> (e) a *person who is responsible for the support* of the victim;
>
> (f) *where the death of the victim has resulted, the victim's dependants* or any of them or the *person who was responsible for the support of the victim immediately before his or her death* or who has, on behalf of the

---

1 RSO 1990, c C.24.

2 Criminal Injuries Compensation Board, "What We Do" (2015), online: <http://www.sjto.gov.on.ca/cicb/what-we-do/>.

> victim or his or her estate and not being required by law to do so, *incurred an expense referred to* in clause 7 (1) (a) or (e) arising from the act or omission. [Emphasis added.]

Individuals can claim compensation from the CICB if they have suffered an injury as a result of a violent crime, in a situation of lawful arrest (or attempted lawful arrest), or while attempting to prevent a crime. Furthermore, individuals seeking compensation do not have to be the victims; the seeker may be a third party, such as a support person or dependant of the victim.

The legislation does not define "crime of violence." As is the case with many terms that are found in legislation, "crime of violence" has been open to interpretation by the CICB. When a term or phrase is not clearly defined by legislation, decision-makers can use case law as an interpretive tool. *Pitters v Criminal Injuries Compensation Board*[3] is one such case that helps with the interpretation of "crime of violence." In the absence of a description by the legislators, the court in *Pitters* determined that whether an act amounted to a "crime of violence" was a matter to be determined by the CICB, based on the evidence provided by the applicant. *Pitters* is summarized at the end of this chapter.

Under the CVCA (s 7(1)), compensation can be awarded for the following:

> (a) expenses actually and reasonably incurred or to be incurred as a result of the victim's injury or death;
> (b) pecuniary loss incurred by the victim as a result of total or partial disability affecting the victim's capacity for work;
> (c) pecuniary loss incurred by dependants as a result of the victim's death;
> (d) pain and suffering;
> (e) support of a child born as a result of rape;
> (f) other pecuniary loss resulting from the victim's injury and any expense that, in the opinion of the Board, it is reasonable to incur.

"Actually" incurred expenses (as mentioned in subsection a) refer to general losses, and aim to restore the victim to his or her pre-injury position or to put the person back in the position in which he or she would have been had the harm not occurred. "**Pecuniary**" losses (as mentioned in subsections b and c), also known as special damages, are easily quantifiable or calculable, such as five physiotherapy sessions costing $50 each for a total monetary loss of $250. "Pain and suffering" is an example of a non-pecuniary award for which a specific amount cannot be calculated, but a general figure is offered. Before the

pecuniary a cost award that is given as compensation for something that is measurable or quantifiable

3 (1996), 95 OAC 325.

completion of a hearing, the CICB can also order **interim compensation** to assist, for example, with ongoing medical expenses, and such compensation is not recoverable, even if the CICB later decides against awarding compensation (s 14). Interim compensation awarded to assist an applicant who is in great financial need throughout the CICB process but who has not yet had a full hearing cannot be clawed-back by the CICB, even if the applicant is eventually denied compensation under the CVCA. This type of compensation is called "interim" because it is awarded in the interim, before the final decision. It is meant as a financial aid for therapy or other medical costs.

A number of items may not be compensable, including damaged or stolen goods and legal fees for related criminal or civil matters.

An applicant who shows that the crime of violence resulted in a criminal conviction will not need to prove to the CICB that a crime of violence occurred; the conviction is proof (s 11). However, the applicant is still required to show the resulting injury. An applicant who is claiming a crime of violence occurred but for which there is no conviction has the additional onus of first proving to the CICB that the crime of violence happened before asserting the injuries. Although compensation can be awarded even without a conviction, the CICB may **stay** the proceedings pending the outcome of an ongoing criminal trial, at the request of a party or on its own motion (s 16(1)).

In determining whether compensation should be awarded, the CICB has broad discretion in the factors it considers. The CVCA requires members to consider "all relevant circumstances," including any behaviour of the victim that may have contributed to their injury (s 17(1)). If the victim's own behaviour contributed to the injury, whether directly or indirectly, the CICB can reduce or completely bar compensation that it might have ordered (s 17(2)). Furthermore, the CICB is entitled to consider subsequent criminal behaviour in determining whether to award compensation (see *Sweet v Ontario (Attorney General)*,[4] discussed later in the chapter under "Case Law").

According to the CVCA, compensation can be awarded to one victim in a lump sum, to a maximum of $25,000, or in multiple payments with a monthly maximum of $1,000 (ss 18, 19(1)). Where multiple or periodic payments are awarded, recipients must notify the CICB of any change in their circumstances that could have bearing on the amount of compensation they receive.[5]

interim compensation assistance awarded before the final determination of the issue

stay when proceedings are placed on hold or paused

4 2011 ONSC 2650.

5 Criminal Injuries Compensation Board, "Rules of Procedure," r 15.2 (24 October 2017), online: <http://www.sjto.gov.on.ca/documents/cicb/Rules_of_Procedure.html>.

When multiple applicants are seeking compensation in the same matter, the CVCA specifies that the total lump sum payment awarded to all cannot exceed $150,000, or $365,000 in installment payments (ss 18, 19(2)).

When there is a history of acts, all of a similar nature and involving the same parties (e.g., in a case of ongoing abuse), the CICB may consider each violent act to be one part of a greater whole; in other words, ongoing acts of abuse may be considered one act for the compensation being awarded (s 19(4)). The CICB may also revisit and vary a periodic payment award.[6] Note that compensation may be varied by the CICB, in accordance with section 25, and this also applies when an applicant has requested a review of a one-member decision. This means that applicants risk having their compensation reduced when they request a review before a two-member panel.

The CVCA specifically allows persons injured as a result of a violent crime to also recover damages in civil court (s 26(1)). However, if damages are awarded in a civil proceeding, the applicant is required to notify the CICB and may be required to reimburse any compensation previously ordered by the CICB (ss 26(2)-(5)).

There is also interplay between CICB compensation awarded and other government assistance programs. For example, if a victim who is awarded compensation by the CICB is a recipient of social assistance through Ontario Works (OW) or the Ontario Disability Support Program (ODSP), his or her social assistance payments may be reduced. Any compensation awarded by the CICB for loss of earnings will be deducted from the individual's OW or ODSP entitlement. However, CICB compensation for pain and suffering will not be deducted from the individual's OW or ODSP entitlement.[7] The CICB is also required to consider other benefits or compensation the victim is receiving when determining possible compensation awards; this requires a consideration of Employment Insurance or Workplace Safety and Insurance Board payments.[8]

A secondary piece of legislation by which the CICB is bound is the *Victims' Bill of Rights, 1995* (VBR).[9] The purpose of this Act is clearly stated in its preamble:

> The people of Ontario believe that victims of crime, who have suffered harm and whose rights and security have been violated by crime, should be treated with compassion and fairness. The people of Ontario further believe that the justice system should operate in a manner that does not increase the suffering of victims of crime and that does not discourage victims of crime from participating in the justice process.

---

6 *Ibid*, r 15.3.

7 O Reg 134/98, General, s 54.4; and O Reg 222/98, General, s 43.4.

8 CVCA, s 17(3).

9 SO 1995, c 6.

The VBR outlines foundational principles for the treatment of victims, including courtesy, compassion, respect, privacy, and access to information (ss 2(1)1, 2(1)2). It also details the Victims' Justice Fund Account (s 5) and establishes the Office for Victims of Crime (s 5.1), both of which further support victims.

There are no regulations made pursuant to the CVCA. One regulation exists under the VBR, which is very limited and serves the sole purpose of identifying what crimes under the *Criminal Code*[10] are "prescribed" according to specific sections of the VBR.

Application Process

The CVCA gives an individual seeking compensation two years from the date of the injury (or death) to submit an application, except in circumstances of violent sexual assault or assault arising from an intimate relationship, which have no time limit (ss 6(1), (2)). The CVCA will allow for an extension beyond the two years when applications to the CICB are made requesting an extension (s 6(1)).[11] However, the CICB Rules of Procedure (the Rules) also state that failure to apply to the CICB within the two-year timeframe is grounds for dismissal of an application (r 2.4(c)).

Applications for compensation must be submitted to the CICB using the prescribed forms, which are available on the CICB website.[12] There are two applications forms, one for a crime that resulted in injury and one for a crime that resulted in death. The CICB website is a useful tool for applicants to refer to when starting their application. For example, it lists a number of documents that the applicant should consider submitting with an application, including restraining orders, victim impact statements, and medical records. More in-depth guides are available for review and download. The application must be printed and mailed in to the CICB to start the process.

Once the application is received by the CICB, a preliminary review is completed to ensure that the information is sufficient and complete and that the matter falls within the CICB's jurisdiction, according to the Rules (r 2.3). Applications may be denied at this stage for inadequate information, if no claim is available under the CVCA, or if the limitation period has expired (subject to the discussion above) (r 2.4). If an application is refused, the applicant will receive notice of the decision and the grounds on which that decision was based (r 2.6). An application may also be dismissed without a hearing for a number of factors, some of which are identified by the Rules, such as a matter representing an abuse of process, being beyond the jurisdiction of the CICB, involving trivial injuries, or having no prospect of succeeding (r 2.11).

10 RSC 1985, c C-46.

11 Criminal Injuries Compensation Board, *supra* note 5, r 2.8.

12 Criminal Injuries Compensation Board, "Application and Hearing Process" (2015), online: <http://www.sjto.gov.on.ca/cicb/application-hearing-process/>.

Of course, the parties must be notified of any decision to dismiss the application and be given an opportunity to respond, at which time the CICB may reconsider its decision (r 2.12). At this early stage, the CICB may also request additional medical reports from the applicant and will pay directly for medical reports to a maximum of $100. The CICB will take it upon itself to request police records, as necessary.

Hearing Process

The CVCA states that hearings are open to the public, unless there is a possibility of a prejudicial impact to an ongoing criminal trial or where it would be contrary to the interests of the victim or the victim's dependants, in cases of sexual assault or child abuse (s 12). Hearings may be held before one or two members (s 8). Notice of the hearing is required to be provided to the parties at least ten days before the hearing date, specifying the time, date, and place of the hearing (ss 9(1), (2); see also r 3.3). Note the additional requirements for notice of hearings as mandated by the *Statutory Powers Procedure Act* (SPPA).[13] Interestingly, the offender is one party that requires notice under the CVCA (s 8; see also r 3.1). Where there are multiple offenders named in one application, the CICB may divide the hearing into separate parts (r 8.6).

When a party does not appear for a hearing and proper notice has been served, the Rules allow the CICB to proceed in the absence of the party, and that party is not entitled to any further notice of proceedings (r 3.4).

Hearings may be written, oral, electronic, or any combination of these. Written hearings are common; however, parties can request an oral hearing if they object to a written one. This might be the case if they feel that their case could be prejudiced by the lack of an oral hearing. An applicant may be prejudiced by not appearing for an oral hearing, if the content and context of their testimony is best shared verbally. Where a written hearing is determined, members must give procedural direction to the parties involved (r 7.1). Electronic hearings (r 7.2) are a possibility, but oral hearings are more likely.

In June 2017, the CICB proposed a draft practice direction on recording hearings and asked for stakeholder feedback before the release of the final practice direction. The proposed practice direction is brief; however, the wording suggests that recording proceedings is an administrative function, and it will not allow for a recording to be listened to or released to a party or hearing participants. The proposed exception is for appellants for whom a transcript of the hearing will be provided only after a notice of appeal has been received.

The CICB need only wait 20 minutes for an absent party before either proceeding in the party's absence or moving for an adjournment (r 8.7).

The hearing process itself is typically divided into particular subcategories as a means of information gathering. For example, it is likely that the

13 RSO 1990, c S.22, s 6.

adjudicator(s) will want to hear about each of the following factors separately: the incident itself, the resulting injuries, and then the expenses being claimed. The burden of proof rests with the applicant to show that a "crime of violence" has in fact been suffered as per the requirements of the legislation. The applicant must show this on a balance of probabilities.

Decisions, Reconsiderations, and Appeals

Decisions are rendered in writing and given to each party in the proceeding; however, the rules draw an interesting distinction between the "decision" and the "reasons." Therefore, while there is a requirement for a written decision to be provided, parties who want to receive the written reasons for the decision must request them in writing within 14 days of the hearing. Written reasons are a requirement if the party opts for an appeal or a review of the decision (r 14.1).

Re-hearings may occur as the result of a board-directed order, without the parties' consent. This may occur in cases showing "substantial defect," and Rule 9.1 provides some guidance as to what might constitute such an error:

a. There has been improper notification to parties;
b. An individual with interest in the proceedings has not been notified or otherwise afforded an opportunity to participate;
c. Relevant material evidence has been withheld by a party;
d. Relevant material information has not been disclosed to a party; or
e. There has been a substantive defect in the proceedings.

Reviews of single-member decisions must be requested within 15 days of service of the decision, and the second hearing will be before a two-member panel, without the original member.[14]

Decisions of the CICB may be appealed to Divisional Court.[15]

Other Notable Rules of Procedure

Some rules have already been identified in the context of the application or hearing processes. A practitioner must consider a number of other key rules and practice directions. The Rules for the CICB are online and outline the expected procedures for parties. As discussed in Chapter 1, tribunals are based on principles of fairness and accessibility, and such guiding principles are highlighted in Rule 1.2, which promotes "timely completion of applications," "fair and just resolution of matters," assessment of and proportionality between conduct and complexity of a hearing, and flexibility "in accordance with the principles of procedural fairness and natural justice." Powers of the

14 CVCA, s 10(1), (3); see also r 9.2.

15 CVCA, s 24; see also r 9.3.

board are outlined in Rule 1.5, which provides discretion by members on matters of setting timelines for disclosure and determining if hearings should be oral, written, or electronic. The CICB also has the power to determine its own processes in circumstances where the Rules are silent (r 1.8).

Other matters that are given consideration in the Rules are motions (rr 5.1-5.4), pre-hearing conferences (rr 5.5-5.7), adjournments (rr 6.1, 6.2), stays (r 6.3), and witnesses (rr 11.1, 11.2).

Admission of evidence is also covered in some detail by the Rules. As we know from the SPPA (s 15), hearsay evidence is generally admissible in tribunal practice. The CICB Rules confirm the admissibility of *relevant* hearsay evidence (r 10.3). There are also Rules concerning disclosure; however, note that there is no strict timeline for disclosure created by the Rules. Rather, discretion is given to the member to establish such guidelines on a case-by-case basis (rr 12.1-12.6).

Practitioners should also note the separate practice directions on the CICB website[16] pertaining to the following topics: representation before SJTO, litigation guardians, pre-hearing motions, and public access to hearings.

Case Law

The CICB does not publish their decisions. Therefore, accessing CICB case law can be difficult, but it is not impossible. The website directs interested parties to complete a freedom of information (FOI) request under the *Freedom of Information and Protection of Privacy Act*[17] to have a specific decision released. FOI requests can be made by completing the SJTO form or through a letter.

While accessing decisions can be difficult, there are a few key cases stemming from the CICB that you should be familiar with:

Pitters v Ontario (Criminal Injuries Compensation Board) (1996), 95 OAC 325

The *Pitters* decision is important to defining what a "crime of violence" is under the CVCA because the Act is silent on this. In *Pitters*, the applicant before the CICB had suffered a gunshot wound to the abdomen as a result of an accidental act by a friend (at para 4). The CICB found that she was ineligible for compensation because an accident could not amount to a "crime of violence" (at 10). Pitters appealed the decision to Divisional Court, which allowed the appeal. The court considered the wording of the Act, including who is a "victim" and what is an "injury," to determine what would allow for the kind of compensation envisioned under the Act (at 13-15). Close attention was paid to the term "crime of violence," as the basis of the appeal was whether there

16 Criminal Injuries Compensation Board, "Rules of Procedure: Practice Directions," 2015, online: <http://www.sjto.gov.on.ca/en/rules-of-procedure/>.

17 RSO 1990, c F.31

was an error of law in the CICB failing to define "crime of violence" in a way that would include accidental injury (at 16).

The court recognized the lack of guidance given by the legislature in defining what "crime of violence" should mean and therefore concluded that the meaning must flow from the section of the Act in which it appears (s 5) and from the general rules of statutory construction (at 45). The court concluded that the finding of whether or not a "crime of violence" has occurred rests with the CICB and is not predetermined by evidence submitted to the CICB from a related criminal trial. The court stated (at 55):

> Under the legislation, it is the Board that is required to decide whether a relevant offence, "a crime of violence", has taken place. The matter is not determined by the initial categorization of the offence by police investigators. It is not decided by the charge(s) laid against an offender. It is not resolved by the charge(s) upon which the prosecutor chooses to proceed to trial or other disposition. It is not pre-empted by the decision of the criminal court. It is for the Board to decide the matter, on the evidence adduced before it, and upon proper construction of its statutory mandate.

A number of cases have cited *Pitters* as the discussion around legislative interpretation of the Act continues.[18]

Sweet v Ontario (Attorney General), 2011 ONSC 2650

In this case, the Divisional Court upheld the reasoning of the CICB in its consideration of subsequent criminal conduct of an applicant to determine compensation under the CVCA. Sweet applied to the CICB for compensation for abuse he suffered as a youth at a training school (at 1). The CICB heard evidence of the applicant's criminal history, including a conviction for rape, which occurred after the abuse he suffered in his early years (at 6).

The CICB denied his application for compensation. The issue before the court on appeal was "whether the Board is entitled to consider an applicant/victim's subsequent criminal behaviour when deciding entitlement to compensation" (at 3). The court found that the CICB is entitled to consider the subsequent criminal behaviour of an applicant, pursuant to section 17 of the Act, which requires that "all relevant circumstances" be considered when awarding compensation (at 22). The court specifically pointed to section 17(2), which appears to include some element of "post-occurrence conduct" (at 34), as well as established legislative interpretation principles that require avoidance of an absurd result (at 36). Section 17 of the Act states the following:

18 See *Raba v Criminal Injuries Compensation Board*, 2015 ONSC 5893; *Park v Criminal Injuries Compensation Board*, 2013 ONSC 6673; and *SD v Criminal Injuries Compensation Board*, 2010 ONSC 5808.

> (1) In determining whether to make an order for compensation and the amount thereof, the Board shall have regard to all relevant circumstances, including any behaviour of the victim that may have directly or indirectly contributed to his or her injury or death.
>
> (2) The Board may, in its discretion, refuse to make an order for compensation or order a reduced amount of compensation where it is satisfied that the applicant has refused reasonable co-operation with, or failed to report promptly the offence to, a law enforcement agency.
>
> (3) In assessing compensation, the Board shall take into consideration any benefit, compensation or indemnity paid or payable to the applicant from any source other than social assistance.

Ontario (Attorney General) v Ontario (Criminal Injuries Compensation Board) (1995), 22 OR (3d) 129 (Gen Div)

This case, on appeal to the Divisional Court, began when three victims applied to the CICB for compensation after engaging in sexual intercourse with a man who knowingly carried HIV and failed to disclose this information to each of his sexual partners. Each woman contracted the virus. The man had previously been charged with criminal negligence causing bodily harm in relation to his encounters with these three women; however, he died before a verdict was delivered in the criminal trial (at 12). The CICB awarded $15,000 in compensation to each victim.

In failing to award a greater amount, the CICB reasoned that the victims had contributed to the injuries. The CVCA sets a maximum lump sum amount at $25,000 (s 19(1)(a)); therefore, the victims each received less than the maximum amount compensable. The Divisional Court found that the CICB had held the victims to an unreasonably high standard in finding that they acted carelessly in having unprotected sex with a man that they did not know very well and that the compensation scheme only requires that applicants' actions be "reasonable and prudent" (at Part VIII, 1). As a result, the court determined that there was an error of law, based on a serious error of fact, and the compensation awards were increased to $25,000.

BC v Criminal Injuries Compensation Board, 2014 ONSC 7860

In this case, the applicant applied to the CICB for compensation relating to injuries resulting from two sexual assaults at a high school graduation party. The CICB denied her claim on the basis that the criminal investigation determined there was insufficient evidence. The applicant appealed the CICB decision to the Divisional Court, which overturned the decision of the CICB. The court found that the reasons given by the CICB for the denial of the application were insufficient and that there were gaps in the evidence on which the decision was based. More specifically, the court stated (at 63):

> The Board's reasons fail to give an adequate explanation for its order. Neither the applicant nor this Court could reasonably understand why the Board made its findings of fact and why it issued the order in appeal. This failure thereby resulted in a denial of procedural fairness and natural justice as described in C.P., quoted in paragraph 7, above.

Paragraph 7 of the case, as referenced in the quotation above, provides the basis for the requirement of written reasons as being an integral part of the principles of procedural and natural justice and quotes further from the *Baker*[19] decision of the Supreme Court of Canada to highlight this point.

The matter was remitted back to the CICB for a new hearing, with a new panel.

SD v Criminal Injuries Compensation Board, 2010 ONSC 2562

This case highlights an instance of Divisional Court support for the findings of the CICB when it denied compensation to an applicant. The applicant alleged the following of a man who was her boyfriend at the time: (1) that he forced her to use marijuana, which negatively interacted with her prescribed anti-psychotic medication, causing her to be hospitalized; (2) that following an excessively forceful hug, she suffered from breathlessness and bruising on her back; and (3) that an act of consensual sex turned rough and subsequently was considered by her to be an assault (at 3).

The CICB was not persuaded that these incidents amounted to violent crimes under the CVCA. The applicant appealed the decision on a basis that there was an error of law in the CICB decision, and that the CICB discriminated against her based on her mental disability (at 4). In its decision, the court clearly states, "Not every crime that results in injury is covered by the legislation; it is only crimes of violence that can result in an award" (at 5). The court also found that the CICB adequately relied upon all the evidence that was presented and that no error of law occurred.

The applicant alleged that the CICB discriminated against her based on her mental disability because it found she lacked credibility in her testimony (at 10). The CICB is required to adhere to the *Ontario Human Rights Code* and to take

19 *Baker v Canada (Minister of Citizenship and Immigration)*, [1999] 2 SCR 817.

into consideration any factor that might impact a witness's ability to recall events (at 11, 12). The court noted that "it would be discriminatory to conclude that a person is not credible because he or she has a history of psychiatric illness" (at 11). The CICB, however, was not guilty of such discrimination in this instance. Having considered all of the evidence before it, and finding that some of the applicant's testimony was unreliable, the court found that the CICB "could not conclude on a balance of probabilities that the alleged offender had committed a sexual assault" (at 15). The court denied the appeal.

KEY LEGISLATION

Compensation for Victims of Crime Act
Criminal Code
Statutory Powers Procedure Act
Victims' Bill of Rights, 1995

KEY TERMS

interim compensation, 102
pecuniary, 101
stay, 102

REVIEW QUESTIONS

1. What is the main piece of legislation that governs the CICB?
2. Does a CICB compensation payment have any effect on government benefits?
3. Does every applicant who files an application with the CICB have to prove that a crime of violence occurred for compensation to be awarded?
4. What is the limitation period for applying to the CICB?
5. What three types of injuries are compensable under the legislation?
6. What section of the legislation outlines compensable injuries?
7. What is the monetary amount of compensation that can be awarded as a (1) lump sum and (2) periodic or monthly payment?
8. Can the CICB consider behaviour of the applicant in determining a compensation award?
9. List three types of compensation that may be awarded under the legislation.
10. Aside from the main piece of legislation, addressed in question 1 above, what other statute applies to the CICB?

SCENARIOS

1. Emma has filed an application with the CICB pertaining to an assault that took place one year prior. Emma is seeking compensation for damages following an incident at a mall. Emma and another shopper, Leah, got into a verbal altercation that escalated into a pushing and shoving match over a shoe sale. Emma alleges that Leah attacked her with a pair of four-inch stilettos, leaving a laceration above her right eyebrow and knocking out a tooth. Do you believe that Emma has suffered a crime of violence for which compensation under the CVCA should be awarded?
2. In addition to the CICB claim, there are other related legal matters ongoing as a result of the shoe sale brawl. Leah is facing criminal charges. Emma has also started a tort action against Leah in the civil court system. Pretend that you are Leah's paralegal, representing her in both the criminal and the civil matters. You feel that compensation will be rightfully dealt with in the civil case, and you are concerned about the outcome of this CICB hearing prejudicing your client's criminal trial. Therefore, you want to bring a motion before the CICB to ask that the matter be dismissed, or in the very least, delayed until the outcome of the civil trial. What authorities do you rely upon?
3. If Leah is awarded compensation by the CICB and subsequently is awarded damages in the civil trial, can the CICB request the award back from Leah? Explain your answer with reference to the guiding authorities.

CHAPTER 6

Local Planning Appeal Tribunal

History and Overview 116

Legislation and Regulations 120

Application Process 123

Expropriation Matters 126

Hearing Process 127

Decisions, Reconsideration, and Appeals 129

Case Law 130

Key Terms 133

Review Questions 133

Scenario 134

History and Overview

The Local Planning Appeal Tribunal (LPAT) is a tribunal that many are unfamiliar with, yet the work of the tribunal often affects our daily lives. It came into effect on April 3, 2018 through the enactment of the *Local Planning Appeal Tribunal Act* (LPATA).[1] The LPAT replaces the tribunal formerly known as the Ontario Municipal Board (OMB). The main work of the LPAT falls under the *Planning Act* (PA)[2] and includes resolving disputes related to such things as **zoning by-laws** and the approval of housing subdivisions and condominiums. Another common component of the LPAT's work falls under the *Expropriations Act* (EA)[3] and involves resolving disputes related to **compensation** to homeowners for land that has been used by the province or municipality for **infrastructure** purposes (i.e., the government has paid a homeowner for land that was expropriated to expand a road or highway).

The LPAT is one of six tribunals in the Environment and Land Tribunals of Ontario cluster, which was created under the *Adjudicative Tribunals Accountability, Governance and Appointments Act, 2009*.[4] It is also one of Ontario's oldest tribunals, having been enacted in 1906 when it took over from the Office of the Provincial Municipal Adjudicator and the Railway Committee of the Executive Council and was named the Ontario Railway and Municipal Board (ORMB). The legislation that enabled the ORMB was the *Ontario Railway and Municipal Board Act*.[5] The board was initially enacted to oversee the corporate and accounting practices of **municipalities** and to supervise the rail transportation system between and within municipalities.

If any issues arose related to how municipalities conducted their business or if they were accused of breaching agreements or contracts, the ORMB had the jurisdiction to adjudicate such matters. In addition to dealing with concerns related to the relationship between railways and municipalities, the ORMB was also responsible for resolving any labour disputes that would arise between railway companies and their employees.

zoning by-laws regulations established by a government on the acceptable use of an area of land

compensation consideration paid from one party to another for damages caused

infrastructure the physical assets, such as roads, bridges, and utility power lines, owned by governments or corporations for the benefit of an organized society

municipalities legal entities incorporated as boroughs, villages, towns, or cities

1 *Local Planning Appeal Tribunal Act, 2017*, SO 2017, c 23, Schedule 1.

2 RSO 1990, c P.13.

3 RSO 1990, c E.26.

4 SO 2009, c 33, Schedule 5.

5 SO 1906, c 31.

In 1932, the board name was changed to the Ontario Municipal Board under the *Ontario Municipal Board Act* (OMBA).[6] The OMBA repealed three key pieces of legislation: the *Municipal and School Accounts Audit Act*, the *Railway and Municipal Board Act*, and the *Bureau of Municipal Affairs Act.*[7] The OMB maintained its responsibilities to adjudicate railway matters because this new Act stipulated in section 3 that interpretations under the Railway Act still applied to the OMBA. Responsibilities of the OMB also included overseeing the bookkeeping of **public utilities**, ensuring uniformity in municipal administration, and collecting information and statistics from municipalities.[8]

By the 1970s, the OMB had rarely been required to hear contentious railway issues, and instead its scope related to municipalities expanded[9] to include:

- conducting hearings under the *Assessment Act*,[10]
- approving zoning by-laws, and
- overseeing the affairs of municipalities and using its delegated authority to act on contraventions.[11]

Over time, the responsibilities of the OMB were modified or expanded based on the feedback from stakeholders (i.e., developers, municipalities, and the public) through public inquiries and consultations.

Beginning in 2003, the Ontario government began introducing reforms that expanded the responsibilities and decision-making powers of municipalities. This had the correlational result of expanding the scope of the OMB. These reforms included:

- **Greenbelt** designation and reform in the form of the *Greenbelt Protection Act, 2004*,[12] *Greenbelt Act, 2005*,[13] and Greenbelt Plan;[14]

public utilities providers of public services, such as energy, gas, telecommunications, waste disposal, or water

greenbelt 7,200 square kilometres of protected green space, such as forests, farmland, and watersheds, surrounding the Golden Horseshoe region of Ontario; created by the Ontario government through legislation in 2005

6 SO 1932, c 27.

7 JC McRuer, *Ontario Royal Commission Inquiry into Civil Rights*, Part V, Report 3, Chapter 125 (Toronto: William Kinmon, 1971), online: <https://archive.org/stream/royalcommissioni05onta#page/2012/mode/2up>.

8 *Ibid* at 2014.

9 *Ibid.*

10 *Ibid.*

11 Environment and Land Tribunals Ontario—Local Planning Appeal Tribunal, "About LPAT" (2018), online: <http://elto.gov.on.ca/tribunals/lpat/about-lpat>.

12 SO 2004, c 9 [repealed].

13 SO 2005, c 1.

14 Ontario, *Greenbelt Plan (2017)*, online: <http://www.mah.gov.on.ca/AssetFactory.aspx?did=18549>.

- The *Strong Communities (Planning Amendment) Act, 2004*;[15]
- The *Places to Grow Act, 2005*;[16] and
- The *Planning and Conservation Land Statute Law Amendment Act, 2006*.[17]

This expansion of scope meant that the OMB was now responsible for ensuring that growth and development were in line with the collective values of preserving our greenbelt, overseeing land conservation initiatives, and building accessible, interconnected, and healthy communities.

In December 2015, Ontario enacted the *Smart Growth for Our Communities Act, 2015* (Bill 73)[18] as a result of its review of the OMB. The Act expanded the allowable uses for monies received from development charges, required demonstrated public input into the official plans of municipalities, and removed the ability to appeal some matters to the OMB.[19] These changes came about because municipalities demonstrated that previous restrictions on the use of development charge monies were too prohibitive and adversely affected a municipality's ability to use development dollars for innovative infrastructure development. It was also mandated that municipalities demonstrate how they actively consulted their citizens and community members when creating official plans for their town or city. This ensures that communities are responsive to their citizens and create infrastructure that is meaningful to them.

In 2016, the province embarked on further stakeholder and public consultations that resulted in recommendations that the OMB be phased out to make way for a new tribunal with less scope. Bill 139 proposed that the Local Planning Appeal Tribunal (LPAT) and corresponding new legislation, the *Building Better Communities and Conserving Watersheds Act* (BBCCWA)[20] be introduced to eliminate the OMB and give a stronger voice to municipalities and communities. The BBCCWA received royal assent on December 12, 2017 and was enacted on April 3, 2018. The passing of the BBCCWA[21] included the introduction of the *Local Planning Appeal Tribunal Act, 2017*, the *Local Planning Appeal Support Center Act, 2017*,[22] and changes to the PA, the *Conservation Authorities Act*,[23] and other applicable legislation. The OMB continued to

---

15 J Taylor, *Report No 2 of the Planning and Economic Development Committee* (21 February 2013), online: <http://archives.york.ca/councilcommitteearchives/pdf/-9.pdf>.

16 SO 2005, c 13.

17 SO 2006, c 23.

18 SO 2015, c 26.

19 Ontario Ministry of Municipal Affairs and Ministry of Housing, "Backgrounder on *The Smart Growth for Our Communities Act, 2015*" (7 March 2016), online: <http://www.mah.gov.on.ca/Page11014.aspx>.

20 SO 2017, c 23.

21 SO 2017, c 23, Schedule 1.

22 SO 2017, c 23, Schedule 2.

23 RSO 1990, c C.27.

operate in its full capacity until April 3, 2018. In addition to the LPAT, the province also created the Local Planning Appeal Support Centre (LPASC) (see <https://www.lpasc.ca>). Similar to the Human Rights Legal Support Centre, the LPASC is mandated to "provide free information and support for citizens who want to participate in the land use planning appeal process."[24]

New Process Under the Local Planning Appeal Tribunal

Many changes came with the passing of Bill 139 and the BBCCWA. The Act changed the OMB's legislative framework, eliminated the OMB, and created a new tribunal: the LPAT. The provincial government also updated the PA to eliminate de novo hearings. This means that when a matter is before the LPAT, the tribunal is not hearing the matter anew. The proposed hearing process starts off very similarly to that of the former OMB in that there needs to be a land use planning decision made by a municipality. If there is discontent with the decision, the concerned party must appeal to the tribunal by filing the record of the municipality's decision.

That is where the similarities in process end. After the LPAT receives the record of decision, it will issue a notice of appeal and mandatory case conference. Case conferences are required by the LPAT and are designed to give the parties an opportunity to settle the matter. The parties can choose mediation, or they can simply use the case conference to have discussions that may identify, define, or narrow the issues. If mediation is successful, the resolution on all the issues goes back to the LPAT for final determination without the need for a hearing. Upon conclusion of the case conference (or if mediation was successful only in part), the matter is sent to a hearing in which a panel makes a determination. Of importance to note are the following:

- The scope for the LPAT is to determine if the decision of the municipality is consistent with provincial or local plans. That is the test and will be the only consideration of the panel.
- There is no examination or cross-examination of witnesses in the LPAT hearing process.

The tribunal will then determine whether the initial municipal decision is consistent with provincial or local plans. If inconsistent, the matter is sent back to the municipality for reconsideration, and, if consistent, the LPAT upholds the decision of the municipality.

This new process has been lauded for rebalancing the power dynamic between developers and municipalities and giving a voice back to municipalities to prevent development that is inconsistent with the vision for the province's towns and cities.

24 Ontario Ministry of Municipal Affairs, News Release, "Building Better Communities and Conserving Watersheds" (30 May 2017), online: <https://news.ontario.ca/mma/en/2017/05/building-better-communities-and-conserving-watersheds.html>.

Legislation and Regulations

The LPAT is responsible for mainly dealing with matters related to:

- the PA, including appeals relating to official plans, subdivision plans, ward boundary issues, zoning by-laws, **minor variances**, and development charges; and
- the EA, including compensation claims relating to the **expropriation** of land.

Nine acts define the jurisdiction and scope of the LPAT,[25] along with all the public and private statutes that are created by individual municipalities:

- The LPATA is the enabling legislation that establishes the authority of the tribunal and outlines its jurisdiction.
- The PA oversees **land use planning** and development in Ontario. The PA also provides guidance on appeal procedures.
- The *Municipal Act, 2001*[26] outlines the responsibilities that municipalities owe to their taxpayers.
- The *Development Charges Act, 1997* (DCA)[27] enables municipalities to charge fees to developers to compensate for the services and infrastructure required for the growth of municipalities.
- The EA provides guidance related to expropriation of land for development and to fair compensation to be paid to those who have had land expropriated by a municipality or the province.
- The *Ontario Heritage Act*[28] protects archaeological sites and designated heritage buildings. It also empowers municipalities and the province to preserve heritage within the province.

minor variances procedural requests made by individuals or corporations to be exempt from a specific zoning by-law because of hardship or circumstance

expropriation the act of a municipal, regional, provincial, or federal government to reclaim private property for government use

land use planning an assessment process intended to provide guidance in the inherent conflict between rural land use, urban development, and industrial expansion by selecting the land uses that will best serve the needs of the people while protecting scarce resources

---

25 Environment and Land Tribunals Ontario—Local Planning Appeal Tribunal, "Legislation and Rules" (2018), online: <http://elto.gov.on.ca/tribunals/lpat/legislation-and-rules>.

26 SO 2001, c 25.

27 SO 1997, c 27.

28 RSO 1990, c O.18.

- The *Aggregate Resources Act* (ARA)[29] provides standards for the aggregate and petroleum industries. The role of the Act is to manage aggregate and petroleum resources and to reduce the physical and environmental impact of these industries on the public.
- The *Consolidated Hearings Act* (CHA)[30] allows for collaboration among tribunals that hold related hearings to streamline the hearing process.
- The *Environmental Assessment Act* (EAA)[31] is an example of an Act that falls under the CHA; it allows board members of various tribunals to be cross-appointed.
- The *Statutory Powers Procedure Act* (SPPA)[32] is the overarching framework that every tribunal references to ensure compliance when determining its rules.

In addition to these acts, the LPAT has its Rules of Practice and Procedure[33] made pursuant to section 91 of the LPATA and section 25.1 of the SPPA. The rules offer guidance and information on providing effective representation before the LPAT. The rules set out such things as the initiating of proceedings, the service and filing of documents, motions, settlement, mediations, and the conduct of hearings. It is important to be familiar and up-to-date with the rules because failure to follow them can result in detrimental consequences for your client.

The LPAT also publishes four appeal guides to assist parties filing appeals with the tribunal. Appeal Guide A applies to the following PA matters:

- First appeals filed under:
  - Section 17 (24)—Appeals of a council decision to adopt or amend an official plan
  - Section 17 (36)—Appeals of a decision by an approval authority to approve a decision adopting or amending an official plan
  - Section 22 (7)—Appeals of a council decision to refuse a private amendment to an official plan or non-decision of a private amendment application
  - Section 34 (11)—Appeals of a council decision to refuse a private amendment to a municipal zoning bylaw or non-decision of a private amendment application
  - Section 34 (19)—Appeals of a decision by a council to adopt a zoning bylaw or zoning bylaw amendment

29 RSO 1990, c A.8.

30 RSO 1990, c C.29.

31 RSO 1990, c E.18

32 RSO 1990, c. S.22.

33 Environment and Land Tribunals Ontario—Local Planning Appeal Tribunal, "Legislation and Rules" (2018), online: <http://elto.gov.on.ca/tribunals/lpat/legislation-and-rules/>.

- Appeals filed under:
  - Section 17 (40)—Appeals of a non-decision by an approval authority
  - Section 51 (34)—Appeals of a non-decision on a subdivision.[34]

Appeal Guide B also pertains to the PA and assists with the following matters:

- Second Appeals filed under:
  - Section 17 (24)—Appeals of a council decision to adopt or amend an official plan
  - Section 17 (36)—Appeals of a decision by an approval authority to approve a decision adopting or amending an official plan
  - Section 22 (7)—Appeals of a council decision to refuse a private amendment to an official plan or non-decision of a private amendment application
  - Section 34 (11)—Appeals of a council decision to refuse a private amendment to a municipal zoning bylaw or non-decision of a private amendment application
  - Section 34 (19)—Appeals of a decision by a council to adopt a zoning bylaw or zoning bylaw amendment
- Appeals filed under:
  - Section 41—Appeals of a non-decision of a site plan application by council or requirements imposed on a site plan application by the municipality/county or by the regional metropolitan/district municipality
  - Section 45—Appeals of a Committee of Adjustment decision to approve or refuse a minor variance application
  - Section 53—Appeals of a decision to approve or refuse a consent/severance application, conditions imposed or changed for a consent/severance application or a non-decision of a consent/severance application by an approval authority.[35]

Appeal Guide C addresses matters that fall under the other enabling statutes (*Expropriations Act*, *Municipal Act*, etc.) and Appeal Guide D deals with matters that are now referred to as legacy appeals. These are matters that were filed with the OMB prior to the inception of the LPAT and would follow the same procedure as matters that had been under the OMB.

It is important to note that effective May 3, 2017 the City of Toronto created the Toronto Local Appeal Body (TLAB) under Toronto Municipal Code, Chapter 142.[36] Minor variance and consent appeals from the Committee of

34 Environment and Land Tribunals Ontario—Local Planning Appeal Tribunal, "LPAT Process" (2018), online: <http://elto.gov.on.ca/tribunals/lpat/lpat-process/>.

35 *Ibid.*

36 See the Toronto Municipal Code online at <http://www.toronto.ca/legdocs/municode/toronto-code-142.pdf>.

Adjustment are now heard by the TLAB rather than the LPAT.[37] The City of Toronto amended its municipal code to gain more control over infrastructure decisions in the city. According to the LPAT, if you are appealing a minor variance or consent decision at the TLAB, but you also have a planning application that would normally be dealt with by the LPAT, you must still submit your appeal to the municipality (TLAB), which will then forward the appeal.

Application Process

Generally, in order to initiate a proceeding with the LPAT, you must either have made an oral submission before or have provided a written submission to the municipality to have the standing to file an appeal with the LPAT. (Exemptions, for example, would include non-decision matters under sections 17(40) and 51(34) of the PA).[38] To make an appeal, you must file either an A1 or A2 application (whichever is applicable) with the board, along with the $300 filing fee. The LPAT website has a comprehensive table[39] to guide you on the necessary appeal deadlines and related forms corresponding to the type of appeal. Rule 5 outlines what must be included in the application and represents a good checklist to ensure that your application is complete, and Rule 6 provides appeal filing deadlines. In addition to filing an appeal form there are sections under the PA (and other legislative forms) that require the filing of a submission form from the municipality or another approval authority, if it falls under the jurisdiction, for example, of a regional government or band council.[40]

After your appeal has been received, the tribunal will send you an acknowledgment letter along with information regarding how to contact the planner assigned to your matter.

The LPAT makes a distinction in process depending on whether you are filing a first appeal or second appeal. First appeals filed under sections 17(24), 17(36), 17(40), 22(7), 34(11), 34(19) and 51(34) of the PA are required to go through a process involving a mandatory case management conference. This process is outlined in Appeal Guide A. Second appeals filed under sections

---

37 Toronto Local Appeal Body, "Filing an Appeal," online: <https://www.toronto.ca/city-government/planning-development/committee-of-adjustment/appeals/filing-an-appeal/>.

38 Environment and Land Tribunals Ontario, "Local Planning Appeals Tribunal (LPAT): Appeal Guide A," online: <http://elto.gov.on.ca/wp-content/uploads/2018/05/2018_05_10-LPAT-Guide-A.pdf> at 6.

39 Environment and Land Tribunals Ontario—Local Planning Appeals Tribunal, "Appellant/Applicant Forms" (2018), online: <http://elto.gov.on.ca/tribunals/lpat/forms/appellant-applicant-forms/>.

40 PA, ss 17(24), (36), (40); s 22(7); ss 34(11), (19); s 38(4); s 45(12); ss 53(19), (27), (14); and ss 51(34), (39), (43), (48). See also DCA, ss 14, 19(1), 22(1), 22(2), 47, 50; *Education Act*, RSO 1990, c E.2, ss 257.65, 257.74(1), 257.87(1), 257.87(2); ARA, ss 11(5), (11), 13(6), 16(8), 18(5), 20(4).

17(24), 17(36), 22(7), 34(11), 34(19), 41, 45, 51, and 53 of the PA can go straight to the hearing phase once the file passes the screening process. This process is outlined in Appeal Guide B. If filing a first appeal the appellant must:

> include which part of the decision of the municipality/approval authority being appealed:
>
> - Is inconsistent with the Provincial Policy Statement;
> - Fails to conform with or conflicts with a provincial plan; or,
> - Fails to conform to an applicable Official Plan.[41]

Appeals under sections 22(7) and 34(11) of the PA must also demonstrate how the initial application would either conform or be consistent with the provincial policy statement, the provincial plan, a municipality's Official Plan or another applicable official plan.

Staff at the LPAT will then screen the application and corresponding documentation to see if they have been filed within the right time frame, in accordance with statutory requirements, and with the correct information as outlined above (r 26.05). If all is well, the appeal will be deemed valid and you will receive a Notice of Commencement from the registrar. It is important to note the date indicated on the Notice of Commencement because this will help you determine your timelines for a final decision to be made. Essentially, the Notice of Commencement triggers the decision timelines.

It is also at this time that the Registrar will schedule a mandatory case management conference. You will be given at least 75 days' notice of the case management conference date and all requirements will be outlined in the Appointment of Hearing that is received. Rules 26.11 through to 26.16 outline the requirements of the Appeal Record, Case Synopsis, and responding documents.

At the case management conference, parties are not expected to provide oral evidence but they should come prepared to discuss the merits of the appeal. Generally, the case conference is designed to:

> (a) identify persons other than the Appellant [and] the municipality or approval authority who wish to participate in the appeal, based on written submissions provided by these persons to the Tribunal;
>
> (b) determine, from the written submissions provided, whether a person may participate in the appeal as an additional party, or participant, on such terms as the Tribunal may determine;
>
> (c) identify facts or evidence the parties may agree upon or on which the Tribunal may make a binding decision;
>
> (d) identify, define or narrow the issues raised in the appeal;

---

41 Environment and Land Tribunals Ontario, "Local Planning Appeals Tribunal (LPAT): Appeal Guide A," *supra* note 38 at 6.

(e) obtain admissions that may simplify the hearing, which may include the examination of persons by the Tribunal as part of the case management conference;

(f) provide directions for disclosure of information among the parties or persons who may participate in the appeal;

(g) provide directions that a person or persons attend the hearing for examination by the Tribunal, including persons to provide expert opinion evidence;

(h) discuss opportunities for settlement, including the possible use of mediation or other dispute resolution processes;

(i) fix a date and place for the hearing and estimate its length;

(j) determine the format of a hearing, including whether a hearing be conducted in writing and any applicable dates to exchange documentation or submissions;

(k) discuss issues of confidentiality, including any need to hold a part of the hearing in the absence of the public or to seal documents;

(l) address the production and cost sharing of joint document books; and

deal with any other matter that may assist in a fair, just, and expeditious resolution of the issues

(m) or proceeding.[42]

If filing a second appeal the appellant must:

include which part of the decision of the municipality/approval authority being appealed:

- Is inconsistent with the Provincial Policy Statement;
- Fails to conform with or conflicts with a provincial plan; or,
- Fails to conform to an applicable Official Plan.[43]

Appeals under sections 22(7) and 34(11) of the PA must also demonstrate how the initial application would either conform or be consistent with the provincial policy statement, the provincial plan, a municipality's Official Plan or another applicable official plan.

Staff at the LPAT will then screen the application and corresponding documentation to see if they have been filed within the right time frame, in accordance with statutory requirements, and with the correct information as

42 LPAT, r 26.20.

43 Environment and Land Tribunals Ontario, "Local Planning Appeals Tribunal (LPAT): Appeal Guide A," *supra* note 38 at 6.

outlined above (r 26.05). Once the review is complete, the matter is scheduled for hearing. If the case management officer deems the case complicated or requiring direction from the tribunal (especially if it is scheduled for more than five days), the matter may be referred to have a pre-hearing conference scheduled. Pre-hearing conferences are not a mandatory component of the process but if the tribunal schedules one, the parties are required to attend. They act like case management conferences in that they help to narrow the issues and provide clarity and direction for the parties. Rule 19 provides guidance on the requirements for pre-hearing conferences.

It is also possible that the parties may identify an opportunity for mediation in order to resolve the matter. The parties can request mediation at any time (r 18) and mediation can also be ordered as a result of the case management conference as a next step. Mediations are confidential, and, in general, the member who presides over the matter will not preside over the hearing, unless the parties request it (r 18.03). If, after mediation, the parties are unable to settle the matter to their satisfaction, the tribunal schedules the matter for hearing and a different member will preside over the hearing.

If a hearing lasts more than five days, the Board requires that expert witness statements and reports be served and filed at least 30 days before the hearing (r 7.04). This is a good practice (and may be required of the parties), even if the matter will not extend beyond five days. It is also good practice to submit witness statements for non-experts (r 7.06).

With respect to exhibits, any graphics should be on paper and not glued to boards (r 7.02), and, if using a board for demonstration at the hearing, any graphics must be removed after the hearing and folded to 8.5 × 11 inches. If using any three-dimensional models, you will be required to take a picture of them to submit them as an exhibit.

Finally, the LPAT allows service by fax or email (electronically) between 8:00 am and 4:30 pm (r 7.10). Anything sent after 4:30 pm is deemed served or filed the next business day (r 7.11). A confirmation page received by the sender is sufficient for proof of transmission of the document (r 7.12). If the materials were successfully transmitted, there is no requirement to provide hard copies of said documents unless requested to do so (r 7.13).

Expropriation Matters

For expropriation matters, the rules provide guidance on how to proceed starting at Rule 28. The person making a claim for compensation for expropriation is required to serve a notice of arbitration and statement of claim on the respondent and then file proof of service with the board within ten days of service (r 28.03). The notice should indicate how much compensation is requested along with how this amount was calculated and the facts supporting the claim. The responding party (generally the province or municipality) has 20 days to respond to the claim by serving the claimant and filing proof of service at the LPAT (r 28.04). In the reply, the respondent must identify grounds upon which the claimant is not entitled to compensation as outlined in Rule 28.08. If the responding party feels that the claimant is entitled to compensation, the respondent may make an offer of compensation pursuant to section 25 of the Act (r 28.09).

The parties can also choose to request a pre-hearing conference, and the LPAT may direct the parties to attend as per Rule 28.14. If unable to settle the matter, the board will issue a notice of hearing to the respondent for an **arbitration** hearing to take place (r 28.17). The respondent is required to serve the notice of hearing on all registered owners and any person known to be an owner who is claiming entitlement to compensation (r 28.19). It would be good practice to obtain expert reports supporting the claim for compensation as the respondent will definitely have documentation to support the compensation amount initially proposed. The decision of the arbitrator is binding.

Hearing Process

Rule 19.10 indicates that hearings before the LPAT can be oral, electronic, or written. It is up to the board to make a determination regarding the appropriate method for the hearing. It is possible to file objections to the hearing format, but you must be clear as to why the scheduled hearing format would be prejudicial to your client. All hearings are also open to the public unless the board makes a determination that the matter should be held *in camera* because of the confidential or sensitive nature of the hearing (r 22.01).

Matters before the LPAT are adjudicated by one member appointed by the chair. This member is the sole decision-maker and will weigh all evidence introduced and referred to in the hearing to make a determination. Hearings are not as formal as court hearings, but they follow a more regimented procedure than in other tribunals. For first appeal matters under sections 17(24), 17(36), 22(7), 34(11), and 3(19) of the PA, parties will have up to 75 minutes to make oral submissions. Witnesses (if any) are only questioned by the member and there is no opportunity for either side to conduct examinations or cross-examinations. Generally, you would only be making submissions regarding evidence and documents that had been before the municipality when the original decision was made.[44] If the member requires more information, they will advise the parties and request that witnesses are available to speak to the particular issue.

arbitration one of the four components of alternative dispute resolution (negotiation, mediation, and collaborative law being the other three) meant to attain a legal settlement outside of the court room; arbitrator hears legal arguments from both sides and determines an award for one party; result is legally binding (although some exceptions exist)

44 Environment and Land Tribunals Ontario, "Local Planning Appeals Tribunal (LPAT): Appeal Guide A," *supra* note 38 at 17.

For first appeal matters that fall under sections 17(40) and 51(34) of the PA, the format of hearing remains the same with the exception that parties will have 75 minutes to make submissions and participants will have 25 minutes to make submissions to the tribunal. The stipulations on the calling of witnesses and the ability to examine and cross-examine remain the same.

For all other matters (i.e., second appeals, expropriation matters), hearings are not as formal as court hearings, but they follow a more regimented procedure than in other tribunals. It is common to see examination-in-chief (both sides), cross-examinations (of each witness on both sides), and final submissions by both parties at these hearings.

Because of the nature of the LPAT's jurisdiction, many matters require expert witnesses, like urban planners, architects, and environmental experts. Any exhibits referred to in the hearing will be kept for 180 days after the board renders its decision. You can request the return of your exhibits after the 180-day hold has passed; otherwise, they remain in the board's possession and become board property (r 7.09).

The LPAT will issue costs against a party if the board believes that the party acted in bad faith or exhibited unreasonable, frivolous, or vexatious conduct (r 23.09). Requests for costs must be made at the end of the hearing before a determination is made. If this is not done, the party requesting costs must notify the board of its intention to request costs within 30 days of receiving the written decision (r 23.01).

At the conclusion of the hearing (after final submissions), the adjudicator may render a decision that will be followed by a written decision. Generally adjudicators reserve their decision in order to carefully weigh all of the evidence, make a determination of the facts, and render a decision. For matters that fall under sections 17(24), 17(36), 22(7), 34(11), and 34(19), the LPAT will make a determination within ten months of the Notice of Commencement, whereas for sections 17(40) and 51(34), members determination will come within 12 months. Members are allowed to deviate from these timelines if they deem it necessary.

For other matters, "the LPAT is required to make a decision within 6 months of the issuance of the Tribunal's acknowledgement letter (to confirm the commencement of the time period), unless the Member(s) decided that more time was necessary."[45]

45 Environment and Land Tribunals Ontario, "Local Planning Appeals Tribunal (LPAT): Appeal Guide B," online: <http://elto.gov.on.ca/wp-content/uploads/2018/05/2018_05_10-LPAT-Guide-B.pdf> at 29.

Decisions, Reconsideration, and Appeals

With respect to first appeals, matters dealing with sections 17(24), 17(36), 22(7), 34(11), and 34(19) can result in the member confirming whether or not the municipality/approval authority met the test of conformity and consistency, and if their decision:

- Was consistent with the Provincial Policy Statement;
- Conforms with or conflicts with a provincial plan; or,
- Conforms to an applicable Official Plan.[46]

If the member makes a determination that the municipality did not meet the test, they will refer the matter back to the municipality for consideration.

Additionally, for first appeals dealing with sections 17(40) and 51(34) of the PA, the member will make a determination with respect to consistency and conformity to provincial policies and municipal plans. They will decide to either approve, modify, or deny the application. For these matters, there is no opportunity for a second appeal. The decision of the LPAT stands.

A decision of the LPAT is not final until it becomes an order. Sometimes the decision includes components or requirements that must be complied with, and, until such matters are resolved, the decision will not become an order. Typically, the tribunal will issue a decision and order at the same time.

Municipalities can enforce the order, or they may be required to file the order with the Superior Court to have it enforced. Anyone who disagrees with a decision of the LPAT can request a review pursuant to Rule 25.02, which must be filed within 30 days of the date of hearing (r 25.03). The tribunal will review the request to ensure that it includes the correct information, that it is a new request made by a party with standing (or a good reason why they do not have standing), and that it is filed within the 30-day limitation period (unless an extension was requested and provided) (r 25.04).

The tribunal may require responding documentation from the other side. If so, they must file a response within the timeframe requested by the tribunal pursuant to Rule 25.05. Upon review, the chair may either deny or grant the request, in whole or in part, by ordering a rehearing or a ordering a motion to review the request (r 25.06). To grant the request, as outlined in Rule 25.07, the chair would have to have grounds to believe that the board:

> (a) acted outside its jurisdiction;
>
> (b) violated the rules of natural justice or procedural fairness, including those against bias;
>
> (c) made an error of law or fact such that the Board would likely have reached a different decision;

46 Environment and Land Tribunals Ontario, "Local Planning Appeals Tribunal (LPAT): Appeal Guide A," *supra* note 38 at 27.

(d) heard false or misleading evidence from a party or witness, which was discovered only after the hearing and would have affected the result; or

(e) should consider evidence which was not available at the time of the hearing, but that is credible and could have affected the result.

If there is a finding that the tribunal erred as outlined, the LPAT will determine if there will be a rehearing of the matter (either in whole or in part) and it "will review, rescind, change, alter or vary any decision, approval or order made by the Board" (r 25.10).

Until 2009, decisions of the OMB could be appealed by making an application to the Lieutenant-Governor-in-Council. In 2009, the province introduced the *Good Government Act, 2009*,[47] which repealed sections 6, 18, 19, and 20 of the OMBA and repealed and replaced section 95. As a result, OMB decisions, and now LPAT decisions, are final and can be appealed only to the Divisional Court on a question of law with leave of the court.[48] You must bring a motion to Divisional Court seeking leave to appeal.[49] An applicant will have to satisfy the following tests to obtain leave to appeal an LPAT decision:

- The proposed appeal relates to a question of law.
- The question of law is of sufficient importance to merit the attention of the Divisional Court.
- There is reason to doubt the correctness of the decision.[50]

Case Law

Richmond Hill (Town) v Elginbay Corporation, 2016 ONSC 5560

The Town of Richmond Hill, with the support of Oakville, Mississauga, Markham, and Vaughn as intervenors, successfully appealed a decision of the OMB to the Divisional Court regarding the OMB's application of section 42 of the PA. This is one of the few recent decisions in which a town has been successful at the Divisional Court level.

47 SO 2009, c 33, s 54.

48 Environment and Land Tribunals Ontario, "Local Planning Appeals Tribunal (LPAT): Appeal Guide A," *supra* note 38 at 30.

49 *Ibid.*

50 "Conflicting Court Decisions on OMB Appeals," *Novae Res Urbis* [GTA Edition] (21 November 2007), online: <http://www.weirfoulds.com/conflicting-court-decisions-on-omb-appeals>.

Antrim Truck Centre Ltd v Ontario (Transportation), 2013 SCC 13, [2013] 1 SCR 594

The appellant owned a parcel of land off Highway 17 in Antrim, Ontario (in the Ottawa area) where they operated a thriving truck stop, which included a restaurant and gas station. When the province decided to build Highway 417, this caused significant adverse effects on the business, eventually requiring the Appellant to close the business. The Appellant went to the OMB to seek compensation under expropriation provisions and was awarded $58,000 for business loss and $335,000 for loss of market value on the land. The Divisional Court upheld the decision, but the Court of Appeal set aside the decision because it felt that the board's test of reasonableness was lacking. The Supreme Court allowed the appeal and upheld the decision of the OMB citing that:

> It was reasonable for the Board to conclude that in all of the circumstances, the appellant should not be expected to endure permanent interference with the use of its land that caused a significant diminution of its market value in order to serve the greater public good.

CHC MPAR Church Holdings Inc v Toronto (City)[51]

In this proceeding, a developer wanted to build a 32-storey building on a corner that would replace a parking lot. The proposed building would be close to buildings that were designated as heritage buildings under the *Ontario Heritage Act*. The City of Toronto refused to rezone the lot to allow the developer to build the tower, and the developer appealed the city's ruling to the OMB. The city was successful in this case. The OMB ruled that new developments must respect properties with a heritage designation. This is a precedent setting case of the OMB from 2015 in which it deals with the issue of adjacency (i.e., a proposed development close to designated heritage buildings or in a heritage district). Although the policy regarding adjacency was created in 2005, there were no OMB decisions that dealt specifically with adjacency until this one.

---

51 Ontario Municipal Board, "Decision: Case No PL141140" (23 December 2015), online: <http://www.omb.gov.on.ca/e-decisions/pl141140-dec-23-2015.pdf>.

KEY LEGISLATION

Planning Act
Expropriations Act
Ontario Municipal Board Act
Municipal Act, 2001
Development Charges Act, 1997
Ontario Heritage Act
Aggregate Resources Act
Consolidated Hearings Act
Statutory Powers Procedure Act
Environmental Assessment Act
City of Toronto Act, 2006
Local Planning Appeal Tribunal Act, 2017
Local Planning Appeal Support Centre Act, 2017

KEY TERMS

arbitration, 127
compensation, 116
expropriation, 120
greenbelt, 117
infrastructure, 116
land use planning, 120
minor variances, 120
municipalities, 116
public utilities, 117
zoning by-laws, 116

REVIEW QUESTIONS

1. What is the purpose of the LPAT?
2. What are the main pieces of legislation that provide the LPAT with its jurisdiction and scope?
3. What does the term "expropriation" mean?
4. How do you initiate a proceeding with the LPAT?
5. What role does mediation play at the LPAT?
6. On what grounds can a chair grant a review of a decision of the LPAT?
7. Under what grounds can you appeal a decision of the LPAT?
8. Where would you appeal a decision of the LPAT? Describe the process.
9. What effect did the *Building Better Communities and Conserving Watersheds Act* have on the LPAT and its process?
10. What is the role of the Local Planning Appeal Support Centre?

SCENARIO

John is a developer who purchased a 16-hectare parcel of land in a rural section outside of Anytown, Ontario. He would like to build a housing development that would include 200 freehold townhomes, 100 semi-detached homes, and 100 detached homes. Anytown is a small community of 20,000 people and a popular tourist destination. Typically, as a retirement town, Anytown is also well known for its cultural events and wineries. Over the summer, the population of Anytown swells to more than 100,000 people as visitors and short-term residents take in the sights and sounds of the area. While the town and business owners appreciate the revenue that comes from tourism, many residents are retirees and oppose development of any kind.

When John sought approval from the town to commence work on this development project, he characterized the development as one that would bring young families to the area as the anticipated price points would be much lower than the average home cost in Anytown. The town recognized this as a mutually beneficial characteristic as it had identified a need to diversify the population base of the town. The local school board had been closing schools at a rapid rate, and the town had already lost a high school and a few elementary schools, which made it difficult to attract new long-term residents. A diverse population base would also help the town attract more investments, businesses, and further development.

The required public consultations for this new development proposed by John resulted in fierce opposition from many residents in town who expressed concerns about the strain on services and infrastructure, the inconvenience of the project, the inappropriateness of the location for such a large development, and the aesthetics of the proposed homes not matching the area. As a result, the town approved the development with the conditions that there be only 100 townhomes, 50 semi-detached homes, and 50 detached homes; that the developer create greenspace for the local residents; and that the aesthetic match the local area characteristics.

While John was happy about the approval, he didn't see how the project could remain profitable with the proposed number of units halved. John's attempts to have the town reconsider its decision have failed.

How would John go about appealing this decision?

CHAPTER 7

Assessment Review Board

Overview and History 136

Legislation and Regulations 137

Application Process 142

Assessment Appeals 143

Tax Appeals 143

Hearing Process 145

General Proceedings 145

Summary Proceedings 146

Adjournments and Mandatory Meetings 146

Streaming 147

Settlement Conferences 148

Mediation 149

Decisions, Reconsiderations, and Appeals 150

Case Law 151

Key Terms 155

Review Questions 155

Scenarios 156

Overview and History

The Assessment Review Board (ARB) is one of the six tribunals clustered under Environment and Land Tribunals Ontario. The ARB was established under the *Assessment Review Board Act* (ARBA)[1] and hears appeals about property **tax assessments** and **property classification**.

A few bodies are involved in the property assessment process. The ARB is the adjudicative body that decides disputes between, for example, property owners and the Municipal Property Assessment Corporation (MPAC) about the valuation of a property. MPAC's role in the province is to undertake property assessments and notify property owners of the assessed value of their land. This assessment forms the basis of the municipal tax that owners pay on the property. Therefore, the ARB process is integrally linked to MPAC and the municipalities who set and collect taxes, as well as to the Ministry of Finance, through which the property assessment laws are established. MPAC receives its authority under the *Municipal Property Assessment Corporation Act, 1997*.[2] Paralegals may find themselves representing either individual property owners in an appeal of the established tax rate or working for MPAC to defend against property tax appeals.

MPAC calculates property taxes and classifies properties into categories (i.e., farm land or residential). The valuation of the property is provided to municipalities on annual assessment rolls.[3] The assessments given are based on a current value of a property on a specific date.[4] Section 19.2(1)3 of the *Assessment Act* (AA) establishes the date of valuation for each taxation year. For example, for the taxation years of 2013-2016, the date of valuation is set in the Act as January 1, 2012. For the taxation years of 2017-2020, the date of valuation as set in the Act is January 1, 2016.[5] This means that each property is given a certain value as of January 1, 2016, and that value is what the municipality uses as a base for taxation, once it sets the tax rate for 2017-2020. Once MPAC

tax assessment the value of a property as determined by the Municipal Property Assessment Corporation for the purposes of paying taxes to the municipality

property classification the categories into which properties may be placed, for the purposes of assessment, such as farm or residential

1 RSO 1990, c A.32.

2 SO 1997, c 43, Schedule G.

3 Environment and Land Tribunals Ontario, "Municipal Property Assessment Corporation (MPAC)" (2018), online: <http://elto.gov.on.ca/mpac>.

4 *Assessment Act*, RSO 1990, c A.31, s 19(1).

5 Assessment Review Board, "Introduction to Property Assessment" (2018), online: <http://elto.gov.on.ca/tribunals/arb/assessment-cycle-2017-2020/introduction-to-property-assessment/>.

establishes the value of a property, they send a property assessment to the owners.

In Ontario, property assessment dates back centuries, even before the province as we now know it, to the late 1700s. In the 1970s, the provincial government took over the role of property assessment from the municipalities, creating the Assessment Review Court. This court was renamed to the ARB in the 1980s. At one time, ARB appeals could go to the board formerly known as the Ontario Municipal Board (OMB), now replaced by the Local Planning Appeal Tribunal (LPAT). Now, ARB decisions are final, with an appeal option to Divisional Court only for errors of law and if leave is granted by the court.[6]

The ARB works efficiently to process thousands of appeals every year. The first half of 2017 alone saw a staggering caseload of over 53,000, with just under 7,000 new appeals being filed in the first quarter of the calendar year. This was a marked increase from the first quarter of 2015 (1,072 appeals) and 2016 (1,260), and close to the overall totals for those years, with 7,068 in 2015 and 6,251 in 2016.[7] To assist with behind-the-scenes policy, the Appeal Management Advisory Committee (AMAC) supports the ARB by developing best practices and coordinating with municipalities.[8]

Legislation and Regulations

While the ARB's enabling legislation is the ARBA, additional jurisdiction is gleaned from other statutes, including the AA, the *Municipal Act* (MA),[9] the *City of Toronto Act* (CTA),[10] the *Provincial Land Tax Act* (PLTA),[11] the *Condominium Act* (CA),[12] the *Education Act* (EA),[13] and the *Statutory Powers Procedure Act* (SPPA).[14]

The ARBA doesn't so much create the ARB as it does continue its existence from previous legislation (s 2). This Act also outlines the more mundane but necessary features of the ARB, such as:

- the composition of one chair and a number of vice-chairs and members (s 3),

---

6 See Assessment Review Board, "Your Guide to the Assessment Review Board" at 1, online: <http://elto.gov.on.ca/wp-content/uploads/2017/01/ARB-Guide.pdf>.

7 Assessment Review Board, "Assessment Review Board, Resources" (2018), online: <http://elto.gov.on.ca/tribunals/arb/resources/annual-reports-statistics/>.

8 Assessment Review Board," Appeal Management Advisory Committee (AMAC)" (2018), online: <http://elto.gov.on.ca/tribunals/arb/assessment-cycle-2017-2020/amac>.

9 SO 2001, c 25.

10 SO 2006, c 11, Schedule A.

11 SO 2006, c 33, Schedule Z.2.

12 SO 1998, c 19.

13 RSO 1990, c E.2.

14 RSO 1990, c S.22.

- a **quorum** for the ARB is one member (s 5),
- the oath for every board member, which is to "honestly decide the appeals" (s 7),
- the ARB's ability to establish fees for various proceedings and administrative matters (s 8.1), and
- the power to dismiss a complaint or an appeal (s 8.2).

There are no current regulations pursuant to the ARBA.

The AA is a large piece of legislation that forms the basis for much of the ARB's work. The AA is the legal base for property assessment in Ontario (s 3(1)1) and provides for exemptions. Land exempted from property taxation includes Crown lands (s 3(1)1), cemeteries (s 3(1)2), churches (s 3(1)3), public education institutions under the *Education Act* (s 3(4)), hospitals (s 3(1)5), and care homes (s 3(1)7), along with a variety of other exceptions provided for under the AA. Aside from property assessment, this Act also provides the authority to classify property into at least seven categories: residential, multi-residential, commercial, industrial, pipeline, farm, and managed forests (ss 7(2)1-7).

MPAC's duty to create an assessment roll for each municipality arises out of the AA (s 14). An assessment roll contains information about the property (ss 14(10)1-9). This Act contains sections pertaining to different types of assessments, such as easements (s 9), Crown lands (s 18), water and power companies (s 24), and pipelines (s 25(4)). A notice of assessment is sent to the property owner any time there is a change in the information reflected in the assessment rolls.[15] Importantly, section 43 of this Act outlines the powers and duties of the ARB and equates its assessment capabilities with MPAC's.

Two regulations exist pursuant to the AA: O Reg 574/06, Generation Facilities; and O Reg 282/98, General. The Generation Facilities regulation is focused on the property classes and assessed value of three generation stations (Bruce, Pickering, and Darlington) and is therefore a very specific regulation that does not require further discussion, as its application to general practice is so limited. The General regulation is very detailed and a key tool in interpreting and defining the different classes of property. For example, section 2 of this regulation identifies the general property classifications, all 15 of them, ranging from residential and commercial use of property to retail and sports facilities. Each of these classifications is further detailed (i.e., what is and what isn't a part of this class) in the sections to follow (ss 3-17.3). Subclasses are also outlined in sections 19 to 22. This regulation contains guidance on matters relating to exemptions from taxation for certain properties (ss 23.1-26),

quorum the base number or minimum number of people required to be present to proceed

15 SPPA, s 31.

assessments of specific lands (ss 32.1, 32.2, 41-42.6), and disputes about certain property classifications (ss 29-32 and 33-40).

The MA is a very large piece of legislation, and only some provisions fall under the auspices of the ARB. The purpose of the statute is to empower municipalities as functioning bodies under the province's power (ultimately, municipalities are not considered separate levels of government in Canada's *Constitution Act* but rather are part of the provincial governments). The provisions relating to municipal taxation powers fall under sections 306 to 338. Therefore, these provisions are central to the property assessment and taxation scheme in Ontario, and for the process of appeals made to the ARB. As voluminous as the statute itself is, so too are the regulations that exist pursuant to the MA. Once again, only certain regulations in the long list apply specifically to municipal taxation matters, some of those being:

- Tax Matters—Regional Municipality of Peel, O Reg 103/09,
- Municipal and School Capital Facilities—Agreements and Tax Exemptions, O Reg 603/06,
- Tax Matters—Notice Under Subsection 365.1(5) of the Act, O Reg 274/04,
- Municipal Tax Sales Rules, O Reg 181/03,
- Tax Matters—Special Tax Rates and Limits, O Reg 73/03,
- Tax Matters—Eligible Property Under Section 364 of the Act and Land Prescribed Under Subsection 357(1.1) of the Act, O Reg 325/01,
- Tax Ratios—City of Owen Sound, O Reg 311/01,
- Property Tax Bills, O Reg 75/01,
- Tax Related Matters, O Reg 406/98,
- Tax Matters—Charity Rebates, O Reg 389/98,
- Tax Matters—Taxation of Certain Railway, Power Utility Lands, O Reg 387/98,
- Tax Matters—Allowable Ranges for Tax Ratios, O Reg 386/98,
- Tax Matters—Transition Rations and Average Transition Ratios, O Reg 385/98,
- Tax Matters—Universities and Other Institutions, O Reg 384/98,
- Tax Matters—Farm Land Awaiting Development Subclasses, Tax Reduction Percentages, O Reg 383/98,
- Payments in Lieu of Taxes, Distribution, O Reg 382/98, and
- Prescribed Tax—International Bridges, O Reg 33/98.

From this long list of regulations alone, you can see just how complex the property taxation scheme can be. Remember the relationship between MPAC, which assesses property values, and the role of the municipality in setting tax rates and taxing properties accordingly with the assessed values as set by MPAC.

The CTA mirrors the provisions in the MA, but governs strictly the City of Toronto. Similarly, taxation provisions fall toward the end of the Act, beginning at section 267. There are also various taxation regulations.[16]

The PLTA outlines exemptions from tax on non-municipal territory in the province, including, for example, "Indian land," and mining lands in section 3(1). This Act also enables appeals before the ARB (ss 8(4), 9(4), and 10(4)) and empowers the ARB to restore property taxes (s 9(1)). Two regulations are made pursuant to the PLTA: O Reg 229/09, General; and O Reg 224/09, Tax Rates. The General regulation details further the particulars around tax collection, refunds, deferrals, and rebates. The Tax Rates regulation sets rates for different classes of land that are subject to the PLTA.

The CA states the following for the purposes of property assessment:

> 15(1) Each unit, together with its appurtenant common interest, constitutes a parcel for the purpose of municipal assessment and taxation.
>
> (2) Subject to subsection (3), the common elements of a corporation that is not a common elements condominium corporation do not constitute a parcel for the purpose of municipal assessment and taxation.
>
> (3) A part of the common elements of a corporation that is not a common elements condominium corporation constitutes a separate parcel for the purpose of municipal assessment and taxation if it is leased for business purposes under section 21, the lessee carries on an undertaking for gain on it and it is in the commercial property class prescribed under the *Assessment Act*.
>
> (4) The common elements of a common elements condominium corporation constitute a parcel for the purpose of municipal assessment and taxation within each municipality in which the common elements or a part of them are located and the municipal taxes levied on the parcel or parcels shall form part of the common expenses of the corporation.

These provisions allow for municipal assessment and taxation of a condo unit, taking into consideration a portion of value for the common areas of the condo as well. These common areas are typically pools, games rooms, meeting rooms, etc. The "common elements" are strictly defined in the CA as being "all the property except the units" (s 1). The common elements alone, unless they are part of a "common elements condominium corporation" (CECC), are not included as a parcel for the purposes of taxation, unless they are leased for business purposes, qualifying it as commercial property. The common elements of a CECC are considered a parcel for the purposes of municipal taxation. What is a CECC? A CECC is defined in the Act as being a registered

16 Property Tax Bills, O Reg 122/07; Traditional Municipal Taxes, Limits and Taxation, O Reg 121/07; Municipal and School Capital Facilities, O Reg 598/06; Toronto Tax Sales Rules, O Reg 579/06.

property that creates common elements but does not divide the land into separate units (ss 138(1) and (2)) and is a type of freehold estate (s 6(2)). The CA allows municipal tax amounts to be calculated in an occupancy fee charged to persons who agree to interim occupancy of a condominium unit (s 80(4)).[17]

The EA includes provisions relating to the types of school boards that an individual can financially support (s 257.4), in accordance with the AA provisions, and describes education taxes in relation to the AA (ss 257.5-257.29). Individuals may support a specific school by requesting a portion of their taxes be allocated (s 16(4)), as indicated on the annual assessment roll (s 14(1.1)2). Specific regulations also detail further municipal tax matters.[18] For example, special notice is required within 30 days from the "commencement day" in summary proceedings for matters pertaining to (i) a change in property classification that raises the tax rate, (ii) a higher property assessment than MPAC's determination, (iii) use of section 40(18) of the AA (i.e., an appeal raised where burden of proof falls on the appellant to prove correctness of the current assessment with certain factors at stake), or (iv) if issue estoppel is raised.[19]

The ARB's Rules of Practice and Procedure (the Rules) have recent amendments, with the current version dated April 1, 2017.[20] The ARB website outlines these amendments, highlighting significant changes, including new, updated, and discarded rules.[21] The Rules are comprehensive and offer valuable guidance to both new and seasoned practitioners. The rules pertaining to advocates outline the ARB's authority to remove any representative by order or pursuant to Rule 12, which allows for removal of unauthorized representatives (r 13). In addition, the Rules allow representatives to act as witnesses (r 14), which is unusual in court proceedings. All notices referred to in the Rules must be in writing (r 10). The Rules state that hearings may be conducted in English, French, or as bilingual proceedings. Sign-language interpretation is also available (r 74). Hearings that are required to be conducted entirely in French or with a sign-language interpreter present require that a 25-day notice

---

17 See s 80(2) of the CA for a definition of "interim occupancy."

18 Tax Matters—Limitation on Tax Increases in Territory Without Municipal Organization, O Reg 259/17; Tax Matters—Rates Under Subsection 255 (1) of the Act, O Reg 712/98; Tax Matters—Tax Rates for School Purposes, O Reg 400/98; Tax Matters—Definition of Business Property and Residential Property, O Reg 394/98; Tax Matters—Eligible Theatre Definition, O Reg 393/98; Tax Matters—Taxation of Certain Railway, Power Utility Lands, O Reg 392/98; Tax Arrears in Annexed Areas, O Reg 366/98; Deemed District Municipalities (District School Board Jurisdiction)—Tax Rates, O Reg 468/97; Deemed District Municipalities (School Authority Jurisdiction)—Tax Rates, O Reg 467/97.

19 Assessment Review Board, "Rules of Practice and Procedure," r 40 (2018), online: <http://elto.gov.on.ca/tribunals/arb/legislation-and-rules/>.

20 *Ibid.*

21 Assessment Review Board, "Legislation and Rules" (2018), online: <http://elto.gov.on.ca/tribunals/arb/legislation-and-rules/>.

be provided to the registrar (r 75). Hearings may be combined where matters are united with similar questions of facts or law (rr 78-80). Conversely, combined matters may be severed to avoid complicating factors (r 81). In addition, a Practice Direction on Combined Proceedings[22] should be read in conjunction with the governing rule. Practice directions also exist for the topics of appeals management,[23] mediation,[24] and settlement conferences.[25] The last two are discussed later in this chapter. The Appeals Management Practice Direction is notable in that it discusses the purpose of **commencement days** and how they are assigned to each appeal. More importantly, it addresses the appointment of complaints representatives, who assist parties in meeting the **schedule of events** dates so as to keep the appeal on track and on time.[26] This practice direction also outlines the role of the Appeals Management Advisory Committee to assist the ARB with "the timely completion of appeals."[27]

Application Process

The first step in applying to the ARB is to file an appeal. Individuals who disagree with a property assessment notice, as received from MPAC, can file an assessment appeal. Individuals disputing a tax bill can file a tax appeal. Fees to file an appeal vary from $25 to $300 according to the type of appeal and the Act from which it originates. A fee chart is available online.[28] There is no fee for appeals made on the basis of sickness or poverty under the MA. There are

commencement days the date assigned by the ARB as the start date of the appeal and from which all further events are scheduled in accordance with the schedule of events

schedule of events a timeline of how proceedings will flow from the commencement day, highlighting events such as disclosure

22 Assessment Review Board, "Practice Direction Combined Proceedings" (2017), online: <http://elto.gov.on.ca/wp-content/uploads/2017/06/Practice-Direction-Combined-Proceedings-1.pdf>.

23 Assessment Review Board, "Practice Direction, Appeals Management" (2017), online: <http://elto.gov.on.ca/wp-content/uploads/2017/06/ARB-Appeals-Management-Practice-Direction.pdf>.

24 Assessment Review Board, "Practice Direction, Mediation" (2017), online: <http://elto.gov.on.ca/wp-content/uploads/2017/06/ARB-Mediation-Practice-Direction.pdf>.

25 Assessment Review Board, "Practice Direction, Settlement Conferences" (2017), online: <http://elto.gov.on.ca/wp-content/uploads/2017/06/ARB-Settlement-Conference-Practice-Direction.pdf>.

26 *Supra* note 23.

27 *Ibid.*

28 Assessment Review Board, "Fee Chart" (2018), online: <http://elto.gov.on.ca/tribunals/arb/fee-chart/>.

numerous appeal forms, one of which is required to begin an appeal process at the ARB. Some of these are the Assessment Appeal Form (can be filed online to save $10 off the fee); the MA Appeal Forms (various); and the CTA Appeal Forms (various). Determining if you are at the appeal stage in a file and what path to pursue at the ARB can be complicated. It is not as simple a process as, for example, filing an appeal at the Social Benefits Tribunal, where one appeal form is used for all appealable tribunal matters.

If the property in question received a classification from MPAC as either (1) residential, (2) farm, (3) managed forest, or (4) conservation land, then before you can file an appeal with the ARB, you must file a request for reconsideration directly with MPAC. Only after you receive a reconsideration decision can you pursue an appeal with the ARB.[29] This appeal to the ARB must be filed within 90 days of the mailing date of the reconsideration decision.[30]

Properties classified as any other type can either file a request for reconsideration or go directly to the ARB with an appeal. If you forgo the reconsideration option, then the deadline to make an appeal depends on the type of assessment in question: for annual assessment appeals the deadline is March 31, and for other types of assessment appeals the deadline is 90 days from the notice date.[31]

The different types of appeals are outlined below.

Assessment Appeals

Assessment appeals result from sections 32, 33, 34, or 40 of the AA. Section 32(1) allows MPAC to correct an error or omission in an assessment and update the assessment roll accordingly. Section 33(1)2 allows for land previously omitted from the tax roll to be assessed and included in the roll. Section 34(1) allows for a new assessment and alteration of the tax roll where a property has changed in value (perhaps because of an addition to a home) or classification. Appeals of this nature can be e-filed through the ARB website with a $10 cost savings.

Tax Appeals

Tax appeals arise out of the MA or the CTA. The legislation that applies is determined by the location of the property. If the property is in Toronto, then the appeal arises under the CTA. If it arises elsewhere in Ontario, then it is under the MA. The basis of a tax appeal is a dispute over the amount of tax on a property and therefore occurs after the property assessment by MPAC has been given. CTA appeals to the ARB begin after a tax appeal application has been made to the city first. Tax appeals in the City of Toronto may request a

29 AA, ss 40(3), (3.1).

30 AA, s 40(5)1.

31 AA, s 40(6).

cancellation, refund, or reduction of taxes and are made to the Treasurer.[32] After a decision has been received by the city (technically, the Toronto City Council in the form of the Government Management Committee), parties can appeal this decision to the ARB within 35 days.[33] If a decision is not made by September 30 of the year following that to which the application pertains (i.e., if the appeal application is filed with the treasurer on February 15, 2017 for the previous 2016 assessment, then a decision should be given by council no later than September 30, 2017), then the applicant can file an appeal directly to the ARB no later than October 21 of that year.[34]

Various tax applications and appeal forms apply to both Acts, so practitioners must ensure that they choose the correct form in pursuing an appeal at the ARB. All forms are available on the ARB website.[35] Tax appeals can also stem from requests for exemption because of poverty or illness,[36] which are forwarded directly from a city treasurer to the ARB.[37] The MA appeals follow a very similar process to those outlined under the CTA (s 334). Appeal applications should be made to the municipality first, and the party should await a decision from the municipal council before filing an appeal with the ARB.[38] CTA and MA appeals cannot be e-filed on the ARB website; these must be filed with the board and served on the other party.[39] Once an appeal is received by the ARB, an acknowledgment letter will be sent to the parties, a commencement day will be established, and a schedule of events will be assigned.[40] These last two procedures are instrumental to the appeal process and hearing readiness. They are discussed further in the next section.

For both assessment and tax appeals, the following rules apply to the early phase of appeals at the ARB, or the first steps in the appeal process:

- Rule 18—Form of Appeal: appeals must be initiated in the correct form and comply with ten requirements, including full contact information

32 CTA, ss 323(1)-(3); see also City of Toronto, "Property Tax Appeal: Cancellation, Reduction or Refund of Taxes," online: <https://www.toronto.ca/services-payments/property-taxes-utilities/property-tax/property-tax-rebates-and-relief-programs/property-tax-appeal-cancellation-reduction-refund-of-taxes/>.

33 CTA, s 323(7).

34 CTA, s 323(8).

35 Assessment Review Board, "City of Toronto Act Appeals" (2018), online: <http://elto.gov.on.ca/tribunals/arb/filing-an-appeal/city-of-toronto-act-appeals/>.

36 CTA, s 323(1)(e).

37 City of Toronto, "Property Tax and Utility Relief and Rebate Programs" (2018), online: <https://www.toronto.ca/services-payments/property-taxes-utilities/property-tax/property-tax-rebates-and-relief-programs/>.

38 MA, ss 357(2), (3), (7), (8).

39 *Supra* note 19, rr 19, 27.

40 Assessment Review Board, "Filing an Appeal" (2018), online: <http://elto.gov.on.ca/tribunals/arb/filing-an-appeal/>. See also *supra* note 19, rr 32, 33.

for the appellant, the property's roll number, the fee, and proof of service of the appeal;

- Rule 19—Special Legislation: appeals made under the MA, CTA, and PLTA include additional requirements to initiate proceedings;
- Rule 20—Administrative Screening: failure to comply with statutory requirements will result in a bar to the appeal proceeding;
- Rule 24—Dismissal of Appeals: the ARB may dismiss an appeal before weighing the merits of the case if, for example, there is no jurisdiction to hear the appeal (other reasons set out in rule); and
- Rule 26—Late Appeals: late appeals may be accepted only in strict circumstances with affidavit evidence.

Hearing Process

After an appeal is filed, it will proceed along the path of either summary proceeding or general proceeding. According to Rule 32, "All proceedings are general proceedings, unless the Board specifies a proceeding as a summary proceeding." Therefore, we will review the general proceeding path first.

General Proceedings

General proceedings appear to be the norm, according to Rule 32. However, the board has stipulated, also in accordance with Rule 32, that all AA appeals that deal with property classified as residential, farm, or managed forest property will *not* be heard in the general proceeding stream. In addition, MA or CTA appeals will proceed in the general stream only if the same property has an AA appeal underway in the general stream.[41] As mentioned above in the Application Process section, after an appeal is commenced and accepted by the ARB, a commencement date and schedule of events will be determined. A commencement date is defined in the Rules as the day the schedule of events commences, as set by the ARB.[42] The schedule of events for general proceedings then flows from this date and is set out in Schedule A to the Rules (r 34(a)). The schedule of events for general proceedings is detailed and includes processes that are absent from the summary proceeding stream. For example, the schedule of events identifies the following required processes: initial disclosure from MPAC (weeks 1-4) all the way through to gathering and disclosure of expert reports (weeks 63-104), with over ten steps between the starting and ending point.

41 Assessment Review Board, "Proceedings" (2018), online: <http://elto.gov.on.ca/tribunals/arb/assessment-cycle-2017-2020/proceedings/>.

42 *Supra* note 19, r 33.

Summary Proceedings

Summary proceedings apply to AA appeals, where the property in question is classified as residential, farm, or managed forest property, or MA appeals and CTA appeals (unless the latter two also have properties that are the subject of a hearing under the AA in the general proceeding stream). The ARB has assisted appellants by providing a list on its website of all properties classified as falling into the summary proceeding stream.[43] The list is organized according to property code and description. For example, the following properties appear on the list:

200—Farm property without any buildings/structures,
222—Farm with a winery,
306—Boathouse with residence above, and
366—Student housing off-campus.

Therefore, any appeal pertaining to property that is classified in one of those categories would begin the ARB process in the summary proceeding stream. As with the general proceeding process, a commencement date and schedule of events are assigned to each appeal. The schedule of events for summary proceedings can be found at Schedule B to the Rules (r 34(b)) and is less complex than its general proceeding counterpart. It begins with the parties full disclosure exchange (weeks 1-4) and ends with the parties' filing of documents (week 13-14), with only a few steps in the interim (Schedule B). Summary proceedings are electronic, unless the ARB determines otherwise (r 35).

Adjournments and Mandatory Meetings

The procedure around adjournments and mandatory meetings apply equally to both the general proceeding and summary proceeding streams. The granting of adjournments is an unlikely occurrence. The information sheet on adjournments says, "All requests for adjournments must be submitted before the due date or appearance before the ARB. Adjournments will only be granted in exceptional circumstances."[44] Nevertheless, as counsel you must sometimes request an adjournment for the sake of your client, even in the most unlikely circumstances. In such a case, complete the Expedited Board Proceedings Form, providing the reasons for your adjournment request, three possible dates for rescheduling, and confirmation you have notified the other parties who in turn consent to the adjournment.[45] In determining whether to grant an adjournment request, the ARB will consider:

43 *Supra* note 41.

44 Assessment Review Board, "Information Sheet Adjournments" (2018), online: <http://elto.gov.on.ca/wp-content/uploads/2017/05/Info-Sheet-Adjournments.pdf>.

45 *Ibid.*

- the interests of the parties in a full and fair proceeding;
- the impact of the adjournment on parties and other persons;
- the integrity of the Board's process, including the Board's ability to efficiently resolve all appeals filed with the Board within the current four year cycle;
- the circumstances giving rise to the need for an adjournment;
- the timeliness of the request for the adjournment;
- the position of the other parties;
- the public interest in the delivery of the Board's services in a just, timely and cost effective manner; and
- any practice directions issued by the Board.[46]

Rules 82-85 also state the exceptional nature of adjournment requests being granted, the required elements of such a request, the factors the ARB will consider, and the power of the ARB to impose any conditions that it deems appropriate.

Mandatory meetings are a requirement for both general proceeding appeals (at 52 weeks after commencement day) and summary proceeding appeals (at 12 weeks after commencement day). The mandatory meeting is an opportunity for parties to discuss issues and possibly come to an agreement on matters. After the meeting, a mandatory meeting outcome form must be filed with the ARB to provide an update on what was decided in the meeting and how the appeal will proceed. A specific Mandatory Meeting Form must be completed and filed by MPAC (not available online).[47]

Streaming

Streaming is another board process used to categorize hearings and manage application flow. After the ARB receives an appeal, it is placed either in the direct hearing (DH) or standard hearing (SH) stream, in accordance with the chair's streaming strategy.[48] DH matters are scheduled to a full hearing and have already proceeded through a request for reconsideration with MPAC. SH matters undergo a set order of pre-hearing processes.[49] Some other defining points of each of the processes are outlined below.

---

46 *Ibid*, as taken from r 84.

47 *Supra* note 41.

48 Assessment Review Board, "Chair's Streaming Strategy" (2016), online: <http://elto.gov.on.ca/wp-content/uploads/2016/01/ARB-Chairs-Streaming-Strategy.pdf>.

49 *Supra* note 41.

DH matters:

- pertain to "all new Residential, Farm, Managed Forest and Conservation Land appeals that require the mandatory filing of Requests for Reconsideration, regardless of value";[50]
- include non-residential properties with a property value of less than $6 million in the GTA or Ottawa regions, or $3 million in the rest of the province;
- have appeals set within six months of the filing date;
- receive at least 60 days for a notice of hearing with input from parties;
- do not require pleadings or discovery;
- allow for notice requirements to be waived; and
- aim for resolution of the appeal within a year of filing.

SH matters:

- pertain to non-residential appeals with a property value greater than $6 million in the GTA or Ottawa regions, or $3 million in the rest of the province; and
- have greater disclosure requirements and increased procedural and pre-hearing requirements.

After the appeals have been received and processed according to streaming requirements, they may proceed through a settlement conference, mediation, or a full hearing.

Settlement Conferences

Settlement conferences proceed in accordance with Rules 56-60 and the Practice Direction on Settlement Conferences. These occur before a hearing, under the direction of a board member, and attempt to have the parties agree on and narrow issues before a hearing and hopefully replace a hearing altogether. Parties are required to serve and file a settlement conference brief, in accordance with the schedule of events. The brief must include particulars, such as the issues, the party's position, and reasons for their position:

> For example, if the appeal is pursuant to s. 40 of the *Assessment Act*, where the issue in dispute is the correct current value of the property under appeal, it is not sufficient for the parties to each simply state their conclusion as to what the current value should be. They also need to further clarify the specific issues to be addressed by the Board, by explaining precisely how their underlying assessments of property value differ, e.g. each party applied a

50 *Supra* note 48 at 2.

different capitalization rate or fair market rent, or made different assumptions respecting functional or economic obsolescence, etc.[51]

All matters discussed in a settlement conference are confidential and may not be raised in a subsequent hearing.[52] If a settlement is not reached, the board member will encourage the use of mediation.

Mediation

Mediation is governed by Rules 86-89 and is "strongly encouraged"[53] by the ARB. Mediation is presided over by a board member who, with the active participation of the parties, seeks to resolve the dispute and avoid a hearing. Mediation, like a settlement conference, is confidential. It also requires that a mediation brief be served and filed, outlining the issues, the party's position, and the reasons for their position.[54]

Hearings occur as a last resort, when parties are unable or unwilling to settle or mediate the matter. At the ARB, hearings occur via teleconference, videoconference, or in person. Rules 90-95 govern electronic (teleconference or videoconference) hearings, and Rules 96-102 govern written hearings. Objections to either format can be made no more than 10 days after the notice of the written or electronic hearing.[55] Many matters will proceed in person.

The hearing proceeds in a similar matter to most traditional hearings. On the hearing day, matters are called on a first-come-first-served basis.[56] At the start of the hearing, the board member will introduce himself or herself and explain the expectations of procedure. Typically, MPAC offers evidence outlining the assessment process and an explanation of how the property in question received its assessment. The property owner/disputant will have the opportunity to cross-examine MPAC and then present any evidence against the assessment. The disputant will then be subject to cross-examination from MPAC. The municipality, if present, may also give evidence and be subject to cross-examination. The parties have the chance for re-direct, to allow for clarification of issues that arose in any cross-examinations. The hearing will then draw to a close, with the parties presenting closing statements. The ARB will either provide an oral decision or reserve the decision and provide a written one later.[57]

---

51 *Supra* note 25 at 2.

52 *Supra* note 19, r 59.

53 *Supra* note 24 at 1.

54 *Ibid* at 2.

55 *Supra* note 19, rr 91, 98.

56 *Supra* note 6 at 5.

57 Assessment Review Board, "Hearing Process" (2018), online: <http://elto.gov.on.ca/tribunals/arb/assessment-cycle-2017-2020/hearing-process/>.

Practitioners, appellants, and the public, can access the hearing schedule, including location, for each municipality online.[58] This is an invaluable resource for students or junior practitioners who want to observe some hearings before appearing before the ARB. Hearings are open to the public, according to Rule 103. Appellants and representatives can check the status of the appeal and hearing online by entering the 19-digit roll number that appears on the Notice of Assessment.[59] The ARB website hosts 17 information sheets for different appeal hearings[60] on topics ranging from pre-hearing requests for reconsideration and scheduling policy to a post-hearing request for review or reinstatement.

Decisions, Reconsiderations, and Appeals

Decisions may be given orally on the day of the hearing, or the board member may reserve his or her decision for later release. Typically, oral decisions are rendered on the day of the hearing.[61] If the decision is granted orally, written confirmation will follow. Parties can request written reasons for the decision, either at the hearing or through a formal request sent within 14 days of the hearing.[62] If a party is seeking a **review** of a decision, the party must include this review request with the written reasons. Reviews, accompanied by written reasons, may be requested within 30 days of the date of the decision[63] and in the following circumstances:

> Whether a material error of law or fact was made, which, if corrected, would have a significant effect on the decision; [w]hether any other person has relied upon or acted on the decision; and [w]hether the rights of a party other than the requester will be prejudiced if the decision is changed.[64]

review a request to the ARB to internally review a decision of the ARB

58 Assessment Review Board, "E-Calendar" (2018), online: <http://elto.gov.on.ca/tribunals/arb/e-calendar/>.

59 Assessment Review Board, "E-Status" (2018), online: <http://elto.gov.on.ca/tribunals/arb/e-status/>.

60 Assessment Review Board, "Information Sheets" (2018), online: <http://elto.gov.on.ca/tribunals/arb/assessment-cycle-2017-2020/information-sheets/>.

61 *Supra* note 7 at 7.

62 *Supra* note 19, r 112.

63 *Ibid*, r 120.

64 Assessment Review Board, "Decisions" (2018), online: <http://elto.gov.on.ca/tribunals/arb/assessment-cycle-2017-2020/hearing-process/decisions/>. See also "Rules," *supra* note 19, r 121.

The request must include the $125 filing fee and indicate whether a judicial review has been filed or leave to appeal has been sought at Divisional Court. Appeals from the ARB to Divisional Court are made possible by section 43.1 of the AA, section 331(18) of the CTA, and section 364(18) of the MA. From April 1, 2017 to June 30, 2017, the ARB received 17 review requests.[65]

In 2015 the ARB issued a staggering 37,159 decisions. In 2016 it issued 37,578.[66] And 2016 was a busy year for new appeals filed because it was an assessment year, meaning that the value of properties assessed in 2016 were the basis of taxation for the new assessment cycle of 2017-2020.[67]

Case Law

Olsheski v Municipal Property Assessment Corp, Region 9, [2017] OARBD No 101

Olsheski appealed to the ARB following a property assessment by MPAC of her two-and-three-quarter storey, semi-detached, 2,503-square-foot home in Toronto. The assessment was $1,100,000 for the 2016 calendar year. Olsheski argues it should be valued between $878,000 and $950,000. The two issues in the appeal are, "Does the assessment of $1,100,000 reflect the current value of the land; and should the assessment be adjusted to make it equitable with the assessments of similar lands in the vicinity?" (at 4). Valuation of the property is required by section 44(3)(a) of the AA and can be adjusted according to section 44(3)(b) (at 5, 7). The land is assessed at its current value according to section 19(1) of the AA (at 6). The ARB determined that MPAC had assessed the value of $1,100,000 correctly, taking into consideration the direct sales comparison approach of similar properties nearby (at 13, 14, 19, 21-31, 41-42).

MM v Toronto (City), [2017] OARBD No 68

This appeal to the ARB is based on section 323(1)(e) of the CTA. MM brought the appeal, requesting that her property tax of $6,785.12 for the calendar year of 2015 be cancelled because of her inability to pay because of sickness or poverty (at 3-4). An applicant appealing under this section must first satisfy the test outlined in the Act (at 7):

> In order for the Applicant to qualify for relief under this section of the Act, the Board must first determine whether sickness or extreme poverty exists. If neither sickness nor extreme poverty exists, then the application fails. If

---

65 *Supra* note 7.

66 *Ibid.*

67 David Tang, "Review Your Property Tax Situation Before 2016 Ends" (December 2016) <http://www.millerthomson.com/en/publications/communiques-and-updates/real-estate-report/december-2016-real-estate/review-property-tax-situation-2016-ends/>.

either is present, the Applicant must demonstrate an inability to pay all or part of the taxes.

MM provided evidence that her 25-year-old autistic son required her full care and attention; both the City and the ARB were convinced that this satisfied the test for sickness under the Act (at 10-12). MM provided evidence of her inability to work and her monthly income and spending to show that she was not in a financial position to afford property tax. The City did not support MM in this part of the test; however, the ARB found that she met the test for extreme poverty under the Act. MM's property tax was completely cancelled for 2015 (at 22-23).

Drennan Farms Ltd v Municipal Property Assessment Corp, Region 24, [2017] OARBD No 98

This is a decision from a Request to Review an assessment decision based on farm land. Section 40 of the AA is the applicable legislative provision. Drennan requested a review of an ARB decision on the following grounds (at 4):

1. The presiding members did not properly consider the evidence regarding the devaluation of suggested comparable properties.
2. The presiding members denied the requester natural justice and procedural fairness by allowing MPAC to submit a book of authorities at the hearing.
3. The presiding members acted in a biased manner toward the requester.

Though the review request was one week late, the ARB made a discretionary decision to accept the request (at 1). On the first issue, Drennan submitted that the ARB failed to properly consider assessment-to-sale ratios of comparable properties as submitted by MPAC. The ARB found that the presiding board member had considered this evidence and that members have discretion in assessing evidence. In this case, no error had been made, and board members are extended deference in their decision-making (at 14, 15). On the second issue, Drennan argued that he was denied natural justice and procedural fairness through the ARB's acceptance of MPAC's book of authorities. The ARB found that Drennan had sufficient time to review MPAC's book of authorities and that submitting such evidence did not amount to unfairness for an opposing party (at 17, 18). On the third issue, Drennan claimed bias based on a statement made by an ARB member in the original decision in which they relied upon a previous decision of the board. In the review decision, the board considered the test for bias: "whether a fully informed reasonable person viewing the Presiding Members' conduct practically and realistically would conclude that it is more likely than not that the Presiding Members did not decide the matter fairly" (at 20). The board concluded that the member's statements did not meet the threshold for showing a reasonable apprehension of bias (at 21). For these reasons, the request to review was denied (at 24).

KEY LEGISLATION

Assessment Act

Generation Facilities, O Reg 574/06

General, O Reg 282/98

Assessment Review Board Act

City of Toronto Act, 2006

Property Tax Bills, O Reg 122/07

Traditional Municipal Taxes, Limits and Collection, O Reg 121/07

Municipal and School Capital Facilities—Agreements and Tax Exemptions, O Reg 598/06

Toronto Tax Sales Rules, O Reg 579/06

Condominium Act, 1998

Education Act

Tax Matters—Limitation on Tax Increases in Territory Without Municipal Organization, O Reg 259/17

Tax Matters—Rates Under Subsection 255(1) of the Act, O Reg 712/98

Tax Matters—Tax Rates for School Purposes, O Reg 400/98

Tax Matters—Definition of Business Property and Residential Property, O Reg 394/98

Tax Matters—Eligible Theatre Definition, O Reg 393/98

Tax Matters—Taxation of Certain Railway, Power Utility Lands, O Reg 392/98

Tax Arrears in Annexed Areas, O Reg 366/98

Deemed District Municipalities (District School Board Jurisdiction)—Tax Rates, O Reg 468/97

Deemed District Municipalities (School Authority Jurisdiction)—Tax Rates, O Reg 467/97

Municipal Act, 2001

Tax Matters—Regional Municipality of Peel, O Reg 103/09

Municipal and School Capital Facilities—Agreements and Tax Exemptions, O Reg 603/06

Tax Matters—Notice Under Subsection 365.1(5) of the Act, O Reg 274/04

Municipal Tax Sales Rules, O Reg 181/03

Tax Matters—Special Tax Rates and Limits, O Reg 73/03

Tax Matters—Eligible Property Under Section 364 of the Act and Land Prescribed Under Subsection 357(1.1) of the Act, O Reg 325/01

Tax Ratios—City of Owen Sound, O Reg 311/01

Property Tax Bills, O Reg 75/01

Tax Related Matters, O Reg 406/98

Tax Matters—Charity Rebates, O Reg 389/98

Tax Matters—Taxation of Certain Railway, Power Utility Lands, O Reg 387/98

Tax Matters—Allowable Ranges for Tax Ratios, O Reg 386/98

Tax Matters—Transition Rations and Average Transition Ratios, O Reg 385/98

Tax Matters—Universities and Other Institutions, O Reg 384/98
Tax Matters—Farm Land Awaiting Development Subclasses, Tax Reduction Percentages, O Reg 383/98
Payments in Lieu of Taxes, Distribution, O Reg 382/98
Prescribed Tax—International Bridges, O Reg 33/98

Municipal Property Assessment Corporation Act, 1997

Provincial Land Tax Act, 2006

General, O Reg 229/09
Tax Rates, O Reg 224/09

Statutory Powers Procedure Act

KEY TERMS

commencement days, 142
property classification, 136
quorum, 138
review, 150
schedule of events, 142
tax assessment, 136

REVIEW QUESTIONS

1. Name the four bodies that are integral to the property assessment and taxation process.
2. What important features of the Assessment Review Board are outlined in the *Assessment Review Board Act*?
3. Identify which piece of legislation governs the following ARB appeals: (a) City of Toronto tax appeal; (b) City of Ottawa tax appeal; (c) City of Peterborough tax appeal.
4. What is the "special legislation" rule in the Rules of Practice and Procedure, and what additional requirement does it impose for initiating proceedings?
5. What matters are heard in the general stream versus the summary stream?
6. Define "commencement date." What rule applies?
7. Define "schedule of events." What rule applies?
8. Using the Fee Chart (online at <http://elto.gov.on.ca/tribunals/arb/fee-chart>), identify the cost of the following appeals:
   a. *Assessment Act*, section 34, farm property
   b. *City of Toronto Act, 2006*, section 326
   c. *Municipal Act, 2001*, section 331
   d. *Assessment Act*, section 40, Industrial property, e-filing
9. How would you seek an adjournment for your client, and what authorities would you rely upon?
10. How would you seek a review of an ARB decision, and what authorities would you rely upon?

SCENARIOS

1. Using O Reg 282/98, section 2, identify what proceeding stream (general, G, or summary, S) each class of property would fall into. In other words, if you were bringing an appeal to the ARB on the basis of a property assessment for 2.1 Residential Property Class, it would be a summary proceeding. Assume they are all AA appeals. Identify the following:
   - **a.** The multi-residential property class
   - **b.** The commercial property class
   - **c.** The industrial property class
   - **d.** The pipe line property class
   - **e.** The farm property class
   - **f.** The managed forests property class
   - **g.** The new multi-residential property class
   - **h.** The office building property class
   - **i.** The shopping centre property class
   - **j.** The parking lots and vacant land property class
   - **j.1** The residual commercial property class
   - **k.** The large industrial property class
   - **l.** The professional sports facility property class
   - **m.** The resort condominium property class
   - **n.** The landfill property class
2. Assume that your client has a number of related appeals before the ARB and wants to combine them into one proceeding. Unfortunately, MPAC does not agree on the basis that different evidence is required for each matter. According to the Rules and the Practice Direction on Combined Proceedings, will you be successful in requesting that the proceedings be combined?
3. Grace Stenovski approaches you in desperation after receiving her last tax bill from the City of Markham, knowing she can't afford to pay it after falling ill last year and being out of work since then. What do you advise, and what authorities do you rely upon?

CHAPTER 8

The Licence Appeal Tribunal and Automobile Accident Benefits Service

Overview ... 158
Licence Appeal Tribunal General ... 158
LAT AABS ... 158
What Types of Benefits Are Available? ... 159
Legislation ... 161
The Insurance Act ... 161
The SABS—Statutory Accident Benefits Schedule ... 161
LAT Common Rules of Practice and Procedure ... 162
Superintendent's and Commissioner's Guidelines—Auto Insurance SABs ... 163
Decisions and Case Law ... 163
The AABS Dispute Resolution Process ... 164
Case Law ... 179
Key Terms ... 186
Review Questions ... 186
Scenario 1 ... 187
Scenario 2 ... 188
Scenario 3 ... 188

Overview

Licence Appeal Tribunal General

The Licence Appeal Tribunal (LAT) is an adjudicative tribunal established under the *Licence Appeal Tribunal Act, 1999* (LATA).[1] The LAT's mandate is to resolve appeals regarding compensation claims and licensing decisions made by a variety of regulators and in accordance with the appeal rights set out under several statutes.

The tribunal receives appeals, conducts hearings, resolves disputes, and makes decisions on numerous matters. The LAT currently hears appeals from decisions pursuant to over 25 statutes, which are listed on its website at <http://www.slasto.gov.on.ca/en/lat/Pages/The-Law/Legislations.aspx>. Some of the most common LAT cases involve liquor licences, new home warranty claims, medical suspension of driver's licences, impoundment of motor vehicles, and the regulation of some occupations and businesses.

Some recent additions to the LAT include adjudicative responsibility for beer-in-grocery-store licensing appeals and appeals relating to horse racing licences.

Since April 1, 2016 the LAT has accepted applications to the new Automobile Accident Benefits Service (AABS) system that aims to quickly resolve disagreements between individuals and insurance companies about accident benefits. These disputes were previously heard by the **Financial Services Commission of Ontario (FSCO)**. AABS applications at LAT now represent the largest number of appeals that the LAT receives—more than 800 applications per month.

This chapter will focus on LAT AABS statutory accident benefits cases and procedure.

LAT AABS

The AABS assists people who are injured in a motor vehicle accident, have made a claim for statutory accident benefits, and have had their claim denied by an insurance company. Drivers, passengers, pedestrians, or family members of a person who is injured or dies may all have a potential claim for benefits. If an insurer denies a claim for benefits, an applicant can apply to LAT AABS for help in resolving the dispute.

These disputes were previously heard by the FSCO and the Superior Court of Justice. Since April 1, 2016 disputes regarding accident benefits can no longer be started at the FSCO or the court. FSCO will continue to be responsible for all files remaining open as of March 31, 2016. Parties can also file a notice of appeal at FSCO, if FSCO received the application for arbitration before April 1, 2016. All other accident benefits disputes must be filed with LAT AABS.

1 SO 1999, c 12, Schedule G.

What Are Statutory Accident Benefits?

Statutory accident benefits are benefits available for people who have been injured or killed in an automobile accident. They are also known as "no-fault benefits" because they are available regardless of who is at fault for an accident. If your client was injured in an accident that arose directly out of the use or operation of an automobile, then he or she may be entitled to these no-fault accident benefits.

What Types of Benefits Are Available?

Statutory accident benefits coverage pays for things such as medical treatment, income replacement if as a result of the accident a person is not able to work, and the cost of attendant care in more serious cases.

Some of the benefits available include the following:

- *Income replacement benefits (IRB):* If your client cannot work as the result of an auto accident, he or she may be eligible for weekly income replacement benefits of 70 percent of their gross income, up to $400/week.
- *Caregiver benefits:* If your client can no longer provide full-time care to a dependant—for example, a child or other person—as a result of a catastrophic injury, your client may be eligible for caregiver benefits to be reimbursed for expenses in hiring someone to take over for him or her. This benefit is available only to claimants whose impairment meets the definition of "catastrophic" or who have purchased optional benefits.
- *Non-earner benefits (NEB):* If your client's injuries result in a complete inability to carry on a normal life, and he or she does not qualify for income replacement benefits or was a full-time student at the time of the accident, then your client may be eligible for non-earner benefits of $185/week.

Financial Services Commission of Ontario (FSCO) a regulatory agency of the Ministry of Finance that regulates insurance, pension plans, loan and trust companies, credit unions, caisses populaires, mortgage brokering, and co-operative corporations in Ontario

statutory accident benefits benefits provided to persons in Ontario injured by the use or operation of a motor vehicle; governed by the Statutory Accident Benefits Schedule, which is a regulation made under the *Insurance Act* of Ontario (also called no fault benefits)

- *Medical and rehabilitation benefit:* These benefits cover costs such as massage, chiropractic, physiotherapy, prescriptions, counselling, and transportation to medical appointments not covered by OHIP or private group insurance plans.
- *Attendant care benefit (ACB):* These benefits cover the need for an attendant to care for your client, either at home or in a healthcare facility, if he or she has been seriously injured in an auto accident. ACBs are not available if the impairments are considered to be minor injuries.

Some additional categories of benefits are:

- lost education expenses
- housekeeping and home maintenance
- death and funeral expenses
- visitor's expenses
- damage to clothing
- interest.

Who Is Eligible for Accident Benefits?

Anyone injured in an accident may be eligible for benefits.

An applicant's injuries must be *caused by the accident* and the circumstances causing the impairment must meet the definition of accident:

> "accident" means an incident in which the use or operation of an automobile directly causes an impairment or directly causes damage to any prescription eyewear, denture, hearing aid, prosthesis or other medical or dental device.[2]

There are some circumstances, however, that may limit a claim for benefits or make an applicant ineligible. For example:

- driving without a valid driver's licence,
- driving a vehicle without the owner's consent,
- being a passenger in a vehicle driven by someone without the owner's consent,
- driving without valid insurance,
- driving while impaired or refusing to provide a breath sample, and
- using a vehicle in connection with a criminal activity.

2 Statutory Accident Benefits Schedule, O Reg 34/10, s 3(1).

Legislation

The LAT, like all administrative tribunals, aims to provide clear and flexible appeal processes and dispute resolution services that are accessible to the public. The tribunal is subject to the rules of natural justice and the requirements of the Statutory Powers Procedure Act (SPPA).[3] The members appointed to the tribunal conduct fair, efficient, and impartial hearings during which they consider all evidence presented and make a decision with written reasons. Most tribunal decisions are subject to appeal to the Superior Court of Justice (Divisional Court). All tribunal proceedings are subject to judicial review under the Judicial Review Procedure Act.[4]

The Insurance Act

The enabling statute governing the AABS is the *Insurance Act* (IA).[5] Section 280 of the Act states that:

> 280(1) This section applies with respect to the resolution of disputes in respect of an insured person's entitlement to statutory accident benefits or in respect of the amount of statutory accident benefits to which an insured person is entitled.
>
> Application to tribunal
> (2) The insured person or the insurer may apply to the Licence Appeal Tribunal to resolve a dispute described in subsection (1).

Sections 279-288 of the IA set out the dispute resolution process.

The SABS—Statutory Accident Benefits Schedule

The Statutory Accident Benefits Schedule (SABS)[6] is a regulation under the IA that sets out the benefits and compensation that may be available to someone injured in an accident. The benefits set out in the SABS are standardized among all Ontario insurance companies.

The date of the accident, also referred to as the **date of loss**, is key in determining which SABS Schedule applies (see Table 8.1). The available benefits and rules that apply differ depending on the date of the accident.

date of loss date the accident occured

3 RSO 1990, c S.22.

4 RSO 1990, c J.1.

5 RSO 1990, c I.8.

6 O Reg 34/10 is the current schedule.

TABLE 8.1 Summary of SAB Schedules

Date of Accident	Originating Legislation	Applicable Schedule
Accidents after September 1, 2010	O Reg 34/10	Statutory Accident Benefits Schedule—Effective September 1, 2010
Accidents on or after November 1, 1996 to August 30, 2010	O Reg 403/96	Statutory Accident Benefits Schedule—Accidents on or After November 1, 1996
Accidents on or after December 31, 1993 and before November 1, 1996	O Reg 776/93	Statutory Accident Benefits Schedule—Accidents After December 31, 1993 And Before November 1, 1996
Accidents before January 1, 1994	RRO 1990, Reg 672	Statutory Accident Benefits Schedule—Accidents Before January 1, 1994

LAT Common Rules of Practice and Procedure

The Safety, Licensing Appeals and Standards Tribunals Ontario (SLASTO) is a cluster of five adjudicative tribunals: the Animal Care Review Board, Fire Safety Commission, Licence Appeal Tribunal, Ontario Civilian Police Commission, and Ontario Parole Board. Effective October 2, 2017, three of the constituent tribunals adopted an updated **Common Rules of Practice and Procedure**. The Rules are made pursuant to section 25.1 of the SPPA and also under section 6 of the LAT. These Common Rules also apply to the LAT AABS.

The Rules should be read and understood together with the SPPA and the SABS. If there is a conflict between the Rules and any statute or regulation, the provisions of the statute or regulation prevail.

Rule 3.1 provides that the Rules are to be liberally interpreted and applied and may be varied or applied to facilitate a fair, open, and accessible process and to allow effective participation by all parties and ensure efficient, proportional, and timely resolution on the merits of the proceeding. Rule 3.1 may

Common Rules of Practice and Procedure Effective October 2, 2017, the Licence Appeal Tribunal, Animal Care Review Board, and the Fire Safety Commission adopted the Common Rules of Practice and Procedure, which will apply to all tribunal proceedings filed on or after October 2, 2017; previous versions of the Rules will continue to apply to matters filed before October 2, 2017

prove to be important in circumstances where technical compliance with the Rules is not achieved but is nevertheless appropriate in the circumstances.

The Rules set out the basic processes and procedures for tribunal proceedings such as:

- definitions
- parties
- serving of documents
- notice
- representation
- summons
- disclosure
- witnesses
- motions
- adjournments
- reconsideration
- costs

Superintendent's and Commissioner's Guidelines—Auto Insurance SABs

Although FSCO no longer hears new disputes, several superintendent's Guidelines are still in effect. The Guidelines have been issued by the superintendent of financial services and the former commissioner of the Ontario Insurance Commission (OIC) on the interpretation and operation of the SABS. They set out the rights and responsibilities of insurers and claimants when dealing with statutory accident benefits claims relating to auto insurance, and set out the rules for such matters as the filing of documents, time limits, and payments of fees and expenses.

Each Guideline is issued as part of an Auto Insurance Bulletin. The FSCO website has a complete list of all superintendent's Guidelines. Some of the commonly used Guidelines include:

- 2017
  - No 03/17: Attendant Care Hourly Rate Guideline (Bulletin A-04/17)
- 2016
  - No 04/16: Transportation Expense Guideline (Bulletin A-14/16)
  - No 02/16: Cost of Goods Guideline (Bulletin A-09/16)
- 2014
  - No 03/14: Professional Services Guideline (Bulletin A-08/14)
  - No 01/14: Minor Injury Guideline (Bulletin A-01/14)

Decisions and Case Law

All LAT AABS decisions are published on the Canadian Legal Information Institute website (CanLII). After a hearing is complete, the AABS adjudicator will consider everything that he or she heard or read and make a decision. After the decision is made, a copy of the decision with reasons is sent to the parties.

LAT adjudicators are not bound by FSCO decisions; however, it is still important to know the FSCO decisions that deal with the issue in your case. Although the FSCO decisions are not binding, they have been considered persuasive in LAT decisions to date. FSCO decisions can be accessed on the FSCO website at <http://www.fsco.gov.on.ca/en/drs/Pages/arbitration_appeal_decisions.aspx>.

The AABS Dispute Resolution Process

Filing an AABS Application

The person injured by the accident can file an application with AABS if there is a dispute about the injured person's entitlement to accident benefits or the amount of benefits. Application forms are available on the SLASTO website.

An insurance company can also file an application with AABS if it is seeking a repayment from an insured person. If an insurance company believes an individual has been paid too much under his or her policy, the company can file an AABS application to have the money returned.

AABS *does not* hear disputes about:

- damages for pain and suffering,
- damage to cars or other property,
- who was at fault in the accident, and
- which insurer is responsible for a claim.

Two-Year Limitation Period

If an insurance company denies or stops paying benefits to an insured person, it must provide a *written notice of this decision* that includes the reason(s) for its decision. If an applicant wants to dispute the denial of their claim, he or she must file an AABS application within *two years after the denial notice* from the insurance company. This is set out in section 56 of the SABS Schedule:

> Time limit for proceedings
>
> 56. An application under subsection 280 (2) of the Act in respect of a benefit shall be commenced within two years after the insurer's refusal to pay the amount claimed.

To trigger the two-year limitation period, the denial or stoppage of benefits must be "clear and unequivocal."[7]

7 *Zeppieri and Royal Insurance Company of Canada*, QIC A-005237, Arbitrator Naylor, February 17, 1994; *Turner v State Farm Mutual Automobile Insurance Company* (2005), 195 OAC 61 (CA); *Monks v Dominion of Canada*, P09-00018, Director's Delegate Blackman, December 10, 2009.

The leading case in defining what constitutes "proper notice" is the Supreme Court of Canada's decision in *Smith v Co-operators General Insurance Co.*[8] In that case, the majority of the Supreme Court held that an insurer's refusal must include an adequate description of the SABS dispute resolution process. The court held that it was necessary to do so in "straightforward and clear language, directed towards an unsophisticated person."

Completing an AABS Application

When completing an AABS application (see Table 8.2), provide as much detail as possible about the disputed claims and benefits. Be specific about:

- the type of benefit claimed,
- time period for the claim,
- names of service providers, and
- amount in dispute.

For example: The applicant claims physiotherapy treatment in the amount of $1,500 provided by Dr Kessel. The claim was provided to ABC Insurance on March 5, 2017 and denied by ABC Insurance on March 10, 2017.

TABLE 8.2 The Application Process

• Complete an AABS application form (available on the SLASTO website).
• Send a copy of the application form to the other party or the party's representative.
• Complete an AABS certificate of service form (available on the SLASTO website).
• Send the application and certificate of service forms to AABS and pay the AABS application fee.

E-Filing for AABS Applications

Online filing for AABS applications and responses is available. If you have questions about AABS e-File, contact SLASTOinfo@ontario.ca.

8 [2002] 2 SCR 129.

Filing an AABS Response

If your client is served with a completed AABS application form, he or she must file a response. All forms are available from the SLASTO website. The responding party is usually the insurance company, but sometimes the injured person must respond to an application that was started by the insurance company.

An insurance company must complete the response by an insurance company form. A claimant must complete the response by an injured person form.

Table 8.3 outlines the steps to responding to an AABS application.

TABLE 8.3 Responding to an AABS Application

• Complete the response form (available on the SLASTO website).
• Send a copy to the other party or the party's representative and to the tribunal within ten business days.
• Send the response to AABS and complete a certificate of service to tell AABS how you have sent the response to the other party.

Preliminary Issues

There may be preliminary issues raised that need to be resolved before the main issues in dispute can be decided. These are often the determination of a question of law, which can be isolated from factual issues. Preliminary issues are typically raised in the response as a defence to the entire claim.

A common preliminary issue is whether the applicant has applied to the LAT within the two-year limitation period. The hearing will typically be bifurcated to deal with the preliminary issue first. If the tribunal finds that the applicant has not applied within the required time, then there is no need for a subsequent hearing on whether the applicant is entitled to the benefits claimed.

Another common AABS preliminary issue involves the question of whether an insured attended at a required insurer examination. Section 55 of the SABS states that an insured person cannot apply to the LAT under subsection 280(2) of the IA if the insurer has provided the insured person with proper notice to attend an examination under section 44, but the insured person has not complied with that section.

When preliminary issues are raised in a response, it is still necessary to schedule a case conference and a hearing if the issues do not settle in order for an adjudicator to decide on the preliminary issue.

The Case Conference

AABS will schedule a **case conference** after receiving the response or when the time for filing a response has lapsed. A case management officer (CMO) will schedule a one-hour case conference for the parties with an AABS adjudicator. Case conferences usually take place within 45 to 60 days of the response being received. The case conference usually takes place *by telephone* unless the parties request that it be in person. Case conferences are not open to the public.

A case conference is an opportunity for the parties to discuss the dispute with an adjudicator and attempt to settle the claim. If the case does not settle at a case conference, the adjudicator will assist the parties in preparing for and scheduling a hearing date.

Parties must participate at the case conference even if they have a representative. The focus of the case conference is to attempt to settle the case; therefore, all parties must be present. They cannot simply send their representatives to attend without seeking permission from the tribunal (r 14.6).

Before attending a case conference, the injured person and insurer should each complete and submit an AABS case conference summary form. A copy of the completed case conference summary, and any relevant documents, must be sent to the other party. This exchange and disclosure helps parties understand each other's differences and may assist in settlement.

The case conference is your first opportunity to present your client's position to the adjudicator and the other party. This is also an opportunity to use your advocacy skills not only to list the issues in dispute but also to state your argument and the evidence you have in support of the claim and your position. Good advocacy and preparation will assist in the early settlement of a case.

The case conference summary is due at least ten days before the scheduled case conference. Rule 20.4 sets out the requirements for the case conference summary:

> Each party shall file an AABS Case Conference Summary, in such form as may be required by the Tribunal, with the Tribunal at least 10 days before a scheduled Case Conference. An AABS Case Conference Summary shall include:
>
> (a) A list of key documents in the party's possession which he or she intends to use in a hearing;
>
> (b) Verification that the documents listed in (a) have been disclosed and have been provided to the other parties;

case conference the first meeting between the parties in a dispute and an adjudicator. This is an opportunity for the parties to discuss the dispute with an adjudicator and attempt to settle the claim; if the case does not settle, the adjudicator will assist the parties in preparing for and scheduling a hearing date

(c) A list of key documents that the party intends to seek from other parties pursuant to the disclosure Rules set out at Rule 9;

(d) A list of any information the party is seeking from non-parties and requests for issuance of summonses;

(e) The party's preference of hearing type with reasons for the preference;

(f) A list of anticipated witnesses, including expert witnesses, that the party intends to call at a hearing in electronic or in-person format and a brief description of each witness' anticipated testimony;

(g) An explanation of the necessity of calling more than two expert witnesses to provide opinion evidence, if a party seeks to call more than two such experts; and

(h) Details of the most recent settlement offer that is open for acceptance.

What Happens If the Issues Do Not Settle at the Case Conference?

Parties should come to the case conference prepared to try to settle the issues. During the case conference, the adjudicator will try to narrow the differences between the parties by asking questions and explaining how the SABS have been applied in similar cases. However, if the issues do not settle, the adjudicator will set a date for a hearing and make an order as required. The adjudicator who conducts the case conference is not the same adjudicator that hears the case.

Parties must come prepared to discuss the following:

- *Clarification of the issues in dispute.* The case conference adjudicator will identify and clarify the issues in dispute that will be proceeding to a hearing. Parties should advise the adjudicator and each other if any of the issues have changed since filing the application or response and provide details.
- *Disclosure.* **Disclosure** covers the documents that each party wants and what each party may want to use as evidence at the hearing, such as medical assessments and records, employment records, and tax returns.
- *Witnesses.* Witnesses are individuals who have information and knowledge relevant to the issues in dispute. Witnesses can appear in person at a hearing or provide evidence through an affidavit.

disclosure providing to the other party a copy of the evidence that one party plans to use during a hearing

- *Format of the hearing.* AABS hearings can be held in writing, by telephone, in person, or in a combination of these formats. Complex cases are typically held in person.
- *Hearing date.* The adjudicator will canvass dates for a hearing, typically 90 days or less from the date of the case conference.

Disclosure

At the case conference parties often disagree about which documents they should produce or share with the other side. The test for admissibility at the hearing is *relevance*. If there is a document that you want the opposing side to produce, then come prepared to argue why that document is relevant to the case.

After the case conference and up to the start of the hearing, there is an ongoing obligation to ensure the timely and complete exchange of documents that are reasonably necessary to determine the issues in dispute. Any new reports or evidence that are relevant to your client's case and that you plan to submit at the hearing should be disclosed to the other party and the tribunal as soon as possible. Any unreasonable or unnecessary delay in exchanging relevant evidence may result in the hearing adjudicator deciding that you cannot rely on the document or thing as evidence, or call the witnesses to give evidence, without the consent of the tribunal. This is set out in Rule 9.2, Disclosure of Documents:

> A party to a hearing shall, at least 10 days before the hearing, or at any other time ordered by the Tribunal or undertaken by the party:
>
> (a) Disclose to the other parties the existence of every document and anything else the party intends to present as evidence at the hearing;
>
> (b) Disclose a list of witnesses whom the party may call to give evidence at the hearing and a brief description of each witness' anticipated testimony; and
>
> (c) Serve a copy of the documents, numbered consecutively, on the other parties.

A typical applicant disclosure request includes the insurance adjuster's complete file, including adjuster's log notes, emails, letters of instruction, correspondence, surveillance and investigation reports, and any other documents relevant to adjusting the file. Any documents in the insurance adjuster's file after the date when an application has been filed at LAT are considered privileged and not disclosed.

A typical respondent disclosure request includes all clinical notes and records by the applicant's treating medical practitioners and OHIP records at least one year pre-accident. This period may be extended if there are any pre-existing injuries or impairments.

The tribunal will send the parties a **case conference report and order** after the case conference. These will set out the issues discussed and the outcome, as well as any orders made.

How Do I Ask for an Adjournment? (Rule 16)

Given the tight timelines, the LAT will grant adjournments of hearings only in special circumstances where fairness requires an **adjournment**. For example, illness or the unavoidable and unexpected absence of a party or witness, or where the interests of fairness can be addressed only by an adjournment.

The first step is to contact the other party to see if the party will consent to the request and if there are other dates that both parties can agree on.

The next step is to fill out the request for an adjournment, file it with the LAT, and serve the Request on all parties as soon as possible. Forms are available from the SLASTO website.

A request for an adjournment of a case conference or hearing must be in writing, be served on the other parties, and include:

- the reason for the request;
- written agreement for the adjournment from the other parties or their representatives, if given; and
- at least three alternative dates, within 30 days of the case conference date or hearing date to be adjourned, that are agreeable to all parties (r 16.1).

Withdrawing an Application

If your client decides not to proceed with the application, or if the case has settled at any time before a hearing, you can withdraw the application. Complete the AABS notice of withdrawal form (available from the SLASTO website), and send it to both the AABS and the other party.

After you withdraw the application, AABS will close the file and cancel any case conference or hearing dates that have been set.

case conference report and order issued after a case conference by the adjudicator and sets out any orders made, such as the date and format of the hearing, the specific witnesses who will give evidence, and any documents that must be exchanged or produced

adjournment the postponement of a case conference or hearing until some future date (the LAT Rules describe how to request an adjournment and the circumstances when an adjournment may be granted by the tribunal)

What Is a Motion?

A motion is a request for an order or a decision from the tribunal to (a) rule on its jurisdiction, (b) give directions concerning its procedures, or (c) make an order for any other purpose necessary to carrying out its functions.

Some examples of when you may need to bring a motion at LAT AABS include:

- to make a change to a case conference order,
- to add a witness,
- to add a new issue or defence to a scheduled hearing, or
- to introduce new evidence at the hearing that was not discussed at the case conference.

Rule 15 requires that a party bringing a motion will deliver a notice of motion (available from the SLASTO website) setting out:

- the decision or order that the party is requesting from the tribunal;
- the grounds to be argued, including a reference to any statutory or regulatory provision, rule, or case law relied on;
- the evidence in support of the motion; and
- the proposed format of the motion (r 15.1).

The Hearing

AABS hearings are held only if the mandatory case conference does not result in an agreement between the parties.

All parties receive a notice of hearing that includes the date, time, and location of the hearing. The hearing will be scheduled within 60 to 90 days after the case conference. The notice will also set out the hearing format.

AABS hearings are conducted in writing, electronically (by videoconference or teleconference), in person, or by any combination of these methods (r 12.1). Hearings are open to the public, unless the adjudicator decides that all or part of the hearing should be closed for privacy reasons allowed by law.

How to Prepare for the Hearing

The applicant has the onus to prove his or her case. In preparation of a hearing, consider the following:

- What are the specific issues in dispute?
- What is the test you need to meet and what elements do you need to prove to meet the test?
- What evidence do you have in support of your position?

- How will you present that evidence before the adjudicator? For example, the evidence might be submitted as
  - documents,
  - reports,
  - affidavits, or
  - witness testimony.
- Do you have any case law that supports your argument?

Disclosure for the Hearing

Rule 9.2 requires the disclosure of every document and anything else the party intends to present as evidence at the hearing *at least ten days before the hearing*, unless the case conference adjudicator has made an order setting out a different time.

Once you have determined which documents you are relying on for the hearing, start to prepare a document brief. It should be indexed, tabbed, and bound, and the pages should be numbered for easy reference during the hearing. To keep the hearing focused, you may consider creating a **joint document brief** with the other party. This is a collection of documentary evidence that both parties agree is relevant and should be put before the decision-maker for the hearing. Having parties work together to organize the key documents helps keep the hearing more organized and focused and the volume of paper down.

What Happens at an AABS Hearing

At the beginning of the hearing, the hearing adjudicator will again canvass the possibility of settlement with the parties. If the parties do not settle, the hearing will go ahead.

An AABS hearing is a legal proceeding led by an independent adjudicator. The claimant and the insurance company will each have an opportunity to deliver a brief opening statement setting out their understanding of the case and the important issues. Parties will then use evidence—for example, documents and witnesses—to present their position.

Participants

The participants in an AABS hearing include:

- the adjudicator;
- the injured person (in most cases, this is the applicant or claimant);

joint document brief a collection of documentary evidence that both parties agree is relevant and should be put before the decision-maker for the hearing, the organization of which keeps the hearing more organized and focused and the volume of paper down

- a representative of the insurance company;
- any representatives of the participants (lawyer, paralegal, or other representative);
- witnesses;
- interpreters, if required, for language interpretation or sign language interpretation (if a party or a witness requires an interpreter in a language other than English or French, the party must notify the tribunal at least 14 days before the hearing or case conference; rr 4.2 and 20.6); and
- support persons, if needed.

The adjudicator who leads the hearing will not be the same adjudicator as at the case conference and will not know what happened at the case conference.

The Role of the Adjudicator

The **adjudicator** controls the hearing, and parties must follow the directions of the adjudicator. Adjudicators are neutral and independent; they cannot provide legal advice to either party. Adjudicators will sometimes ask questions during the hearing when the claimant and the insurance company present evidence to support their positions.

Presenting a Case

During the hearing, representatives for the injured person and the insurance company will explain their positions to the adjudicator, question witnesses, and introduce documents as evidence. The parties can make arguments about the facts and the law.

Evidence versus Submissions

Evidence is documents or things that the adjudicator accepts as part of what the adjudicator can consider in deciding the case. Evidence is also the testimony of witnesses—that is, what witnesses say at the hearing. Evidence from witnesses can also be contained in a document called an affidavit. In an affidavit, the witness swears or affirms that the information given is the truth.

Examples of evidence in a motor vehicle accident case may include the police accident report, employment records, or a report from a doctor or other type of medical professional.

adjudicator a decision-maker who presides over (or hears) formal disputes between parties and makes a decision

evidence testimony and presentation of documents, records, objects, and other such items relating to the existence or non-existence of alleged or disputed facts being decided by a court or tribunal

Submissions are the arguments you make about the evidence. Remember that as a representative you cannot directly give the adjudicator evidence. You must enter it using a document or witness. You can, however, use your submissions to explain to the adjudicator why the evidence is important and how it helps your case.

Witnesses

If the hearing is scheduled to be heard electronically or in person, you may call a witness to provide evidence. A witness is someone with personal knowledge about events relevant to the case. A person can be his or her own witness and testify at the hearing. The adjudicator will ask witnesses to make an affirmation or swear an oath that they will tell the truth. Persons who are called by one party to testify as witnesses may be questioned by the other party—this is called cross-examination. The tribunal's adjudicator may also pose questions to any witness.

Expert Witnesses

Many of the AABS hearings involve medical evidence provided by expert witnesses or in reports. An **expert witness** can provide technical information or an opinion at the hearing. The tribunal can decide who is an expert witness, based on the expert's qualifications and experience. In accident cases, doctors who examine injured parties after an accident are often expert witnesses.

Parties must exchange information about their expert evidence. This information is usually set out in written reports or witness statements and called "expert reports." These reports provide a summary of what the experts will say and explain briefly why they believe they are right.

Rule 10.2 sets out the requirements for calling an expert witness:

> A party who intends to rely on or refer to the evidence of an expert witness shall provide every other party with the following information in writing:
>
> (a) The name and contact information of the expert witness;
>
> (b) A signed statement from the expert, in the Tribunal's required form, acknowledging his or her duty to:
>
> (i) Provide opinion evidence that is fair, objective, and non-partisan;
>
> (ii) Provide opinion evidence that is related to matters within his/her area of expertise; and

submissions legal documents or closing oral remarks that summarize the arguments in a legal dispute

expert witnesses specialists in a subject, often technical, who may present an expert opinion in a legal proceeding (procedures for using expert witnesses are set out in the Rules)

(iii) Provide such additional assistance as the Tribunal may reasonably require to determine a matter in issue.

(c) The qualifications of that expert witness, referring specifically to the education, training and experience relied upon to qualify the expert;

(d) A signed report that sets out the instructions provided to the expert in relation to the proceeding, the expert's conclusions, and the basis for those conclusions on the issues to which the expert will provide evidence to the Tribunal; and

(e) A concise summary stating the facts and issues that are admitted and those that are in dispute, and the expert's findings and conclusions.

Costs

Rule 19.1 provides that costs may be requested in a proceeding where a party believes that another party in a proceeding has acted unreasonably, frivolously, vexatiously, or in bad faith. **Costs** awards are meant to discourage improper conduct and not compensate parties for their involvement and expenses in a proceeding.

Rule 19.1 allows for costs only when the impugned party's conduct occurs in a proceeding before the tribunal. Behaviour by the parties that occurred before a LAT proceeding is not subject to a costs award.

What Are the Steps to Follow When Requesting Costs?

A request for costs is made in accordance with the procedure set out in Rule 19. A party can request costs in writing or orally at a case conference or hearing or at any time before the decision or order is released.

Some Costs Case Law

In *PB v RBC Insurance Company*[9] the adjudicator commented on the purpose of costs awards:

> Cost awards under Rule 19 are to maintain civility and order during proceedings, to deter conduct that threatens the orderly and civil resolution of an application, and to ensure that the Tribunal's process and the other participants are respected. They are not to compensate parties for the cost of bringing or defending claims or to punish.

costs expenses that can be claimed by either party after a legal proceeding (allowable costs and test for awarding costs are set out in the Rules)

9 2017 CanLII 9816 (Ont LAT).

BF v Wawanesa Mutual Insurance Company[10] is an example of where costs were awarded by the tribunal. It involved an application for various benefits, where the insurer failed to produce documents pursuant to two case management orders. Arbitrator Lester ordered $250 in costs against the insurer stating that "the Tribunal's rules and orders must be respected and followed promptly and responsively."

After the Hearing

After a hearing, the hearing adjudicator will make a final decision about the case, which will usually be sent to the parties later as a written decision. The tribunal decisions are legally binding and must be followed by both the claimant and the insurance company.

Orders

AABS adjudicators can make orders during the case conference, at the hearing, or as part of their final decision. The adjudicator's orders are legally binding and have to be followed.

What If a Party Does Not Follow an Order?

If either party believes that the other party is not obeying an order, or if a party is having trouble getting the remedy that the adjudicator ordered, the order can be registered with the Superior Court of Justice. It is then enforceable, as if it were an order of that court.

After the Decision: What If My Client Did Not Get the Remedy He or She Was Seeking at the Hearing?

Reconsideration

After receiving a decision, either party can request that the executive chair of the tribunal reconsider the decision. The party requesting **reconsideration** must provide its reasons for the request within 21 days of the decision (r 18).

reconsideration a party can request that the tribunal reconsider a decision made by the tribunal and issue a new or different decision in light of that review (procedures and test for a reconsideration of a LAT AABS decision are set out in the Rules)

10 2017 CanLII 9821 (Ont LAT).

The criteria for granting a reconsideration are as follows:

- The tribunal acted outside its jurisdiction or violated the rules of natural justice or procedural fairness.
- The tribunal made a significant error of law or fact and would likely have reached a different decision had the error not been made.
- The tribunal heard false or misleading evidence from a party or witness, which was discovered only after the hearing and likely affected the result.
- There is new evidence that could not have reasonably been obtained earlier and would have affected the result (r 18.2).

All parties will have an opportunity to make submissions before any order is made. After reconsidering a decision of the tribunal, the executive chair may dismiss the request; confirm, vary, or cancel the decision or order; or order a rehearing on all or part of the matter.

Appeal and Judicial Review

Section 11 of the LATA sets out that a party to a LAT AABS proceeding may appeal from its decision or order to the Divisional Court in accordance with the rules of court. An appeal from a decision of the tribunal relating to a matter under the IA may be made on a *question of law only*. A party can also bring an application to Divisional Court requesting judicial review of the decision.

Judicial review is different from an appeal. It is the process that allows courts to review the decisions of administrative tribunals and supervise how they exercise their statutory powers. Individuals can challenge the decisions made by public bodies, such as tribunals, to ensure they have stayed within the powers delegated to them by the government and the law has not been misapplied. It is important to note that bringing an application for judicial review is meant to be a last resort; parties should generally exhaust any internal appeal or reconsideration options that may exist within the tribunal first.

judicial review a process that allows courts to review the decisions of administrative tribunals and supervise how they exercise their statutory powers. Individuals can challenge the decisions made by public bodies, such as agencies, boards, and tribunals, to ensure they have stayed within the powers delegated to them by the government and the law has not been misapplied. It is important to note that bringing an application for judicial review is meant to be a last resort and parties should generally exhaust any internal appeal or reconsideration options that may exist within the tribunal first

BE PREPARED!

Timelines at LAT AABS are quite short after an application has been submitted. The tribunal aims to have the entire case completed within six months. Applicants should be well prepared before submitting an application and come to the case conference knowing their case well. If the case does not settle at the case conference, there are only 60 to 90 days from the date of the case conference to the date of the LAT hearing.

WRITTEN HEARINGS

Some LAT AABS hearings are conducted completely in writing. At the case conference, the adjudicator will set out a schedule of when each party's evidence and submissions are due. You must adhere to these timelines unless you have sought permission from the tribunal.

Written hearings can be challenging in a document-heavy case. It is important not to do a document dump on the tribunal. Be sure that the evidence you submit is relevant to the issues in dispute *and* that you indicate to the adjudicator where to find important documents and evidence (e.g., TAB 5, pages 12-17). Do not expect that the adjudicator will sift through hundreds of pages of records if he or she has not been directed to a specific reference and with an explanation of why it helps your case.

Also remember that you can use your submissions to explain to the adjudicator why the evidence is important and how it helps your case, but don't forget to also include the actual evidence. Submissions are not evidence!

Case Law

Limitation Periods

Smith v Co-operators General Insurance Co, 2002 SCC 30, [2002] 2 SCR 129

The Supreme Court decision of *Smith v Co-operators* stands for the proposition that the Statutory Accident Benefit Schedule is consumer protection legislation. The insurer is considered a sophisticated party that must ensure that its dealings with insureds are clear, unequivocal, and fair.

The court in Smith confirmed that a Notice terminating benefits may be invalid, even if approved by the superintendent of insurance, if the insurer does not take steps to ensure that all of the required and relevant information to be communicated to the insured person is included.

16-003034 v Economical Mutual Insurance Company, 2017 CanLII 59507 (Ont LAT)

In this preliminary issue decision, the tribunal decided that the applicant was precluded from proceeding with her application for ongoing entitlement to attendant care, housekeeping, and home maintenance benefits because she missed the statutory two-year time limit to dispute the respondent's denial, despite the applicant's catastrophic impairment designation.

Applying *Smith v Co-operators General Insurance Co*, the tribunal found that the insurer's denial notice met the requirements and therefore started the two-year limitation period. The notice stated that the benefits would no longer be paid as of a specified date and confirmed that the stoppage was based on section 18 and section 22 of SABS.

The applicant did not dispute the insurer's denial until six years after her benefits were denied.

Limitation Defences and Section 7 of the LATA

AF v North Blenheim Mutual Insurance Company, 2017 CanLII 87546 (Ont LAT) [Reconsideration decision]

Section 7 may be applied at the tribunal's discretion to extend any time limit in the IA or the SABS.

The tribunal must be satisfied that there are reasonable grounds for applying the extension and for granting relief.

In determining whether to grant an extension of time under section 7 of the LATA, the tribunal generally weighs the following four factors:

1. The existence of a bona fide intention to appeal within the appeal period;
2. The length of the delay;
3. Prejudice to the other party; and
4. The merits of the appeal.

The above are not strict rules but rather are to be used as a guide. Whether to grant an extension depends on the specific facts of each case.

Technical Non-Compliance

Stranges v Allstate Insurance Company, 2010 ONCA 457 [leave to appeal to the Supreme Court of Canada denied]

In *Stranges*, the Court of Appeal held that the merits of a case still take precedence over procedural irregularities.

The lower court held that the insurer had provided an improper notice of termination of income replacement benefits. On account of this procedural error, the court ordered benefits to be paid retroactively and continuously until such time as a proper notice was provided.

At the same time the court also found that the claimant did not continue to suffer a substantial inability to perform the essential tasks of her employment as she had recovered from all of her injuries.

Accordingly, the court found that despite the fact that the claimant did not meet the test for disability on substantive reasons, she was still entitled to income replacement benefits because of procedural ones (technical over substantive).

The Court of Appeal disagreed. On appeal the court found that the inadequate notice did not automatically entitle the insured to payment of benefits. The Court of Appeal relied on the Supreme Court of Canada decision of *Smith v Co-operators* (2002).

Section 55 Defences

IK v Primmum Insurance Company, 2018 CanLII 13162 (Ont LAT) [Reconsideration]

In this reconsideration decision the tribunal commented on the importance of insurer examinations (IEs). The decision notes that the SABS provides insurers with a number of tools to adjust files. One of those is the ability to request an insurer's examination (IE) under section 44, in essence a medical assessment of an insured person's condition. Using an IE, an insurer can more accurately assess whether an insured is eligible to receive the benefits for which he or she applies. Put simply, IEs help insurers make the decisions they need to make.

NH v Aviva Insurance Company, 2018 CanLII 13175 (Ont LAT) [Reconsideration]

The applicant failed to attend two IEs, and the tribunal required her to attend them before advancing her application, applying the bar in section 55(1)2.

The applicant requested a reconsideration and the tribunal upheld the decision. The insurer was well within its rights under the SABS to request an IE:

it had very limited information about her psychological condition. An in-person IE was entirely appropriate to determine whether the assessment was reasonable and necessary.

Definition of "Insured Person"

GK v Security National Insurance Company, 2017 CanLII 81584 (Ont LAT), aff'd 2018 ONSC 3556 (Div Ct) [Reconsideration]

If the accident occurs outside of Ontario, the injured party must be a resident of Ontario or a resident of Ontario at any time during the 60 days before the accident to be considered an "insured person" under the Schedule.

Exclusion Defences

16-000024 v Economical Mutual Insurance Company, 2016 CanLII 106912 (Ont LAT)

The tribunal found that the insurer was not required to pay an income replacement benefit because the applicant was driving without a valid driver's licence at the time of the accident (it was expired).

Repayment

An insurer is able to attempt to claim benefits back pursuant to section 52 of the Schedule, but there are specific notice requirements outlined in section 52(3). If the insurer does not provide the required notice of repayment "within 12 months after the payment of the amount that is to be repaid," the insured no longer has to repay those benefits to the insurer unless they were paid out as a result of willful misrepresentation or fraud.

- LAT Cases
  - *Unifund Assurance Company v 17-001773*, 2018 CanLII 13168 (Ont LAT)
  - *16-003709/AABS v Unifund Assurance Company*, 2018 CanLII 2302 (Ont LAT)

The Minor Injury Guideline

- LAT Cases
  - *17-002907 v Aviva Insurance Company*, 2018 CanLII 13153 (Ont LAT)
  - *16-000143 v Aviva Canada Inc*, 2016 CanLII 96167 (Ont LAT)
  - *16-000098 v Aviva Insurance Canada*, 2016 CanLII 93136 (Ont LAT)

Chronic Pain and the Minor Injury Guideline

Arruda v Western Assurance, FSCO A13-003926

The applicant was involved in a motor vehicle accident and sustained psychological and soft tissue injuries as a result.

The applicant's position was that her injuries did not fall within the Minor Injury Guideline (MIG) because she had pre-existing back injuries related to her pregnancy, which occurred before the motor vehicle accident, and that she had developed soft tissue and psychological injuries as well as chronic pain.

Western agreed that the applicant suffered soft tissue injuries but took the position that the applicant's psychological injuries were merely minor difficulties and that these injuries fell within the scope of the MIG.

The arbitrator determined that the applicant was diagnosed with chronic pain syndrome (one and a half years after the accident), which had not yet resolved. This, in the arbitrator's opinion, put her injuries outside the MIG.

IRB Disability Test—Post 104 Weeks

The test for income replacement benefits post 104 weeks after the accident is a complete inability to engage in any employment for which the person is reasonably suited by education, training, or experience. The case law has found that there must be "suitable employment." A helpful list of factors to consider regarding the definition of suitable employment follows:

1. What constitutes suitable employment is fact specific. The work must be suitable for that person, viewed fairly and realistically in the context of his or her educational and employment background.
2. If the job is substantially different in nature, status, or remuneration, it may not be an appropriate alternative.
3. The insured's age, qualifications and technical training, and expertise are relevant.
4. The primary focus is on an applicant's functional limitations; however, job-market considerations are relevant in determining suitable employment. For example, this may include geographic and economic considerations.

- FSCO Case
  - *Horne v CIBC Insurance*, FSCO A00-00291 at para 16, 2001 CarswellOnt 5206
- LAT Cases
  - *16-004619 v State Farm Insurance*, 2018 CanLII 13165 (Ont LAT)
  - *16-000082 v Echelon General Insurance Company*, 2016 CanLII 82874 (Ont LAT)

NEB Disability Test

Heath v Economical Mutual Insurance Company, 2009 ONCA 391; Galdamez v Allstate Insurance Company of Canada, 2012 ONCA 508

The leading principles for the non-earner disability test come from the Court of Appeal decisions in *Heath v Economical Mutual Insurance Company* and *Galdamez v Allstate.*

Under *Heath*, the Court of Appeal found that to determine a complete inability, an analysis must be made with regard to the activities the claimant was ordinarily engaged in before the accident *in actuality*, and not whether the individual suffers a complete inability to engage in the activities people would normally engage in.

This contextual approach endorsed in *Heath* was furthered in the Court of Appeal's recent *Galdamez* decision, where it found that a claimant may earn money pre- and post-accident and still qualify for NEBs, which in effect widened the door to NEB entitlement.

- LAT Cases
  - *16-003195 v State Farm Insurance Company*, 2017 CanLII 99136 (Ont LAT)
  - *16-000283 v Co-operators General Insurance Company*, 2017 CanLII 9815 (Ont LAT)

Reasonable and Necessary Test

16-001934 v Aviva Insurance Company of Canada, 2017 CanLII 59514 (Ont LAT) [Reconsideration]

This is a case-by-case determination. The standard of proof is the balance of probabilities (more probable than not). The tribunal must assess the evidence and determine whether, on a balance of probabilities, the examination/assessment claimed is reasonable and necessary.

Interest

16-001985 v Aviva Insurance Company of Canada, 2017 CanLII 39728 (Ont LAT) [Reconsideration]

The tribunal clarified the interest rates under the current SABS. Section 51 provides that where a schedule-related claim becomes the subject matter of an application to the tribunal, the applicable interest rate on an overdue payment varies; there is a separate interest rate for (1) before an application is commenced (1 percent per month, compounded monthly), and (2) after an application is commenced (calculated at the prejudgment interest rate described in section 128(3) of the *Courts of Justice Act*).[11]

Section 10 Ontario Regulation 664

Section 10 states:

> If the Licence Appeal Tribunal finds that an insurer has unreasonably withheld or delayed payments, the Licence Appeal Tribunal, in addition to awarding the benefits and interest to which an insured person is entitled under the Statutory Accident Benefits Schedule, may award a lump sum of up to 50 per cent of the amount to which the person was entitled at the time of the award together with interest on all amounts then owing to the insured (including unpaid interest) at the rate of 2 per cent per month, compounded monthly, from the time the benefits first became payable under the Schedule.[12]

17-001627 v Certas Direct Insurance Company, 2017 CanLII 99139 (Ont LAT)

The insurer delayed until the eve of the hearing to pay treatment and assessment expenses and waited two years to pay the applicant's benefits claims.

The tribunal ordered an award, taking into account the applicant's youth, the severity of her injuries, and her unsettled family situation.

11 RSO 1990, c C.43.

12 RRO 1990, Reg 664: Automobile Insurance.

KEY LEGISLATION

Insurance Act

Statutory Accident Benefits Schedule—Effective September 1, 2010, O Reg 34/10

Statutory Accident Benefits Schedule—Accidents on or After November 1, 1996, O Reg 403/96

Statutory Accident Benefits Schedule—Accidents After December 31, 1993 and Before November 1, 1996, O Reg 776/93

Statutory Accident Benefits Schedule—Accidents Before January 1, 1994, RRO 1990, Reg 672

Automobile Insurance—in particular section 10, RRO 1990, Reg 664

Judicial Review Procedure Act

Licence Appeal Tribunal Act, 1999

Statutory Powers Procedure Act

Other Related Legislation

Compulsory Automobile Insurance Act

Motor Vehicle Accident Claims Act

Automobile Insurance Rate Stabilization Act, 2003

KEY TERMS

adjournment, 170
adjudicator, 173
case conference, 167
case conference report and order, 170
Common Rules of Practice and Procedure, 162
costs, 175
date of loss, 161
disclosure, 168
evidence, 173
expert witnesses, 174
Financial Services Commission of Ontario (FSCO), 159
joint document brief, 172
judicial review, 177
reconsideration, 176
statutory accident benefits, 159
submissions, 174

REVIEW QUESTIONS

1. Your client has been in a motor vehicle accident and feels that her car is a complete writeoff; however, the insurer takes the position that it can be repaired. Your client also claims to have whiplash and would like to get some chiropractic and massage treatment, which the insurer has denied. Can LAT AABS hear this dispute?
2. Your client was in an accident on July 1, 2009. Which SABS Schedule applies?
3. You realize that you have submitted your reply submissions one day late. Which rule can you refer to in asking the tribunal to still consider your submissions?
4. After the case conference, you realize there is another key witness that you would like to have testify at the hearing. What steps can you take to add the witness?
5. You have done such a great job in preparing your client's application and case conference summary form that the insurer has paid the benefits your client has requested. You no longer require a case conference date. Do you still need to attend? What steps, if any, should you take?
6. Your client requires an interpreter to participate at the hearing. What is the process for obtaining one?
7. After the hearing, your client receives a decision that is not in her favour. Two weeks later she obtains the results of an MRI that shows a new and more serious impairment that was not known at the time of the hearing. What can your client do?

8. You have been successful at the hearing in proving your case. You would like to make a request for compensation for your legal costs. Is this possible?
9. Will an adjournment be automatically granted if both you and the other party want one and can agree on a date?
10. In preparing for a hearing, you have identified both a FSCO case and a recent LAT AABS case that supports your case. Will the adjudicator have to follow these cases and decide in a similar way?

SCENARIO 1

You are representing a client, Ella, in a claim for accident benefits. Since her motor vehicle accident, Ella has been unable to go back to work. She was a personal support worker before the accident. Her job was very physical. WeCare Insurance (WCI) paid Ella income replacement benefits for 12 months. They sent her to an assessment that determined that she was able to return to her pre-accident employment. Ella disagrees and so do her doctors. WCI sent Ella a denial and explanation of benefits on March 1, 2017. WCI submitted an application on June 1, 2018 bringing a claim for repayment of some of the IRBs because it had miscalculated the amount.

You represent Ella.

1. What LAT AABS form do you use to respond to the application?
2. How long do you have to respond to the claim?
3. What advice would you give Ella about her obligation to repay her IRB? Make reference to the applicable section of the SABS.
4. Would your advice to Ella be different if the reason for the repayment was that she had gone back to work one month post-accident and had not advised the insurer?

SCENARIO 2

Amanda was in a motorcycle accident on July 15, 2016. She received medical and rehabilitation benefits, as well as psychological counselling, to assist in her recovery. On February 1, 2017 the insurer sent her an explanation of benefits stating, "Our assessments show you no longer require massage therapy and therefore your request for the treatment plan for the medical benefits is denied."

On April 1, 2018 Amanda comes to you to represent her. She would still like to make a claim for those same massage benefits that were denied in the previous treatment plan, as she says she is still experiencing pain.

She indicates that about six months ago she was also in a snowboarding accident, which seemed to aggravate her symptoms; however, she knows that her main symptoms are a result of the accident, as they had not gone away completely.

You agree to file an application at LAT AABS on her behalf.

1. What is the test for medical benefits? Make reference to the applicable section of the SABS.
2. Are there any preliminary issues you may need to address?
3. Amanda advises that she is waiting for the results of a chronic pain assessment that will help her case. You would like to request an adjournment so that you have this information before the hearing. What steps do you need to take?

SCENARIO 3

Sam was a passenger in a car that was rear ended. ProtectUs Insurance approved treatment for Sam within the Minor Injury Guideline (MIG). The MIG provides a framework for the treatment and benefits of motor vehicle accident victims who sustain minor injuries.

Injuries that fall within the MIG are defined as "one or more of a sprain, strain, whiplash associated disorder, contusion, abrasion, laceration or subluxation and includes any clinically associated sequelae to such an injury." There is a $3,500 cap on medical and rehabilitation benefits for minor injuries.

After Sam exhausted the $3,500 limit for treatment, he felt he needed more treatment because he was still in pain and had not fully recovered. Sam comes to you for help asking how he can obtain more treatment.

How will you advise Sam?

CHAPTER 9

Ontario Labour Relations Board

Overview and History 190

Legislation and Regulations 193

Application Process 198

Hearing Process 201

Decisions, Reconsiderations, Appeals 203

Case Law 204

Key Terms 208

Review Questions 208

Scenarios 209

Appendix 9.1 Form A-1, Application for Certification 210

Appendix 9.2 Form A-14, Application for Interim Order 221

Overview and History

The Ontario Labour Relations Board (OLRB) plays a fundamental role in the administrative justice scheme in Ontario. It is a well-established and well-functioning tribunal, with roots that date back to the early 1900s. The OLRB is focused on the resolution of labour and employment matters and has jurisdiction stemming from multiple statutes. The current board was created under section 2 of the *Labour Relations Act, 1948*[1] but is currently empowered by section 110(1) of the *Labour Relations Act, 1995* (LRA).[2] Staff are appointed under the *Public Service of Ontario Act, 2006*.[3]

The OLRB refers to itself as "fundamental" in labour relations, encouraging "harmonious relations between employers, employees and trade unions" while "dealing with matters before it as expeditiously and as fairly as reasonably possible."[4] Indeed, a large part of the OLRB's work is in the area of trade union activity that falls under the LRA. One example of an application that comes before the OLRB pursuant to the LRA is certification of a trade union as a bargaining agent. **Trade unions** act as agents in bargaining rights for workers (members of that particular trade union) vis-à-vis the management. For a trade union to act for a group of workers, they must be certified in accordance with board processes. Other examples of applications will be discussed later in this chapter, under the Application Process section.

This board works smoothly likely because of the nature of the applications before it and the conglomerate of legislative provisions that apply to it. The OLRB offers information bulletins to be read in conjunction with the Rules of Procedure for any applications affected by the specifics in a bulletin. For example, there is a bulletin on the duty of fair representation[5] and another on termination of bargaining rights.[6] In total there are 36 information bulletins. In addition, the OLRB places updates to its processes on the website. These news flashes inform visitors to the homepage. For example, in spring 2017, the

trade unions collections of workers who unite to promote favourable working conditions, including negotiation of fair employment contracts (collective agreements)

1 SO 1948, c 51.

2 SO 1995, c 1, Schedule A.

3 SO 2006, c 35, Schedule A.

4 Ontario Labour Relations Board, "About Us" (2013), online: <http://www.olrb.gov.on.ca/english/aboutus.htm>.

5 Ontario Labour Relations Board, "The Duty of Fair Representation—What Does It Mean?" *Information Bulletin 12* (June 2014), online: <http://www.olrb.gov.on.ca/english/infob/infbul12.pdf>.

6 Ontario Labour Relations Board, "Termination of Bargaining Rights under Section 63 of the *Labour Relations Act*," *Information Bulletin 2* (October 2014), online: <http://www.olrb.gov.on.ca/english/infob/infbul02.pdf>.

OLRB posted a notice about a change in jurisdiction, allowing it to hear applications for review of notices of contravention under the *Ontario College of Trades and Apprenticeship Act, 2009* (OCTAA).[7]

If a **notice of contravention** is issued under the Act, the OLRB has jurisdiction to hear an appeal from a party.[8] A notice of contravention may be issued if people present themselves as tradespeople and practise a trade without a certificate of qualification.[9]

Furthermore, the OLRB offers insight into other processes, including:

- the removal of translators because of funding; only a French interpreter is provided for mediation and adjudication;[10]
- specific guidelines around summons procedure, which incorporates requirements in the *Statutory Powers Procedure Act* (SPPA),[11] section 12, and the *Rules of Civil Procedure* with respect to appearance payment and travel allowance;[12] and
- the availability of a video magnifier for individual use or TTY.[13]

Additionally, useful information is available on the website, including:

- recent decisions of interest;
- daily hearings schedule;
- link for e-filing (though not yet available);
- notices to the community, such as the accessibility policy;
- links to tribunal accountability documents, such as the ethics plan, as referred to in Chapter 1, Understanding the Tribunal Landscape; and
- new items of interest, such as changes to board jurisdiction.

The OLRB's growth is characteristic of its rich history, which is marked by ever-evolving processes and jurisdiction. The OLRB's website provides a thorough history of its beginnings under the auspices of the Ontario Labour

notice of contravention issued pursuant to the *Ontario College of Trades and Apprenticeship Act, 2009* against an uncertified person practising a trade

7 SO 2009, c 22.

8 OCTAA, ss 2, 4, 59.1. See also Rule 22A and "Applications for Review of a Notice of Contravention under the *Ontario College of Trades and Apprenticeship Act, 2009*," *Information Bulletin 36* (5 June 2017), online: <http://www.olrb.gov.on.ca/english/infob/infbul36.pdf>.

9 OCTAA, ss 2, 4, 59.1.

10 Ontario Labour Relations Board, "Notice the Community" (2011), online: <http://www.olrb.gov.on.ca/english/notices/not0806.htm>.

11 RSO 1990, c S.22.

12 *Supra* note 10.

13 Ontario Labour Relations Board, "Video Magnifier and Teletypewriter" (2004), online: <http://www.olrb.gov.on.ca/english/tty.htm>.

Court, pursuant to the 1943 *Collective Bargaining Act*. The OLRB's jurisdiction was somewhat limited until the 1960s. Until this time, the board could declare an illegal strike or lockout but had no real enforcement power. The 1960s was a time of growth; board orders could be filed with the court and therefore made enforceable, and the construction industry was brought under the Act. The next few decades saw increased powers of the OLRB through the appointment of a labour relations officer to investigate complaints (1970s), the power to make cease and desist orders for unlawful strikes or lockouts (1970s), the introduction of contract arbitration when **collective bargaining** negotiations broke down (1980s), and the extension of the Act to domestic workers and some categories of professionals (1990s), although the latter was again removed under the 1995 Act. In particular, 1986 was a notable year, as the Act was updated to reflect anti-discrimination practices under the Ontario *Human Rights Code*[14] and the *Canadian Charter of Rights and Freedoms*.[15] Essentially, the inclusion of these anti-discrimination principles prohibited certification being granted to a union that had discriminatory practices.[16]

The OLRB has numerous relationships beyond the scope of its internal dispute-resolution mandate. It holds jurisdiction to oversee the Pay Equity Hearings Tribunal, as of 2008, and provide support through administration, mediation, and legal means. The Pay Equity Hearings Tribunal hears and decides pay equity disputes.[17] Vice-chairs of the OLRB also have roles as adjudicators or vice-chairs on the College of Trades Review Panels and the Human Rights Tribunal of Ontario.[18] The relationship of external bodies is one factor to keep in mind when discussing the case route with a client. Some legal issues elusively shelter another legal issue within the first and most obvious one.

For example, you may have a client come to you with what appears to be an employment-related issue. Before rushing to the OLRB and searching through the multiple applications to find the right one, consider whether this is the correct venue. If your client's legal issue is linked to discrimination in employment, it is likely better off being heard before the Ontario Human Rights Tribunal (or Canadian Human Rights Tribunal if the person is employed in a federally regulated industry). Sometimes employment matters should proceed

collective bargaining the process when a trade union negotiates new contract terms with an employer as the basis of a new collective agreement

14 RSO 1990, c H.19.

15 Part I of the *Constitution Act, 1982*, being Schedule B to the *Canada Act 1982* (UK), 1982, c 11.

16 Ontario Labour Relations Board, "About Us" (2013), online: <http://www.olrb.gov.on.ca/english/aboutus.htm>.

17 *Ibid.*

18 *Ibid.*

with a complaint under the *Employment Standards Act* (ESA)[19] (initiated through Employment Standards) as opposed to the OLRB. Where a matter proceeds depends on the jurisdiction of the body. Therefore, as a practitioner, you will want to become familiar with the jurisdiction of the OLRB to ensure you are in the right place to have your matter resolved.

Most paralegals and lawyers who find themselves before the OLRB are there because of their union employer. Because of the nature of the proceedings before the OLRB (i.e., the high volume of unionized matters), you would likely be appearing before this board if you were employed as counsel to the union or to the employer. However, some applications are filed by an individual applicant, such as the Application for Religious Exemption from paying union dues, where paralegals might find themselves in the role of representative. Many paralegal firms represent clients in matters before the OLRB. Representatives or self-represented individuals may also come to the OLRB by way of an application for review from an order of an Employment Standards Officer, following a complaint from an employee under the ESA.

The OLRB functions as a result of the following personnel:[20]

- director/registrar,
- deputy director/deputy registrar,
- legal staff,
- field services manager,
- labour relations specialists,
- labour relations officers,
- conciliators,
- chair,
- alternate chair,
- vice-chairs, and
- member representatives of labour and management.

Legislation and Regulations

As mentioned above, the LRA forms the basis of the OLRB. This Act not only "continues" the existence of the OLRB (initially created in 1948) but also enables the board to act by outlining its structure (ss 110(2)-(5)), mandate (ss 114, 115),[21] and powers (s 111).

19 SO 2000, c 41.

20 Ontario Labour Relations Board, "Members of the Board—Administration" (2015), online: <http://www.olrb.gov.on.ca/english/staffadm.htm>; "Members of the Board—Field Services" (2016), online: <http://www.olrb.gov.on.ca/english/stafffs.htm>; "Members of the Board—Order in Council" (2014), online: <http://www.olrb.gov.on.ca/english/staffoic.htm>.

21 See also LRA, s 2.

The Act explicitly removes itself from a portion of the requirements under the SPPA by stating its own supremacy (s 110(21)) regarding rules made governing **expedited proceedings** on various matters (s 110(18)). The board is granted the power to create rules for efficient practice and procedure (s 110(7)).

Other key features of the LRA are easily identified through a variety of sections, some of which are:

- the establishment of bargaining right by **certification** (ss 7-15);
  - Trade unions have to receive certification to represent a group of workers in collective bargaining. The trade union must apply to the OLRB for certification (s 7 and Rules of Procedure r 9) and provide notice to the employer of the application (s 7(11) and Rules of Procedure r 9). Part of the certification process involves a vote by the employees, which confirms the desire for representation by the trade union (s 8). The board will then determine if certification will or will not be granted (ss 10, 15).
- **collective agreements** (e.g., negotiation (ss 16-44), contents (ss 45-52), operation (s 45(1));
  - A collective agreement is essentially a shared contract among employees with their employer. Historically, workers were at a disadvantage in trying to negotiate fair work contracts with employers, hence the need for a trade union to intervene and negotiate on behalf of a group. Negotiation of a collective agreement does not come easily, as there are numerous measures and intricate details to the process, as is evidenced by the 28 sections of the LRA that govern this process. The Act requires specifics as to what content must be incorporated into the collective agreement. For example, there must be recognition of the trade union as the exclusive bargaining agent (s 45(1)), and a provision detailing that there will be no strikes or lockouts for the duration of the operating agreement (s 46), among others. Finally, the Act stipulates how the collective agreement must operate. One requirement of a collective agreement is that it cannot discriminate against an individual in accordance with the *Human Rights Code* or the *Canadian Charter of Rights and Freedoms* (s 54). The Act also limits the existence of a collective agreement to one, at any one time, between an employer and trade union (s 55). There is also an imposed term of one year for the operation of a collective agreement, if a term is unspecified or stated as less than one year (s 58).

expedited proceedings an internal process through which applications can be fast-tracked through the standard hearing process

certification a trade union's status to negotiate on behalf of a group of workers

collective agreements shared contracts among members of trade unions vis-à-vis their employers

- the termination of bargaining rights (ss 62-66);
  - Termination of bargaining rights means that a trade union is no longer authorized to undertake collective bargaining on behalf of employees. An application for termination must be made to the OLRB by an employee.[22]
- unfair practices (ss 70-88);
  - Unfair practices include employer's interference with trade union formation and intimidation or threats toward employees (s 70), bargaining rights (s 72), or other employee rights (s 23). Conversely, union interference with the employer's organization is also prohibited (s 71). The Act also imposes duties of fair representation and referral on trade union practices (ss 74, 75). This part of the Act includes many other prohibited practices that require representatives to be duly aware of, just a few being: strikes or lock-outs during an operating collective agreement (s 79) and causing or authorizing such illegal activity (ss 81-83).
- enforcement (ss 96-106);
  - Labour relations officers are appointed and dispersed for the investigation of complaint for a report back to the OLRB, following an attempt at settlement (s 96). If a settlement is not reached, the board may make an order that will affect the desired result of the grieving party (s 96(4)). The order may be enforceable through the processes of the Superior Court, once filed (s 96(6)). Superior Court filing is also supported for declarations of unlawful strikes or lockouts (ss 100-102). The LRA also imposes fines on individuals, trade unions, or employers' organizations that contravene the Act (s 104).
- construction industry provisions (ss 126-150); and
  - The construction industry provisions incorporate within them their own interpretative guidelines for certain terms and principles (s 126). Some of the provisions that have specific application to the construction industry prevail over other conflicting sections of the Act (s 126.1(3)).
- province-wide bargaining (ss 151-168);
  - Province-wide bargaining occurs in certain sectors when the employers enter into united negotiations with all unions in that one sector. Provisions were adopted in the 1970s to allow for province-wide bargaining in some sectors.[23] Province-wide bargaining in the construction industry occurs every three years as a requirement under the LRA (s 148(1)).[24]

---

22 LRA, ss 63, 65, 66; Ontario Labour Relations Board, "Rules of Procedure—Rule 10: Termination of Bargaining Rights under Section 63 of the Act" (January 2018), online: <http://www.olrb.gov.on.ca/english/Rules_of_Procedure.pdf>.

23 *Supra* note 16.

24 See also Unionized Construction Works, "Stability," online: <http://unionizedconstructionworks.com/stability/>.

Other important features of the Act are:

- The establishment of what is NOT covered under the LRA (s 3), including certain workers, such as an employee under the *Agricultural Employees Protection Act, 2002*[25] or police under the *Police Services Act*;[26] and
- Freedoms,[27] such as joining and participating in a trade union or an employer's organization.

Like any other statute, the regulations pursuant to the LRA play an important role in fleshing out the bones of the Act. There are five current regulations under the LRA: Deemed Abandonment of Bargaining Rights—Sarnia Working Agreement (O Reg 98/16), General (O Reg 94/07), Arbitration—Residential Sector of the Construction Industry (O Reg 522/05), Deemed Abandonment of Bargaining Rights (O Reg 105/01), and Ontario Construction Secretariat (O Reg 187/93). A practitioner will certainly want to be familiar with the provisions of the General regulation (O Reg 94/07), and the others when necessary to their client's matter before the OLRB (as the latter deal with more specific topics). The General regulation is brief but outlines procedures around the filing of arbitration agreements (O Reg 94/07, s 1(1)) and specifics around board forms (O Reg 94/07, s 3 and Schedule 1).

The OLRB has jurisdiction over numerous other statutes.[28] These statutes may not form the basis of your standard application when appearing as a paralegal before the OLRB, but it is important to be familiar with the extent of the board's jurisdiction regardless of whether your matter stems from one of these statutes. In addition, this familiarity will help you to recognize legal issues when a client comes to you with a complaint arising from one of these statutes. "Limited jurisdiction" means that the OLRB does not have power to adjudicate over every section of the following acts, only over sections as specified. Those statutes of limited jurisdiction are:

- *Colleges Collective Bargaining Act, 2008*:[29] duty of fair representation (s 56) and employee freedom (s 23);
- *Smoke-Free Ontario Act*:[30] unlawful reprisals (s 9(4) and O Reg 48/06, s 16), meaning an employee cannot be punished by an employer for trying to assert any rights or obligations under the Act;
- *Environmental Protection Act*:[31] unlawful reprisals (s 174(2));

25 SO 2002, c 16.

26 RSO 1990, c P.15.

27 LRA, ss 5-6.

28 Ontario Labour Relations Board, "Does Your Concern Fall Under the Board?" (2007), online: <http://www.olrb.gov.on.ca/english/concern.htm>.

29 SO 2008, c 15.

30 SO 1994, c 10.

31 RSO 1990, c E.19.

- *Environmental Bill of Rights Act, 1993*:[32] unlawful reprisals (ss 2(3)(d), 104-116);
- *Public Service Labour Relations Transition Act, 1997*:[33] determination of bargaining rights (s 17); and
- *Crown Employees Collective Bargaining Act, 1993*:[34] determination of essential services (ss 30-42) and some broad application (ss 2-21).

The OLRB Rules of Procedure are made pursuant to the LRA sections 110 (16)-(22). The Rules were revised and amended, effective January 2018, to address some changes to the legislation. Specifically, impacted topics are:

- revisions to Rule 9A (Employee Lists) and Rule 9B (Certification—Specified Industry), and indirectly, revisions to Rules 6.4, 6.9(a), 6.11, and 7.3(c);
- revisions to Rule 12 due to amendments in the LRA sections 43 and 43.1 (first collective agreement by mediation-arbitration);
- revisions to Rule 19 due to changes to section 98 (Board's interim order powers).

The Rules are available online to download.[35] An excellent resource for practitioners, particularly new counsel to the board, is the Annotated Rules, also available online.[36] The Annotated Rules provide key cases that have interpreted each rule. For example, under Rule 9.1, which covers the requirements for an application for certification, the case of *TWD Roads Management*[37] is included with the following summary:

> Where the Board received the membership evidence, list of employees and Form A-4, one day after receiving the application (the letter accompanying the application indicated the documents would follow by courier), the Board treated the application as being filed on the date it was complete.[38]

Rule 18.1, which covers requests for reconsideration, states the following: "A request for reconsideration must include complete written representations in

32 SO 1993, c 28.

33 SO 1997, c 21, Schedule B.

34 SO 1993, c 38.

35 Ontario Labour Relations Board, "Rules of Procedure" (January 2018), online: <http://www.olrb.gov.on.ca/english/Rules_of_Procedure.pdf>.

36 Ontario Labour Relations Board, "Annotated Rules of Procedure" (March 2016), online: <http://www.olrb.gov.on.ca/english/Annotated_Rules.pdf>.

37 *Labourers' International Union of North America v TWD Roads Management Inc*, 2006 CanLII 42012 (Ont LRB).

38 *Supra* note 36, r 9.1 at 17.

support of the request."[39] Following this rule, the case summary for *MacMillan Bathurst Inc v Canadian Paper-workers' Union, Local 1497*[40] appears, which further discusses the importance of written representations. The summary of this case in the annotated rules states: "The Board usually determines reconsideration requests on the basis of written material submitted, rather than an oral hearing."[41] You can see how useful these annotated rules are, but don't rely on the case summary alone; if you do rely on this rule and this case to make an argument before the OLRB, read the entire case so that you understand its nuances and how it is best applied to your client's situation.

Application Process

Applying to this board requires you to pinpoint the exact form required for your legal issue. This is a different procedure than you may have read about in other chapters of this book; for example, the Social Benefits Tribunal has only one appeal form for initiating a proceeding. It is, however, similar to some processes that you have read about, such as the Landlord and Tenant Board, which requires that applicants proceed with the form that fits their specific need. The OLRB has over 45 different applications.

One example of an application is Form A-1 (see Appendix 9.1), which is required when a trade union is seeking certification for bargaining rights for an exclusive group of employees. Another example is Form A-14 (see Appendix 9.2), which you would use to request that the OLRB make a determination on some preliminary matter before the final disposition of a case. For example, you might require that the board determine if it has jurisdiction over a certain type of application before proceeding with the matter.

Some other types of applications before the OLRB are:

- applications concerning a trade union's duty of fair representation of its members;
- applications for a religious exemption from having to pay dues to a trade union;
- applications concerning illegal strikes or lockouts;
- applications concerning early termination of collective agreements;
- referrals of grievances to arbitration in the construction industry;
- applications for accreditation in the construction industry; and
- requests for reconsideration of board decisions.[42]

39 *Supra* note 36, r 18.1 at 32.

40 1988 CanLII 3686 (Ont LRB).

41 *Supra* note 36, r 18.1 at 32.

42 *Supra* note 28.

Rule 7.1 and 7.2 speak generally about applications, such as what details are required to be included in applications (name, address, etc.) and how delivery to the respondent should occur.[43] In most cases, the applicant is required to serve the other side with the application documents, and the responding party has a similar duty to file a response with the OLRB and the applicant.[44] In addition, specific rules that apply to various types of applications should be read in conjunction with the general procedure outlined in Rule 7. For example, Rules 9.1 to 9.4 outline specific requirements for applications for certification.[45] Rules 10.1 to 10.4 outline similar requirements for termination of bargaining rights applications.[46] Further still, part IV of the Rules (12 to 22) covers requirements for other types of applications before the OLRB, such as applications for interim order[47] or duty of fair representation applications.[48] Therefore, it is essential that practitioners are cautious about visiting all sections of the Act and Rules that apply to their proceeding.

Responses to an application are required in accordance with Rules 7.3 to 7.5. The timeline for filing a response varies according to the application type and can be from one to ten days after the application is served or at another established date.[49] As with the applications, there are specific requirements for the filing and serving of responses. Rule 9.5 is specific to responses that flow from applications for certification. Rule 10.5 is specific to requirements for responses to applications for termination of bargaining rights. Rule 12.2 and 12.3 outline greater detail about responses to applications dealing with first collective agreement arbitration. And there are further examples throughout the Rules.

There are a number of forms that can now be e-filed, though this convenient service is offered as an option only, and not a requirement. Therefore, the other methods of filing are still acceptable. Representatives can complete the e-filing on behalf of clients. Some Rules of Procedure were amended with the e-filing changes (see, for example, Rules 6.2, 7.2(c)-(e), 16.2). Rule 6.2 now states that signatures are not required on forms that have been e-filed.

In addition to the Rules and application form, the OLRB also provides its Procedural Guide for applications. This guide is available online[50] or from the board office. A complete package for applicants is offered in person at the

43 *Supra* note 35, rr 7.1, 7.2 at 6.

44 *Supra* note 35, r 7.3 at 6-7.

45 *Supra* note 35, rr 9.1-9.4 at 8-9.

46 *Supra* note 35, rr 10.1-10.4 at 13-14.

47 *Supra* note 35, r 19 at 20-21.

48 *Supra* note 35, r 16 at 19.

49 *Supra* note 35, r 7.3 at 6-7.

50 Ontario Labour Relations Board, "Procedural Guide" (June 2015), online: <http://www.olrb.gov.on.ca/english/Procedural-Guide.pdf>.

board office (in downtown Toronto) and includes an application, the Rules of Procedure, information bulletins, and the Procedural Guide. In addition to what you now know about the application for certification from the Rules of Procedure, keep in mind the other information about these applications that you would glean from the information bulletins and Procedural Guide. "Certification of Trade Unions," *Information Bulletin 1*, specifically states:

> This Information Bulletin describes the procedures that must be followed when a union applies to represent a group of employees at a workplace. … It is important that the parties involved in a certification application read and comply with the directions in this Bulletin and the Board's Rules of Procedure. Failure to do so may result in the application or other materials not being processed by the Board.[51]

This information bulletin proceeds to give clear direction on this application process. It provides definitions to terms, such as "day," "delivered," and "filed" (at 1-2) It also provides detailed instructions on such topics as delivery of the package to the employer (at 2), the employer's obligation to notify employees (at 5-6), voting arrangements (at 8-9), and much more.

The Procedural Guide is an all-in-one document that offers an overview of what is required for each specific application.[52] For each type of application, the following information is provided in an easy-to-read chart form:

- special rules that apply;
- material to be delivered by the applicant;
- manner of delivery by the applicant;
- time limit for filing by the applicant;
- number of copies of the application to be filed;
- manner of filing by the applicant;
- material to be filed by the responding party;
- manner of delivery by the responding party;
- time limit for filing by the responding party;
- number of copies of response to be filed; and
- manner of filing by the responding party.

The applications discussed thus far have been those under the jurisdiction of the LRA. Of course, other applications come before the OLRB based on its limited jurisdiction over other statutes. The *Occupational Health and Safety*

51 Ontario Labour Relations Board, "Certification of Trade Unions," *Information Bulletin 1* (October 2014), online: <http://www.olrb.gov.on.ca/english/infob/infbul01.pdf>.

52 *Supra* note 50.

Act[53] provides a basis for applications concerning unlawful **reprisals** for exercising rights under the Act (s 50), appeals of Ministry of Labour inspectors' orders (s 61(1)),[54] and requests for suspension of Ministry of Labour inspectors orders (s 61(7)).[55] Applications also stem from the *Employment Standards Act*[56] for a review of an employment standards officer's order to pay or refusal to issue an order to pay (s 116).[57]

Aside from the application forms, numerous other forms are available online,[58] such as notices and general forms created under other acts than the LRA, such as the *Freedom of Information and Protection of Privacy Act*.[59] One notice in this section is Form C-1, Notice to the Employer of Application for Certification. This is required to be served on the employer of the group or workers for which a trade union is seeking certification.

Hearing Process

Mediation is one process of dispute resolution at the OLRB. Mediation may be conducted in person or through a telephone call by labour relations officers (LROs). LROs are not adjudicators; rather they are considered experts in the field because of their backgrounds in labour and employment law. LROs are considered neutral arbiters. Mediation is a confidential process, and the notes created during mediation are not shared in board proceedings if the matter goes to adjudication. If a settlement is reached, then the contents of mediation will likely be embodied in a board order.[60]

If a settlement is not reached, then the parties proceed to adjudication. Before adjudication, a pre-hearing conference might occur. These may also be conducted via telephone or in person. They are typically quite short proceedings and are used for preliminary matters (such as agreement on the facts), or to narrow issues for a hearing. Both routes can result in less time allotted to the hearing, which helps to eliminate tribunal delay and backlog. A vice-chair

reprisal punishment of a worker by an employer for exercising rights

53 RSO 1990, c O.1.

54 See also Rule 22.

55 See also Rule 22.

56 SO 2000, c 41.

57 See also Rule 21; *supra* note 28.

58 Ontario Labour Relations Board, "Board Processes: Forms" (2017), online: <http://www.olrb.gov.on.ca/english/bdocs.htm>.

59 RSO 1990, c F.31.

60 Ontario Labour Relations Board, "Board Processes: Mediation" (2004), online: <http://www.olrb.gov.on.ca/english/mediat.htm>.

will typically conduct the pre-hearing conference, and a decision or memo will follow.[61]

At this stage, a notice of hearing will be sent to the parties. The notice of hearing will likely be written, but it may be verbal, and it may be for either a consultation or hearing (rr 38.1 and 38.2). As is the case with many tribunals, consultations and hearings can be written (r 38.4) or electronic (r 38.5), but they are typically in person. Written consultations occur through a back-and-forth written exchange between the parties and the tribunal. Electronic consultations may be via teleconference or videoconference. There is a small difference between consultation and hearing process. Consultations are less formal and less costly to the parties than a hearing and may dispose of the matter entirely without having to proceed to full adjudication. Consultations are presided over by the vice-chair or by a panel. How the matter proceeds varies from case to case but typically the vice-chair or panel will:

> (1) question the parties and their representatives; (2) express views; (3) define or re-define the issues; and (4) make determinations as to what matters are agreed to or in dispute. The giving of evidence under oath and the cross-examination of witnesses are normally not part of a consultation, and when they are, it is only with respect to those matters that are defined by the Board.[62]

Because the consultation is expedited (shorter than a full hearing), there is no time to call witnesses and enter evidence. Therefore, parties rely on written submissions (provided in the application and response).[63] It is essential to include all material facts that you will rely upon in your submissions, otherwise you may not be able to raise an issue or point later.

The hearing process before the OLRB is more formal than the consultation process and one of the more formal hearing processes in the administrative tribunal scheme (though still less formal than a court room). Hearings are open to the public, unless there is some reason for one to be closed (perhaps a privacy concern); however, they are not recorded and there are no transcripts.[64] OLRB hearings follow a fairly standard adversarial approach to dispute resolution. The applicant will be allowed to present their case with witnesses and evidence, followed by a cross-examination. The respondent will then follow suit. OLRB matters have become more complex over time, as the case law and Rules have evolved, and legal representation is often required to make the tough legalistic arguments. Hearings are usually conducted with

61 Ontario Labour Relations Board, "Board Processes and Forms: Hearings" (September 2004), online: <http://www.olrb.gov.on.ca/english/hearing.htm>.

62 *Ibid.*

63 *Ibid.*

64 *Ibid.*

multiple members (at least three)[65] but may be governed by the chair or vice-chair alone.[66]

Decisions, Reconsiderations, Appeals

Decisions are typically issued sometime after the hearing in writing to all parties. It may be that an oral decision is rendered on the day of the hearing, from which the written order will follow. If a decision has not been rendered within six months of the final hearing day, a party to the application may request that the chair terminate the proceeding.[67]

Reconsiderations by the OLRB of its own decisions and orders are made possible under section 114(1) of the LRA, and governed by Rule 18. Reconsiderations are commenced with Form A-49, Requests for Reconsideration, within 20 days after the date of the decision, and notice must be served on the opposing party using Form C-24, Notice of Request for Reconsideration. There is also an Information Bulletin 19—Requests for Reconsideration that must be read by the parties. More often than not, requests for reconsideration are denied:

> Generally, the Board will not reconsider its decision unless the requesting party has new evidence that would be practically conclusive of the case and *that it could not have reasonably obtained earlier*, or the party has *new* objections or arguments *that it had no opportunity to raise earlier.*[68]

The information bulletin also highlights:

> The panel that decided the case originally is usually the panel that decides the reconsideration request. This is because the reconsideration power is not an "appeal" where the entire matter is reheard—the question is whether there is any new information, and the panel that heard the case originally is in the best position to make that determination.[69]

Section 116 of the LRA states the OLRB decisions are final and not reviewable by a court. Judicial review by the Superior Court of a board decision is made possible under the *Judicial Review Procedure Act*.[70]

---

65 LRA, s 110(9).

66 LRA, ss 13, 14.

67 LRA, s 115.1.

68 Ontario Labour Relations Board, "Requests for Consideration," *Information Bulletin 19* (June 2014), online: <http://www.olrb.gov.on.ca/english/Infob/infbul19.pdf> at 1.

69 *Ibid* at 2.

70 RSO 1990, c J.1.

Case Law

Durham District School Board, Rainbow District School Board and Peel District School Board v Ontario Secondary School Teachers' Federation, 2015 CanLII 30160 (Ont LRB)

This case began as an application to the OLRB pursuant to section 100 of the LRA, which allows for the OLRB to declare an unlawful strike. The application was brought by three school boards: Durham District School Board, Rainbow District School Board, and Peel District School Board, for a declaration that the Ontario Secondary School Teachers' Federation fuelled an unlawful strike. At dispute in this application is a complicated matter of what strike action constitutes "local" versus "central" as it relates to the collective bargaining process. The governing legislation allows for the "two-tiered" bargaining process by which central issues are decided at the central bargaining table and local issues are decided at the local bargaining table. A local strike must only be related to a local bargaining issue; therefore, an employee cannot strike based on a central bargaining issue unless certain conditions are met (at 26). In this case, the school boards argue that the strikes are illegal because they were local strikes based on central bargaining issues when a central strike was not yet "legal" according to the legislation (at 27). The OLRB was forced to read the provisions of the Act in accordance with rules of statutory interpretation and concluded that the overall scheme of the legislation and the direct wording of the statute prohibited the strike that had occurred (at paras 58, 59, 63, 98).

Communications, Energy and Paperworkers Union of Canada, Local 87-M v Ming Pao Newspapers (Canada) Ltd, 2012 CanLII 3525 (Ont LRB)

An application was brought before the OLRB based on unfair labour practice toward the employees of Ming Pao Newspapers, a Chinese-language newspaper in Toronto. The employees union received certification to enter into collective bargaining, which it did so in January 2011. When collective bargaining failed, a legal strike began in September 2011. Concerns about the employer's conduct arose out of activities during the organizing drive (at paras 11-148) and a series of layoffs (at paras 49-100). The OLRB found that the employer contravened sections 70, 72, 76, and 86 in a number of ways: it threatened employment security and laid-off employees, which amounted to reprisal; it started an employee committee during the organizing campaign; and it increased salaries to urge employees to rebuke the union, among other things (at para 101). Consequently, the OLRB ordered that the employer reinstate the laid-off employees and pay them the wages for the period of their layoff, as well as return their clients to them. In addition, the employer was ordered to post the Notice to Employees to inform them of the results, and keep it posted for 30 days (at para 102).

Corporation of the City of Toronto v Toronto Civic Employees Union, Local 416, 2012 CanLII 974 (Ont LRB)

An application was brought by the City of Toronto, pursuant to the *Ambulance Services Collective Bargaining Act, 2001*,[71] to receive a determination about the number of ambulance workers considered "essential" (required to work) in the event of a strike or lockout. The precipitating event was that the employer was considering a lockout (at para 3). The Act requires that both sides enter into good faith negotiations toward establishing an essential ambulance services agreement (EASA), yet no agreement was reached (at paras 6-11). The OLRB summarized its jurisdiction in the scope of this application:

> Lock-outs and strikes affecting paramedics are permitted. ... the Legislature requires that "essential ambulance services" must be provided whether or not a strike or lock-out occurs. A responsibility of the Board is to decide the number of ambulance workers who are required to provide "essential ambulance services" as contemplated by the Act—if the parties fail to agree. (At paras 16-17)

The City of Toronto made the argument that the interpretation of essential ambulance service should cover all emergency services provided by the City (at paras 43-44). The union submitted that the status quo should not be altered from the findings of a 2002 decision by then Chair Whitaker, which considered adequate numbers of ambulances as essential services. The union was seeking that only certain types of calls be considered essential for the purposes of responding during a strike (at paras 64-67). While the collective-bargaining process will undoubtedly put pressure on public service, resulting in negative outcomes during strikes or lockouts, it also requires that some essential services be maintained (paras 89-91). The OLRB determined that there should be an increase in ambulance services from the 2002 decision, but that there should not be a blanket approach to providing ambulance services, as the City suggested (para 136). The order provided for 85 percent of ambulance workers to be present during the event of a strike or lockout, equalling about 272 paramedics on weekdays and 233 paramedics on weekends (at para 140). The decision was based on statistical evidence provided to the OLRB about service volumes, emergency versus non-emergency calls, previous ability during strike action, and general respect for the collective bargaining process, as well as public need.

International Brotherhood of Electrical Workers Local 1739 v International Brotherhood of Electrical Workers, 2007 CanLII 65617 (Ont Div Ct)

The Ontario Divisional Court heard this Judicial Review application, brought by the International Brotherhood of Electrical Workers, Local 1739, on the basis that the decision of the OLRB was *ultra vires* (beyond the jurisdiction of

71 SO 2001, c 10.

the board) and breached the principles of natural justice and procedural fairness (at paras 1-2). The Local had requested an expedited proceeding but thereafter believed that it was denied procedural fairness when the OLRB proceeded by way of consultation, thereby making findings of fact without hearing from witnesses. The Divisional Court upheld the OLRB's use of the expedited proceeding, stating that the board "operates in a complex, dynamic, and highly fluid environment where expeditious rulings and informal and accessible procedures are often essential to maintaining the delicate balance between the parties' various interests" (at para 44).

This is an important case from the perspective of how the reviewing court considered the board's internal rules. This case, however, received negative treatment from the Ontario Court of Appeal in a subsequent decision.[72] The later decision is not specifically concerned with the rule and jurisdiction over expedited proceedings, as was the focus of this highlighted case, but rather the OLRB's issuance of supplementary reasons. This case is referenced in the later decision as a basis for the court's ruling that the OLRB did not have jurisdiction to issue supplemental reasons.[73]

Amalgamated Transit Union Local 113, 2007 CanLII 59152 (Ont Div Ct)

This Divisional Court decision also considered and upheld the OLRB's internal processes. A Judicial Review application was brought by Amalgamated Transit Union Local 113 (ATU), citing unfairness in the OLRB's process and decisions (at para 1). Following an alleged unlawful strike by the Toronto Transit Commission (TTC) workers (represented by ATU), the TTC brought an application seeking a cease and desist order from the OLRB (at para 11). The TTC appeared to make various attempts at serving the documents on ATU and made numerous phone calls in attempts to notify it (at paras 12-20). The OLRB chair also made numerous attempts to contact ATU to inform it of the pending hearing on the application (at para 20). The hearing proceeded in the absence of the union, and a cease and desist order was granted as per the TTC's application request (at para 21). ATU complained that the timing of the hearing had been "unilaterally imposed" and that it had "denied it full opportunity to make submissions" (at para 25), and the Judicial Review application was filed. The Divisional Court found that the abridgment of time and procedures for scheduling the application hearing was justified in the circumstances, because of "the urgency of the underlying public transportation shutdown" (at para 150) and was not a breach of fairness.

72 *Jacobs Catalytic Ltd v International Brotherhood of Electrical Workers, Local 353*, 2009 ONCA 749.

73 *Ibid* at 6.

KEY LEGISLATION

Labour Relations Act, 1948
Labour Relations Act, 1995
Public Service Act
Ontario College of Trades and Apprenticeship Act, 2009
Statutory Powers Procedure Act
Rules of Civil Procedure
Collective Bargaining Act
Human Rights Code
Canadian Charter of Rights and Freedoms
Employment Standards Act
Agricultural Employees Protection Act, 2002
Police Services Act
Colleges Collective Bargaining Act, 2008
Smoke-Free Ontario Act
Environmental Protection Act
Environmental Bill of Rights Act, 1993
Public Service Labour Relations Transition Act, 1997
Crown Employees Collective Bargaining Act, 1993
Occupational Health and Safety Act
Freedom of Information and Protection of Privacy Act
Judicial Review Procedure Act

KEY TERMS

certification, 194
collective agreements, 194
collective bargaining, 192
expedited proceedings, 194
notice of contravention, 191
reprisal, 201
trade unions, 190

REVIEW QUESTIONS

1. Is the construction industry governed by the provisions of the LRA?
2. Can a trade union discriminate against an employee on the basis of gender?
3. What is an information bulletin and how would you use it as a practitioner?
4. The case of *MacMillan Bathurst Inc* is included in the discussion of the Annotated Rules above with respect to reconsiderations. Why is this case important in this context?
5. What four options exist in the hearing process at the OLRB?
6. What is an unfair practice?
7. Name two acts, other than the LRA, from which applications to the OLRB may arise?
8. Does the OLRB have sufficient control over its internal proceedings and rules? Support your answer.
9. What is the Pay Equity Hearings Tribunal?
10. What use does the Procedural Guide serve for practitioners?

SCENARIOS

1. Kate Wrong, a summer student at your paralegal firm, has had a client approach her about a concern with paying union dues. The client feels that paying the dues is contrary to her religious beliefs. How do you recommend Kate advise the client on procedure before the OLRB?
2. You have just received an OLRB order from a consultation you conducted for your client last month. You strongly believe that the OLRB misapplied important evidence that you discussed in the consultation process; unfortunately, you were unable to call a witness due to the nature of this proceeding. What do you do?
3. Jeremy Forrest is a licensed paralegal providing legal advice to a union on the termination of bargaining rights under section 63 of the LRA. What process required for termination of rights, as well as the statutory authority, must Jeremy be aware of before giving advice?

APPENDIX 9.1 Form A-1, Application for Certification

Form A-1

LABOUR RELATIONS ACT, 1995

APPLICATION FOR CERTIFICATION

BEFORE THE ONTARIO LABOUR RELATIONS BOARD

Between:

Applicant,

- and -

Responding Party.

PLEASE READ INFORMATION BULLETIN NO. 1 – CERTIFICATION OF TRADE UNIONS BEFORE COMPLETING THIS FORM.

The applicant applies to the Ontario Labour Relations Board for certification of the employees of the responding party in a unit described below.

1. (a) Name, address, telephone number, facsimile number and e-mail address of the applicant:

   (b) Name, address, telephone number, facsimile number and e-mail address of a contact person for the applicant (Please Note: this individual **must** be regularly available by phone during the five (5) days leading up to the date set for the vote. Your contact person should be an individual with the authority to enter into agreements on your behalf.):

(p. 1 of 11) (February 2018)

Form A-1

(c) E-mail address of representative and assistant (if any):

□ **Counsel:** **Assistant:**

□ **Paralegal:** **Assistant:**

□ **other:** **Assistant:**

[Periods of time referred to in this application, in other Board forms and notices, and in the Board's Rules of Procedure do not include weekends, statutory holidays, or any other day that the Board is closed.]

(d) Name, address, telephone number, facsimile number and e-mail address of the responding party and contact person:

[Before you file your application with the Board, you must deliver to the responding party: a copy of your application, a blank response form (A-2, including Schedules A and B and the Instructions for filing Excel Schedules with the Board, found at Tab 4 of the Spreadsheet, a blank Confirmation of Posting (A-124) , a Notice to Employer of Application for Certification (Form C-1) with the names of the parties and the date inserted, a copy of Information Bulletin No. 1 -- Certification of Trade Unions, a copy of Information Bulletin No. 3 -- Vote Arrangements, a copy of Information Bulletin No. 4 -- Status Disputes in Certification Applications, and a copy of Part III of the Board's Rules of Procedure. You must also complete the attached Certificate of Delivery.]

2. Detailed description of the unit of employees of the responding party that the applicant claims to be appropriate for collective bargaining, including the municipality or other geographic area affected:

(p. 2 of 11) (February 2018)

Form A-1

3. Number and addresses of locations where affected employees work (Please list):

4. The number of employees the applicant believes to be in the proposed unit (Please provide a breakdown by location listed in paragraph 3):

5. General nature of the responding party's business:

6. Does the proposed bargaining unit include guards?

   [ ] Yes
   [ ] No

7. Name, address, telephone number, facsimile number and e-mail address of any trade union known to the applicant which claims to represent any employee(s) who may be affected by this application:

[Before you file your application with the Board, you should deliver to the union(s) named in paragraph 7: a copy of this application, a blank intervention form, a copy of Information Bulletin No. 1 -- Certification of Trade Unions, a copy of Information Bulletin No, 3 -- Vote Arrangements, a copy of Information Bulletin No. 4 -- Status Disputes in Certification Applications, and a copy of Part III of the Board's Rules of Procedure. You must also complete the attached Certificate of Delivery.]

(p. 3 of 11) (February 2018)

Form A-1

8. Membership evidence relating to this application accompanies this application and

[ ] does
[ ] does not

represent membership evidence on behalf of 40 percent or more of the employees in the proposed bargaining unit.

[Section 7(13) of the Act provides that the application for certification shall be accompanied by a list of names of union members in the proposed bargaining unit and evidence of their status as union members, but the trade union shall not give this information to the employer.]

9. Other relevant statements (attach additional pages if necessary):

Vote Arrangements (Please read Information Bulletin No. 3 - Vote Arrangements before completing this portion of the form.)

10. Do you assert that a vote should take place on the fifth day after the date on which this application is filed with the Board?

[ ] Yes
[ ] No

If no, please explain fully. As well, please state the date on which you believe the vote should take place, and explain why:

(p. 4 of 11) (February 2018)

Form A-1

11. Please list your proposed hours for the vote specifying start and finish times and either a.m. or p.m.:

    Please explain the reasons for your proposed vote times (e.g., shift change, employee start times etc.):

12. Please indicate the location you propose for the poll(s):

    Poll #1

    Room, or other description of the location:

    Floor:

    Address:

    City:

    Poll #2 (only if multiple locations are necessary):

    Room, or other description of the location:

    Floor:

    Address:

    City:

    Please explain the reason for your proposed poll location(s):

Form A-1

13. Please state the name of the Scrutineer you have selected to represent you at each poll:

    Poll #1:

    Poll #2 (only if multiple locations are necessary):

14. Please state the name of the Agent you have selected to represent you at the counting of the ballots:

15. Please indicate the name of the applicant as you wish it to appear on the Notice in the voting booth (and, in a displacement application, on the ballot):

DATED ______________________

____
Signature for the Applicant

(p. 6 of 11) (February 2018)

Form A-1

ATTACHMENTS

THE FOLLOWING DOCUMENTS MUST ACCOMPANY THIS APPLICATION WHEN IT IS FILED WITH THE BOARD:

(A) ANY MEMBERSHIP EVIDENCE RELATING TO THIS APPLICATION;

(B) ONE COPY OF A LIST OF EMPLOYEES, IN ALPHABETICAL ORDER, CORRESPONDING WITH THE MEMBERSHIP EVIDENCE FILED; AND

(C) A COMPLETED DECLARATION VERIFYING MEMBERSHIP EVIDENCE (FORM A-4)

NOTE: THE MEMBERSHIP EVIDENCE, LIST OF EMPLOYEES CORRESPONDING WITH THE EVIDENCE, AND THE DECLARATION VERIFYING EVIDENCE ARE NOT TO BE DELIVERED TO THE EMPLOYER OR ANY AFFECTED TRADE UNION.

(p. 7 of 11) (February 2018)

Form A-1

CERTIFICATE OF DELIVERY

1. I certify that the following documents were delivered to the employer, as follows:

   - a copy of the Application for Certification (Form A-1);
   - a blank copy of a Response to Application for Certification (Form A-2) including Schedules A & B (List of Employees);
   - a blank Confirmation of Posting (A-124);
   - a completed copy of the Notice to Employer of Application for Certification (Form C-1), **with the names of the parties and the date inserted**;
   - a copy of Information Bulletin No. 1 -- Certification of Trade Unions;
   - a copy of Information Bulletin No. 3 -- Vote Arrangements;
   - a copy of Information Bulletin No. 4 -- Status Disputes in Certification Applications; and
   - a copy of Part III of the Board's Rules of Procedures.

______________________________	______________________________
Name of Organization and name title of person to whom documents were delivered	Address or facsimile number to and which documents were delivered

2. **[Complete this section only if you identified an affected trade union in paragraph 7 of the application.]**

   I certify that the following documents were delivered to the trade union(s) named in paragraph 7 of the application, as follows:

   - a completed copy of the Application for Certification (Form A-1);
   - a blank copy of an Intervention in Application for Certification (Form A-3);

(p. 8 of 11) (February 2018)

Form A-1

- a copy of Information Bulletin No. 1 -- Certification of Trade Unions;
- a copy of Information Bulletin No. 3 -- Vote Arrangements;
- a copy of Information Bulletin No. 4 -- Status Disputes in Certification Applications; and
- a copy of Part III of the Board's Rules of Procedure.

______________________	______________________
Name of Organization and name and title of person to whom documents were delivered	Address or facsimile number to which documents were delivered

[Complete either section 3 or section 4 below.]

3. The documents were delivered by [ ] facsimile transmission or [ ] hand delivery on ______________ (Date) at ____________ a.m./p.m.

4. The documents were given to ______________________ (Name of Courier) on ______________ (Date), and I was advised that they would be delivered not later than ______________ (Date), at ____________ a.m. /p.m.

NAME: ______________________

TITLE: ______________________

SIGNATURE: ______________________

(p. 9 of 11) (February 2018)

Form A-1

IMPORTANT NOTES

The Board's forms, Notices, Information Bulletins, Rules of Procedure and Filing Guide may be obtained from its website www.olrb.gov.on.ca or by calling 416-326-7500 or toll-free at 1-877-339-3335.

FRENCH OR ENGLISH

Vous avez le droit de communiquer et recevoir des services en français et en anglais. La Commission n'offre pas de services d'interprétation dans les langues autres que le français et l'anglais.

You have the right to communicate and receive services in either English or French. The Board does not provide translation services in languages other than English or French.

CHANGE OF CONTACT INFORMATION

Notify the Board immediately of any change in your contact information. If you fail to do so, correspondence sent to your last known address (including email) may be deemed to be reasonable notice to you and the case may proceed in your absence.

ACCESSIBILITY AND ACCOMMODATION

The Board is committed to providing an inclusive and accessible environment in which all members of the public have equitable access to our services. We will aim to meet our obligations under the *Accessibility for Ontarians with Disabilities Act* in a timely manner. Please advise the Board if you require any accommodation to meet your individual needs. The Board's Accessibility Policy can be found on its website.

FREEDOM OF INFORMATION AND PROTECTION OF PRIVACY

Personal information is collected on this form under the authority of the Board's governing legislation to assist in the processing of cases before it. Information received in written or oral submissions may be used and disclosed for the proper administration of the Board's legislation and processes. Any relevant information that you provide to the Board must in the normal course be provided to the other parties to the proceeding. The *Freedom of Information and Protection of Privacy Act* may also address the collection, use and disclosure of personal information. If you have any questions, contact the Solicitors' Office at the numbers listed above or in writing to the OLRB, 505 University Ave., 2nd floor, Toronto, ON M5G 2P1.

(p. 10 of 11) (February 2018)

Form A-1

E-FILING AND E-MAIL

The Rules of Procedure and Filing Guide set out the permitted methods of filing. Forms and submissions may be filed with the Board by a variety of methods including the Board's e-filing system, but not by e-mail. Note that the efiling system is not encrypted and e-filing is optional. Contact the Client Services Coordinator at the numbers listed above if you have questions regarding e-filing or other filing methods. If you provide an e-mail address with your contact information, the Board will in most cases communicate with you by e-mail from an out-going only generic account. Incoming emails are not permitted.

HEARINGS AND DECISIONS

Hearings are open to the public unless the Board decides that matters involving public security may be disclosed or if it believes that disclosure of financial or personal matters would be damaging to any of the parties. Hearings are not recorded and no transcripts are produced.

The Board issues written decisions, which may include the name and personal information about persons appearing before it. Decisions are available to the public from a variety of sources including the Ontario Workplace Tribunals Library and www.canlii.org. Some summaries and decisions may be found on the Board's website.

(p. 11 of 11) (February 2018)

APPENDIX 9.2 Form A-14, Application for Interim Order

Ontario

ONTARIO LABOUR RELATIONS BOARD
APPLICATION FOR INTERIM ORDER
Labour Relations Act, 1995
Fire Protection and Prevention Act, 1997
Statutory Powers Procedure Act

Print Blank Form | Clear Form | Save Form

Form A-14

Fields marked with an asterisk (*) are mandatory.

Between: *

Applicant(s)

- and -

Responding Party(ies)

- Review the Filing Guide and the Board's Rules of Procedure on acceptable methods of delivery and filing **before** completing this form to avoid any delay in processing.
- All forms, Notices, Information Bulletins, the Filing Guide and the Rules of Procedure may be obtained from the Board's website (http://www.olrb.gov.on.ca).
- To print a paper copy of this form, use **only** the "Print" buttons located within the form.
- Save a copy of your completed form and any attachments as the Board will not return them to you. To save the form at any time, use the "Save" buttons located within the form.
- If there is insufficient space on the form, attach additional pages clearly identifying the relevant section of the form. For e-filing, you may attach files by selecting the "Attach documents electronically" option.

Part A Contact Information

Instructions

- Provide the contact information for each Applicant, Responding Party and Affected Party below. If you wish to add additional parties, use the "Add" button or attach a separate page if completing the form by hand.
- If a party is an organization, provide the name and contact information of an individual who will be able to respond on behalf of that organization. When adding multiple individuals at the same organization, "Add" an additional contact section, repeat the organization name and provide that individual's contact information (e.g. name, email address, phone number).

A-14E (2017/03) Disponible en français Page 1 of 8

1 (a). Applicant Collapse List

Applicant 1

Type * ☐ Organization ☐ Individual

Organization Name

First Name	Last Name	Position/Title

Full Address (Number, Street, Unit/Apartment, Building Name)	Other Address Details (e.g. PO Box, R.R. #, c/o)

City/Town	Province/State	Country	Postal/Zip Code

Telephone Number Ext.	Fax Number	Email Address

Additional Contact Information, if any (Assistant's Email Address, Alternate Telephone Numbers)

Add

1 (b). Representative/Contact Person for the Applicant Collapse List

Add

2 (a). Responding Party Collapse List

Responding Party 1

Type * ☐ Organization ☐ Individual

Organization Name

First Name	Last Name	Position/Title

Full Address (Number, Street, Unit/Apartment, Building Name)	Other Address Details (e.g. PO Box, R.R. #, c/o)

City/Town	Province/State	Country	Postal/Zip Code

Telephone Number Ext.	Fax Number	Email Address

Additional Contact Information, if any (Assistant's Email Address, Alternate Telephone Numbers)

Add

2 (b). Representative/Contact Person for the Responding Party, if known Collapse List

Add

3 (a). Affected Party Collapse List

Contact information for any person, trade union, employer or employer's organization which may be affected by the application must be provided below.

Add

3 (b). Representative/Contact Person for the Affected Party, if known Collapse List

Add

A-14E (2017/03) Page 2 of 8

3 (c). The person, trade union, employer or employers' organization named above is affected by the application for the following reason(s):

2000 characters remaining

Part B Material Facts and Relief Sought

4(a). The Applicant states that the following section(s) of the *Labour Relations Act, 1995* relate to this application:

4(b). If any other statute relates to this application, state the applicable statute and sections below:

5. The Applicant requests the following interim orders:

Describe in detail what you wish the Board to order as a result of this application. If you require more space, attach a separate document.

2000 characters remaining

6. The Applicant must attach four Schedules as part of this application:

(1) **Schedule A** must contain one or more declarations signed by persons with first-hand knowledge, detailing all of the facts upon which the Applicant relies. Each signed declaration must include the following statement: "This declaration has been prepared by me or under my instruction and I hereby confirm its accuracy."

(2) **Schedule B** must contain complete written representations in support of the Applicant's request for the interim order. The Applicant must include **all** of the submissions that it wishes the Board to consider.

(3) **Schedule C** must contain a copy of the pending application in relation to which the interim order is being requested. If the pending application has already been filed with the Board, the Board File Number must be indicated.

(4) **Schedule D** must contain any other relevant statements that the Applicant wishes to make.

7. Attached documents:

Provide a list of the documents you are filing together with this form as instructed below.

Name your documents/attachments so that they are easily identifiable.

If you are e-filing this form, select the "Attach documents electronically" option below and attach each document using the "Add File" button.

If you are filing in a manner other than e-filing, provide the numbered list of documents in the box below.

☐ Attach documents electronically

Documents

IMPORTANT NOTES

The Board's forms, Notices, Information Bulletins, Rules of Procedure and Filing Guide may be obtained from its website http://www.olrb.gov.on.ca or by calling 416-326-7500 or toll-free at 1-877-339-3335.

FRENCH OR ENGLISH

Vous avez le droit de communiquer et recevoir des services en français et en anglais. La Commission n'offre pas de services d'interprétation dans les langues autres que le français et l'anglais.

You have the right to communicate and receive services in either English or French. The Board does not provide translation services in languages other than English or French.

CHANGE OF CONTACT INFORMATION

Notify the Board immediately of any change in your contact information. If you fail to do so, correspondence sent to your last known address (including email) may be deemed to be reasonable notice to you and the case may proceed in your absence.

ACCESSIBILITY AND ACCOMMODATION

The Board is committed to providing an inclusive and accessible environment in which all members of the public have equitable access to our services. We will aim to meet our obligations under the *Accessibility for Ontarians with Disabilities Act* in a timely manner. Please advise the Board if you require any accommodation to meet your individual needs. The Board's Accessibility Policy can be found on its website.

FREEDOM OF INFORMATION AND PROTECTION OF PRIVACY

Personal information is collected on this form under the authority of the Board's governing legislation to assist in the processing of cases before it. Information received in written or oral submissions may be used and disclosed for the proper administration of the Board's legislation and processes. Any relevant information that you provide to the Board must in the normal course be provided to the other parties to the proceeding. The *Freedom of Information and Protection of Privacy Act* may also address the collection, use and disclosure of personal information. If you have any questions, contact the Solicitors' Office at the numbers listed above or in writing to the OLRB, 505 University Ave., 2nd floor, Toronto, ON M5G 2P1.

E-FILING AND E-MAIL

The Rules of Procedure and Filing Guide set out the permitted methods of filing. Forms and submissions may be filed with the Board by a variety of methods including the Board's e-filing system, but not by e-mail. Note that the e-filing system is not encrypted and e-filing is optional. Contact the Client Services Coordinator at the numbers listed above if you have questions regarding e-filing or other filing methods. If you provide an e-mail address with your contact information, the Board will in most cases communicate with you by e-mail from an out-going only generic account. Incoming emails are not permitted.

HEARINGS AND DECISIONS

Hearings are open to the public unless the Board decides that matters involving public security may be disclosed or if it believes that disclosure of financial or personal matters would be damaging to any of the parties. Hearings are not recorded and no transcripts are produced.

The Board issues written decisions, which may include the name and personal information about persons appearing before it. Decisions are available to the public from a variety of sources including the Ontario Workplace Tribunals Library and www.canlii.org. Some summaries and decisions may be found on the Board's website.

A-14E (2017/03) Page 5 of 8

Documents to be Delivered

Before you file your application with the Board, you must deliver the following documents to each Responding Party and Affected Party named in Part A of this application:

- A completed copy of this Application for Interim Order (Form A-14), **including the four Schedules and all documents you are filing with this form**; and
- A Notice to Responding Party and/or Affected Party of Application for Interim Order (Form C-11) **with the names of the parties and the date inserted.**

Note to each Responding Party and Affected Party: The documents listed above should have been delivered to you by the Applicant. The applicable response/intervention form is **Form A-15.**

Once the above-listed documents have been delivered to the other parties, you must complete the following Certificate of Delivery before filing the completed form and attachments with the Board.

☐ I have reviewed this form to confirm it is complete *	Date (yyyy/mm/dd) *

Save Print

Note: The "**Print**" button above will print the form only up to and including this page.

A-14E (2017/03) Page 6 of 8

Certificate of Delivery

I, ______________________ (Name *), ______________________ (Title),

certify that the documents identified above were delivered to each of the parties as set out below:

Note: You must complete delivery information for each party separately.

Use the "Add" button below if completing electronically.

Delivered To

Name of organization (if applicable) and name and title of person to whom the documents were delivered *

Address or fax number to which the documents were delivered *

Method of delivery *

☐ Hand Delivered ☐ Courier ☐ Fax ☐ Regular Mail ☐ Other

Add

File with the Board

- File the completed form and any attachments using a method permitted by the Board's Rules of Procedure.
- Save and Print a copy of your completed form and all attachments as the Board will not return them to you.
- To e-file, click the "Submit" button below. You will receive a confirmation email once the form has been successfully submitted.
- If you choose not to e-file, print this form by clicking on the "Print" button below and then file with the Board together with any attachments.

For E-Filing only

You must provide a valid email address in order to file this form electronically so that a confirmation email may be sent to you. If you do not have a valid email address, file a paper copy of this form using an alternative method permitted by the Board's Rules of Procedure.

Submitted By:

First Name *	Last Name *
Email Address *	Confirm Email Address *

Print Save Submit

A-14E (2017/03)

Page 8 of 8

CHAPTER 10

Workplace Safety and Insurance Board/Workplace Safety and Insurance Appeal Tribunal

Overview and History 230

Authority and Jurisdiction of the WSIB 231

The Workplace Safety and Insurance Appeals Tribunal 234

Legislation, Regulations, and Other Sources Relevant to WSIB and WSIAT 235

Disputes at WSIB and WSIAT 237

Appearing Before the Workplace Safety and Insurance Appeals Tribunal 241

Decisions, Reconsideration, and Judicial Review 244

Case Law 247

Key Terms 252

Review Questions 252

Scenarios 253

Overview and History

Workplace safety and insurance in Ontario is a "no fault" system, meaning benefits are provided to an injured employee regardless of how the workplace injury or disease was caused. Originally introduced in the early 1900s, the system is founded on the principle of collective employer liability, ensuring certainty of payment for injured **workers** while removing the risk of litigation and bankruptcy for employers. The system and its laws evolved significantly over 100 years. This chapter deals with the current state of the law.

Ontario's modern no fault workplace safety and insurance system is governed by the *Workplace Safety and Insurance Act, 1997* (WSIA) and managed by the Workplace Safety and Insurance Board (WSIB) formerly known as the Workers' Compensation Board (WCB). The WSIA establishes a no-fault system of mandatory insurance for most employers within Ontario and a benefit scheme financed by employers (through premiums) for compensation for workers of those employers who are injured or ill in the course of their employment.

As a result of the insurance and compensation system, commonly referred to as "workers' compensation," a worker's right to commence a civil action relating to the injury is either taken away or is significantly restricted.

Workplace Law

Before representing or advising a client, it is important to have an understanding of the overlap between the WSIA and other areas of workplace law. Although the right to commence an action for compensation relating to a workplace injury may be taken away, the WSIA does not displace a worker's rights under the *Human Rights Code*,[1] the *Employment Standards Act, 2000*,[2] the *Labour Relations Act, 1995*,[3] the *Occupational Health and Safety Act* (OHSA),[4] a collective agreement in place between the worker's union and employer, or common law rights to commence an action for wrongful dismissal. A worker's entitlement to benefits under the *Employment Insurance Act*,[5] the Canada Pension Plan, or under private disability plans are not reduced by virtue of the WSIA.

1 RSO 1990, c H.19.

2 SO 2000, c 41.

3 SO 1995, c 1, Schedule A.

4 RSO 1990, c O.1.

5 SC 1996, c 23.

Authority and Jurisdiction of the WSIB

To qualify for workplace insurance benefits and services, an injured or ill worker must meet the requirements set out in the WSIA and submit a claim to the WSIB, the provincial agency that oversees the workplace insurance scheme in Ontario. The WSIB has its head offices in Toronto and regional offices all over Ontario. It has two departments: the Operating Services Division includes claim-management and employer-account services; the Corporate Services Division includes compliance and prosecution, appeals, and policy departments.

The WSIB is created by and derives all of its authority from the WSIA. The WSIB has the exclusive jurisdiction to decide all matters arising out of the WSIA, except where the WSIA provides otherwise.[6]

Who Is Covered Under the WSIA?

Most workers are covered under the WSIA from the moment they are hired because the WSIA applies to most, but not all, industries operating within Ontario. For those that are not automatically covered (i.e., sole proprietors, partners and their spouses, and executive officers), there is the option to apply for coverage and opt in.

The WSIB has the authority to develop a scheme of classification of **employers**.[7] An employer whose business activity falls within Schedule 1 is liable to contribute to the collective insurance fund under the WSIA. Such employers are referred to by the WSIB as "Schedule 1 employers."[8] Schedule 2 sets out a list

workers defined under the WSIA as persons who have entered into or are employed under a contract of service or apprenticeship, including (1) a learner, (2) a student, or (3) an auxiliary member of a police force

employers defined under the WSIA as persons having in their service under a contract of service or apprenticeship another person engaged in work in or about an industry, including (1) trustees, receivers, liquidators, executors, or administrators who carry on an industry; (2) persons who authorize or permit a learner to be in or about an industry for the purpose of undergoing training or probationary work; or (3) deemed employers

6 See Community Legal Education Ontario, "Worker's Compensation: Making a Claim" (June 2017), online: <https://www.cleo.on.ca/en/publications/makeclaim> for a clear guide that explains how to make a claim and what happens after a claim is made.

7 The industries that are subject to the WSIA are identified in Schedules 1 and 2 of General, O Reg 175/98, made under the WSIA.

8 A Schedule 1 employer's failure to register with the WSIB or failure to pay premiums as are required does not affect that employer's workers' rights under the WSIA.

of further industries that do not fall within Schedule 1.[9] An employer whose business activity falls within the list set out in Schedule 2 is commonly referred to as a "Schedule 2 employer." A Schedule 2 employer is directly liable to pay for the cost of benefits to its workers, but the WSIB administers the claims of Schedule 2 workers, and in addition to the cost of benefits, a Schedule 2 employer is also liable to pay to the WSIB an administration fee.

If a business activity does not fall within the list of industries identified in Schedule 1 or Schedule 2, then that business is not subject to the mandatory coverage of the WSIA (for example, the insurance industry and banking industry). Of those businesses that are not in Schedule 1 or Schedule 2, most are eligible to apply for voluntary coverage under the WSIA subject to all of the same obligations under the WSIA that apply to Schedule 1 employers.

Administration and Adjudication by WSIB

The WSIB is responsible for the administration and benefit adjudication of a worker's claim. This includes registering the claim and initiating the process of investigating and adjudicating the worker's claim.

A worker's claim arises when a worker is injured as a result of an accident in the course of and arising out of that worker's employment. The worker must file a claim no more than six months after the accident, although the WSIB may permit an extension of time if it is just to do so (s 22 of the WSIA). If any of three reports of the worker's accident—the employer's report of accident (Form 7), the worker's report of accident (Form 6), or the health care professional's first report (Form 8)—are delivered to the WSIB, it will register the claim and start investigating and adjudicating the claim.

The adjudication process begins with the assignment of the claim to an eligibility adjudicator. This person will determine whether the accident reported occurred in the course of the employment and whether the injuries reported were caused by the employment. As a claim becomes more complex, other members of the WSIB's claims services team become involved with the management of the case. These may include a nurse consultant, physician consultant, return-to-work specialist, or work-transition specialist. A decision as to whether a worker is permanently impaired is made by the long-term case manager.

Generally, the WSIB has broad authority to determine the following:

- Causation: whether a person's injury (or death) was caused by an accident or illness that arose out of or in the course of employment;

9 A partial list of these industries includes municipalities; public utilities; police boards; school boards; construction and operation of railways; shipping and marine navigation; construction and operation of federally regulated telephone businesses; airlines who operate international passenger service; and the Province of Ontario and provincial Crown agencies and corporations.

- Degree of impairment: whether a permanent impairment resulted from an injury;
- Entitlement to benefits and **quantum of benefits**: whether loss of earnings resulted from an injury, the amount of a worker's average earnings and net average earnings;
- Return to work: whether the workplace parties are cooperating in a **return-to-work plan** or **work-transition plan**; and
- Survivor benefits: whether a person is a spouse, child, or dependant of an injured worker.

If an injured worker or employer feels that he or she has been unfairly treated or served by the WSIB, he or she may make a complaint to the Fair Practices Commission, the ombudsman for the WSIB. To resolve the fairness issue, the commission may make suggestions to the WSIB to, for example, offer an apology, act on a delay, correct an omission, or develop a procedure. The commission cannot make or vary a WSIB decision or assist with an appeal.

Appealing a WSIB Decision

Either or both of the worker or the employer can object to any benefit decision made by the WSIB regarding the worker's claim. The WSIA requires, however, that an objection must be filed with the WSIB in writing within a certain time. It is important, therefore, to promptly identify any limitation periods and meet them. For an objection to a return-to-work or work-transition decision, the objection must be filed with the WSIB within 30 days of the decision. For all other issues, an objection must be filed within six months of the decision (WSIA, s 120(1)). The WSIB has the discretion to extend this time limit, but will only do so in exceptional circumstances

A worker who objects to a decision made by the WSIB will receive a copy of his or her claim file following the filing of the objection.[10] If the employer elects to participate in the worker's appeal, it will be provided with a copy of

quantum of benefits the monetary amount of the benefit

return-to-work plan a proactive, formal plan that helps injured workers remain at work or safely return to suitable work and outlines the steps that workers, supervisors, and others within the organization need to take if an injury occurs

work-transition plan a plan to assist an injured worker's transition back into work and outlines the assistance and services required to enable the worker to return to the previous employer in the identified suitable and available work or, if required, to re-enter the labour market in the identified suitable occupation

---

10 A worker has a right of access to his or her claim file at any time (s 57). The worker need only make a written request to the WSIB for access.

the worker's claim file. Similarly, if an employer objects to a decision made in the worker's claim, it will also receive a copy of the worker's claim file to fairly participate in its own appeal. Whenever an employer or its representative receives claim-file information from the WSIB, it is bound by the WSIA to keep all health information confidential (s 59(6)). It may not use that health information in any other proceeding. To breach this duty of confidentiality is an offence under the WSIA (s 150).

There are two separate levels of appeal. The first appeal from a primary adjudication decision is to the Appeals Services Division of the WSIB. At this level, the appeal is heard by an appeals resolution officer (ARO) of the WSIB and the decision is considered a final decision of the WSIB (s 118(3)).[11] The second appeal from the decision of the ARO is to the Workplace Safety and Insurance Appeals Tribunal.

The Workplace Safety and Insurance Appeals Tribunal

The Workplace Safety and Insurance Appeals Tribunal (WSIAT) has been around since October 1, 1985 and was first called the Workers' Compensation Appeals Tribunal. Before the creation of the tribunal, all decisions concerning workers' compensation matters were made by the Workers' Compensation Board (WCB), now the WSIB, which possessed two levels of internal appeal. There was no external appeals body in the workers' compensation system. Finality in decision-making was difficult to achieve as decisions were often disputed by appellants and taken to the minister of labour, individual MPPs, the ombudsman and the courts for review and relief.

The tribunal was created to replace the board's internal appeal process with an external independent appeals body within the workers' compensation system. The tribunal's general mandate was, and continues to be, to hear the appeals of workers and employers who were dissatisfied with the final decisions of the board.

The hallmarks of this newly created tribunal were its adjudication model and expertise in decision-making. This new tribunal would adjudicate cases by tribunal panels. Instead of a single adjudicator hearing the case, the tribunal was composed of three members: a neutral vice-chair, a member drawn from the employer community, and a member drawn from the worker community.

The legislation also created a roster of independent medical practitioners to advise the tribunal on medical matters. Other significant initiatives included

11 The WSIB's practice and procedure related to applications, proceedings, mediation, and appeals process is detailed in the Appeals Services Division's Practice and Procedures. These guidelines are amended periodically and should be reviewed on a regular basis.

the creation of new advisory services for workers and employers by establishing the Office of the Worker Adviser (an independent agency of the Ministry of Labour that advises and represents non-unionized injured workers and their survivors in their workplace insurance cases) and Office of the Employer Adviser (which provides Ontario employers with expert, free, and confidential advice, representation, and education on all workers' compensation issues under the WSIA and on unjust reprisal issues under OHSA), both still in existence today.

Although initially viewed with skepticism, the tribunal quickly earned respect and became a leader among administrative agencies, boards, and tribunals. The tribunal's specialized expertise, and the quality of its well-reasoned judgments, is demonstrated in the respect that has been accorded to it by the courts. The decisions of the tribunal are consistently accorded the highest standard of deference, that of reasonableness.

Legislation, Regulations, and Other Sources Relevant to WSIB and WSIAT

The WSIAT is created by and derives all of its authority from the WSIA. It is located in Toronto and conducts most hearings there, but regional hearings are held in Thunder Bay, Timmins, Sault Ste. Marie, Sudbury, Windsor, London, Kitchener, Hamilton, Oshawa, and Ottawa. The WSIAT has the exclusive jurisdiction to hear appeals of final decisions of the WSIB. The WSIAT also has the exclusive jurisdiction to hear applications brought by a party to civil litigation to determine whether the plaintiff's right to sue has been taken away by the WSIA.

The Right to Sue

A worker who suffers an accident in the course of his or her employment and whose injury arises out of the employment cannot commence a civil action against his or her employer or against any of his or her co-workers (s 26).

Where the employer is a Schedule 1 employer, the worker also may not sue any other Schedule 1 employer or worker of that other Schedule 1 employer (s 28(1)). This additional prohibition against litigation applies only if the worker of the other Schedule 1 employer was engaged in his or her employment at the time of any alleged negligence that led to the accident.

Where the employer is a Schedule 2 employer, the worker may not sue the employer or any co-worker (s 28(2)). The worker may, however, sue any other party who may be responsible for the accident. This is the case even if the other party is a Schedule 1 or Schedule 2 employer or a worker of such an employer who was engaged in his or her employment at the time of the accident. In this case, the employee must choose whether she or he wishes to make a claim for benefits under the WSIA or to commence a civil action. The worker cannot do both. If the worker chooses to claim benefits under the WSIA, then the right to sue passes to the employer.

Where a person commences a civil action in circumstances where it is in doubt as to whether the right to sue is taken away by the WSIA, any party to that proceeding may bring an application to the WSIAT to determine whether the right to sue was taken away (s 31(1)). Only the WSIAT has jurisdiction to make such a determination (s 31(2)).

The Legislative Frameworks and Recent Amendment

There have been two major changes to workers' compensation legislation since the creation of the tribunal. As the Act in force at the time of a worker's injury continues to apply to the determination of that worker's benefits, not only has the tribunal had to apply the three different legislative frameworks in its history, but it continues to hear cases under all three acts.

More recent amendments took place in 2017 with respect to mental stress and chronic pain in the workplace. In May 2017, Bill 127, *Stronger, Healthier Ontario Act (Budget Measures)* received royal assent. Under Schedule 33 of the Bill, sections 13(4) and (5) of the WSIA were repealed effective January 1, 2018 and replaced. The new section 13(4) provides that workers are entitled to benefits for chronic and traumatic mental stress arising out of and in the course of the worker's employment, subject to section 13(5). Section 13(5) provides that workers are not entitled to mental stress caused by "decisions or actions of the worker's employer relating to the worker's employment." The WSIB has also introduced new policies pertaining to traumatic and chronic mental stress.

On December 14, 2017, Bill 177, *Stronger, Fairer Ontario Act (Budget Measures)*, received royal assent. This Bill amended the WSIA and specifically introduced transitional provisions with respect to claims for mental stress. These transitional provisions came into effect on January 1, 2018. Two of these transitional provisions relate specifically to appeals at the WSIAT.[12]

Relevant Sources

The sources that you should be familiar with if you represent clients in workers' compensation cases include the following:

12 Under the new section 13.1(8), claims for entitlement for mental stress pending at the WSIAT on January 1, 2018 had to be referred back to the WSIB. These claims will then be decided by the WSIB in accordance with section 13(4) of the WSIA as it reads at the time the decision is made, regardless of the date on which the mental stress occurred. Similarly, the new section 13.1(9) states that notice of appeals with the WSIAT of a final decision of the WSIB made before January 1, 2018 regarding claims for entitlement to benefits for mental stress had to be referred back to the WSIB. These claims will also be decided by the WSIB in accordance with section 13(4) as it read at the time the decision was made.

- WSIA, including amendments and previous acts.
- *Practice Direction and Guidelines:* The tribunal has exercised its powers of practice and procedure under section 131 of the WSIA to adopt practice directions and practice guidelines. In the event of a conflict between a practice direction and a guideline, the practice direction prevails.
- *The WSIB Operational Policy Manual:* This manual contains matters of policy and law, such as worker coverage, filing claims, benefits, work reintegration, employer coverage, premiums, experience rating, health care, and occupational diseases. It is important to stay current with respect to this source. In December 2017, the WSIB's Operational Policy Branch and Permanent Impairment Program jointly released a memorandum regarding pre-existing conditions and permanent impairments. The purpose of the memo was to clarify the WSIB's application of its policies on non-economic loss benefits. As set out in the memorandum, starting December 15, 2017 the WSIB will no longer reduce benefits for people with an asymptomatic pre-existing condition if it is non-measureable. In addition, the WSIB also confirmed that it would be reviewing approximately 4,500 decisions made between January 2012 and December 15, 2017 where there was a reduction because of an asymptomatic pre-existing condition. Information about the WSIB's review for workers and employers is available on the WSIB's website.
- *WSIAT Medical Discussion Papers:* These papers provide general information on medical issues. Each paper is written by a recognized expert in the field selected by the WSIAT, and each expert is asked to present a balanced view of the current medical knowledge on the topic.

Disputes at WSIB and WSIAT

Various types of benefits and WSIB determinations are disputed before the WSIAT:

- health care benefits
- **loss-of-earnings (LOE) benefits**
- **non-economic loss (NEL) benefits**
- independent-living and personal-care allowance
- work reintegration and work-transition services
- survivor benefits

non-economic loss (NEL) benefits an award from the WSIB for workers who have a work-related permanent impairment that recognizes the permanent effects of a workplace injury on a worker's life outside work

loss-of-earnings (LOE) benefits payments from the WSIB intended to replace some of the future wages the worker lost as a result of the work-related injury or illness

Benefits

Health Care

A worker who sustains an injury is entitled to such health care as may be necessary, appropriate, and sufficient as a result of the injury and is entitled to make the initial choice of health professional (WSIA, s 33(1)). Health care includes services of a registered health care practitioner, hospital, or health care facility, drugs, attendant care, modifications to a home or vehicle to facilitate independent living, assistive devices and prostheses, extraordinary transportation to obtain health care, and appropriate measures needed to improve the quality of life of a severely impaired worker (s 32).

Loss of Earnings (LOE)

A worker who suffers a loss of earnings (LOE) as a result of the injury is entitled to benefits equal to 85 percent of the difference between the worker's net average earnings before the accident and the worker's net average earnings after the accident (WSIA, ss 43(1)-(3)). The benefits are payable only until age 65.[13] LOE benefits are payable only if a worker is cooperating in appropriate health care measures and his or her early and safe return to work. The benefits are payable only so long as the worker has a loss of earnings and the worker remains impaired as a result of the injury (s 43(3)). In addition to LOE benefits, a worker who is not yet 64 years of age and has been in receipt of LOE benefits for 12 continuous months is also entitled to a benefit for loss of retirement income (s 45).[14]

Non-Economic Loss (NEL)

If a worker's injury results in permanent impairment, the worker is entitled to compensation for his or her NEL (WSIA, s 46(1)). The WSIB determines the degree of impairment with reference to either the existing health records in the worker's claim file or based on an independent medical assessment specifically requested by the WSIB for this purpose (s 47).[15] The amount payable is paid either as a lump sum or, if the amount is greater than $11,452.07,

13 If a worker was injured in an accident after the age of 63, then benefits are payable for no more than 24 months following the date of accident (ss 43(1)(b)-(c)).

14 The WSIB will set aside a further amount equal to 5 percent of the worker's LOE benefits as a retirement benefit. The worker may also elect to contribute an additional 5 percent of his or her LOE benefit into this retirement fund, which is then deducted from the worker's LOE benefit.

15 The WSIB uses the American Medical Association's guidelines to measure a worker's impairment. The amount of the NEL benefit is then calculated as the percentage of permanent impairment times a base amount that is adjusted depending on the worker's age at the time of the accident (s 46(2)).

in equal monthly payments unless the worker elects to be paid in a lump sum (s 46(3)).

Work Reintegration and Transition

Both the worker and the employer are required to cooperate in the worker's early and safe return to work (WSIA, s 40).[16] In addition, an employer with at least 20 employees and where the worker was employed for a continuous period of at least 12 months before the date of injury (WSIA, s 41) has a further obligation to re-employ a worker who has been absent from work as a result of an injury. A breach of the re-employment obligation is presumed to have occurred when a worker's employment is terminated within six months of the worker's return to work and may result in a penalty against the employer. The employer may rebut this presumption by demonstrating that the worker's termination was not related to the injury (s 41(10)). The WSIB does not have the authority to order the reinstatement of the worker.

The duty to cooperate is not exhausted after any specified period of time, but the re-employment obligation ends 24 months following the date of injury (s 41(7)). The return to work and re-employment obligations are in addition to any obligation that might arise under a collective agreement, employment agreement, or the *Human Rights Code*.

When it is apparent that a return to the pre-injury workplace is not achievable, the WSIB will determine whether the worker requires further assistance to re-enter the workforce or to transition into new employment (s 42). These services may include retraining or re-education, assistive devices or equipment, or assistance in developing job-search skills and techniques. If a worker is found to be unable to return to the pre-injury workplace but is not unemployable, the WSIB will ultimately determine a suitable occupation for that worker.[17]

Independent Allowance and Personal Care Allowance

A worker who is severely impaired as a result of an injury may also be entitled to further annual allowances to facilitate the worker's independence or to provide financial support for a worker that requires attendant care. The

---

16 This obligation requires the parties to maintain regular communication and to work together to identify suitable work that would allow the worker to return to employment. If a worker fails to cooperate in return to work, the WSIB may suspend or reduce the worker's benefits during the period of non-cooperation (s 43(7)). Similarly, if an employer fails to cooperate, the WSIB can level a monetary penalty against the employer (s 86).

17 After a suitable occupation is determined and any work-transition services are complete, the WSIB deems the worker to be able to earn wages based on the earnings for that occupation established with economic statistics for that market. These deemed earnings are then applied as though the worker were actually employed in the occupation (s 43(4)).

WSIA does not set out any specific financial benefit payable to a worker in such circumstances, rather the availability of benefits is described as part of the health care to which a worker is entitled.[18]

A personal-care allowance is calculated based on the nature of a worker's degree of impairment and need for specific personal care. The WSIB does not arrange for that personal attendant care but provides a monthly economic benefit based on its assessment of the probable cost of that care.[19]

Survivor

Survivor benefits are payable when a worker dies as a result of an accident or because of the illness or injury. Survivors who may be eligible for benefits in the event of a worker's death include the worker's spouse, child or children, and any of the following persons who were dependent in whole or in part on the worker's earnings at the time of the worker's death (WSIA, s 2(1)): parent, step-parent, or person who stood in the role of parent to the worker; sibling or half-sibling; grandparent; or grandchild.

Survivor benefits include a significant lump-sum death benefit, burial costs, and periodic payments made to specific survivors depending on which persons are survivors at the time of the worker's death (s 48).[20] When a worker's death is not immediate as a result of an accident, it is likely that the worker will be entitled to other benefits under the WSIA including health care, LOE, and NEL benefits. In cases where benefits are payable but not yet paid at the time of death, these benefits are payable to the worker's estate. Where retained by the worker directly and the worker subsequently dies, it is important to confirm the continuation of any retainer with the estate trustee before taking steps on behalf of the estate.

---

18 The WSIB has operational policies that address the threshold for entitlement to such allowances and the manner in which they are calculated (Operational Policy Manual [OPM], Independent Living Allowance and Personal Care Allowance).

19 The type of care is determined based on a direct assessment of the worker, usually including a home visit, and is classed in one of three levels of care: general attendant care, personal attendant care, or skilled attendant care. The calculation of the benefit is based on a fixed hourly rate for each level of care and the estimated number of weekly hours required to provide care.

20 The primary survivor is the worker's spouse, then children who are 18 or younger or who are 30 or younger and continuing in their education (OPM, Child 19 Years or Older Continuing in Education). If none of these persons are alive at the time of the worker's death, then benefits are payable to the class of dependants described above (s 48(21)).

Appearing Before the Workplace Safety and Insurance Appeals Tribunal

A final decision of the WSIB may be appealed to the WSIAT (s 125(1)). The WSIAT sets its own practice and procedure. Unlike other administrative tribunals, including the WSIB, the WSIAT has not developed a single, consolidated practice and procedure guideline. It has, however, developed several practice directions that explain the process through which appeals are heard and determined, all of which are available on the WSIAT website.

Starting the Appeal

An appeal is initiated by filing a written notice of appeal form with the WSIAT (s 125(2)). The notice of appeal must identify the specific appeals resolution officer (ARO) decision under appeal, the WSIB claim file, and the issues under appeal. A copy of the ARO decision must also be filed along with the notice of appeal. The notice of appeal must be filed within six months of the ARO decision (s 125(2)). If an appeal is filed after this six-month limitation period, the appellant must also request an extension of the time to appeal. Extensions are granted by the WSIAT in exceptional circumstances.

Once the notice of appeal is filed, the appellant must file a readiness form indicating that the appeal is ready to proceed. The appellant will then receive a bound copy of a WSIAT case record, which contains a full copy of the WSIB claim file under appeal and any other related claim file of the worker, copies of the relevant WSIB operational policy, and copies of all WSIAT correspondence. The WSIAT has commissioned the preparation of a number of medical discussion papers addressing common medical issues and injuries. When an issue under appeal appears related to one of these medical discussion papers, the WSIAT will include the related discussion paper within its case record. The entire case record is part of the evidentiary record before the WSIAT panel or vice chair when the appeal is determined.

Confirmation of Appeal

After the appellant receives the case record, the appellant must then file a confirmation of appeal form (WSIAT Practice Direction Confirmation of Appeal and Hearing Ready Letter). This form, which is similar to the WSIB's appeal readiness form, must identify any additional relevant documentary evidence, have copies of such evidence attached, and identify any witnesses that the appellant intends to call along with will-say statements for each witness (WSIAT Practice Direction Disclosure, Witnesses and the Three-Week Rule). If the appellant requires that a witness be summoned to testify, the need and rationale for that summons must be identified on the confirmation of appeal form (WSIAT Practice Direction Summonses and Production of Documents).

The confirmation of appeal must be filed no later than 24 months from the time the notice of appeal is filed.

At this stage, the respondent is provided with a copy of the case record. The respondent must also complete and file the confirmation of appeal, identifying and producing additional relevant documentary evidence and anticipated witnesses. This must be done within two weeks of receiving the appellant's confirmation of appeal.

Mediation

Section 130 of the WSIA grants the authority to the WSIAT to provide mediation services in such circumstances as it considers appropriate. The mediation is intended either to resolve all or some of the appeal issues or to address factual and evidentiary issues that can be agreed upon before an oral hearing. The parties to an appeal (the worker and the employer) may jointly request a **mediation** of the appeal issues (WSIAT Practice Direction Mediation). A request for mediation can be made at any time before a hearing of the appeal is scheduled. Both parties must agree to participate, and the WSIAT must agree that the matter is appropriate for mediation in order for a matter to proceed to a mediation. In such a case, the WSIAT will provide its specially trained mediation staff to act as the mediator.

At the outset of any mediation, the parties are required to sign a consent form agreeing to participate in mediation and an acknowledgement that the substance of the mediation is subject to confidentiality.

All disclosures, admissions, and other communications made while the case is in the mediation process will be made **without prejudice** and only for the purposes of resolving an appeal. These communications do not form part of the case record before the WSIAT and may not be used in the appeal hearing or in any other proceeding. There are some exceptions to this rule, most notably that the disclosure of new medical evidence during mediation will be added to the case file.

In preparation for a mediation, it is important for the paralegal to thoroughly prepare a client by reviewing the purpose of the mediation, the interests of the client, and the opportunities to resolve parts of an appeal case that would otherwise be in dispute.

mediation a way of settling an issue without going to a hearing by the parties discussing possible settlements with a mediator; if a settlement is reached it goes to a vice-chair for approval, after which the case can be closed

without prejudice communications that are precluded from being disclosed or referred to in any subsequent proceedings, such as communications made between the applicant and respondent during a WSIAT mediation; they are therefore inadmissible as evidence at any subsequent proceeding, such as the hearing

Any agreement reached by the parties in mediation is only effective once it has been reviewed and approved by a vice chair of the WSIAT. In addition, any such agreement must be consistent with the evidence and the WSIA. Parties cannot reach an agreement that would waive a worker's right to benefits since this is prohibited by section 16 of the WSIA. For example, a worker may not agree to withdraw his or her appeal in exchange for a cash settlement.

A hearing of an appeal may still occur if the parties cannot reach an agreement or there are outstanding issues that the mediator and the parties agree should be referred to a hearing.

Pre-Hearing

Once both parties have filed their confirmation of appeal forms, the matter is referred for scheduling of an **oral hearing**. On selected cases, the WSIAT may direct that the hearing be conducted in writing (WSIAT Practice Direction Written Appeals). After the hearing is scheduled, the parties are entitled to present new documentary evidence or identify additional witnesses to provide oral evidence. To do so, a party must provide copies of all new documentary evidence to the WSIAT and the opposing party at least three weeks before the hearing. Similarly, notice of any new witnesses must be provided at least three weeks before the hearing (WSIAT Practice Direction Disclosure, Witnesses and the Three-Week Rule).

Hearing

Most hearings before the WSIAT are scheduled as an oral hearing for a half day. An oral hearing before the WSIAT is a **hearing de novo**. Although the entire claim file, including the ARO's decision, is part of the evidence before the WSIAT, the parties must present their cases on a fresh basis. A hearing before the WSIAT proceeds in essentially the same format as a hearing before the WSIB's Appeals Services Division.

The primary difference in the two levels of appeal is that a hearing before the WSIAT can take place before a panel of three adjudicators, whereas a hearing before the WSIB is always before a single ARO.

Hearings are conducted in French or English. When a party or witness does not speak or understand either of these languages, the WSIAT will provide interpreters for the hearing.

oral hearing the proceeding whereby the applicant/appellant is provided the opportunity to verbally tell the WSIB/WSIAT why he or she is entitled to the benefits and the respondent is allowed to respond to the claims

hearing de novo a hearing in which the adjudicator deals completely afresh with a matter that has already been heard once before

Expert Evidence

The WSIAT has the further authority to seek the assistance of a health care practitioner to provide expert evidence to assist the panel or vice chair in making a decision on the facts (s 134). This additional tool affords the WSIAT decision-makers the opportunity to obtain oral evidence from the witnesses, to make preliminary findings of fact, and to then refer focused questions to a medical assessor for the purpose of such assistance (WSIAT Practice Direction Post-Hearing Procedure).

In such a case, both parties are usually consulted regarding the nature and scope of the questions to be presented to an assessor and are provided with an opportunity to make further written submissions in response to the opinion of the assessor.

Assessor reports, along with the medical discussion papers of the WSIAT, are persuasive pieces of evidence that are, in practice, accorded a high degree of weight in many appeals. Become familiar with the medical discussion papers and consider whether challenging medical issues in the appeal might merit the use of a medical assessor. If so, you should address with your client the need to obtain a comprehensive expert report in advance of the appeal hearing. Where the opinions expressed in a medical discussion paper are contrary to the position of your client, the likelihood for success on the appeal may well turn on the quality of any expert evidence that the appellant (and paralegal) is able to present.

Effective advocacy will not ignore the challenges of the opposing case or the opposing expert opinions, but will directly address these issues and differences of opinion.

Stay current on WSIAT's process and practice directions by reviewing them regularly through WSAIT's website.

Decisions, Reconsideration, and Judicial Review

Decisions

The WSIAT does not render decisions orally on the day of the hearing. A written decision of the WSIAT is generally released within 120 days of the conclusion of the hearing (s 127). The decision is binding on the WSIB and is forwarded to the WSIB for implementation. All WSIAT decisions are then published in an anonymized format and posted to the WSIAT decision database, which is accessible through its website. Take care to review the WSIAT decision database, particularly when dealing with a novel issue in dispute.

Reconsideration

Although the decision of the WSIAT is a final decision, the WSIAT has the authority to reconsider its decision and may confirm, vary, or revoke it at any time that it considers appropriate (WSIA, s 129). A party may apply to the WSIAT to reconsider its decision (WSIAT Practice Direction Reconsiderations). Such a request should not simply be an attempt to reargue the appeal or to express dissatisfaction with the outcome of an appeal. It is important, therefore, when explaining this process to a client to make clear that the purpose of a reconsideration request is limited and the test to meet is difficult and that reconsiderations are rarely granted. While there is no established time limit in the WSIA for a reconsideration of a decision, the WSIAT has decided that as a general rule it will consider a request that is made within six months of a decision. A further delay will weigh against a finding that a decision should be reconsidered.

To request a **reconsideration** of a decision, a party must file a reconsideration/clarification request form with the WSIAT, setting out the basis upon which a reconsideration is requested. Any new evidence argued in support of the request must be provided at the time the form is filed.

A reconsideration involves two steps. First, WSIAT must decide whether it is advisable to reconsider the decision. This is called the threshold test. Second, if the threshold test is met, the WSIAT will decide whether the previous decision should be changed and, if so, how it should be changed. This is called the decision on the merits. In any request for reconsideration, a party must first satisfy a threshold test that demonstrates that there is a good reason to reconsider a decision. In particular, the party must demonstrate one of the following:

- Significant new evidence has been discovered that was not available at the original hearing and would likely have changed the outcome. Information that was available but not obtained or not presented by a party will fall short of this test.
- The decision overlooks an important piece of evidence, as opposed to rejecting the evidence or distinguishing it. If the decision indicates that all evidence was reviewed and considered but does not specifically refer to a particular piece of important evidence, then this test might not be met. A complete omission of a reference to a key piece of evidence, however, might satisfy this test.
- The decision contains a clear error of law. This might occur if the decision fails to reference a key provision of the WSIA or operational policy of the WSIB.
- The decision contains a jurisdictional error (for example, the WSIAT decided an issue for which it did not have legal authority, such as an issue for which there was no final decision from the WSIB).

reconsideration the process by which a party dissatisfied by the WSIAT's decision can request that the tribunal look at its decision again, which can result in a change in the decision

If the WSIAT decides that there is no reasonable chance of success that a request for reconsideration meets the threshold test, it will dismiss the application by way of a reconsideration decision without submissions from the other party.

If it decides that there is an arguable case that the threshold has been met, then both parties are provided with a reconsideration case record. The responding party is then granted three weeks to provide submissions on the threshold test. The applicant is granted two weeks to provide a reply. A decision is then made as to whether the threshold test has been met.

If the WSIAT decides that the threshold test has been met, the case will be referred to a vice chair or panel for a further hearing on the issues to be reconsidered. The WSIAT may give instructions about the procedure to be followed on the decision on the merits. For example, if credibility is not an issue, it may not be necessary to hold an oral hearing on the merits. Unless otherwise ordered, the decision on the merits will be made by the vice chair or panel who decided the threshold question. In some cases, it may be appropriate to combine the hearings on the threshold test and the merits. Following the conclusion of a reconsideration hearing, a final reconsideration decision is rendered in writing.

Judicial Review

There is no right of appeal from a decision of the WSIAT. Occasionally, a dissatisfied party will bring an application for a judicial review of a tribunal decision. A party who brings an application for **judicial review** may be liable to pay an award of court costs to the other parties, including the tribunal, if the judicial review is dismissed by the court. The amount of court costs assessed against the losing party on a judicial review is often several thousand dollars.

The courts have stated many times that on applications for judicial review, they will treat decisions of the tribunal with deference, so that a court will only interfere with a tribunal decision if it is "irrational."[21]

One reason the courts are reluctant to interfere with tribunal decisions is section 123 of the WSIA. Section 123 is a **privative clause**, which states that tribunal decisions are not open to question or review in a court. The Court of Appeal has stated that even without a privative clause a decision of the

judicial review the process by which a court reviews an administrative body's exercise of its statutory duties; there is no right of appeal of a WSIAT decision, but a dissatisfied party may bring an application for judicial review for the court to review the decision

privative clause a statutory provision that limits the availability of appeal or review of the decision of an administrative body (e.g., s 123 of the WSIA)

21 See the Ontario Court of Appeal's decision in *Rodrigues v Ontario (Workplace Safety and Insurance Appeals Tribunal)*, 2008 ONCA 719, 92 OR (3d) 757.

tribunal is still subject to deference. A very important reason the courts give great deference to tribunal decisions is because the tribunal is recognized as an expert body with special expertise in workplace safety and insurance matters.

On many occasions the courts have found that the tribunal's decisions are not only *not* unreasonable, they are correct.[22]

Case Law

The following is a selection of WSIAT cases from 2017. WSIAT decisions are available from LexisNexis Quicklaw (fee-based database), CanLII, and the Ontario Workplace Tribunal Library.

Decision No 3291/16, 2017 ONWSIAT 3225

- Dependency benefits (common law spouse)
- Words and phrases (conjugal relationship)

The worker was a firefighter from 1976 to 1988. He was diagnosed with a brain tumour in 1988 and died in 1990. In 2006, the board granted entitlement for the brain tumour, with an accident date in 1988. The board paid $74,000 in benefits to the estate. The board also determined that the surviving spouse was entitled to $392,000 of survivor benefits. The employer appealed the determination regarding the surviving spouse, and the appeals resolution officer found that the woman was not a spouse. The woman appealed to the tribunal.

The Act and board policy provide that a spouse includes a man or woman who, at the time of the death of the worker, was not married to the other but had cohabited for at least one year. The test for cohabitation has been accepted as living together in a conjugal relationship, which includes matters such as financial interdependence, sexual relationship, common principal residence, and shared obligations regarding the home.

The panel reviewed the evidence and concluded that the appellant had not cohabited with the worker in a conjugal relationship for at least one year at the time of his death: the appellant and the worker had their own separate residences; they did not share the majority of household expenses; they filed tax returns as single persons; the appellant was not covered by any of the worker's benefits; the appellant did not change the address on her driver's licence; a contemporaneous social work report indicated that the worker was divorced,

---

22 *Rogers and Malfara v WCAT*, Decision No 258/90, 1990 CanLII 4395 (Ont WSIAT); *Stelpipe v Franyo and WCAT*, Decision No. 298/88, 1988 CanLII 2207 (Ont WSIAT); *Canada Post v Johnson*, Decision No 1480/98, 2002 ONWSIAT 2247, *Canadian Pacific Railway v WCAT and Minshall*, Decision 647/95, [2000] OJ No 500 (QL); *Canada Post Corp v Smith* (1998), Decision 716/91, 40 OR (3d) 97 (CA), leave to appeal to SCC dismissed, [1998] SCCA No 329; *Dionne v Ontario Hydro*, Decision 1118/07, [2008] OJ No 4337 (QL).

lived alone, and had a girlfriend; permission for an autopsy was obtained from the family, not from the appellant; the worker did not name the appellant as a beneficiary in his will; an addendum to the will left a small amount to the appellant, whom he described as his lover, confidant, and best friend; the worker's sister testified that when she cleaned out the worker's apartment after his death, there was no evidence that the appellant was living there. The appellant was not a spouse and was not entitled to survivor benefits. The appeal was dismissed.

Decision No 1675/17I, 2017 ONWSIAT 2411

- Procedure (venue)

The worker and employer appealed a decision of the appeals resolution officer regarding ongoing entitlement for an accident. The employer also appealed regarding initial entitlement and Secondary Injury Enhancement Fund (SIEF) relief.

In this decision, the vice-chair determined the location for the hearing.

The worker lived in Sarnia and had medical restrictions limiting travel by car to no more than one hour. The tribunal regularly schedules hearings in London, which is about one hour by car from Sarnia. The employer requested that the hearing be scheduled in Toronto, to minimize travel costs for its three witnesses.

The usual practice of the tribunal is to hold the hearing at the location closest to where the worker lives. Some tribunal decisions have applied a balance of convenience, but many of those decisions involve right-to-sue applications, which began in the court system rather than the workers' compensation system. The vice-chair concluded that the hearing should be scheduled in London.

Decision No 960/16, 2017 ONWSIAT 3010

- Aggravation (pre-existing condition; asthma)
- Medical report (varying diagnoses)
- Permanent impairment (NEL)
- Reactive airways dysfunction syndrome
- Evidence (weight; medical report)

The board granted the worker entitlement for aggravation of pre-existing asthma in 2006. The worker appealed a decision of the appeals resolution officer denying an NEL award for permanent aggravation.

From 1998 to 2002, there were various medical reports with references to asthma. There was no indication of assessments from 2002 to 2006. After workplace exposure in 2006, the worker was seen by numerous respirologists, with varying diagnoses, including primary chronic obstructive pulmonary disease (COPD), asthma, and reactive airways dysfunction syndrome (RADS).

The board medical assessor examined the worker and was of the opinion that the worker's condition was primary COPD. However, she made her diagnosis in the absence of detailed reports from four specialists substantiating pre-existing asthma without emphysema. Further, she did not reach a conclusion on work-relatedness and did not specifically comment on temporary or permanent aggravation of the pre-existing condition. Another specialist found that the worker had asthma but did not compare pre-accident and post-accident exposure periods.

The vice-chair preferred the opinion of a tribunal medical assessor, who had the benefit of the full picture over time and who specifically addressed the role of the workplace exposure. This report was detailed, thorough, and reflective of the evidence on file. The vice-chair accepted the tribunal assessor's diagnosis of RADS and found that the RADS permanently aggravated the worker's pre-existing impairment by worsening her lung function through the imposition of RADS on the pre-existing asthma. The worker was entitled to a NEL assessment for the permanent aggravation. The appeal was allowed.

Decision No 2678/17, 2017 ONWSIAT 2826

- Right to sue (claim denied by board)

The worker's estate brought an action against the worker's employer claiming that the worker developed amyotrophic lateral sclerosis (ALS) as a result of negligence of the employer regarding the worker's workplace exposure to chemicals. The defendant applied to determine whether the plaintiff's right of action was taken away.

The estate had claimed benefits from the board, but the claim was denied on the grounds that it had not been established that the worker's condition was related to her workplace exposure.

The core of the civil action was that the worker died as a result of a work-related disease. This is precisely the type of circumstance in which employers have a right to be protected from civil suit by the historic bargain that created the workers' compensation system and remains fully incorporated into the current legislation. The plaintiff's right of action was taken away. The vice-chair noted that he made no finding regarding continuing appeal rights at the board or the tribunal regarding the denied workplace insurance claim, as that issue was not argued on this application.

Decision No 1397/16, 2017 ONWSIAT 1291

- Disablement (nature of work)
- Medical report (opinion of treating doctor preferred)

The board granted the worker entitlement for a right arm injury. The worker appealed a decision of the appeals resolution officer denying entitlement for shoulder and left arm injuries. Modified work provided by the employer after the right arm injury was not suitable for the worker and led to the development of the secondary conditions.

The vice-chair rejected the submission of the employer that the evidence of the worker's treating doctors was partial and should be accorded less weight. The vice-chair noted that these doctors had the benefit of examining the worker and following the course of her condition following the injury. Their reports should be accorded significant weight.

Only in rare circumstances are treating doctors found to have overstepped the boundaries and to have lost their objectivity to such a degree that they may be seen as advocates for their patients. There must be something concrete to indicate that a treating doctor's objectivity has been compromised. In this case, the vice-chair found that the reporting from the treating doctors was reliable. The reports were supported by clear reasons and were provided in a balanced manner. The vice-chair gave little weight to the employer's medical consultant. His reports lacked independence and relied upon information regarding the worker's job duties that the vice-chair rejected. The appeal was allowed.

Decision No 1868/17, 2017 ONWSIAT 1924

- Stress, mental
- Board directives and guidelines (stress, mental; traumatic event)

A truck driver appealed a decision of the appeals resolution officer denying the worker entitlement for traumatic mental stress.

On December 22, 2011 the worker drove his tractor to a location to pick up a trailer, delivered the trailer to its destination, and then went home. That evening, at about 7:30 p.m., he received a call asking him to go to the OPP station. At the station, he was informed that two wheels had come off the trailer and killed a woman driving her car. He did not know the wheels had come off the trailer until that time.

The panel found that the worker experienced a sudden and unexpected traumatic event. He was involved in a motor vehicle accident that resulted in the death of another driver. The panel was satisfied that the circumstances fell within the parameters of board policy. Even if the policy language excluded entitlement because the worker did not witness the events, the panel would have granted entitlement based on the merits and justice of the case. The appeal was allowed.

Decision No 215/17, 2017 ONWSIAT 362

- Suitable employment (factors other than physical capability; shift change)

The worker suffered a shoulder injury in January 2010. The employer appealed a decision of the appeals resolution officer granting the worker LOE benefits from March 2010 to April 2010 and granting the worker entitlement for a Bankart lesion.

The employer operated 24 hours per day, using three shifts. The terms of the worker's employment were that she was required to work on any shift. However, she requested the midnight shift and had been working on that shift since 2007. After the accident, the employer offered modified work on the day shift. The worker advised that she could not work the day shift because of child care obligations. Later, the worker advised that another reason she could not work the day shift was because she was taking courses during the day.

Decision No 137/11 referred to a dichotomy in tribunal case law regarding whether a worker is required to accept modified work on a different shift. That decision sided with the case finding that a change in work schedule is not relevant when considering suitability of modified work.

The vice-chair agreed with the general principle that a modified job should not be considered unsuitable simply because it is offered in a different time slot than the pre-injury job. However, there can be exceptions to this general principle in certain limited circumstances, one of which exceptions will occur when the employer offers a different time slot because of animus to the worker rather than because of unavailability in the pre-accident time slot.

In this case, evidence indicated that the employer could have easily accommodated the worker's request to stay on the midnight shift. Evidence also showed that the employer had developed a hostile approach to the worker's claim and request for accommodation. The vice-chair concluded that the modified work should not be regarded as suitable because the shift change was motivated by hostility to the worker rather than legitimate operational requirements. The worker was entitled to LOE benefits during the period in question. The vice-chair also found that the Bankart lesion was related to the compensable accident. The appeal was allowed.

KEY LEGISLATION

Workplace Safety and Insurance Act, 1997, including amendments, previous acts, regulations, and schedules
Workers' Compensation Act

KEY TERMS

employers, 231
hearing de novo, 243
judicial review, 246
loss-of-earnings (LOE) benefits, 237
mediation, 242
non-economic loss (NEL) benefits, 237
oral hearing, 243
privative clause, 246
quantum of benefits, 233
reconsideration, 245
return-to-work plan, 233
without prejudice, 242
workers, 231
work-transition plan, 233

REVIEW QUESTIONS

1. Workplace safety and insurance in Ontario is a "no fault" system. What does that mean?
2. Who is covered by the WSIA?
3. What workers or category of workers are excluded from coverage of the WSIA?
4. Can a worker not automatically covered by the WSIA apply for workers' compensation?
5. Is a worker employed by a Schedule 1 employer entitled to pursue a civil action for damages in respect to the worker's injury or disease?
6. How much time does a worker have to file a complaint with the WSIB?
7. What is the purpose of mediation?
8. What are the two levels of appeal from a WSIB decision?
9. How does a worker appeal a final WSIB decision to the WSIAT?
10. Can a worker or employer appeal the decision of the WSIAT?

SCENARIO 1

Tony, a technician employed by Tech Nation, was installing a software program on his colleague's computer at work. While installing the program, Tony suddenly starting seizing. He was taken to the emergency room where he was diagnosed with encephalitis. He claimed the condition was a result, to a significant degree, of the prolonged time he spends in front of computers. Dr Khan, the neurosurgeon who assessed Tony's injuries, explained that prolonged use of a computer screen is not generally a cause of encephalitis.

1. Does the section 13(2) presumption apply to Tony's accident?
2. In your opinion, is Tony entitled to benefits under the insurance plan?

SCENARIO 2

Felicia died while operating heavy machinery during her employment at a cement factory. At the time of her death, she was engaged to Naveed. She and Naveed had lived together for the past 13 months. They had not filed their tax returns together, but two days prior to Felicia's death, they scheduled an appointment at the bank to create a joint bank account. Naveed applied to the board for survivors' benefits.

Was Naveed a spouse or common law spouse of the deceased worker at the time of her death?

SCENARIO 3

Stephanie worked at Glyming, a mining company, for ten years. Because of constant exposure to asbestos while on the job, she developed lung cancer. She claimed workers' compensation benefits, and the WSIB awarded her $500,000. She later brought a civil action for damages against Glyming, claiming that her lung cancer was a result of Glyming's negligence. Glyming brought a right to sue application to the WSIAT under section 31 of the WSIA, seeking a determination that Stephanie is barred from bringing an action against it.

Is Glyming's application likely to succeed?

CHAPTER 11

Law Society Tribunal

Overview and History 256

Legislation and Regulations 258

The Hearing Division 259

The Appeal Division 260

Application Process: Hearing Division 265

Hearing Process: Hearing Division 267

Decisions, Reconsiderations, and Appeals 270

Case Law 273

Key Terms 275

Review Questions 275

Scenarios 276

Overview and History

The Law Society Tribunal (LST) was created by the Law Society of Upper Canada, now the Law Society of Ontario (LSO), as an independent adjudicative body that hears applications and appeals on licensee regulation matters, such as conduct and capacity. This tribunal is still in its infancy; it came into existence in 2014 through the *Modernizing Regulation of the Legal Profession Act, 2013* (MRLPA).[1] This new tribunal replaced the Law Society Hearing Panel and Appeal Panel. The LST has two divisions: the hearing division and the appeal division.[2] The hearing division hears notices of application relating to conduct, capacity, licensing, and reinstatement of a licence. The appeal division hears appeals stemming from decisions of the hearing division, brought by either the licensee or the LSO.

LST members are either **benchers** or other appointed individuals, be they lawyers, paralegals, or members of the public.[3] Benchers are basically the government of the LSO. Section 10 of the *Law Society Act* (LSA) says "benchers shall govern the society." Most benchers are elected (they must be licensed lawyers to qualify, although newer rules allow for five licensed paralegals to sit as benchers; see s 15(1)), but some are appointed through the office they hold (such as the minister of justice; s 12(1)1), and some are honorary benchers (s 11). There are 72 LST members, plus two vice-chairs (one each for the hearing division and the appeal division) and one chair. Appointments to the LST are for two years.[4] Members are held to the Adjudicator Code of Conduct, a three-part document (Part I: Introduction, Part II: Conflict of Interest and Reasonable Apprehension of Bias, and Part III: Adjudicator Responsibilities) that guides:

> the conduct and the *professional and ethical responsibilities of the Law Society's adjudicators*. … the purpose of the guide is to reflect *accepted principles of behaviour*. Law Society adjudicators should familiarize themselves with the content of this document in addition to the legislation, rules, practice directions and procedures established to ensure that the Law Society Tribunal's processes are *consistent, transparent and fair*.[5]

benchers elected licensees or appointed officials who sit on convocation and govern the LSO; some sit as LST members

1 SO 2013, c 17—Bill 111.

2 *Law Society Act*, RSO 1990, c L.8, s 49.20.1(2) [LSA].

3 LSA, ss 49.21(2)(3), 49.29(2)(3).

4 Law Society Tribunal, "Tribunal Members" (2017), online: <https://lawsocietytribunal.ca/Pages/tribunalmemberbio_en.aspx>; see also LSA, s 49.21(3).

5 Law Society Tribunal, "Adjudicator Code of Conduct" (2017), online: <https://lawsocietytribunal.ca/Pages/Mainpage.aspx#114> (emphasis added).

This code is meant to guide and govern adjudicators from the beginning of their term and to cover any responsibilities that might extend after their term expires. Some topics covered in the code are:

- conflicts of interest,[6]
- bias,[7]
- conduct during proceedings,[8]
- decision-making responsibilities,[9]
- responsibilities to the panel, and[10]
- responsibilities to the tribunal, such as ongoing education requirements.[11]

The LST's mission statement ensures the processing, hearing, and deciding of cases "in a manner that is fair, just and in the public interest,"[12] and is governed by the four core values of (1) fairness, (2) transparency, (3) quality, and (4) timeliness:[13]

> *Fairness*: We will be fair and impartial in our processes and proceedings, treating all with respect, courtesy and dignity.
>
> *Quality*: We strive for excellence, acting with dedication and professionalism. We aim for continuous improvement, valuing diverse perspectives. We commit to an atmosphere that enables all to perform at their best.
>
> *Transparency*: We will act in a manner that bears the closest scrutiny. Our decisions, rules, processes and policies will be available to licensees and the public, accessible and easily understandable.
>
> *Timeliness*: We are guided by the importance of timely resolution of all matters. We will schedule hearing and continuation dates expeditiously and complete written reasons promptly.[14]

---

6 *Ibid*, "IV. Definitions" at paras 6-8.

7 *Ibid*, "IV. Definitions" at para 9.

8 *Ibid*, "VII. Conduct During the Proceeding" at paras 38-42.

9 *Ibid*, "VIII. Decision-Making Responsibilities" at paras 46-48.

10 *Ibid*, "X. Responsibilities When Sitting as a Panel."

11 *Ibid*, "XI. Responsibilities to the Tribunal" at paras 53-60.

12 Law Society Tribunal, "Legislation, Rules and Forms" (2017), online: <https://lawsocietytribunal.ca/Pages/Mainpage.aspx#121>.

13 Law Society Tribunal, "Message from the Chair" (2017), online: <https://lawsocietytribunal.ca/Pages/Mainpage.aspx#111>.

14 Law Society Tribunal, "Mission and Core Values" (2017), online: <https://lawsocietytribunal.ca/Pages/Mainpage.aspx#112>.

These core values are highlighted in the annual report for 2016,[15] which includes a comprehensive review of the LST's accomplishments to date and its ongoing plans for development. The report highlights efficiencies, such as enhanced case management, pre-hearing conferences, and fewer adjudicator hours.[16] Since the LST's inception in 2014, three pillars of achievement have been showcased: independence, adjudicative excellence, and enhanced processes.[17]

According to the report, tribunal independence is demonstrated in the mission statement, core values, logo, separate website, and off-site location from the LSO, and in its own annual reports. Adjudicative excellence is seen through the diversity and skills of its members, ongoing training and professional development, a self-evaluation scheme, and increased efficiency with hearings and decisions. Enhanced processes include more efficient scheduling practices, re-drafted Rules of Practice and Procedure, use of assistive listening devices and cameras for video and web conferences to enhance access and transparency, and plans for a new electronic case management system.[18]

Future plans include incorporation of the Truth and Reconciliation Commission of Canada's final report recommendations urging "constructive action in addressing First Nations, Métis and Inuit peoples' experiences with the administration of justice."[19] Achievement of this recommendation is found in the 2016 mandatory member education session on Indigenous issues: "We recognize that it is important to ensure that proceedings at our Tribunal fairly and respectfully deal with Indigenous people and issues that affect them in the administration of justice."[20] In addition, efforts have been made to include Elders and traditional ceremonial practices, such as smudging circle seating and the use of eagle feathers, which are available for LST hearings on request.[21]

Legislation and Regulations

The LST was created by the MRLPA and is governed by the LSA, O Reg 167/07: Hearings Before the Hearing and Appeal Divisions, and the *Statutory Powers Procedure Act*.[22]

15 Law Society Tribunal, "Annual Report 2016" (2017), online: <https://lawsocietytribunal.ca/Document%20Resources/Tribunal-AR-2016-English.pdf>.

16 *Ibid* at 2.

17 *Ibid* at 5.

18 *Ibid*.

19 *Ibid* at 10.

20 *Ibid*.

21 *Ibid*.

22 RSO 1990, c S.22.

The MRLPA allows for amendments to the LSA and the *Solicitors Act* (SA);[23] the amendments to the latter Act enable the creation of the LST. For example, it adds the definition of the "Appeal Division," meaning the Law Society Tribunal Appeal Division, to the LSA.[24] Numerous sections remove portions of the LSA. Sections 8 to 10 pave the way for the LSO to raise conduct, capacity, and competence applications before the tribunal. Provisions relating to suspensions of licensees are also embedded (s 12). The amended provisions pertaining to the establishment of the LST begin at section 15 and are to be embedded into the LSA at section 49.20.1(1). This section states that the "Law Society Tribunal is established under the name Law Society Tribunal in English and Tribunal du Barreau in French" (s 15). The remaining aspects of the MRLPA predominantly provide the word-for-word account of what sections are to be incorporated into the LSA, with the exception of a small portion at the end that governs the amendments made to the SA. As such, we will focus now on the LSA.

The LSA is a large piece of legislation that details matters beyond the LST. For example, Part I outlines the makeup of the LSO, provisions concerning benchers, the paralegal standing committee, and the advisory council. The Act has three additional parts, with the LST provisions placed under Part II, sections 49.20.1 through 49.53.

The Hearing Division

As mentioned above, the LST is created under the MRLPA, with the statement of its establishment appearing at section 49.20.1(1) of the LSA. The hearing division is governed by provisions 49.21 to 49.28 and is empowered to determine any question of law that comes before it (s 49.25). The hearing division may also hear **interlocutory orders** (s 49.27(1)) on a motion by the LSO, as authorized by the rules;[25] however, it shall not make such an order to suspend a licence or restrict a licensee's practice "unless there are reasonable grounds for believing that there is a significant risk of harm to members of the public, or to the public interest in the administration of justice, if the order is not made and that making the order is likely to reduce the risk."[26] Furthermore, a one-member panel is not permitted to suspend a licensee's licence or permit a licensee to surrender his or her licence.[27]

interlocutory orders interim orders; do not dispose of the matter

23 RSO 1990, c S.15.

24 MRLPA, s 1(1).

25 Law Society Tribunal, "Hearing Division Rules of Practice and Procedure," r 21, 21 January 2017, online: <https://lawsocietytribunal.ca/Document%20Resources/Hearing_Division_Rules_EN.pdf>.

26 LSA, s 49.27(2).

27 LSA, r 26.02(1).

As an interesting side note to the legislation, this section was recently the focus of an LST decision in the matter of *Law Society of Upper Canada v Siziba*.[28] In this case, the LST dismissed the LSO's motion seeking an interlocutory injunction against Siziba, a licensed paralegal, after allegations that he committed a sexual assault while acting as an Uber driver. The LST was required to consider section 49.27 of the LSA and determine if there was a "significant risk of harm" to the public based on "reasonable grounds," which it did not find. The case is discussed further in the Case Law section at the end of the chapter.

The hearing division also hears applications for reinstatement from licensees whose licences have been suspended by the LST.[29] Applicants can seek a discharge or variance to the order if they can supply new evidence or show a "material change in circumstances."[30] Reinstatement applications cannot be made on the basis of an interlocutory order or summary orders related to non-payment of fees, failure to file a report with the LSO or comply with indemnity requirements, or suspension for incomplete professional development.[31] Cost orders may be made in accordance with section 49.28.

The Appeal Division

The Appeal Division is governed by sections 49.29 to 49.37 of the LSA. Final decisions or orders from the hearing division may be appealed here (s 49.32(1)), including an appeal from a costs order (s 49.32(2)), and summary orders related to non-payment of fees, failure to file a report with the LSO or comply with indemnity requirements, revocation of a licence for any of the foregoing matters, or suspension for incomplete professional development (s 49.32(3)). While a matter is under appeal to the appeal division, the original order of the hearing divisions stands, unless ordered otherwise by the appeal division (49.35(1)). Therefore, if the hearing division suspends your client's licence because of incapacity, and your client wants to appeal that decision, she will remain suspended pending the outcome of the appeal (once a decision has been given by the appeal division), unless you file a motion to request that the hearing division order be stayed during the resolution of the matter. Costs may also be awarded by the appeal division (s 49.37(3)).

The enabling legislation empowers O Reg 167/07 to outline details of hearing composition, such as the number of members assigned to a hearing (s 49.23(3)); this regulation provides the legislative meat for hearings before the hearing division and appeal division. According to section 1(1) of O Reg 167/07, hearing division panels consist of three members, except for some

---

28 2017 ONLSTH 59.

29 LSA, s 49.42(1).

30 *Ibid.*

31 *Ibid*, s 49.42(2).

matters, which may be heard by one member (s 2(1)1). Some matters that could be heard by one member are those concerning a licensee who continues to practise with a suspended licence (s 2(1)1.i), fails to make a payment to the LSO (s 2(1)1.iv), or fails to respond to communication from the LSO (s 2(1)1.vii). The parties to a proceeding on conduct can consent to have one member preside.[32] O Reg 167/07 stipulates that appeal division panels consist of three (s 5(1)) or five (s 6(1)) members, depending on the subject of the appeal. For example, appeals stemming from a final decision of a three-member panel of the hearing division (s 5(1)) or from an interlocutory order suspending a licence (s 5(1)3) will be heard by a five-member appeal panel. Appeals stemming from a final decision by one member of the hearing division (s 6(1)1) or from a summary order for suspension for failure to complete professional development (s 6(1)3) will be heard by a three-member appeal panel.

There are two sets of Rules of Practice and Procedure for the LST, one for the hearing division and one for the appeal division. In addition, there are two practice directions and numerous process guides. The current version of the Hearing Division Rules of Practice and Procedure came into effect on January 1, 2017. These rules cover the expected topics, such as originating process (r 9), service (r 10), motions (r 13), adjournments (r 14), pre-hearing conferences (r 22), and evidence (r 24). There are also some unexpected topics found in this set of rules (compared with other Rules of Procedure as covered throughout this book), such as proceedings management (r 12), access to hearing (r 18), admissions (r 20), interlocutory suspension or restriction (r 21), reprimands (r 28), and retired judge appearing as counsel proceedings (r 29). Some notable features of the rules are discussed below, in addition to some of the identified unexpected topics. Other rules, such as originating process and adjournments, are discussed later in this chapter.

Rule 2 states that non-compliance with a procedural requirement in the rules does not nullify a proceeding or document; however, the LST may make an order for relief to one party, if necessary, or, in the interests of justice, dismiss the entire proceeding or a step in the proceeding (r 2.01(1)(2)). Motions attacking non-compliance with the rules can be made only under certain conditions and with leave of the tribunal (r 2.01(3)). Communication with the panel outside of the hearing is forbidden, except in the presence of all parties and participants or in writing to the tribunal office with all parties and participants copied on the communication (r 5.01(a)(b)). Alternatively, an order directed at case management and communications with the panel may be made by the panel (r 5.02). **Intervenors** to proceedings are able to participate through

intervenors interested parties in the outcome of a case, but neither the applicant nor the respondent, who are granted status by the tribunal to give limited submissions to a hearing panel

32 *Supra* note 25, r 23.01.

Rule 8, either on a motion (r 8.01(1)) or through invitation by the panel as a "friend of the court" (r 8.02).

Rule 28 governs the administration of reprimands, as per section 35(1)19 of the LSA. According to the Act, an order for a licensee to be reprimanded may flow from a Notice of Application for Conduct, where it was found that a licensee engaged in professional misconduct or conduct unbecoming of a licensee (ss 33-35).

The Rules of Practice and Procedure for the Appeal Division are highlighted later in the chapter in the discussion about appeals. The hearing division rules apply to the appeal division, unless stated in the appeal division rules, such as those outlined in Rule 1.2(2).[33] Interlocutory orders from the hearing division cannot be appealed to the appeal division, except for a motion decision from the hearing division for the suspension of a licence or the restriction of a licensee's practice (r 2.1(2)).

The LST offers an online Tribunal Book of Authorities, also governed by a practice direction.[34] The same is available in hardcopy in the hearing rooms. This is a useful resource, providing access to frequently cited case law that the LST often relies upon. Parties may refer to the Tribunal Book of Authorities in their own arguments, rather than reproducing a copy of the case in their own book of authorities.

Finally, the LST provides online guides for different types of hearings. These are referred to as Guides to the Tribunal Process and cover the following topic areas: capacity, competency, conduct, licensing, non-compliance, reinstatement, restoration, terms dispute, and retired judge appearing as counsel proceedings and working with or employing unauthorized persons proceedings. Conduct hearings form the majority of the hearing division's work, with 93 out of 140 current proceedings about conduct.[35] The second most common type of proceeding that occurs is licensing (10 of the 140), and the third most common type of hearing is tied between capacity and interlocutory suspension or restriction of practice (each representing 9 of the 140).[36] All guides include a cautionary statement that they contain only general information and that they must be read in conjunction with the governing legislation, rules, forms, and other user materials available on the LST website.

Conduct proceedings are commenced by the LSO by service and filing a Notice of Application—Conduct and information sheet. To do so, the LSO must receive authorization from the proceedings authorization committee

33 Law Society Tribunal, "Appeal Division Rules of Practice and Procedure" (1 January 2017), online: <https://lawsocietytribunal.ca/Document%20Resources/Appeal_Division_Rules_EN.pdf>.

34 Law Society Tribunal, "Tribunal Book of Authorities" (25 May 2017), online: <https://lawsocietytribunal.ca/Pages/Mainpage.aspx#122>.

35 Law Society Tribunal, "Current Proceedings Chart" (2018), online: https://lawsocietytribunal.ca/Pages/Mainpage.aspx#132>.

36 *Ibid.*

(PAC). PAC receives authority from section 49.20 of the LSA and By-Law 11.[37] The PAC's role is to review any matter referred to it by the LSO and to determine if action should be taken. Referrals from LSO to PAC may pertain to concerns around conduct, capacity, professional competence, or even licence suspension.[38] PAC will give authority to the LSO to proceed with a conduct application where it has reasonable grounds to believe that a licensee has engaged in behaviour that is unbecoming of a lawyer or paralegal.[39] The information sheet, which is a part of the originating process, will contain such information as a hearing date or proceeding management conference date, as well as the location of the hearing.[40]

Licensing proceedings are commenced by the LSO serving and filing a Notice of Referral for Hearing and information sheet.[41] Much of the same process, as indicated in the capacity section above, is outlined in the Guide to Licensing Proceedings. Refusal of a licence can only occur by the LST after a hearing division panel has decided the case based on a referral from the LSO.[42]

Capacity proceedings are commenced by the LSO by serving and filing a Notice of Application—Capacity and the information sheet. PAC authority is once again required for the LSO to proceed (as outlined in the conduct discussion), and this authority is typically granted when the PAC has reasonable grounds to believe that a licensee is incapacitated.[43]

Competence proceedings are initiated by the LSO serving and filing a Notice of Application—Competence and the information sheet. Once again, PAC approval is required before the LSO initiating such proceedings, which will be granted when the PAC sees reasonable grounds to believe that a licensee fails to meet the standards of professional competence.[44]

---

37 Law Society of Ontario, *By-Law 11*, Part VI (amendments current to 25 May 2017), online: <http://www.lsuc.on.ca/uploadedFiles/By-Law-11-Regulation-Conduct-05-25-2017.pdf>.

38 *Ibid.*

39 Law Society Tribunal, "A Guide to Conduct Proceedings" (2017) at 3, online: <https://lawsocietytribunal.ca/Document%20Resources/Guide%20to%20the%20Tribunal%20Process%20-%20Conduct%20(E)%20FINAL.pdf>. See also LSA, ss 33, 34.

40 *Ibid.*

41 Law Society Tribunal, "Guide to Licensing Proceedings" (2017) at 3, online: <https://lawsocietytribunal.ca/Document%20Resources/Guide%20to%20the%20Tribunal%20Process%20-%20Licensing%20(E)%20FINAL.pdf>. See also LSA, s 27.

42 LSA, s 27(4).

43 Law Society Tribunal, "A Guide to Capacity Proceedings" (2017) at 3, online: <https://lawsocietytribunal.ca/Document%20Resources/Guide%20to%20the%20Tribunal%20Process%20-%20Capacity%20(E)%20FINAL.pdf>. See also LSA, ss 37, 38.

44 Law Society Tribunal, "A Guide to Competence Proceedings" (2017) at 3, online: <https://lawsocietytribunal.ca/Document%20Resources/Guide%20to%20the%20Tribunal%20Process%20-%20Competence%20(E)%20FINAL.pdf>. See also LSA, ss 41-43.

Non-compliance proceedings are initiated by the LSO serving and filing a Notice of Application—Non-Compliance and the information sheet. This proceeding is started when the LSO alleges that a licensee has failed to comply with an order under Part II of the LSA.[45] Orders made under Part II of the LSA may stem from failure to pay fees, resulting in suspension (s 46); failure to file a document with the LSO, resulting in suspension (s 47); failure to comply with indemnity requirements for professional liability, resulting in suspension (s 47.1); or failure to comply with professional development requirements, resulting in suspension (s 49).

Reinstatement proceedings are initiated by the licensee under suspension by serving and filing a Notice of Application—Reinstatement and the information sheet.[46] Reinstatement applications can vary or discharge a previous order of the LST to suspend or restrict a licensee's licence on the basis of fresh evidence or a material change in circumstances.[47]

Restoration proceedings are initiated by the LSO by serving and filing a Notice of Referral for Hearing and information sheet.[48] A restoration proceeding is commenced when a licensee who has previously surrendered his or her licence under section 30 of the LSA applies to the LSO to have the licence restored. When the reapplication for license is made, the LSO will refer the matter to the hearing division.[49]

Terms disputed proceedings are commenced by the licensee by serving and filing a Notice of Application—Terms Disputed and information sheet.[50] This type of application would be commenced by a licensee for a determination by the LST that the terms or conditions in a previous LST order have been met.[51]

Retired judge appearing as counsel proceedings must begin with the advocate submitting a Request for Approval for a Retired Judge to Appear as Counsel or Advocate Form, as governed by section 7.7 of the Rules of Professional

45 Law Society Tribunal, "A Guide to Non-Compliance Proceedings" (2017) at 3, online: <https://lawsocietytribunal.ca/Document%20Resources/Guide%20to%20the%20Tribunal%20Process%20-%20Non-compliance%20(E)%20FINAL.pdf>.

46 Law Society Tribunal, "A Guide to Re-instatement Proceedings" (2017) at 3, online: <https://lawsocietytribunal.ca/Document%20Resources/Guide%20to%20the%20Tribunal%20Process%20-%20Reinstatement%20(E)%20FINAL.pdf>.

47 LSA, s 49.42(1).

48 Law Society Tribunal, "A Guide to Restoration Proceedings" (2017) at 3, online: <https://lawsocietytribunal.ca/Document%20Resources/Guide%20to%20the%20Tribunal%20Process%20-%20Restoration%20(E)%20FINAL.pdf>.

49 LSA, s 31.

50 Law Society Tribunal, "A Guide to Terms Dispute Proceedings" (2017) at 3, online: <https://lawsocietytribunal.ca/Document%20Resources/Guide%20to%20the%20Tribunal%20Process%20-%20Terms%20(E)%20FINAL.pdf>.

51 LSA, s 49.43(1).

Conduct (RPC).[52] Section 7.7-1.2 of the RPC, which governs retired judges who return to practice, stipulates:

> A lawyer to whom this Rule applies shall not appear as counsel or advocate in any court, or in chambers, or before any administrative board or tribunal without the express approval of a panel of the Hearing Division of the Law Society Tribunal. This approval may only be granted in exceptional circumstances and may be restricted as the panel sees fit.

Working with or employing unauthorized persons proceedings arise when an applicant wants to work with or hire an unauthorized person. The applicant must complete an application form and submit an Information for a Plan of Supervision Under Rule 7.6-1.1/Subrule 6.01(6) Form.[53] The LSO can commence either of these last two proceedings by serving and filing a Notice of Referral for Hearing.[54]

Application Process: Hearing Division

The Hearing Division Rules of Process and Procedure govern originating process. Originating process includes the requirements of serving and filing the appropriate (1) information sheet, (2) Notice of Application, (3) Notice of Referral for Hearing *or* Notice of Motion—Interlocutory Suspension or Restriction.[55] Therefore, proceedings at the hearing division can be initiated by the following:

- Notice of Application for any of the following: conduct, capacity, competence, non-compliance, reinstatement, or term dispute proceedings (most of which are conduct proceedings);[56]
- Notice of Referral for Hearing for licensing or restoration proceedings; or
- Notice of Motion for an interlocutory suspension or restriction of a lawyer's or paralegal's licence.

---

52 Law Society of Ontario, "Rules of Professional Conduct" (2018), online: <http://www.lsuc.on.ca/list.aspx?id=671>; Law Society Tribunal, "A Guide to Retired Judge Appearing as Counsel Proceedings and Working with or Employing Unauthorized Persons Proceedings" (2017) at 3, online: <https://lawsocietytribunal.ca/Document%20Resources/Guide%20to%20the%20Tribunal%20Process%20-%20JJ%20and%20UA%20(E)%20FINAL.pdf>.

53 "Guide to Retired Judge Appearing as Counsel Proceedings and Working with or Employing Unauthorized Persons Proceedings," *ibid* at 3.

54 LSA, s 27.

55 *Supra* note 25, r 9.01(1).

56 *Supra* note 34.

The following information is also useful foundational knowledge, as outlined in the Guides to the Tribunal Process.

Proceedings are initiated by an applicant. An applicant can be:

- the Law Society of Ontario (Law Society),
- a lawyer or paralegal licensee, or
- a lawyer or paralegal licensee applicant for licence.

The Law Society may initiate these proceedings:

- conduct
- capacity
- competence
- non-compliance
- licensing
- restoration
- retired judge appearing as counsel
- working with or employing unauthorized persons

A licensee may initiate these proceedings:

- reinstatement
- terms dispute[57]

Per the Hearing Division Rules of Practice and Procedure, service is satisfied through hand delivery, mail, registered mail, or courier, or as approved by the LST (r 9.01(2)). Service by the LSO must be filed electronically (r 9.01(3)). Service of other documents, other than originating documents, is governed by Rule 10.

A proceeding management conference is a tool used to further the management of a case proceeding. In particular, it may be used to schedule a pre-hearing conference or another proceeding management conference, schedule or adjourn a hearing, or give directions on any matter that the parties may raise (r 12.04(1)). These are conducted by a member of the panel (r 12.01(1)) and may be requested by a party at any time, with requests being sent to the LST office (r 12.01(2)(3)). These conferences can occur in person, by telephone, or in writing (r 12.02). Whatever the outcome of a proceeding management conference, the member will write an endorsement on the originating process that identifies what resolutions were made and the next steps, if applicable (r 12.04(2)).

57 "Guide to Conduct Proceedings," *supra* note 39.

Pre-hearing conferences enable "the just and most expeditious disposition of a proceeding" (r 22.01(1)) and are typically presided over by one panel member (r 22.03). The panel member facilitates this meeting with the parties by discussing any of the following:

(a) the identification, limitation, or simplification of the issues in the proceeding;
(b) the identification and limitation of evidence and witnesses;
(c) the possibility of settlement of any or all of the issues in the proceeding;
(d) the possibility of the parties entering into an agreed statement of facts with respect to all or part of the facts in issue in the proceeding; and
(e) directions to be given to the parties with respect to the conduct of the proceeding or a motion in the proceeding (r 22.01(2)).

Pre-hearing conferences will be mandated where one party estimates the hearing will last beyond two days, a panel or member directs one to be held, or all parties agree to one (r 22.02). These conferences are most often held in person, but may be held over the telephone with the consent of the parties. A memoranda must be prepared by the parties before the pre-hearing conference, outlining the party's statement of facts and position on the issues (r 22.07(1)). The panelist presiding over the conference must receive the LSO's memorandum at least seven days before, and the licensee's memorandum at least two days before the pre-hearing conference (r 22.07(3)). The outcome of the conference, including any agreements reached and directions to the parties, must be endorsed on the originating process and is binding on the parties (r 22.09).

Hearing Process: Hearing Division

Applications are determined following a hearing at the hearing division.[58] According to the Hearing Division Rules of Practice and Procedure, hearings may be scheduled either by an LST member or the LST office (r 11.01(1)). This practical requirement allows members to schedule hearings in the context of other meetings with the parties (i.e., pre-hearing conferences or motion appearances). It is a practicality that allows for ease of scheduling when the parties can have a face-to-face discussion over available dates. A notice of hearing for a **hearing on the merits** will be sent to all parties and participants

hearing on the merits proceedings in which the panel will entertain the final question of law or fact to be determined and conclude the matter by providing a decision that will dispose of the legal issue up for determination; not an interim proceeding

58 LSA, s 49.23(1).

involved in either oral or electronic hearings (rr 11.02(1)-(3)). All hearings are usually held at one central hearing location, which is the LST in Toronto (r 17.01(1)); however, they can be held elsewhere (rr 17.01(2)-(5)).

Adjournment requests at the hearing division are governed by Rule 14 and a practice direction.[59] The practice direction does not replace the rule but offers additional guidance to parties.[60] In the interests of a "just and expeditious" proceeding, the LST is keen to avoid adjournments where possible:

> When hearing dates have been scheduled, adjournments can interfere with access to justice, waste resources and cause delay and cost to all parties and the Tribunal. As a result parties should use pre-hearing preparation to avoid unnecessary adjournments.[61]

Before the hearing date, adjournment requests must be made to a member at the proceedings management conference at least ten days before the hearing, or on a motion to the panel if a proceedings management cannot be scheduled, or on request to the LST office with the consent of all parties after the request has been heard on a motion.[62] A request can be made directly to the LST office to have an adjournment request placed on the agenda for the next scheduled proceedings management conference.[63] It is preferred that adjournment requests be made as soon as possible and before the hearing date to avoid wasting tribunal resources,[64] such as tribunal scheduling time, the sending of notices of hearing, and member appearances at the tribunal. The closer the request is made to the hearing date, the less likely it is to be granted. The practice direction offers insight into when adjournment requests may not be granted:

> Adjournments will not ordinarily be granted due to late retention of counsel and/or the unavailability of such counsel for the scheduled hearing dates or on the grounds that parties wish to engage in settlement discussions. Settlement discussions are encouraged, but should be part of the prehearing preparation process.[65]

---

59 Law Society Tribunal, "Practice Direction Adjournment Requests to Hearing Division" (2017), online: <https://lawsocietytribunal.ca/Document%20Resources/Practice_Direction_on_Adjournments_(E)_FINAL-s.pdf>.

60 *Ibid.*

61 *Ibid* at 1.

62 *Supra* note 25, rr 14.01(1)(a)-(c).

63 *Supra* note 60 at 1.

64 *Ibid* at 2.

65 *Ibid* at 2.

Of course, adjournment requests can be made on the day of the hearing where necessary and should be requested by way of a motion to the panel.[66] On-the-day requests should be made only in exceptional circumstances, such as the illness of a party.[67] Adjournments may be granted with consideration of the following:

(a) prejudice to a person;
(b) the timing of the request or motion for the adjournment;
(c) the number of prior requests and motions for an adjournment;
(d) the number of adjournments already granted;
(e) prior directions or orders with respect to the scheduling of future hearings;
(f) the public interest;
(g) the costs of an adjournment;
(h) the availability of witnesses;
(i) the efforts made to avoid the adjournment;
(j) the requirement for a fair hearing; and
(k) any other relevant factor.[68]

As identified above in the Hearing Division Rules of Practice and Procedure, hearings may be oral, electronic (telephone or other electronic means) (r 16.02(4)), or written. The default format for a proceeding is oral (r 16.01(1)). If a motion is brought to have a hearing, or part of a hearing, held electronically (r 16.02(2)), the motion will be submitted in writing (r 16.03(1)1), and the LST will consider a number of factors in coming to a decision, including whether the matter is suitable to an electronic format, what evidence is being called, convenience, efficiency, fairness, and accessibility (r 16.02(3)). Motions on consent or requesting adjournment may be made electronically or in written form (rr 16.02(1), 16.03(2)).

All hearings at the LST are open to the public; however, a party may bring a motion requesting that the hearing be closed (rr 18.01, 18.02).

Disclosure by the LSO must be given to the opposing party at least ten days before the hearing (r 19.01(1)). In most proceedings, disclosure by the licensee (or the subject of the matter) is also due at least ten days before the hearing (r 19.01(2)). Disclosure deadlines pertaining to expert witness evidence are 30 and 90 days before the hearing (r 19.02(1)). Any evidence that is not disclosed in the time frames outlined in the rules is barred from being used as evidence in the proceedings, unless leave is granted by the panel (r 19.03). Admissions of truth about a fact or document may be requested by one party of another no later than 30 days before the hearing, and the request must be made using Form 20A (r 20.02(1)(2)).

---

66 *Supra* note 25, r 14.03.

67 *Supra* note 60 at 2.

68 *Supra* note 25, r 14.03.

Evidence before the hearing division is governed by Rule 24 and includes topics such as the exclusion of witnesses from a hearing (r 24.01), evidence accepted by affidavit (r 24.03), admissibility of evidence from a former proceeding (r 24.05), judicial knowledge of facts or other general knowledge (r 24.09), the tendering of documentary evidence (r 24.11), and summons of a witness (r 24.13). Rule 24.02 states that, subject to the content in these rules, the rules of evidence applicable to civil proceedings apply at the LST.

Decisions, Reconsiderations, and Appeals

The hearing division has authority to order costs pursuant to the LSA section 49.28. According to the Hearing Division Rules of Practice and Procedure, costs against the LSO may only be awarded in the case of an unwarranted proceeding for "licensing, conduct, capacity, competence or non-compliance," or by cause of the LSO in the case of, for example, undue delay (r 25.01(1)). Costs against a licensee (or the subject of the proceeding) may be awarded because of the party, as in the case of undue delay, or "where a determination adverse to the subject of the proceeding was made" (r 25.01(2)). In section 49.28, the LSA specifies:

> (2) Costs awarded to the Society under subsection (1) may include,
>
> (a) expenses incurred by the Society in providing facilities or services for the purposes of the proceeding; and
>
> (b) expenses incurred by the Society in any audit, investigation, review, search or seizure that is related to the proceeding.

An example of a cost order under subsection (2)(a) may include reasonable fees for having to hold the hearing off-site, at a location requested by the other party.

A decision or an order by the hearing division is effective on the date it is made and will be endorsed on the originating process or on a piece of paper attached to it.[69] Written reasons are required for any decision or order in a capacity proceeding or for an oral order when a request for written reasons has been made immediately after the order is made or within 60 days of the order being delivered.[70] A notice of decision is sent to each party (or representative) in accordance with Rule 26.06.

An appeal to the appeal division[71] is commenced by filing a notice of appeal on the established form along with an information sheet within 30 days of the order being received by the appellant (or deemed to have been received) and serving the opposing party, according to Rule 3.1 of the Appeal Division Rules

69 *Supra* note 25, rr 26.01(1), (2), 26.02(4), (5)(a).

70 *Ibid*, r 26.04.

71 LSA, s 49.32.

of Practice and Procedure. Along with the notice of appeal, the appellant must include a certificate of the reporting service indicating that copies of the proceeding's transcript have been ordered (r 4.1(1)).

Cross-appeals are allowed in accordance with Rule 5.1 and are commenced by filing and serving a notice of cross-appeal (r 5.1(2)). Cross-appeal materials by the respondent to the cross-appeal (original appellant) are due no later than 14 days before the hearing of the appeal (r 6.6). The appellant is required to file a book of materials known as the appellant's appeal book, which must contain consecutively numbered pages and tabs identifying the materials as outlined in Rule 6.1(1) and be bound front and back in blue card stock (r 6.1(3)). The appellant is required to submit a factum (r 6.2(1)) of no more than 30 pages (r 6.2(4)), also bound front and back in blue card stock (r 6.2(5)), matching the specifications for paper and font size found in Rule 6.2(6). A book of authorities must also be submitted (r 6.3).

The LST office may refuse any of the foregoing appellant requirements for failure to comply with the rules, unless it is in the interests of justice to vary the rules accordingly (r 6.5). The appeal division rules require that this process includes the appellant serving the respondent with a copy of the appeal book, factum, book of authorities, and transcript, and filing the same along with proof of service to the LST (the number of copies depends on the number of panel members) (r 7.1(1)). A certificate of perfection must also be filed with the LST (r 7.1(3)). The above must be accomplished no later than 60 days after the appellant is deemed to have received the hearing division order or have received the transcript (r 7.1(4)).

The respondent is also required to file a respondent's appeal book (r 8.1), factum (r 8.2), and book of authorities (r 8.4), with similar specifications as set out in the appellant's requirements, except bound front and back with green card stock (rr 8.1(3), 8.2(5), 8.4(3)). When there is no cross-appeal, the respondent must serve and file materials no later than 14 days before the appeal hearing (r 8.6(1)). Where a cross-appeal has commenced, the respondent must serve and file materials no later than 30 days after receiving the appellant's materials (r 8.6(2)). Both the appellant and the respondent are required to prepare a compendium, referring to portions of transcript or other documents from the appeal book that will be referred to in the oral argument (r 9). The LST office will schedule the hearing date for the appeal, and if a cross-appeal has been commenced, both will be heard on the same day (r 11.1).

Just as the hearing division is concerned with case management, so too is the appeal division. Hence, for matters on appeal, an appeal management

cross-appeal a new appeal launched by the original respondent to an application against the original applicant; the original respondent becomes the appellant in the cross-appeal, and the original applicant or appellant becomes the respondent for the purposes of the cross-appeal only

conference is mandated (r 12). This conference will be managed by a panel member and may deal with such matters as scheduling another conference, scheduling or adjourning an appeal or motion, or providing further direction as needed for the appeal or motion (r 12.2(1)). The results will be endorsed on the appellant's appeal book or notice of appeal (r 12.2(2)).

A notice of motion is required for the introduction of fresh evidence before the appeal division (r 14.1(1)(2)), and the motion should be heard on the day of the appeal hearing (r 14.1(5)). The parties will be expected to proceed with the appeal hearing regardless of the motion's outcome (r 14.1(6)). The foregoing requirements are removed, however, where both the appellant and respondent agree to the introduction of the fresh evidence, making the only requirement that of including such evidence in their respective appeal materials and ensuring that it is identified as evidence that was not before the hearing division (r 14.2).

At the hearing for the appeal, the time allotted for both the appellant's and respondent's oral arguments, along with their respective replies, is set out by the chair or vice-chair (r 15.1). After the appeal has been determined, written reasons are required by the panel for its decision to dismiss or allow the appeal (r 16.1(1)(a)). Written reasons will also be required for any other decision if a party requests them orally at the time the decision is made or in writing within 60 days of the decision being made (rr 16.1(1)(b), 16.2).

Appeals of summary orders related to non-payment of fees, failure to file a report with the LSO or comply with indemnity requirements, revocation of a licence for any of the foregoing matters, or suspension for incomplete professional development are governed by appeal division Rule 17 (r 17.1(1)).

The appeal division has the power to:

> (a) make any order or decision that ought to or could have been made by the Hearing Division or person who made the order or decision appealed from;
>
> (b) order a new hearing before the Hearing Division, in the case of an appeal from a decision or order of the Hearing Division; or
>
> (c) dismiss the appeal.[72]

Final decisions and orders from the appeal division are appealable to Divisional Court and are governed by sections 49.38 to 49.41 of the LSA.

72 LSA, s 49.35(2).

Case Law

Law Society of Upper Canada v Siziba, 2017 ONLSTH 59 (CanLII)

The LSO brought a motion for an interlocutory order to suspend the licence of Siziba, after he was charged with sexual assault. The alleged sexual assault took place while Siziba was acting in the role of an Uber driver. Siziba was licensed in 2015 and worked at his son's law firm, mostly in the role of a process server. A portion of the LST's reasons were redacted pursuant to an Ontario Court of Justice publication ban. The motion was brought under section 49.27 of the LSA. The LSO must show there are reasonable grounds of a significant risk to the public to succeed with the motion to grant a license suspension. The LST panel found that in the circumstances of this case (Siziba's continued employment under the supervision of his son, undertaking not to meet alone with clients, etc.) there was not a significant risk to the public or the administration of justice, and that being charged with a criminal offence alone was not sufficient to justify an interlocutory suspension. The motion was dismissed.

Law Society of Upper Canada v Davidovic, 2017 ONLSTH 47 (CanLII)

Davidovic applied for a licence to practise law in Ontario. He was a licensed lawyer in Florida before being convicted as a sex offender and spending two years in prison. His application to be licensed was brought before the LST on the basis of whether he had "good character" to qualify as a licensee, as required by section 27(2) of the LSA. Ultimately, the LST panel allowed Davidovic's application, though there was a dissenting opinion. The majority found that the applicant's conduct was "very serious" but that a long time had expired since his misconduct, that he had shown remorse, and that he had rehabilitated his good character. Thus, he passed the "good character" test and his application for licensing was accepted.

Law Society of Upper Canada v Nicolas Xynnis, 2014 ONLSAP 9 (CanLII)

This decision was before the appeal panel, on appeal from a decision of the hearing division by the LSO. The hearing division ordered a publication ban on medical evidence used by Xynnis in defending against a professional misconduct application. There was an agreed statement of facts by the parties at the hearing but different positions argued regarding an appropriate penalty. The penalty included ongoing counselling, and Xynnis, through a telephone conference call, raised the possibility of him bringing a motion for a publication ban. The adjudicator accepted arguments from both sides immediately about a publication ban, dismissing the need for a motion to determine the matter. The adjudicator allowed for certain portions of the order to be redacted, on the basis of protection for Xynnis's career. The LST appeal division reversed the decision of the hearing panel and lifted the publication ban, taking into consideration the "open court" principle and the need for transparency, the importance of written reasons, and a balancing of factors, including risks to the administration of justice.

KEY LEGISLATION

Modernizing Regulation of the Legal Profession Act, 2013, SO 2013, c 17—Bill 111

Law Society Act

Hearings Before the Hearing and Appeal Divisions, O Reg 167/07

Statutory Powers Procedure Act

Solicitors Act

KEY TERMS

benchers, 256
cross-appeal, 271
hearing on the merits, 267
interlocutory orders, 259
intervenors, 261

REVIEW QUESTIONS

1. Name the legislation that (1) creates the LST and (2) empowers the LST.
2. What is a bencher?
3. What is the Adjudicator Code of Conduct and to whom does it apply?
4. Is the LST independent from the LSO?
5. Is non-compliance with a procedural requirement in the rules grounds for dismissal?
6. What steps are required to initiate a conduct proceeding before the hearing division?
7. Who may initiate a proceeding before the LST?
8. The following are all proceedings that occur at the LST. Which two from the list can be initiated by a licensee?
   a. conduct
   b. capacity
   c. competence
   d. non-compliance
   e. licensing
   f. restoration
   g. retired judge appearing as counsel
   h. working with or employing unauthorized persons
   i. reinstatement
   j. terms dispute
9. What is a proceedings management conference, and how does it differ from a pre-hearing conference?
10. Identify one disclosure requirement with a 30-day limitation period.

SCENARIOS

As a successful paralegal, you have made your career out of appearing regularly before the LST. Consider the following scenarios, and provide answers with the authorities that you rely upon.

1. Razy Marino is a paralegal whose licence is subject to suspension. The LSO has brought a motion for an interlocutory injunction before the hearing division. You want to obtain an adjournment for your client, Marino, as you were retained two weeks ago to represent him, and the hearing is scheduled next week. How do you go about requesting an adjournment?
2. Assuming that Marino's case has now been heard before the hearing division and a decision has been rendered upholding Marino's suspension, with which your client disagrees, what are your next steps?
3. What material must you serve and file to support your answer to question 2?

CHAPTER 12

Canadian Human Rights Tribunal

Overview and History 278

Legislation and Regulations 280

Initiating an Application 283

Mediation/Mediation-Adjudication 284

The Hearing Process 286

Decision, Reconsideration, and Appeals 287

Case Law 288

Key Terms 292

Review Questions 292

Scenario 293

Overview and History

The Canadian Human Rights Tribunal (CHRT) was created in 1985 under the *Canadian Human Rights Act* (CHRA).[1] It hears human rights complaints that are filed with the Canadian Human Rights Commission (CHRC) against federally regulated employers, agencies, and service providers. Examples of these complaints would include discriminatory practices in:

- federal government departments, agencies, and Crown corporations, including the Canadian Forces and the RCMP,
- chartered banks,
- airlines,
- television and radio stations,
- interprovincial communications and telephone companies,
- interprovincial transportation companies, and
- Indigenous governments and some other Indigenous organizations.[2]

Before the creation of the CHRA, Canada's long history of restrictive and racist policies had an adverse effect on vulnerable and marginalized populations. In 1882, then prime minister Sir John A Macdonald said in Parliament that the Chinese were "a semi-barbaric inferior race and machines with whom Canadians could not compete." They were needed to build the railways in Canada, however, so a head tax was introduced in 1885 with the passing of the *Chinese Immigration Act: An Act to Restrict and Regulate Chinese Immigration into Canada.*[3] Initially, the head tax was set at $50 per person, and the limit on immigration stipulated only one Chinese immigrant for every 50 tons of a ship's weight. Contrast this $50 head tax with a wage of $1 per day that was being paid to Chinese immigrants. In 1900, the head tax was increased to $100, and by 1903 the head tax was increased to $500.[4] Chinese immigrants were forbidden from bringing their wives with them to Canada, and later, when Chinese immigrants began to establish businesses, it was illegal for them to hire white women.

The *Dominion Elections Act, 1920*[5] excluded visible minorities, Indigenous peoples, and women from having the right to vote in federal elections. In 1928,

1 RSC, 1985, c H-6.

2 Canadian Human Rights Tribunal, "Welcome to the Canadian Human Rights Tribunal" (2016), online: <http://www.chrt-tcdp.gc.ca/index-en.html>.

3 1885, c 71 (2004), online: Canadian Asian Law Centre <http://www.asian.ca/law/cia1885.htm>.

4 Canadian Museum of Immigration at Pier 21, "The Chinese Immigration Act, 1885 (Plus Amendments: 1887, 1892, 1900, 1903)" (2004), online: <https://pier21.ca/research/immigration-history/the-chinese-immigration-act-1885>.

5 See Historica, Expanding the Franchise: The Dominion Elections Act, 1920," online: <http://www.histori.ca/voices/page.do?pageID=311>; and Elections Canada, "The Dominion Elections Act" (October 2016), <http://www.elections.ca/content.aspx?section=res&dir=his&document=chap3&lang=e#a31>.

the Supreme Court of Canada gave white women the right to vote by determining that they were in fact "persons." Japanese Canadians were given the right to vote in 1948 when section 14(2)(i) of the *Dominion Elections Act* was repealed. A special prohibition on voting rights for Japanese Canadians had been in place because of the Second World War.

From 1950 onward, Canada began to make legislative strides toward fairness and equality. In 1953, the *Fair Employment Practices Act*[6] attempted to combat discrimination in the civil service. In 1956, the *Female Employees Equal Pay Act*[7] was introduced to provide provisions for equal pay for equal work in the interests of gender equality. The *Canadian Bill of Rights* (CBR)[8] was introduced in 1960. It was a good start to codifying general principles of human rights, but it was limited in its scope and effectiveness. Also in 1960, Indigenous Canadians were offered the right to vote, and they were no longer required to give up treaty rights and to renounce their status under the *Act to Amend and Consolidate the Laws Respecting Indians*[9] (the *Indian Act*) just so they could vote.

In 1977, the CHRA was created, which also created the CHRC. The Commission's role was to administer this new law and to ensure compliance in federally regulated entities.

On April 17, 1982, the *Canadian Charter of Rights and Freedoms* (the Charter)[10] was created and is now established as a reflection of what we deem to be Canadian values. The Charter is Canada's most important document in upholding rights, freedoms, and values in Canadian society. In 1986, Canada introduced the *Employment Equity Act* (EEA),[11] which ensures access and opportunity for marginalized and disenfranchised groups to federally regulated employers (but not the federal public service).

Since the Charter and EEA, most changes to human rights interpretation has been achieved through case law. Cases like *Stinchcombe* clarified evidence disclosure rights, and, in 1995, three cases (*Miron v Trudel*, *Egan v Canada*, and *Thibaudeau v Canada*)[12] changed our views and definition of the term *spouse*.

---

6 SC 1952-53, c 19. Ontario's act was the *Fair Employment Practices Act, 1951*, SO 1951, c 24.

7 SC 1956, c 38. See also Department of Sociology, University of Alberta, "Canada's Human Rights History: Statutes" (2018), online: <https://historyofrights.ca/wp-content/uploads/statutes/CN_Female_Em.pdf>.

8 SC 1960, c 44.

9 SC 1876, c 18. Department of Canadian and World Studies, Waterdown District High School, "The Indian Act" (2018), online: <http://www.tidridge.com/uploads/3/8/4/1/3841927/1876indianact.pdf>.

10 Part I of the *Constitution Act, 1982*, being Schedule B to the *Canada Act 1982* (UK), 1982, c 11.

11 SC 1995, c 44.

12 *R v Stinchcombe*, [1991] 3 SCR 326, 1991 CanLII 45; *Miron v Trudel*, [1995] 2 SCR 418, 1995 CanLII 97; *Egan v Canada*, [1995] 2 SCR 513, 1995 CanLII 98; *Thibaudeau v Canada*, [1995] 2 SCR 627, 1995 CanLII 99.

Through advocacy, the CHRA was amended in 1996 to include sexual orientation as a discriminatory ground. In May 2017, genetic characteristics was added as a discriminatory ground as a result of the passing of the *Genetic Non-Discrimination Act*,[13] and, in June 2017, gender identity and gender expression were added as well. Human rights legislation will continue to evolve and expand to meet new societal norms.

Legislation and Regulations

The CHRA is the enabling legislation for the CHRT. In addition to the Act, the EEA enables the Employment Equity Tribunal, which is a subset of the CHRT. Before the CHRA came into force, Canada signed to the UN's Universal Declaration on Human Rights, and this important document influenced how the CHRA came into existence. Although the CHRA and the EEA are the enabling legislation for the CHRT, two other key pieces of legislation, the Charter and its predecessor, the CBR, also greatly influenced and shaped federal human rights policy and procedure in Canada.

The CHRA outlines 13 grounds on which discrimination is prohibited in federally regulated entities:

- race,
- national or ethnic origin,
- colour,
- religion,
- age,
- sex (includes pregnancy or childbirth),
- marital status,
- family status,
- sexual orientation,
- gender identity or expression (added June 15, 2017),
- genetic characteristics (added May 4, 2017)
- disability (includes mental or physical disability, disfigurement, and dependence on alcohol or a drug), and
- conviction for an offence for which a pardon has been granted or in respect of which a record suspension has been ordered.[14]

---

13 SC 2017, c 3.

14 Canadian Human Rights Tribunal, "A Guide to Understanding the Canadian Human Rights Tribunal" (2016), online: <http://chrt-tcdp.gc.ca/documents/guide-eng.pdf>.

Additionally, the CHRA also prohibits discriminating against someone by:

- Denying or treating someone unfavourably when offering goods, services, facilities, or accommodation (see s. 5 of the Act).
- Denying or treating someone unfavourably when offering occupancy or accommodation in commercial or residential premises (see s. 6 of the Act).
- Refusing to employ or continue to employ someone (see s. 7(a) of the Act).
- Treating someone unfavourably in the workplace (see s. 7(b) of the Act).
- Using a job application form that expresses or implies any limitation, specification or preference (see s. 8(a) of the Act).
- Publishing job advertisements or making inquiries in connection with employment that express or imply any limitation, specification or preference (see s. 8(b) of the Act).
- Excluding, expelling or suspending a member of an employee organization (for example, a trade union) or unfavourably affecting their status or employment opportunities (see s. 9 of the Act).
- Establishing policies or practices, or entering into an agreement, that deprives people of employment opportunities (see s. 10 of the Act).
- Paying men and women differently when they are doing work of the same value in the same establishment (see s. 11 of the Act).
- Publishing or displaying in public any notice, sign, symbol or emblem that expresses, implies or incites discrimination (see s. 12 of the Act).
- Harassing someone, including sexual harassment, in connection with employment or when offering goods, services, facilities or accommodation (see s. 14 of the Act).
- Retaliating against a person who has filed a complaint (see s. 14.1 of the Act).[15]

The CHRA also indicates that some exceptions allow discriminatory practices. If there is a good faith justification to treat someone differentially when providing goods, services, facilities, or accommodation, this is considered a **bona fide** justification (s 15(1)(g)). Additional good faith exceptions include when an employer's discriminatory actions that result from a bona fide requirement to do the job (s 15(1)(a)); when employment is denied because the individual either has not met the minimum age or has exceeded the maximum age related to the job (s 15(1)(b)); and when employees are given special leave or benefits because of pregnancy, birth, or child care (s 15(1)(f)). Section 15(2) further clarifies that the bona fide occupational justification can only be used when it is established that accommodation of the individual would result in undue

bona fide a Latin term that means "good faith." In the context of the CHRT, this term is usually used in relation to exceptions. Actions that are sincere, honest, and without deceit are considered bona fide

15 *Ibid.*

hardship on the employer. If a respondent relies on this justification, they must show that the discriminatory rule or practice was:

- adopted for a purpose that is rationally connected to the performance of the job or function;
- adopted in the honest, sincere belief that it is necessary for the performance of the job or function; and
- reasonably necessary to accomplish the purpose mentioned above, in the sense that accommodating the needs of the complainant would cause the respondent undue hardship.[16]

The EEA was created in 1995 and in turn created the Employment Equity Review Tribunal under the umbrella of the CHRT. It provides guidance to federally regulated employers on creating an employment equity plan and helping employers to achieve equity and equal representation in the workforce. Section 5 of the EEA states it is the duty of every employer to:

- identify and eliminate employment barriers against persons in designated groups that result from the employer's employment systems, policies and practices that are not authorized by law; and
- institute such positive policies and practices and making such reasonable accommodations as will ensure that persons in designated groups achieve a degree of representation in each occupational group in the employer's workforce that reflects their representation in
  (i) the Canadian workforce, or
  (ii) those segments of the Canadian workforce that are identifiable by qualification, eligibility or geography and from which the employer may reasonably be expected to draw employees.

In addition to both acts, the tribunal also has a series of guidelines and regulations related to age, equal wages, benefits, and immigration investigations:

- Age Guidelines, SI/78-165;
- Canadian Human Rights Benefit Regulations, SOR/80-68;
- Canadian Human Rights Commission, By-law No 3, SOR/78-223;
- Customs and Excise Human Rights Investigation Regulations, SOR/83-196;
- Equal Wages Guidelines, 1986, SOR/86-1082;
- Human Rights Tribunal Appeal Regulations, SOR/80-394;
- Immigration Investigation Regulations, SOR/80-686; and
- Protection of Personal Information Regulations, SOR/78-145.

16 CHRA, s 15(2).

The EEA has an accompanying regulation to further clarify procedure[17] and has regulations particular to procedure relating to the Canadian Armed Forces, the RCMP, and the Canadian Security Intelligence Service.

The CHRT uses Rules of Procedure guides for the CHRT and the EERT, and practice notes to give practitioners guidance on how to effectively practise before the tribunal. Of particular importance are practice note 2, which discusses the obligations and responsibilities of non-lawyer representatives who are providing representation before the tribunal, and practice note 3, which discusses the tribunal's pre-hearing case management process.

Initiating an Application

To commence a proceeding before the CHRT, a complaint has to be made to the CHRC. The CHRC is a separate and independent body from the tribunal. Under the CHRA, the role of the commission is to receive the complaint, attempt to settle the matter, and conduct an investigation if warranted. If the commission finds that the complaint has merit, it is then referred to the tribunal for a hearing. The role of the tribunal is to hear the case, make a finding with respect to discrimination, and determine appropriate remedies.

A complaint can be filed online, via mail, or by phone. Online, the commission has a series of questions to be answered to determine if the CHRT has jurisdiction over the matter. Complaints must be started within 12 months of the discriminatory incident. There is no fee to apply, which ensures accessibility for all who face discrimination. The commission will then contact the complainant within 20 days to discuss the matter, and if the complaint is accepted, a copy of the complaint is sent to the respondent. The commission will attempt to resolve the matter between the parties. It may also choose to investigate. As noted, if the complaint is deemed warranted, the matter is referred to the tribunal.

The tribunal will send an initial letter offering a one-day evaluative mediation within eight weeks. The parties have two weeks to respond to this letter. If mediation is accepted, both parties will be required to file mediation briefs three weeks before the mediation date. It is imperative that the mediation brief outlines the arguments regarding remedies being sought and quantifies monetary compensation. Failure to do so may result in the mediation being cancelled.

If the parties decline mediation, in their response to the initial letter, they must provide their address, phone number, email address, and fax number, along with their language of preference (English or French) and dates of availability. They must also identify preliminary issues and any accommodation or special needs concerns.

17 Employment Equity Regulations, SOR/96-470.

The tribunal will then respond with a confirmation letter indicating dates for reciprocal disclosure (e.g., statement of particulars, list of evidence, and list of witnesses) and the date for the first case management conference call. The file is then sent to the tribunal within three weeks. The case management conference call prepares parties for the hearing and attempts to resolve at least some of the issues to streamline the case.

Mediation/Mediation-Adjudication

Mediation in CHRT matters is common and encouraged. Parties are invited to participate in **evaluative mediation** at the time of referral to the tribunal, and the parties are free to attempt to settle matters even during their hearing, if they so choose. Mediations are offered in locations that are convenient and accessible to the parties, can be conducted on the phone, if the parties want, and are typically allocated one day for resolution. Mediation is conducted by members (also called adjudicators) of the CHRT.

Parties who decide to try mediation are required to sign the tribunal's mediation agreement, which outlines that the discussions are confidential regardless of outcome and ensures that the parties understand that all information exchanged in the mediation process is confidential and not to be used at a hearing (if parties are unable to settle). Typically, the member of the CHRT who is assigned to mediate the case is not the same member who will conduct a hearing if the mediation is unsuccessful.

Parties who opt to try mediation are required to file a mediation brief with the tribunal.

A mediation brief is confidential, cannot be used as evidence in a hearing, and does not form part of the tribunal's official record. It helps the mediator to identify issues and possible areas of convergence and facilitates effective settlement discussions. For applicants, the **mediation brief** should include a statement of facts, an outline of the remedies being sought, and any supporting documentation.[18] For respondents, a mediation brief should include a statement of facts, the respondent's submissions regarding legal issues, and remedies being sought by the complainant.

The mediator will facilitate the settlement discussions by either keeping the parties in the same room or going back and forth between parties held in separate rooms, or both. This depends on the mediator's style and skill, but it is

evaluative mediation a mediation in which the mediator provides their opinion and assessment of the merits of the case

mediation brief a bound book of documents filed in advance of a mediation, which may include things such as the facts, evidence, case law, legal principles, assessment of costs or damages, etc.

18 *Supra* note 14, part 3.5(A).

not uncommon to see a combination of both. Another common practice is for the mediator to provide an opinion or analysis of the matter, which is why the tribunal uses the term evaluative mediation. Given the skill and expertise of the tribunal, members will often provide their opinion and thoughts regarding the merits of the case so that parties have a realistic view of outcomes and possible remedies.

To negotiate effectively, all parties at the mediation should have the authority to settle. Many firms send a junior lawyer or paralegal who has instructions to negotiate only within certain parameters. If the other party's parameters are not congruent to what you are seeking or have the authority to seek (especially if what you are seeking is supported by case law), it would be best to adjourn the matter rather than enter into futile discussions with someone who cannot authorize a potential settlement. If the commission is participating in the hearing, it will also have a representative at the mediation. That representative is there to protect the public interest and does not represent the complainant. If the commission is not participating in the hearing, it will send a mediation practitioner to assist with the process and discussions.

If the parties reach a successful settlement, all parties are required to sign the agreement. Any unrepresented parties are given seven days to contemplate the settlement and seek legal advice. The agreement is deemed accepted after seven days. After the settlement is perfected, the agreement is then sent to the commission for approval.[19] The approval process takes four to six weeks. Once the commission accepts it, it informs the tribunal that the matter has been withdrawn.

If mediation is unsuccessful, the matter continues to the hearing stage; however, the parties are informed of their right to seek further mediation at any time in the process up until the end of the hearing. Even unsuccessful mediations can be useful if the parties are able to identify areas where they agree and obtain some preliminary resolution in those areas.

Sometimes, the parties agree that the member assigned to the mediation will also conduct the hearing if mediation is unsuccessful. This is known as **mediation-adjudication (med-adj)**. When the decision is made to participate in med-adj, the tribunal will ask the parties to sign a special consent, which is separate from the general consent form, to ensure that parties are aware of the inherent issues that arise from the med-adj process. These concerns include the fact that, if mediation was unsuccessful, the parties may have disclosed privileged and confidential issues with the member. Adjudicators are trained to be unbiased and fair regardless of the information they may hear in a

mediation-adjudication (med-adj) an option available at the CHRT to resolve the complaint in which the member who conducts the mediation would hear and adjudicate the matter if mediation was unsuccessful

19 CHRA, s 48.

mediation. Having the mediator become the adjudicator means that you have a decision-maker who has a strong understanding of the case and can make a sounder decision for the parties.

The Hearing Process

Hearings before the CHRT are held from 9:30 a.m. to 5:00 p.m. and can last as long as necessary to conduct the hearing. This depends on how complex the case is and the number of witnesses each party calls to substantiate or defend a claim. On average, a hearing before the CHRT lasts about five days and can take place in either a federal courthouse or in another location that minimizes travel costs for the parties and witnesses. It is common for hearings to be held in hotels and conference centres.

In addition to the member (in some cases there are three members rather than one), applicant, respondent, and their respective legal representatives, a typical hearing before the CHRT would also include a registry officer, a lawyer for the commission, and witnesses that the parties will call. Hearings before the CHRT are open to the public, so if you feel that your client's matter should be closed, you have to request confidentiality or an *in camera* hearing pursuant to section 52(1) of the CHRA.

When you arrive, the registry officer will ask you to provide your name, your party's name and address, and the names of witnesses that will be called to testify on a record of appearance. You must also indicate if the witnesses will be swearing or affirming their testimony so that the registry officer can ensure that a holy book is available when needed.

The registry officer will then call the hearing to order by introducing the member and asking the parties to introduce themselves. Typically, the complainant goes first, followed by the commission, if it has opted to participate in the hearing, the respondent, and any intervenors. The parties are then asked to give opening statements in the same order. You can choose not to provide an opening statement or to give your opening statement when it is your turn to advance your case.

After opening statements are complete, the parties will then present their case by calling witnesses in the same order noted previously. For each witness, each party has a chance to ask questions either by way of direct examination, cross-examination, or re-examination (reply). Introduce your evidence through witness testimony, including evidence in support of the remedies you are seeking. It is through witnesses that you submit evidence to support or refute claims. The evidence is what helps the adjudicator determine the facts of the case and ultimately find in your favour. If a party is unrepresented, it is common to see him or her provide evidence and testimony from the witness box without being questioned, rather than what would typically be seen in direct examination with legal representatives. Also remember that re-examination is only allowed to address issues that have arisen through cross-examination testimony.

After the respondent, who is generally last to present evidence, completes his or her case, the commission and the complainant can be given an opportunity to provide reply submissions. You must ask the member for permission to offer reply submissions. Like re-examination, reply evidence and testimony can only address matters that have come up as a result of the respondent arguing their case.

Following reply, each party is provided with an opportunity to provide final arguments (closing submissions) to persuade the board with regard to findings of fact, based on the evidence provided during the hearing. This also is the time when you provide submissions, in a **Book of Authorities**, regarding the applicable sections of the CHRA and case law to support your claim. It is best to cite decisions from the Federal Court, Federal Court of Appeal, or the Supreme Court, as these decisions are binding on the tribunal. Complainants and the Commission are also expected to provide submissions regarding remedies.

Decision, Reconsideration, and Appeals

Following the hearing, the vice-chair will issue a decision. Most cases before the CHRT are reserved to allow an adjudicator time to write reasons for the decision. This normally takes three to four months from the date of hearing. More complex matters can take longer. The decision will outline the reasons for the determination that the complaint was either substantiated or unsubstantiated. If the decision is in favour of the applicant, the tribunal has the authority to issue remedies that are provided for in the CHRA. Remedies are designed to address the harm that was caused and provide compensation for discrimination that the applicant faced. Remedy orders can include the following:

- Cease the discriminatory practice and take measures to prevent the practice from occurring in the future (see s 53(2)(a) of the CHRA);
- Make available to the victim the rights, opportunities, or privileges that were denied (see s 53(2)(b) of the CHRA);
- Compensate the victim for any lost wages as a result of the discrimination (see s 53(2)(c) of the CHRA);
- Compensate the victim for the additional costs of obtaining alternative goods, services, facilities, or accommodation as a result of the discrimination (see s 53(2)(d) of the CHRA);

Book of Authorities a bound book of case law and/or references to legislation that you will be using to support your client's case in your closing at the hearing before the CHRT

- Compensate the victim up to $20,000 for any pain and suffering experienced as a result of the discrimination (see s 53(2)(e) of the CHRA);
- Compensate the victim up to $20,000 if the discrimination was wilful or reckless (see s 53(3) of the CHRA); and
- Award interest on an order to pay financial compensation (see s 53(4) of the CHRA).[20]

The CHRT cannot award legal expenses or costs to successful complainants. This was determined in 2011 by the Supreme Court of Canada in *Canada (Canadian Human Rights Commission) v Canada (Attorney General).*[21] The complainant, Donna Mowat, had filed a complaint with the commission alleging sex discrimination against the Canadian Forces. She was successful at the tribunal and was awarded $4,000 for pain and suffering and an additional $47,000 for legal costs. The Federal Court upheld the costs determination, but the Court of Appeal overturned this decision on the grounds that the tribunal did not have authority or jurisdiction to grant legal costs under the CHRA. The Supreme Court upheld the Court of Appeal finding and made the final determination that the CHRT does not have the authority to award legal costs. The tribunal has the authority to grant compensation for pain and suffering and lost wages but not to compensate successful complainants for the cost of hiring legal representation.

If your client is unhappy with the decision of the tribunal, the matter can be reviewed by the Federal Court. Within 30 days of receipt of the decision (30 days after the date of first communication to the parties), an application for leave and judicial review can be filed with the Federal Court. There is a $50 filing fee. Judicial reviews by the Federal Court are outside a paralegal's scope of practice; your client will either have to be self-represented or retain a lawyer.

Case Law

First Nations Child and Family Caring Society of Canada v Attorney General of Canada (for the Minister of Indian and Northern Affairs Canada), 2016 CHRT 2

In 2007, the Assembly of First Nations and the First Nations Child and Family Caring Society brought a complaint to the CHRC that was referred to the CHRT for a hearing. The basis of the complaint was that child welfare services provided by the federal government to children living on reserves were significantly underfunded when compared to provincial allocations for non-Indigenous communities. It argued that this persistent underfunding was discriminatory under the CHRA and created a crisis situation for First Nations families. As a result, First Nations children were removed from their homes at

20 CHRA, ss 52(2)-(4).

21 2011 SCC 53, [2011] 3 SCR 471.

a disproportionate rate compared with those in non-Indigenous communities, rather than providing support and resources to First Nations communities.

The tribunal ruled that it did not have jurisdiction to hear the matter and dismissed the case. On appeal, the Federal Court of Appeal determined that the tribunal had jurisdiction and sent the matter back to the tribunal for determination. The hearing took place in 2014 and a final decision was rendered in January 2016. The tribunal found that the underfunding of child welfare services to First Nations communities was discriminatory under the CHRA and ordered the government to cease discriminatory practices, immediately reform the funding system, and immediately implement the full meaning and scope of Jordan's Principle.[22]

Jordan's Principle

"Jordan's Principle provides that where a government service is available to all other children, but a jurisdictional dispute regarding services to a First Nations child arises between Canada, a province, a territory, or between government departments, the government department of first contact pays for the service and can seek reimbursement from the other government or department after the child has received the service. It is a child-first principle meant to prevent First Nations children from being denied essential public services or experiencing delays in receiving them."

—Department of Indigenous and Northern Affairs Canada*

* Government of Canada, Department of Indigenous and Northern Affairs Canada, "Definition of Jordan's Principle from the Canadian Human Rights Tribunal" (14 May 2018), online: <https://www.canada.ca/en/indigenous-services-canada/services/jordans-principle/definition-jordans-principle-canadian-human-rights-tribunal.html>.

This important decision sets a precedent that could result in positive changes to the child welfare system for Indigenous families. As of today, however, there has only been a moderate increase in funding that is still not equivalent to provincial or territorial standards, and the orders of the tribunal have not been fully implemented.

22 Government of Canada, Indigenous Services Canada, "Jordan's Principle" (14 May 2018), online: <https://www.canada.ca/en/indigenous-services-canada/services/jordans-principle.html>; Amnesty International, "First Nations Child and Family Caring Society et al v Canada" (20 November 2016), online: <https://www.amnesty.ca/legal-brief/first-nations-child-and-family-caring-society-et-al-v-canada>.

Public Service Alliance of Canada v Canada Post Corp, 2011 SCC 57, [2011] 3 SCR 572

This matter was initiated in 1983 by the Public Service Alliance of Canada, the union that represents clerical employees at Canada Post. The union filed a complaint with the CHRC asserting that clerical staff (mainly women) were not compensated equally to sorting and delivery staff (mainly men). The assertion was that the work was equal and similar in nature and should be compensated at the same level; otherwise, the wage gap was discriminatory. The commission took seven years to investigate the complaint and referred the matter to the tribunal. The evidence from the investigation was so voluminous that it took ten years to complete the hearing process.[23] The tribunal found in favour of the female employees and ordered Canada Post to pay $150,000,000 to the complainants.

Canada Post appealed the matter to the Federal Court where the decision was overturned. After the matter was dismissed at the Federal Court of Appeal, the commission appealed to the Supreme Court of Canada. The Supreme Court unanimously upheld the decision rendered by the tribunal in 2005.

This "2011 Supreme Court decision marked the end of the longest pay-equity dispute in Canadian history,"[24] according to the CHRC.

Canada (Attorney General) v Johnstone, 2013 FC 113

This matter was initially filed with the CHRC in 2004. The complainant, Fiona Johnstone, had been working on a full-time basis at Canada Border Services Agency (CBSA) since 1998. CBSA agents work on a 24-hour rotational shift for a total of 37.5 hours per week. After the birth of her second child, Ms Johnstone requested a change to her work schedule because of difficulties in finding child care that could not be resolved. She and her husband worked for the CBSA on opposite and overlapping shifts, and family was available only on certain days to assist. Since childcare facilities generally operate on a fixed 7 a.m. to 6 p.m. schedule, the couple would need to purchase a bigger home, which they could not afford, to accommodate a live-in nanny.

The CBSA's policy on accommodation relating to family status was discriminatory on its face in that it required full-time employees to become part-time to receive accommodation, and women were disproportionately affected by this policy. Ms Johnstone requested 3-13 hour shifts in order to accommodate her childcare needs because she wanted to remain full-time and maintain her benefits. All requests related to maintaining full-time status were denied. The complaint was initially dismissed by the CHRC (contrary to the recommendation of the CHRC investigator) but was sent back to the commission for

23 Canadian Human Rights Commission, "Annual Report: Equal Pay for Work of Equal Value" (2012), online: <http://www.chrc-ccdp.gc.ca/eng/content/annual-report-2011-page-6>.

24 *Ibid.*

re-determination by the Federal Court.[25] The commission referred the matter to the CHRT, which found in favour of Ms Johnstone. The CBSA applied for leave and judicial review to the Federal Court, and the decision of the tribunal was upheld (with the exception of the monetary award, which was sent back to the tribunal for re-determination). This case is of importance because it provided further clarity on the duty to accommodate for childcare purposes. It also ensured that childcare obligations would be included in the definition of family status and provided further clarity on the definition of a prima facie case.

KEY LEGISLATION

Canadian Human Rights Act
Employment Equity Act
Genetic Non-Discrimination Act
Universal Declaration of Human Rights, United Nations General Assembly in Paris on 10 December 1948, General Assembly resolution 217 A
Canadian Charter of Rights and Freedoms
Canadian Bill of Rights

25 *Johnstone v Canada (Attorney General)*, 2007 FC 36.

KEY TERMS

bona fide, 281
Book of Authorities, 287
evaluative mediation, 284
mediation-adjudication (med-adj), 285
mediation brief, 284

REVIEW QUESTIONS

1. What is the first step required to have a matter referred to the Canadian Human Rights Commission?
2. What are the discriminatory grounds outlined in the *Canadian Human Rights Act*?
3. Who can make a complaint?
4. What is the jurisdiction of the CHRT? What type of matters can the tribunal hear?
5. Can the tribunal award costs to successful applicants?
6. What types of remedies can the tribunal award?
7. What is the role of the Employment Equity Review Tribunal (EERT)?
8. Why is special consent necessary if the parties would like to participate in med-adj?
9. Section 15 of the *Canadian Human Rights Act* provides that there are exceptions to the discriminatory practices. What are they?
10. What should be done if your client is unhappy with the decision of the CHRT?

SCENARIO

Hazel has worked at the Department of Justice for ten years. She was initially hired right out of university as a legal assistant and is now a law clerk. Hazel is one of the more senior law clerks in terms of knowledge and skill, but there is still room for advancement, and she would like to further her career. She has taken numerous professional development courses, has facilitated training sessions for new staff, and is on the social committee in her office. Hazel is also five months pregnant with her first child. She and her spouse are so excited to be expecting as it has been a difficult journey. She disclosed her pregnancy to the lawyer she works for and those who work with her, but her pregnancy is obvious as she is now clearly showing. Everyone seems genuinely happy for her. Hazel has recently applied for a senior law clerk position at work, and she is hopeful and confident in her prospects. She would really like to take on more responsibility at work and also make more money, especially now that she is expecting.

It has now been eight weeks since Hazel applied for the senior law clerk position, interviews have started, and Hazel was not contacted for further consideration. She is also now seven months pregnant. Some colleagues who have been with the department for a much shorter time are under consideration for the position and have had interviews scheduled. Hazel is disappointed and surprised. She approaches HR to inquire about her application and is told that they did not think she was "suitable" for the job. This makes no sense, and Hazel comes to you for legal advice.

What do you tell her? What options does Hazel have?

CHAPTER 13

Social Security Tribunal

Overview and History 296

Legislation and Regulations 300

Application Process 305

Decisions and Appeals 310

Case Law 311

Key Terms 315

Review Questions 315

Scenarios 316

Overview and History

The Social Security Tribunal (SST) was established in 2013 and hears appeals related to three specific federal programs: Employment Insurance (EI), Canada Pension Plan (CPP), and Old Age Security (OAS), as well as related programs, such as Canada Pension Plan Disability (CPP-D) and the Guaranteed Income Supplement (GIS). Its mandate is to "offer fair, impartial and efficient appeal processes"[1] in these areas for Canadians.

The employment insurance scheme in Canada provides temporary financial assistance to Canadians who have lost their jobs, fallen ill, begun caring for a family member, or begun parental leave. For example, regular benefits are available if you have lost your job through no fault of your own. Maternity and parental benefits apply if you are pregnant or off work to care for your new baby, whether biological or adopted. Sick benefits are available if you are unable to work because of an illness. Compassionate care benefits are available if you are off work to care for a very sick relative. Similar benefits are available for parents who are off work to care for a critically ill child. Fishing benefits are available if you are a self-employed fisher who is actively seeking work. If you apply for any of these benefits through Service Canada, you will receive a decision about your application. Typically, this decision will tell you if you qualify for benefits or not. If you disagree with the decision that you received, you can request a reconsideration directly from Service Canada within 30 days of receiving the decision. In fact, to pursue an appeal to the SST, a reconsideration request at this level is a required first step.

The CPP is a federal pension scheme that almost all workers in Canada, outside of Quebec, contribute to and later benefit from in retirement, or possibly in sickness or death. The financial payment that individuals receive is only a portion of what full earnings would be and varies from individual to individual, based on his or her contributions. Contributions are made from earnings throughout your working life. The different types of pensions or benefits available are as follows:

- retirement pension—available as of age 65, earlier (age 60) with decreased entitlement, or later (age 70) with increased entitlement;
- survivor's pension—paid to a surviving spouse upon the death of an individual contributor;
- disability benefits—available for individuals with severe disabilities who are unable to work;
- death benefits—paid to the estate of a contributor upon their death (one-time payment); and
- children's benefits—paid to the children of a disabled or deceased contributor.

1 Social Security Tribunal, "Achievements Report, 2013-2016" (2017) at 3, online: <http://www1.canada.ca/en/sst/rdl/sst-achievements-2013-2016.pdf>.

Any decision about eligibility or the amount of CPP benefit received can be the subject of a reconsideration request. Reconsideration requests must be made within 90 days of receiving the decision. This is the first step in the appeal process to the SST.

OAS is a pension scheme enabled by the federal government and available to those aged 65 or older. To be eligible, applicants must also meet legal status and residency requirements. This means that you have to be either Canadian citizens or permanent residents, or have lived in Canada for 10 years after the age of 18 if currently living in Canada. Applicants who live outside Canada must show that they were a Canadian citizen or permanent resident on the day before they left Canada and resided in Canada for at least 20 years after the age of 18. Additional benefits are attached to the OAS pension: the GIS for low-income seniors; the allowance for spouses ages 60 to 64 of GIS and OAS recipients; and the allowance for the survivor, available for widowers between the ages of 60 of 64.

Decisions about eligibility for OAS may be the subject of a reconsideration request. The reconsideration request must be made within 90 days of the date of the decision. The next step in the process is an appeal to the SST.

The SST's creation amalgamated the work of four other boards that existed before the SST: the Office of Commissioner of Review Tribunals, Board of Referees, Office of the Umpire, and the Pension Appeals Board.

The SST has two divisions: the general division and the appeal division. The general division is further divided into the income security section and the employment insurance section. Be mindful of the distinction between "division" and "section." "Division" refers to the breakdown between the first-level tribunal and the appeal level. "Section" refers to the differentiated parts of the general division. The income security section hears appeals from CPP and OAS matters. The employment insurance section hears appeals from claims for EI benefits. The appeal division hears appeals from both sections of the general division on matters of CPP, OAS, or EI. There is one chairperson for the SST and three vice-chairs, one for the appeal division and one each for the sections of the general division. There are over 80 members across all three divisions, which is a significant increase from the 26 members that the SST commenced with in 2013.[2]

The SST equips its members with plenty of tools to ensure that they are fulfilling their duties, and the mandate of the tribunal, as thoroughly as possible. Upon hiring, the members undergo an intensive training program, followed by a mentorship with an experienced member and ongoing support from legal services. In addition, members participate in regular conference calls and meetings with the vice-chairs to discuss legal and operational matters, as well as best practices. Annually, members take part in a three-day intensive training and performance review by the vice-chairs to assess the quality and

2 *Ibid* at 2.

quantity of their decisions and their hearing performance.[3] Various instruments are in place to enhance the members' efficiency and effectiveness:

- code of conduct for members—guides expectations to ensure a fair and efficient process, including such topics as conduct and etiquette during a hearing, and acceptance of gifts;[4]
- chairperson's guidelines—provide guidance and advice on various topics, such as requests to participate by videoconference when the member has decided on an in-person hearing,[5] adjournment of a hearing,[6] items to be addressed in opening and closing comments,[7] and notice of intention to summarily dismiss;[8]
- practice directions—outline tribunal procedures (discussed further below); and
- chairperson's directives—communicate administrative matters to members, including such topics as printing, scanning, and disposal of documents,[9] reimbursement of a party's travel or living expenses,[10] and recording of hearings.[11]

---

3 *Ibid* at 5.

4 Social Security Tribunal, "Code of Conduct for Members of the Social Security Tribunal" (23 June 2017), online: <http://www1.canada.ca/en/sst/rdl/memcodcon.html>.

5 Social Security Tribunal, "Chairperson's Guidelines for the Appeal Division: Requests to Participate by Videoconference When the Member Has Decided on an In-Person Hearing" (20 May 2016), online: <http://www1.canada.ca/en/sst/rdl/chairguidad2.html>.

6 Social Security Tribunal, "Chairperson's Guidelines for the Appeal Division: Adjournment of a Hearing" (18 January 2017), online: <http://www1.canada.ca/en/sst/rdl/chairguidad8.html>.

7 Social Security Tribunal, "Chairperson's Guidelines for the General Division Employment Insurance Section: Items to Be Addressed in Opening and Closing Comments" (8 June 2017), online: <http://www1.canada.ca/en/sst/rdl/chairguidei6.html>.

8 Social Security Tribunal, "Chairperson's Guidelines for the General Division Income Security Section: Items to Be Addressed in Opening and Closing Comments" (8 June 2017), online: <http://www1.canada.ca/en/sst/rdl/chairguidei6.html>.

9 Social Security Tribunal, "Chairperson's Directives for the Appeal Division: Printing, Scanning and Disposal of Documents" (2 March 2017), online: <http://www1.canada.ca/en/sst/rdl/1printing.html>.

10 Social Security Tribunal, "Chairperson's Directives for the General Division Employment Insurance Section: Reimbursement of a Party's Travel or Living Expenses or Payment of Any Allowance for Special Reasons Under Section 63 of the Department of Employment and Social Development Act" (24 February 2017), online: <http://www1.canada.ca/en/sst/rdl/2reimbursement.html>.

11 Social Security Tribunal, "Chairperson's Directives for the General Division Income Security Section: Recording of Hearings" (2 March 2017) online: <http://www1.canada.ca/en/sst/rdl/3recording.html>; and *supra* note 1 at 12.

Even though the SST's own "Achievements Report"[12] heralds the successes of the tribunal in its first three years of operation, it acknowledges (briefly) the obstacles that it faced in the early stages.[13] Indeed, the excitement of the SST's early days was overshadowed by its deficiencies. In its haste to open the doors of justice to the public, the government showed significant lapses in planning and spending that led to large backlogs in the tribunal's first year. In August 2014, over one year into the SST's existence, CTV News reported that low case dispositions and high backlog were significant problems, despite the expectations that the "new body [would] provide a more efficient appeal process for employment insurance, Canada Pension Plan and old-age security decisions" and the promise of $25 million per year in savings to taxpayers.[14] Over a year later, and two years after the birth of the SST, CTV followed up with another story that highlighted the board's continuing backlog, citing a quote from an external reviewing company that noted, "The SST is concerned that it is facing a capacity issue."[15] Since that time, the SST has pointed out its successes in an effort to change the story:

- increased members and staff, and[16]
- a steady rise in the number of appeals received and concluded:[17]
  - appeals received:
    - 2013-2014: 2,968;
    - 2014-2015: 3,563;
    - 2015-2016 3,654
  - appeals concluded:
    - 2013-2014: 1,306;
    - 2014-2015: 3,084;
    - 2015-2016: 4,000

The most recent figures suggest a continuing trend toward greater efficiency. From April to June 2017, the general division, income security section received 755 appeals and concluded 1,041.[18] In the same time frame, the general division, employment insurance section received 854 appeals and con-

12 *Supra* note 1 at 12.

13 *Ibid* at 6.

14 Lee-Anne Goodman, "Fewer Hearings Held by New Social Security Tribunal, Backlog Growing," CTVNews (25 August 2014), online: <https://www.ctvnews.ca/politics/fewer-hearings-held-by-new-social-security-tribunal-backlog-growing-1.1975023>.

15 Jordan Press, "Social Security Tribunal Short-Staffed, Error-Prone, and Under Pressure: Report," CTVNews (15 October 2015), online: <http://www.ctvnews.ca/canada/social-security-tribunal-short-staffed-error-prone-and-under-pressure-report-1.2611142>.

16 *Supra* note 1 at 2.

17 *Ibid* at 13.

18 Social Security Tribunal, "Statistics" (18 January 2018), online: <http://www1.canada.ca/en/sst/stats/stats.html>.

cluded 796, and the appeal division received 159 appeals and concluded 253.[19] A total of 2,090 appeals were concluded in these three months, whereas in its first year the SST completed 1,600 appeals.[20]

Legislation and Regulations

Various pieces of legislation and regulations feed the SST. The tribunal was established and empowered through the *Department of Employment and Social Development Act* (DESDA).[21] Part 5 of this Act forms the legislative basis for the SST. Section 44(1) establishes the tribunal and the two divisions—general and appeal—and section 44(2) creates the general division sections of income security and employment insurance. In reality, this means that the tribunal is divided into two tiers. Appeals to the SST are first heard in the general division (s 52), either the income security section for CPP and OAS matters or the employment insurance section for EI matters. If an appellant or a respondent disagrees with the decisions of the General Division, they may then file an application for leave to appeal to the Appeal Division (s 53(3)). Asking for **leave to appeal** is essentially requesting permission for the appeal division to hear the matter. This will be discussed in greater detail in the appeal division section, below.

Members of the SST are appointed by the **Governor-in-Council**, pursuant to section 45(1) of the DESDA. The Governor-in-Council is the term attached when the Governor General acts on the advice of the members of cabinet, also known as the Privy Council. The *Constitution Act*[22] cites numerous other duties that the Governor-in-Council must fulfill. In 2017 the prime minister amended the appointment process for federal tribunals, requiring the Governor-in-Council to take over the role of appointing members.

DESDA also creates, or more accurately continues (because it existed before the DESDA), the ministry or department that oversees the OAS and CPP programs, under the name of Department of Employment and Social Development Canada (previously Human Resources and Skills Development Canada),[23] and outlines the powers and duties of the minister.[24] The Canada

leave to appeal permission for an appeal to be heard; not an automatic right of appeal

Governor-in-Council the Governor General acting on the advice of the members of Cabinet, also known as the Privy Council

19 *Ibid.*

20 *Supra* note 14.

21 SC 2005, c 34.

22 *Constitution Act, 1982*, being Schedule B to the *Canada Act 1982* (UK), 1982, c 11.

23 *Ibid*, s 3(1).

24 *Ibid*, ss 5, 6.

Employment Insurance Commission (CEIC) is continued and empowered under Part 3 of DESDA.

The Social Security Tribunal Regulations, SOR/2013-60 (SSTR), are created pursuant to the DESDA. Three other regulations exist under this statute;[25] however, the Social Security Tribunal Regulations are the most prominent with respect to the inner workings of this tribunal. These regulations detail processes regarding proceedings (s 3), the form of hearings (s 21), the filing of documents (s 5), constitutional issues (s 20), and appeals to each division (ss 23, 24, 39), among other things. Embedded in the regulations is a requirement for the SST to "conduct proceedings as informally and quickly" as "fairness and natural justice will permit" (s 3(1)(a)). This highlights the importance of the fast and fair resolution of matters, which our tribunal system is based on.

The method for requesting an adjournment is outlined in section 11(1) and requires only that the request be filed with supporting reasons. Further adjournments may not be granted, unless justified by exceptional circumstances (s 12(1)). Where separate appeals share a common question of law or fact, they may be joined as long as a party suffers no injustice as a result of the joinder (s 13(a)(b)). If a party wishes to raise a constitutional challenge against any of the legislation under which the SST holds jurisdiction (DESDA, *Employment Insurance Act* [EIA]),[26] *Canada Pension Plan* [CPP],[27] *Old Age Security Act* [OASA][28]), they must file a notice with the tribunal and file the requirements established under the *Federal Courts Act* (FCA),[29] as required by section 20 of the Social Security Tribunal Regulations. An example of a constitutional challenge is a party claiming CPP-D benefits who believes that the requirements for proving a disability under the CPP are discriminatory against a certain type of disability. This would raise a concern with the CPP provisions as being disharmonious with section 15 of the *Canadian Charter of Rights and Freedoms*,[30] which is the equality provision, thereby questioning the validity of these provisions of CPP.

The EIA is a lengthy statute that governs the EI scheme in Canada. Sections 6 through 54 prescribe the requirements for benefits paid to out-of-work Canadians; these are called unemployment benefits. A number of regulations are made under the EIA, but the two most important ones for the purposes of practising before the SST are the Employment Insurance Regulations (SOR/96-332) and

25 Department of Employment and Social Development Regulations, SOR/2005-311; Electronic Documents and Electronic Information Regulations, SOR/2014-117; Social Insurance Number Regulations, SOR/2013-82.

26 SC 1996, c 23.

27 RSC 1985, c C-8.

28 RSC 1985, c O-9.

29 RSC 1985, c F-7.

30 Part I of the *Constitution Act, 1982*, being Schedule B to the *Canada Act 1982* (UK), 1982, c 11.

the Reconsideration Request Regulations (SOR/2013-63). The Employment Insurance Regulations contain specifics of the benefits program, including what is "insurable" employment (s 26), how to make a claim for benefits (s 26), sickness benefits (s 40), pregnancy benefits (s 41), or compassionate care benefits (s 41.1), reconsiderations (s 78), and suspension of benefits pending appeal to the SST appeal division (s 80). This last section suspends benefits payable pursuant to a decision of the EI section of the SST's general division, pending an appeal to the appeal division by the CEIC within 21 days of the general division's decision (s 80). Similarly, benefits are also suspended if the CEIC applies to the Federal Court for a judicial review of an appeal division decision (s 81). The Reconsideration Request Regulations briefly address the extension of time for an EI applicant to request a reconsideration of a decision from the CEIC. This step is necessary before proceeding with an appeal to the SST.

The CPP governs this pension and benefits scheme, to which individuals may apply. If an individual disagrees with a decision, resulting, for example, from a denial of his or her application for CPP benefits, then this decision is appealable to the SST. To qualify for CPP benefits, applicants must first have contributed to the pension scheme through their earnings while in the workforce. The Act identifies what type of employment includes "pensionable earnings" versus employment that is exempt from having earnings deducted and forwarded to CPP (s 6(1)(2)). Section 44 outlines the benefits payable for retirement, death, and disability, and to survivors of deceased contributors, children of disabled contributors, and orphans of deceased contributors. The calculation of eligible benefits is covered in sections 45-59.1. There are also special rules (ss 67-76.1), such as that the disability pension (CPP-D) ceases to be available to a recipient on the day that person turns 65 (s 70(1)(c)) because it is deemed that the individual will receive a retirement pension and that the application for such has been made (s 70(2)).

As with the other statutes mentioned, one main set of regulations is integral to practising before the SST: the Canada Pension Plan Regulations.[31] These regulations further detail the pension scheme and contain aspects such as computation of employee's contribution (s 4), employer's contributions (s 7), cancellation of benefits (s 46.2), application for retirement pension (s 61), determination of disability (s 68), and requests for reconsideration (s 74.1). This last section outlines the details about reconsideration requests, pursuant to section 81 of the CPP. A reconsideration request to the minister is required before an appeal to the SST is launched. For example, if an individual is denied CPP-D benefits on the basis of an application, that person must first seek reconsideration before submitting an appeal with the SST general division.

The OASA creates a system of financial assistance for individuals over the age of 65 through a monthly allowance. The allowance is available to those over 65 years of age who are Canadian citizens or legal residents of Canada on the day of the application (or the day before leaving the country if they are

31 CRC, c 385.

applying from outside of Canada), and who have resided in Canada for either 10 or 20 years after turning 18 (the period depends whether application is made from within or outside Canada) (ss 3-5). The OASA also provides for an additional benefit called the GIS that is available for eligible OAS recipients with low incomes (ss 10-18). An individual who has applied for a benefit under the OASA and been denied, or who has been approved but disagrees about the amount of the benefit, can seek a reconsideration from the minister within 90 days of the date of the received decision (s 27.1). Subsequently, an appeal from a reconsideration request decision proceeds to the SST (s 28(1)).

Many regulations have been made pursuant to the OASA as a result of reciprocal pension agreements with other countries; however, for general representation before the SST, the Old Age Security Regulations[32] are most pertinent. The regulations detail aspects of the OAS scheme, including but not limited to forms for application (s 3), approval of a pension application (s 5), approval of supplement application (s 10), evidence of age and identity (s 18), and requests for reconsideration (s 29). The last subject is covered under sections 29 and 29.1, expanding on section 27 of the OASA, and provides detail about the form of the reconsideration request and the minister's role in accepting late reconsideration requests.

In addition to the legislation, practitioners should be guided by the practice directions published by the SST. Different practice directions apply to each of the SST divisions. The income security section and EI section of the general division each have five applicable practice directions:

- Practice Direction 2015-01: Completing incomplete notices of appeal:[33]
  - For example, an appellant has 30 days to file an appeal with the general division EI section. If the appellant indicates to the SST that he or she intends to file an appeal but not all information is received by the SST within 30 days, the SST will then act in accordance with this practice direction. First, it will send a letter to the appellant requesting that all outstanding information be submitted within 30 days of receipt of the letter. If all information is received within that time, the SST will proceed as if the appeal was commenced on the date of the original (incomplete) appeal filing. If all information is received after the 30 days given in the letter, the SST will proceed as if the appeal was commenced on the date the missing information was received.
- Practice Direction 2015-02: Requesting and issuing a corrigendum (which is the correction of an error in a decision):[34]

32 CRC, c 1246.

33 Social Security Tribunal, "Practice Direction 2015-01: Procedure for Completing Incomplete Notices of Appeal" (8 June 2017), online: <http://www1.canada.ca/en/sst/rdl/eigdpracticedirection2015.html>.

34 Social Security Tribunal, "Practice Direction 2015-02: Procedure for Requesting and Issuing a Corrigendum (the Correction of an Error in a Decision)" (17 July 2017), online: <http://www1.canada.ca/en/sst/rdl/adpd2015ispricorrigendum.html>.

  - For example, this practice direction applies when an appellant believes a decision has a minor recording error, not when the appellant believe an error of law exists (the latter would require an appeal to the appeal division). When an appellant finds a minor error in a decision, perhaps a date of 2015 when it should be 2005, this can be corrected by requesting a corrigendum from the same division from which the decision arose. Therefore, if this date error was in a general division income security section decision, the corrigendum request must be sent to the income security section within 90 days of receipt of the decision, stating the apparent error and how the correction should be made. The income security section would then respond with either a denial of the request, or through issuance of a corrigendum (the corrected decision).
- Practice Direction 2016-01: Dealing with post-hearing documents:[35]
  - For example, if an appellant wants to file a document after the hearing, the member must determine whether or not to admit the document. An appellant may pursue this path if an important document was requested by the member at the hearing but was not available. Procedural fairness allows for the member to consider accepting the document after the hearing but before issuing the decision. If the appellant requests admittance of a late document, he or she must outline how it is relevant to the issue up for determination and explain why it was not available earlier. The member will determine if the document should be admitted; submissions and a hearing may follow.
- Practice Direction 2017-01: Requests to participate as an intervener:[36]
  - For example, if an OAS matter before the general division income security section includes a constitutional challenge, a public interest group may seek intervenor status to be allowed to make submissions because the important legal matter affects the aging Canadian populace. To gain intervener status, the public interest group must file a request that includes a statement about the group or organization, how it wants to be included, how this participation will affect the determination of the matter, and its interest in the outcome. The member may deny or grant the request.

---

35 Social Security Tribunal, "Practice Direction 2016-01: Dealing with Post-Hearing Documents" (30 March 2017), online: <http://www1.canada.ca/en/sst/rdl/gdpd2016eiposthearing.html>.

36 Social Security Tribunal, "Practice Direction 2017-01: Procedure for Requests to Participate as an Intervener" (30 May 2017), online: <http://www1.canada.ca/en/sst/rdl/gdpd2017isintervener.html>.

- Practice Direction 2017-02: Dealing with appeals from deceased appellants:[37]
  - For example, an individual may have applied for CPP-D, been denied both at the application and the reconsideration request stage, and then appealed to the income security section of the general division. But after filing the appeal, the appellant died, and now the estate representative is attempting to continue with the appeal. In such circumstances, the appellant's estate must provide clear documentation, including proof of death and proof that the representative is authorized to act for the estate. The member will determine if the representative is authorized to act, and, if so, the appeal will continue.

The appeal division practice directions cover essentially the same topics, but with relevance to the appeal division procedures.

Application Process

After a reconsideration request has been made to either the CEIC commissioner for EI matters or the minister for CPP and OAS matters, and a decision has been received, either party to the decision may appeal to the SST general division. EI appeals must be filed with the EI section of the general division within 30 days of the reconsideration decision being received.[38] CPP and OAS appeals must be filed with the income security section of the general division within 90 days of the reconsideration decision being received.[39] Extensions of time for late filing can be requested[40] and may be granted at the discretion of the SST, but there is a limit of one year, after which appeals will not be accepted.[41]

The filing of an appeal and all related documents must follow the procedures outlined on the website, as per the regulations.[42] Filing may be done by mail, fax, or email. The appeal must be received on the correct form and with all the required information.[43] Both the EI section and the income security section require the appeal form to be submitted with the reconsideration decision for the appeal to start. Although different appeal forms are identified for EI, CPP, or OAS appeals on the website, the three contain similar require-

37 Social Security Tribunal, "Practice Direction 2017-02: Procedure for Dealing with Appeals from Deceased Appellants" (21 July 2017), online: <http://www1.canada.ca/en/sst/rdl/gdpd2017isdeceased.html>.

38 DESDA, s 52(1)(a).

39 *Ibid*, s 52(1)(b).

40 SSTR, s 25.

41 DESDA, s 52(2).

42 SSTR, s 23.

43 SSTR, s 24.

ments. If the appeal is being requested late, there is space on each form to explain why the appellant is requesting a late appeal. Each appeal form has space to outline the reasons for the appeal if, for example, the appellant disagrees with the minister's decision to deny CPP-D because the appellant believes he or she meets the threshold test for a disability under the CPP, or if an appellant disagrees with the CEIC's decision to deny EI on the basis of being fired for misconduct. The appeal forms require the appellant party to be identified, which in the case of an EI appeal could be an individual or the employer, while in the case of a CPP appeal it could be the individual or the ministry.

The general division may **summarily dismiss** an appeal if there is no reasonable chance of success; written reasons must be provided.[44] The appellant must also be offered time to make written submissions on the pending dismissal.[45] The decision to summarily dismiss an appeal can be appealed to the appeal division.[46]

At the income security section, the minister has 20 days after receiving the appeal form to file documents, including the original CPP or OAS application, any notifications sent to the applicant, and the reconsideration request and decision.[47] After filing an appeal, parties have an entire year to file additional documents that they intend to rely upon or, in the absence of such, to file a notice stating there are no additional documents.[48] After 365 days have passed or the notice is received (whichever comes first), the income security section must make a decision on the documents that are filed or schedule a hearing.[49] This notice is called Notice of Readiness: Form for the Appellant, and after it is signed and returned, it signals to the SST that the appellant wants to proceed only on the documents already submitted. Signing and returning the form early is acceptable; however, if the notice is signed and returned prematurely or carelessly, it can close doors to the appellant and ultimately produce a determination on the merits of the case that discounts evidence that was carelessly or unknowingly left out.

Practitioners must be diligent in the search for evidence or even during the questioning of their client (e.g., Are there any other medical conditions not mentioned in the CPP-D appeal that should be? Are there any other doctors or specialists who have not been contacted for a report?) before being satisfied

summarily dismiss dismiss an application before a hearing on the merits, if the tribunal is satisfied that the application has no reasonable chance of success

44 DESDA, s 53(1)(2).

45 SSTR, s 22.

46 DESDA, s 53(3).

47 SSTR, s 26.

48 SSTR, s 27.

49 SSTR, s 28.

that it is indeed time to file the Notice of Readiness form. At the EI section, the CEIC has seven days after receiving the appeal form to file the decision, reconsideration request and decision, and any additional submissions.[50] After the Notice of Readiness form has been signed and sent to the SST general division, it will respond with a Hearing Information Form for the parties to complete and return. The Hearing Information Form informs the tribunal of the parties' intentions concerning witnesses and representatives, whether there are any further hearing requirements (such as translators or the use of assistive technology), and any problematic dates or hearing formats. Following this, a notice of hearing will be sent by the tribunal. Pre-hearing conferences and early dispute resolution may be initiated by the SST.[51]

Appeals are heard before a single member[52] and are open to the public, although they can be held privately.[53] Hearings may be held in any of the following forms: written, teleconference, video conference, or personal appearance.[54] The SST general division frequently employs the use of technology in handling its high volume of cases, with 63 percent of EI hearings held via teleconference in 2015-2016 and 35 percent by teleconference in the income security section for the same year. Most hearings were held by teleconferencing in that year. In-person and videoconferencing options were the next most frequently used methods.[55] In determining the method of hearing, the general division will consider:

- the complexity of the case;
- the number of anticipated parties/participants;
- whether credibility is a prevailing issue;
- whether videoconference is available close to the area where the appellant lives;
- whether there are gaps in the information in the file; and
- whether a request to address specific needs has been made.[56]

For matters related to CPP or OAS at the general division, members may also decide the matter on the evidence submitted in the file alone, if they feel this is sufficient and that a hearing is not necessary.[57]

Hearings, whether technology based or in person, carry a familiar tone of informality, as do many tribunal hearings mentioned in this text. It is typical

50 SSTR, s 30.

51 SSTR, ss 15, 16.

52 DESDA, s 61.

53 DESDA, s 62.

54 SSTR, s 21.

55 *Supra* note 1 at 15, 19.

56 *Supra* note 1 at 10.

57 *Ibid.*

for either the minister or the CEIC (depending on appeal type and section), or a representative, to be absent from general division hearings. This means that the individual and the member (along with any witnesses) are often the only parties present. The representative's absence does not mean that they have abandoned their position; rather, the hearing will proceed with the individual giving his or her testimony and the member following up with questions for clarification. The member will rely upon the ministry's or CEIC's written submissions for its position on the appeal.

The general division has the power to dismiss, confirm, rescind, or vary a decision of the minister or the CEIC, but must provide written reasons for the decision.[58] While the regulations state that decisions must flow from the hearing without delay,[59] the SST has established service standards for both the EI and income security sections of the general division that state "85% of final decisions will be made within 90 days of the appeal being filed."[60] The general division has largely adhered to this service standard, with most decisions being received within 30 days in the 2015-2016 season.[61]

After a decision has been received from the general division, any party may request leave to appeal through an application to the appeal division.[62] Requesting leave to appeal is asking for permission for the appeal to be heard. Leave must be granted by the appeal division before an appeal can proceed. The only exception is for appeals stemming from general division summary dismissals.[63] If the general division summarily dismissed an appeal on the grounds that there was no reasonable chance of success, the party has an automatic appeal right to the appeal division. In the case of summary dismissal appeals, the appeal must be submitted on the correct form and in accordance with the guidelines outlined on the website and appeal form itself.[64] Within 45 days of filing the summary dismissal appeal, parties may file submissions or a notice that there are no more documents to file.[65] At the end of the 45 days, or when the notice is received, the appeal division must make a decision on the documents received or set a hearing date.[66]

For standard applications seeking leave to appeal, the appeal form and submissions must be filed within 30 days if the appeal stems from the EI section of the general division, or 90 days if from the income security section.[67] There

58 DESDA, s 54(1)(2).

59 SSTR, ss 29, 33.

60 *Supra* note 8.

61 *Supra* note 1 at 16.

62 DESDA, s 55; and SSTR, s 56(1).

63 *Ibid*, s 56(2).

64 *Ibid*; and DESDA, s 53(3).

65 *Ibid*, s 36.

66 *Ibid*, s 37.

67 DESDA, ss 57(1)(a), (b). See also SSTR, ss 39, 40.

is a one-year limitation period for filing applications for leave with the Appeal Division.[68] Within 45 days of filing the application for leave to appeal, parties may file additional documents or a notice that there are no further documents to file.[69] At the end of the 45 days, or when the notice is received, the appeal division must make a decision on the documents received or set a hearing date.[70] The application forms to the appeal division contain much of the same required information as the general division appeal forms; however, because of the nature of the request, you must explain why you believe there is a reasonable chance of success, identify all the reasons that you are filing the appeal (from a list provided), and provide detailed reasons why you believe this to be true. The three reasons[71] offered for seeking leave to appeal are that the general division:

- failed to observe a principle of natural justice or otherwise acted beyond or refused to exercise its jurisdiction;
  - For example, a document that was submitted to the SST was not included in the appeal file and therefore not relied upon in coming to a decision.
- made an error in law in its decision;
  - For example, the general division failed to consider an important case from Federal Court on the same point of law, which would have implications for the outcome of this case.
- made an important error regarding the facts contained in the appeal file;
  - For example, the general division disregarded an important piece of evidence that was submitted and was part of the appeal file.

The requirement to seek leave to appeal at the appeal division plays an important gatekeeping function of weeding out ungrounded appeals and therefore assists the tribunal with time management and scheduling. Hearings at the appeal division are open to the public; however, most hearings in 2016 were conducted via teleconference.[72] There is a significant difference between hearings before the appeal division and those at the general division because the issue on appeal differs from the original fact-finding issue that was before the general division. At the appeal division, appellants cannot introduce new evidence or argue the facts (e.g., that your client is disabled under the CPP, or that your client did not voluntarily leave employment making them ineligible for EI); rather, the appellant's case is limited to explaining the error that was made in the general division decision (e.g., there was a breach of natural justice, or the law was applied incorrectly, or an important fact was disregarded).

68 *Ibid*, s 57(2).

69 SSTR, s 42.

70 SSTR, s 43.

71 DESDA, s 58(1).

72 *Supra* note 1 at 10, 23.

Decisions and Appeals

Decisions from the appeal division must be made in writing and "without delay" at the end of the hearing.[73] The service standards set by the SST indicate the following for the appeal division:

> Decisions on Leave to Appeal: 85% of decisions on leave to appeal will be made within 60 days from filing of leave application.
> Final Decisions—where leave has been granted: 85% of final decisions will be made within 7 months from the date leave to appeal was granted.[74]

If the appeal is allowed, then the appeal division will likely send it back to the general division for a new hearing. If the appeal is denied, then the appellant has no other options, unless there are grounds for a judicial review. A decision of the appeal division may be judicially reviewed in accordance with the *Federal Courts Act.* A judicial review, if requested, will stay a decision where benefits or a pension is payable to a recipient,[75] pending the outcome of the review.

Decisions of the general division or appeal division may be rescinded or amended in accordance with SSTR sections 45-48 and section 66 of DESDA. Rescinding an application is essentially a reversal of the decision. Amending an application may be necessary if only a slight modification is required. Section 66(1) states that an application to rescind or amend a decision may be made if:

> (a) in the case of a decision relating to the *Employment Insurance Act,* new facts are presented to the Tribunal or the Tribunal is satisfied that the decision was made without knowledge of, or was based on a mistake as to, some material fact; or
>
> (b) in any other case, a new material fact is presented that could not have been discovered at the time of the hearing with the exercise of reasonable diligence.[76]

73 SSTR, s 44.

74 *Supra* note 1.

75 OASA, s 28(3); EIA, s 81; CPP, s 83.

76 DESDA, s 66.

Case Law

Belo-Alves v Canada (Attorney General), 2014 FC 1100, [2015] 4 FCR 108

This judicial review was brought against a decision by the SST appeal division after refusing leave to appeal a CPP-D decision stemming from the Office of the Commissioner of Review Tribunals (OCRT). The OCRT was the predecessor tribunal to the SST general division. The SST retained some jurisdiction to hear outstanding appeals from the OCRT upon its creation, hence the application for leave to appeal before the appeal division. The appeal division refused leave stating that it did not have jurisdiction to hear the appeal as it had previously been decided by a different tribunal (*res judicata*). This case has a lengthy history of applications, appeals, and judicial review, stemming from the applicant's third attempt at CPP-D, and previous decisions stating that the matter had already been fully decided on the first application. No new evidence had been supplied in subsequent applications, thereby making the first application determinative of the latter. When the denial of the third application was appealed in December 2012 to the Pension Appeals Board (PAB), which was the predecessor to the SST appeal division, the SST took over jurisdiction with its creation in April 2013 (at 1-22). The application for leave was dismissed on the following grounds: the appeal had no reasonable chance of success, based on a retroactive application of the legislation under the jurisdiction of PAB and the reasonable expectations of the appellant; there was no new evidence presented; and no error of law had been identified (at 32). The applicant requested a judicial review of the decision to deny leave to appeal, on the basis that the SST committed an error in refusing the application for leave because it failed to accept new medical evidence, which breached the duty of procedural fairness and denied her the right to a fair hearing (at 41). The Federal Court found there was no breach of procedural fairness, and although the SST applied the wrong test for determining if there was a reasonable chance of success to her appeal (at 75), ultimately the decision to deny leave to appeal was reasonable because of *res judicata* (at 108). The judicial review application was dismissed (at 79).

Yantzi v Canada (AG), 2014 FCA 193 (CanLII)

The applicant applied for judicial review of a decision from the SST that denied him CPP-D, as he was not found to have a severe condition rendering him disabled according to the CPP. The applicant felt that an error was made because the SST failed to consider all the medical evidence before it as it made its determination. The Federal Court stated that no error was made and that the decision of the SST was reasonable. While the general division's decision did not go through a detailed analysis of each medical report, unless the court can fail to see how the decision was made on the basis of the evidence presented, it will be considered a reasonable decision, however brief it may be (at 4-6).

Bossé v Canada (AG), 2015 FC 1142 (CanLII)

The applicant filed a judicial review of the appeal division's decision not to grant leave to appeal on the basis that the wrong appeal form was used and therefore no reasons were offered. The judicial review application was granted on the basis of a lack of procedural fairness or respect for natural justice (at 2). The applicant claimed that he was not given the opportunity to properly present his reasons for seeking an appeal of the general division EI section that denied him EI (at 37). While the incorrect form was used, the SST's website did not offer sufficient guidance or directions in plain language to promote access to justice (at 39, 40, 42, 45). The SST should have taken steps to contact the applicant, inform him of missing information, and seek the required information (at 44). The decision of the SST was set aside and the applicant was provided a new opportunity to submit the correct form within 30 days from the judicial review decision date (at 47). As a result of this decision, the SST took corrective steps to update its website and practices.[77]

JC v Canada Employment Insurance Commission, 2017 SSTADEI 262

This decision from the SST appeal division stems from the EIA. The appeal was dismissed as abandoned (at 1). Though leave to appeal was granted, the appellant did not attend the scheduled teleconference, for which a notice of hearing was sent by courier (at 3-4). There was one point of contact from the appellant between leave being granted and the hearing date, at which time the appellant provided a change in his contact information (at 4). The day after the hearing, at which the Commission did not object to dismissal of the appeal, the appellant called the tribunal to find out the date of his scheduled hearing. He was notified that he missed the hearing the previous day and was invited to offer a written explanation as to why, but no explanation was provided (at 7-8). After consulting case law, the SST felt it reasonable to conclude that the appeal was abandoned.

HP v Minister, 2016 SSTADIS 482

This decision from the appeal division contemplates whether leave to appeal should be granted based on whether there is a reasonable chance of success. The applicant was denied CPP-D and requested leave from the appeal division. An applicant can convince the tribunal that there is a reasonable chance of success if he or she can show in the application that there is an arguable case (at 6). The applicant must also identify which ground of appeal he or she is pursuing:

a. The general division failed to observe a principle of natural justice or otherwise acted beyond or refused to exercise its jurisdiction;

77 *Supra* note 1 at 30.

b. The general division erred in law in making its decision, whether the error appears on the face of the record; or
c. The general division based its decision on an erroneous finding of fact that it made in a perverse or capricious manner or without regard for the material before it (at 10).

Natural justice is not breached simply because an applicant disagrees with a decision. In its decision, the tribunal stated that "[t]he principles of natural justice are concerned with ensuring that parties are able to present their cases fully; to know the case they have to meet; and to have their cases heard by an impartial decision-maker" (at 18). The general division properly considered the evidence that was before it, and the hearing that was held represented the duty of a fair hearing. An arguable case for appeal was not made, and for these reasons leave to appeal was denied (at 18).

CD v Canada Employment Insurance Commission, 2014 SSTGDEI 138

This general division (EI section) decision found that the appellant's employment was not ended because of misconduct (at 2), and he therefore qualified for EI. The appellant filed a claim for EI stating that his reason for stopping work was due to dismissal or suspension from the employer (at 3). The employer had identified on the record of employment (ROE) submitted to the Commission that the reason for dismissal had been misconduct. The Commission notified the employer that it had not provided sufficient reasons backing up the alleged misconduct (at 4). The employer filed a Request for Reconsideration, pursuant to which the Commission was satisfied of the misconduct claim and disqualified the appellant from benefits (at 5-6). Section 30(1) of the EIA disqualifies individuals from receiving EI benefits if the loss of their job was due to misconduct. The evidence before the SST showed that the appellant had been dismissed because of a violent incident (at 20). Misconduct is not defined in the legislation but is the subject of case law where its meaning is clarified:

> In order to constitute misconduct the act complained of must have been willful or at least of such a careless or negligent nature that one could say the employee willfully disregarded the effects his or her actions would have on job performance.[78]

The concept of "wilful" is discussed further in case law.[79] The SST found that the act of shoving a colleague did not constitute misconduct in the Act (at 32), even though it was "inappropriate and reprehensible" (at 35). Disqualifying the appellant from EI was incorrect (at 51). The appeal was allowed (at 53).

---

78 *Canada (Attorney General) v Tucker*, [1986] 2 FC 329 at 24.

79 *Mckay-Eden v Canada*, 1997 CanLII 17410 (FCA), *Mishibinijima v Canada (Attorney General)*, 2007 FCA 36, and *Canada (Attorney General) v Lemire*, 2010 FCA 314.

MS v Minister, 2015 SSTGDIS 92

This decision stems from one that originated under OCRT jurisdiction and was transferred to the SST income security section of the general division upon its inception in April 2013. The appellant was found eligible for the GIS available through OAS for 2010-2011; she sought a reconsideration on the basis of greater retroactive pay of the GIS. The reconsideration request was denied, and the original decision was upheld. The appellant sought an appeal before the OCRT, which was transferred to the SST (at 1). GIS can be paid for up to 11 months prior to the GIS application being made, and the application is deemed to have been made when it is received by the minister (at 10-11). There is an exception to allow retroactivity of longer than 11 months when the applicant was incapable prior of stating his or her wishes to make an application (at 12). The appellant claimed she should qualify for the exception on the basis that:

> She was dependent upon others (her son, specifically) to apply for GIS sooner, but due to health issues her son was unable to do so; She is in financial desperation for additional GIS; The Appellant herself has had health issues, which have been worsened by her financial stress. (At 17)

The SST found that her inability to apply was not due to incapacity, as there was no evidence showing that she was "incapable of forming or expressing an intention to apply for the GIS" (at 25) before the actual date of her application. For these reasons, the appeal was denied and the original decision to grant GIS minus the greater retroactivity was upheld.

KEY LEGISLATION

Department of Employment and Social Development Act
Social Security Tribunal Regulations, SOR/2013-60
Employment Insurance Act
Canada Pension Plan
Old Age Security Act
Federal Courts Act
Employment Insurance Regulations, SOR/96-332
Reconsideration Request Regulations, SOR/2013-63
Canada Pension Plan Regulations, CRC, c 385
Old Age Security Regulations, CRC, c 1246

KEY TERMS

Governor-in-Council, 300

leave to appeal, 300

summarily dismiss, 306

REVIEW QUESTIONS

1. Describe the divisions and sections of the SST and their respective jurisdictions.
2. What is the Governor-in-Council?
3. What body oversees the administration of (a) CPP and (b) EI?
4. What is the procedure for the SST if it receives an incomplete notice of appeal?
5. What limitation periods apply to filing appeals in the general division?
6. What is the difference between OAS and GIS?
7. What is "leave to appeal" and why is it important to procedures at the SST?
8. On what grounds can you seek leave to appeal?
9. What important decision from the Federal Court assisted in overhauling SST practices, and why?
10. How do hearings before the appeal division differ from those before the general division?

SCENARIOS

1. You represented Lila Delaney before the income security section of the general division and are considering applying for leave to appeal to the appeal division because you believe that the member overlooked an important fact about Lila's residency in Canada, because of which she was ultimately denied OAS. You still have 74 days to file the leave to appeal application, but you noticed an error in one of the dates recorded in the general division decision. What do you do to have the reporting error corrected?
2. You have just been approached by Hari Walker, who wants to appeal his denial of EI benefits to SST. He attempted to do so in person at the SST office in Ottawa last week, but his appeal form was rejected, and he was advised to refer to the online guidance for correct filing of his appeal. How do you tell Hari to proceed?
3. Taylor Tran was denied his CPP pension on July 17, 2015 by the minister. He called your office on April 22, 2016 seeking instructions about how to proceed with an appeal. What do you advise Taylor to do?

CHAPTER 14

Immigration and Refugee Board

Overview and History ... 318

Legislation and Regulations ... 320

Initiating an Application ... 324

Immigration Division ... 324

Refugee Protection Division ... 327

Hearing Process ... 330

Immigration Division ... 330

Refugee Protection Division ... 333

Decisions ... 334

Admissibility Hearings ... 334

Detention Reviews ... 334

Refugee Protection Division ... 334

Appeals ... 335

Immigration Appeal Division ... 335

Refugee Appeal Division ... 337

Federal Court ... 340

Case Law ... 342

Key Terms ... 345

Review Questions ... 345

Scenarios ... 346

Overview and History

The Immigration and Refugee Board (IRB) is a federal tribunal that was established in 1989 under the *Immigration Act, 1976*.[1] The Supreme Court of Canada (SCC) issued a decision in *Singh v Minister of Employment and Immigration*[2] that extended protections and rights under section 7 of the *Canadian Charter of Rights and Freedoms* (the Charter)[3] to those seeking asylum in Canada. Under the *Immigration Act, 1976* and before the Singh decision, refugee claimants were examined under oath by an immigration officer who would then create a transcript that was sent to the Refugee Status Advisory Committee (RSAC) for a decision. The RSAC made decisions based on written submissions. Any appeals of an RSAC determination were then sent to the Immigration Appeal Board (IAB) for claims to be re-determined. If the IAB decided to hear the case, an oral hearing would be granted, but this was discretionary. In *Singh*, the Supreme Court held that the determination of refugee status solely based on written submissions violated procedural fairness provisions. The court determined that only an oral hearing would be adequate to establish credibility of refugee claimants. As a result, the IRB was created, and the previous adjudication scheme for those who apply for refugee status in Canada was dismantled.

The IRB is Canada's largest independent tribunal, and it hears over 40,000 cases per year divided among the three regions (West, Central, and East).[4] It also has four divisions that have distinct specialized functions. The Immigration Division (ID) hears matters such as admissibility hearings and detention reviews, and the Immigration Appeal Division (IAD) hears immigration appeals from the ID and from Immigration, Refugees and Citizenship Canada. The Refugee Protection Division (RPD) holds refugee protection hearings, makes determinations with regard to **convention refugee** status, and identifies those in need of protection. Refugee protection in Canada is based on adherence to the principle of **non-refoulement**. As a signatory to the Convention Relating to the Status of Refugees and the 1967 Protocol Relating to the Status of Refugees, Canada's refugee determination system is designed to

---

1 Canadian Museum of Immigration at Pier 21, "Immigration Act, 1976" (2018), online: <https://www.pier21.ca/research/immigration-history/immigration-act-1976>.

2 [1985] 1 SCR 177.

3 Part I of the *Constitution Act, 1982*, being Schedule B to the *Canada Act 1982* (UK), 1982, c 11.

4 In 2017, the RPD finalized 21,480 new system cases; 1,622 legacy cases; and 75 cessation and vacation cases; the RAD finalized 3,136 cases; the ID finalized 2,111 admissibility matters and conducted 11,067 detention reviews regarding 3,554 individuals (3,485 adults and 69 minors), most dealing with flight risk; and the IAD finalized 6,563 cases. There were over 60,000 cases pending (that had not been heard) at the conclusion of 2017. See Immigration and Refugee Board of Canada, "Statistics" (22 November 2017), online: < http://www.irb-cisr.gc.ca/Eng/res/stat/Pages/index.aspx>.

ensure that we will not remove someone to a country where they will face persecution and irreparable harm. The Refugee Appeal Division (RAD) hears refugee appeals from the RPD.

Hearings are conducted by panel members in each of the divisions. For the ID and RPD, decisions are rendered by public servants who are hired by the federal government through a merit-based process. They are government employees who are skilled, well trained, and able to make determinations. There is no limit to their terms. Appeals of these decisions are made to the IAD and RAD, respectively. The decisions of the IAD and RAD are made by members who are appointed through Governor-in-Council appointments. They are publicly appointed members who also undergo a merit-based process to receive appointment. They are restricted to three-year appointments that can be renewed up to three times. This means that, generally, they cannot be appointed for more than nine years. This maintains impartiality and the arm's-length nature of public appointments.

Canada's Two Refugee Determination Systems

People can be deemed convention refugees in Canada in two ways. The first is by way of the United Nations High Commission for Refugees (UNHCR) and the IRCC's Refugee and Humanitarian Resettlement Program in which thousands displaced by war and persecution are processed overseas and resettled in Canada as permanent residents. This process, which does not require or involve paralegals, immigration consultants, or lawyers, is rigorous and completed directly through the UNHCR in partnership with non-governmental organizations (NGOs).

The second way to be deemed a convention refugee is by way of an inland claim initiated in Canada on arrival (or in some cases at an inland IRCC or CBSA office depending on the circumstances). The RPD is responsible for hearing refugee claims that originate in Canada. A refugee claim that comes before the RPD originates and is initiated at the port of entry (POE) or an inland IRCC office.

convention refugees persons who are outside of their country of birth or habitual residence who are unwilling or unable to return to their country of birth or habitual residence because of a well-founded fear of persecution based on race, religion, political opinion, nationality, or membership in a particular social group

non-refoulement a fundamental principle of refugee law which in essence states that we should not be returning a refugee claimant to a country where they will face persecution. Signatories to international refugee conventions agree that they will not remove someone to a country where they will face persecution and irreparable harm

The *Immigration and Refugee Protection Act* (IRPA)[5] replaced the *Immigration Act* in 2002 and is now the governing legislation for the IRB.

Paralegals are permitted to provide advocacy and representation before all four of the IRB's divisions. This is provided for in section 91(2)(b) of the IRPA and section 21.1(2)(b) of the *Citizenship Act*. Some paralegals are dually licensed as registered Canadian immigration consultants through the Immigration Consultants of Canada Regulatory Council (ICCRC) to comprehensively represent clients in areas outside of the paralegal scope of practice. Currently, this extra step is not necessary if paralegals only want to practise within their scope (matters before the IRB only). Immigration is a very extensive area of practice that is constantly changing and requires that representatives acquire and maintain their skills to provide effective representation. The outcomes for clients in this area of practice can literally be matters of life and death, in the case of refugees and persons in need of protection. In the case of foreign nationals and permanent residents, it could mean continued detention or deportation from Canada.

Legislation and Regulations

The legislative framework that the IRB operates under is extensive. Before the creation of the IRB, the refugee determination system was created through a number of conventions and protocols established by the UNHCR. Canada became a signatory to the 1951 Convention Relating to the Status of Refugees and the 1967 Protocol Relating to the Status of Refugees in 1969. The 1951 convention provided the definition of a convention refugee and detailed refugee rights, as well as the responsibilities of member states. Claimants were assessed based on these criteria.[6] The 1967 Protocol further modified the definition by removing geographical location and timeline restrictions.[7] In 1976, Canada signed the 1966 International Covenant on Civil and Political Rights, which articulates rights that member states can and cannot violate. This further established Canada's role in protecting human rights. Finally, in 1984, Canada became a signatory to the Convention Against Torture and Other Cruel, Inhuman or Degrading Treatment or Punishment. This convention helped to define who met the criteria of a person in need of protection. Canada remains a signatory to these conventions and protocols, and they have been instrumental in defining our refugee determination legislation and system.

The IRB was created in 1989, and the refugee determination system was enabled through the *Immigration Act, 1976*. The *Immigration Act* was replaced in 2002 by the IRPA. In 2005, Canada became a signatory to the Second

---

5 SC 2001, c 27.

6 United Nations High Commission for Refugees, "The 1951 Refugee Convention" (2018), online: <http://www.unhcr.org/pages/49da0e466.html>.

7 *Ibid.*

Optional Protocol to the International Covenant on Civil and Political Rights, Aiming at the Abolition of the Death Penalty. This protocol requires member states to take measures to eliminate the death penalty within their jurisdictions. In 2012, Bill C-31, *Protecting Canada's Immigration System Act*[8] instituted changes to the IRB's legislative framework. As a result, the portions of IRPA that addressed an internal appeals process at the IRB were activated, and the RAD was created.

The IRPA provides guidance with respect to immigration as a whole: the scope and practice of immigration to Canada, refugee determination, inadmissibility, detention, and release. It is separated into five parts. Part 2 specifically focuses on refugee determination, and Part 4 speaks specifically to the IRB, its composition, and scope.

The *Immigration and Refugee Protection Regulations* (IRPR) were written in support of the Act. The regulations are separated into 21 parts and provide clarification regarding practice and procedure. Of particular importance to demonstrating effective advocacy before the IRB and its various divisions, it is useful to be familiar with Parts 3 (Inadmissibility), 4 (Procedures), 8 (Refugee Classes) 9 (Temporary Residents), 13 (Removal), 14 (Detention and Release), 15 (Prescribed Conditions, which deals with Inadmissibility and the IAD), 19.1 (Information Sharing Between Countries), and 20 (Transitional Provisions, Division 5, Refugee Protection, which deals with legacy claims—that is, claims that originated before December 15, 2012).

In addition to the IRPA and IRPR, in 2004 Canada also signed the Agreement Between the Government of Canada and the Government of the United States of America for Cooperation in the Examination of Refugee Status Claims from Nationals of Third Countries, otherwise known as the Safe Third Country Agreement. The agreement stipulates that individuals who pass through a country where they could have made a claim for protection on their way to Canada are obligated to make a refugee claim in that safe country. At the time of writing, this agreement only designates the United States as a **safe third country**. It should be noted that while the IRCC position is that claimants

safe third country a country from which a claim for refugee protection should have been made, when a refugee claimant was passing through it. If someone faces persecution in one country and, while headed to another country to seek asylum, he or she passes through a third country where a claim can be made, he or she must do so. So far, Canada only has a Safe Third Country Agreement with the United States

8 J Béchard & S Elgersma, "Legislative Summary, Bill C-31" (4 June 2012), online: <https://lop.parl.ca/About/Parliament/LegislativeSummaries/bills_ls.asp?ls=c31&Parl=41&Ses=1>.

who come directly or indirectly from a safe third country are ineligible to be referred to the RPD, there are many exceptions to this policy.[9]

The ID hears cases related to admissibility and detention. For further clarification beyond what is covered in the provisions of the IRPA, the ID provides Rules and Commentaries to assist parties and legal representatives. The rules are separated into three parts. The rules outlined in Part 1 are specific to admissibility hearings. The rules in Part 2 relate to detention reviews, and Part 3 is applicable to both types of hearings. They touch on topics such as how and when to file documents, how to change the date or time of hearing, and how to join or sever hearings. The rules are further clarified by commentaries to the rules. The IRB also publishes a 14-chapter guide to hearings before the ID that assists readers by familiarizing them with the procedures to follow before the ID.

Matters that are unsuccessful before the ID, or where the minister is unsatisfied with the decision, are appealed to the IAD. The IAD also has its own set of Rules and Commentaries to guide parties and practitioners. Additionally, there are archived documents related to sponsorship appeals and removal orders that provide clarification and guidance. The IRB provides them as legal references, but the documents have not been updated since being archived, so it is imperative to be accurate and aware of the current context when using these documents.

The RPD conducts refugee protection hearings, makes determinations about convention refugee status, and identifies those who are in need of protection. The RPD requires you to have familiarity with a number of references and resources to successfully advocate for your clients.

The RPD rules outline practice and procedure before the RPD. Another very useful resource is the Interpretation of the Convention Refugee Definition in the Case Law document.[10] It is a comprehensive legal reference which covers issues including but not limited to persecution, statelessness, nexus grounds, state protection, and Internal Flight Alternative (IFA). You should also obtain and review the National Documentation Package (NDP) for the country relating to the originating claim. The IRB publishes NDPs on its website. They are updated monthly in accordance with a schedule to enhance accuracy. NDPs are "a compilation of publicly available documents that report on country conditions such as political, social, cultural, economic, and human rights conditions. Each NDP includes full citations to help users locate the documents that are not available on the IRB website."[11] To assist with the

9 Government of Canada: Immigration, Refugees, and Citizenship Canada, "Processing In-Canada Claims for Protection: The Safe Third Country Agreement" (12 March 2018), online: <http://www.cic.gc.ca/english/resources/tools/refugees/canada/processing/stca.asp>.

10 Immigration and Refugee Board of Canada, "Interpretation of the Convention Refugee Definition in the Case Law" (31 December 2010), online: <http://www.irb.gc.ca/Eng/BoaCom/references/LegJur/Pages/RefDef.aspx>.

11 Immigration and Refugee Board of Canada, "National Documentation Packages (NDPs)" (22 April 2016), online: <http://www.irb.gc.ca/Eng/ResRec/NdpCnd/Pages/index.aspx>.

research process, the IRB also publishes the results of research and information requests (RIRs) by country.[12] RIRs allow the IRB to obtain information from NGOs and experts in the field to ascertain the validity and credibility of claims for refugee protection. Once you identify the country and topic that interests you, you then enter your subject or key term into the searchable database. This should prompt results related to the topic you have identified.[13]

Unsuccessful claims from the RPD are appealed to the RAD. The RAD also has its own set of rules. Part 1 applies to appeals made by the claimant (the person who is the subject of the appeal), Part 2 provides guidance regarding appeals made by the minister, and Part 3 applies to both types of matters. The rules detail how to perfect an application before the RAD and the timelines associated with the process.

The IRB also provides jurisprudential guides,[14] chairperson's guidelines,[15] and policies,[16] which can enhance your competency.

Matters that are unsuccessful before the RAD and IAD can be appealed to the Federal Court for judicial review. Appeals to the Federal Court fall outside the jurisdiction of paralegals. It is still important to understand the appeals process and understand the impact that representation and advocacy before the IRB will have on the Federal Court appeals process. The Federal Courts have their own rules[17] and have rules specific to immigration and refugee appeals.[18]

Anticipated regulatory changes are published in the Forward Regulatory Plan.[19] Proposals include moving the pre-removal risk assessment process to the RPD from IRCC. Additionally, the IRCC often makes changes to practices and protocols, so it is wise to subscribe to RSS feeds or regularly check the website and keep track of the news regarding immigration. Although

---

12 Immigration and Refugee Board of Canada, "Responses to Information Requests (RIRs)" (5 January 2016), online: <http://www.irb.gc.ca/Eng/ResRec/RirRdi/Pages/index.aspx>.

13 *Ibid.*

14 Immigration and Refugee Board of Canada, "Jurisprudential Guides" (20 July 2017), online: <http://www.irb-cisr.gc.ca/Eng/BoaCom/references/pol/jurisprud/Pages/index.aspx>.

15 Immigration and Refugee Board of Canada, "Chairperson's Guidelines" (1 May 2017), online: <http://www.irb-cisr.gc.ca/Eng/BoaCom/references/pol/GuiDir/Pages/index.aspx >.

16 Immigration and Refugee Board of Canada, "Policies" (21 December 2017), online: <http://www.irb-cisr.gc.ca/Eng/BoaCom/references/pol/pol/Pages/index.aspx>.

17 Government of Canada, "Federal Courts Rules (SOR/98-106)" (24 April 2018), online: <http://laws.justice.gc.ca/eng/regulations/SOR-98-106/>.

18 Government of Canada, "Federal Courts Citizenship, Immigration and Refugee Protection Rules (SOR/93-22)" (24 April 2018), online: <http://laws.justice.gc.ca/eng/regulations/SOR-93-22/>.

19 Government of Canada, Immigration, Refugees, and Citizenship Canada, "Forward Regulatory Plan: 2018–2020" (9 April 2018), online: <https://www.canada.ca/en/immigration-refugees-citizenship/corporate/mandate/acts-regulations/forward-regulatory-plan.html>.

paralegals cannot generally practise immigration as a whole (e.g., visa applications, sponsorship applications), it would be wise to maintain a general knowledge about all things immigration in order to provide effective representation. You could review IRCC protocols to understand its policies and procedures. For example, the IRCC's enforcement operational manual ENF 3 is its protocol and guideline for immigration officers regarding detention reviews, so familiarity with this document would be essential to providing effective representation before the ID.

Initiating an Application

Immigration Division

The ID holds inadmissibility hearings and detention reviews, and can issue removal orders. To understand how a person comes before the ID, you have to understand the requirements and responsibilities of foreign nationals and permanent residents, and the powers vested in immigration officers under the IRPA.

Section 11 of IRPA requires that **foreign nationals** make an application to an officer before entering Canada and must remain "**in status**" (legally entitled to remain in Canada) to remain. To be granted entry, an officer must be satisfied that the foreign national is not inadmissible and meets the requirements of the Act. When permanent residency is granted, **permanent residents** are required to live in Canada for a set time to meet residency requirements and follow all Canadian laws or risk losing status and being removed from Canada.

The division of powers between the Minister of Immigration, Refugees, and Citizenship Canada (IRCC) and the Minister of Public Safety and Emergency Preparedness (PSEP) is important to understanding the enforcement responsibilities of officers. According to section 4 of IRPA, the minister of IRCC is responsible for:

- immigration policy development,
- the annual immigration plan (s 94 IRPA),

foreign national according to section 2(1) of the IRPA, a person who is not a Canadian citizen or a permanent resident, including a person who is stateless

in status legally entitled to remain in Canada; to maintain status means to renew visitor's visas, student visas, work permits, etc., and to not stay in Canada beyond the time limits or dates indicated on immigration documents

permanent resident according to section 2(1) of the IRPA, "a person who has acquired permanent residency status and has not subsequently lost that status under section 46." Permanent residents have the right to live, work, and study anywhere in Canada; apply for citizenship; receive most of the social benefits that Canadian citizens receive, including health care coverage; and are protected under Canadian law and the Charter

- immigration programs related to temporary and permanent immigration,
- settlement and integration of newcomers,
- resettlement of refugees, and
- policies related to admissibility.

IRPA gives authority to immigration and CBSA officers in sections 15, 138, 139, 140, 141, 142, and 143 to examine, enforce the Act, search, seize documents or goods, take and receive evidence, and execute orders and warrants. Before entry into Canada, visa officers (who are employed by IRCC) examine applications to make determinations regarding eligibility and admissibility. At the POE, CBSA officers can question individuals and search and seize documents and goods. Both IRCC and CBSA officers possess enforcement authority to arrest, detain, or remove individuals.

Admissibility Hearings

When a foreign national or permanent resident is identified as having admissibility issues (at the POE or otherwise), an officer has the discretionary authority to write an inadmissibility report (also known as a s 44(1) report), which can then be referred to the ID for consideration. Under the IRPA there are 11 grounds of inadmissibility:

- security (s 34),
- human or international rights violations (s 35),
- criminality (s 36(1)),
- serious criminality (s 36(2)),
- organized criminality (s 37),
- health grounds (s 38),
- financial reasons (s 39),
- misrepresentation (s 40),
- cessation of refugee protection (s 40.1),
- non-compliance with the IRPA (s 41), and
- inadmissible family member (s 42).[20]

The officer takes a number of factors into consideration when determining if a section 44(1) report is required:

- Is the person already the subject of a removal order or an inadmissibility report?
- Is he or she a foreign national or permanent resident?
- Will the person be leaving Canada shortly?
- Do they have a record of non-compliance?

20 Immigration and Refugee Board of Canada, “Admissibility Hearing Statistics” (22 September 2017), online: <http://www.irb-cisr.gc.ca/Eng/AdmEnq/stats/Pages/index.aspx>.

The IRCC's ENF 5 operational manual on section 44(1) reports provides valuable guidance with respect to officer discretion, grounds for a section 44(1) report, factors under consideration, and procedure.[21]

To initiate an inadmissibility hearing, the minister must file the section 44(1) report along with a request for an inadmissibility hearing and supporting evidence with the ID, pursuant to Rule 3. The individual receives notice of the admissibility hearing in the mail detailing the date, time, and location. They are the respondent. If the respondent has legal status in Canada, the onus is on the hearings officer to prove the allegations of inadmissibility. If the respondent is without status, the onus is on the respondent to show that he or she is not inadmissible. There are no forms.

The IRCC's ENF 1 operational manual on inadmissibility,[22] ENF 3 operational manual on admissibility hearings and detention review proceedings,[23] and ENF 4 on port of entry examinations are useful tools to gain insights into the IRCC's position and procedure regarding inadmissibility. A review of these documents will enhance your ability to effectively advocate for your client.

Detention Reviews

After a person enters at a POE, a CBSA officer may determine that there are serious grounds for detention and refer the person for a detention review or both an admissibility hearing and a detention review. IRCC officers may also encounter individuals that must be referred to the ID for detention reviews (e.g., someone who has fallen out of status or has been identified for removal, and there is a concern that the person is a flight risk). ID members may also issue a detention order at an admissibility hearing based on evidence presented to them during the hearing. This triggers the need for a detention review. There are several possible grounds for detention:

- The person in question is a danger to the public.
- The person in question is a flight risk (i.e., on a balance of probabilities the person isn't likely to appear for examination, removal, an admissibility hearing, or another type of proceeding that may result in a removal order).
- The minister is investigating an individual for potentially serious inadmissibility grounds.
- There are concerns regarding the person's identity (i.e., difficulty establishing identity).[24]

---

21 Immigration and Citizenship Canada, "ENF 5 Writing 44(1) Reports" (20 August 2013), online: <http://www.cic.gc.ca/english/resources/manuals/enf/enf05-eng.pdf>.

22 Immigration and Citizenship Canada, "ENF 1 Inadmissibility" (4 September 2013), online: <http://www.cic.gc.ca/english/resources/manuals/enf/enf01-eng.pdf>.

23 Immigration and Citizenship Canada, "ENF 3 Admissibility, Hearings and Detention Review Proceedings" (29 April 2015), < http://www.cic.gc.ca/english/resources/manuals/enf/enf03-eng.pdf>.

24 Immigration and Refugee Board of Canada, "Detention Review Statistics" (22 September 2017), online: <http://www.irb-cisr.gc.ca/Eng/detention/stats/Pages/index.aspx>.

The role of the ID is to examine the grounds identified for detention and determine whether, under the Act, the detention should continue. The ID may order the release of the person (with or without conditions) or the person's continued detention. If an individual is detained pending a hearing (an inadmissibility hearing on more serious grounds) or pending action by the IRCC/CBSA (i.e., as a result of a warrant for arrest and detention to proceed with removal from Canada), the minister must file a request for detention hearing under Rule 8 to initiate a detention review. Detention hearings must occur within the first 48 hours of detention. The Rules require that further detention reviews must take place at 7 days, 30 days, and every 30 days thereafter. The timelines can be expedited but not delayed.

In some cases hearings are open to the public and held at the IRB's offices, but for a detainee, the matter can be held in an immigration holding centre, jail, or penitentiary. Otherwise, the rule requires attendance at a location identified by the tribunal, unless other circumstances preclude this from happening. An application can be made to change the location of a hearing under Rule 42(1). Under section 56(1) of the IRPA, an officer is authorized to release a foreign national or permanent resident from detention before the first detention review by the ID, if the officer believes that there is no longer a need for detention. Officers also have the authority to impose any conditions on the individual that they deem necessary. These could include having the person pay money or obtain a guarantor to ensure compliance with conditions.

IRCC operational manuals ENF 3, "Admissibility Hearings and Detention Review Proceedings," and ENF 20, "Detention,"[25] are additional resources to consult to enhance your knowledge and skill with regard to detention reviews.

Refugee Protection Division

Canada became a signatory to both the 1951 refugee convention and the 1967 protocol in 1969. As such, Canada agreed to take in displaced persons from around the world and to provide a refugee determination system. A convention refugee is defined under section 96 of the IRPA as:

> a person who, by reason of a well-founded fear of persecution for reasons of race, religion, nationality, membership in a particular social group or political opinion,
>
> (a) Is outside each of their countries of nationality and is unable or, by reason of that fear, unwilling to avail themselves of the protection of each of those countries, or
>
> (b) Not having a country of nationality, is outside the country of their former habitual residence and is unable or, by reason of that fear, unwilling to return to that country.

25 Immigration and Citizenship Canada, "ENF 20 Detention" (12 February 2018), online: <http://www.cic.gc.ca/english/resources/manuals/enf/enf20-eng.pdf>.

To be granted refugee status, a refugee claimant must meet four criteria: **alienage**, a well-founded fear, persecution, and **nexus** (to one of the five grounds of persecution listed under s 96).

Additionally, a person in need of protection is defined in section 97 of the IRPA as:

> (1) …a person in Canada whose removal to their country or countries of nationality or, if they do not have a country of nationality, their country of former habitual residence, would subject them personally
>
> (a) to a danger, believed on substantial grounds to exist, of torture within the meaning of Article 1 of the Convention Against Torture; or
>
> (b) to a risk to their life or to a risk of cruel and unusual treatment or punishment if
>
> (i) the person is unable or, because of that risk, unwilling to avail themself of the protection of that country,
>
> (ii) the risk would be faced by the person in every part of that country and is not faced generally by other individuals in or from that country,
>
> (iii) the risk is not inherent or incidental to lawful sanctions, unless imposed in disregard of accepted international standards, and
>
> (iv) the risk is not caused by the inability of that country to provide adequate health or medical care.
>
> (2) A person in Canada who is a member of a class of persons prescribed by the regulations as being in need of protection is also a person in need of protection.

These definitions are imperative to understand to effectively advocate for a client.

In Canada, there are two ways that a person can become a refugee. The first is through the UNHCR and the IRCC's Refugee and Humanitarian Resettlement Program. Each year millions of people are displaced all over the world through war and persecution. There are over 65 million forcibly displaced persons, 22.5 million refugees, and over 10 million stateless persons in the

alienage one of the four components of refugee determination: refugee claimants must be outside their country of nationality or country of former habitual residence and unwilling or unable to return to said country because of a fear of persecution and the belief that they are unable to avail themselves of state protection

nexus a connection between, or intersection with, more than one thing. To be deemed a convention refugee, the person must show that the well-founded fear of persecution is connected (or has a nexus) to race, religion, political opinion, nationality, or membership in a particular social group (see convention refugee)

world.[26] Generally, those affected will either flee or be sent to refugee camps in neighbouring countries. The UNHCR has the mandate of resettling refugees around the world. It works with 130 countries[27] to resettle individuals and families. Since Canada is a signatory to the convention and the protocol, many are resettled in Canada. This process happens overseas, and when resettled individuals arrive in Canada, they arrive as permanent residents. This process, which does not require or involve paralegals, immigration consultants, or lawyers, is rigorous and completed directly through the UNHCR in partnership with NGOs and the IRCC. For more information about this process and system, consult resources published with the UNHCR,[28] especially the "Handbook and Guidelines on Procedures and Criteria for Determining Refugee Status Under the 1951 Convention and the 1967 Protocol Relating to the Status of Refugees"[29] and the website Refworld.org.[30]

The second way to be deemed a convention refugee is to initiate a claim with a CBSA officer in Canada upon arrival (or in some cases at an inland IRCC or CBSA office, depending on the circumstances). The RPD is responsible for hearing refugee claims that originate in Canada. A refugee claim that comes before the RPD originates and is initiated at the POE or an inland IRCC office. The officer who receives the initial claim for refugee protection must receive it in person and conduct an oral interview. There are no exceptions to this; a claim must be made in person. The officer will obtain information that will help to establish or confirm identity and have the claimant fill out the generic application form for Canada (IMM 0008).[31] The officer will then assess whether there are any issues regarding identity, inadmissibility (possibly issuing a section 44 report regarding inadmissibility), and eligibility. This includes conducting background checks, running biometrical information, and checking for the claimant's history in Canada (e.g., Had the claimant made an unsuccessful refugee claim before? Are they currently in status?). It is also possible that the officer will issue a removal order that will be stayed if the matter is referred to the RPD and recommence if the claim is unsuccessful.

26 United Nations High Commission on Refugees, "Figures at a Glance" (2018), online: <http://www.unhcr.org/figures-at-a-glance.html>.

27 *Ibid.*

28 See the United Nations High Commission on Refugees website at <http://www.unhcr.org>.

29 United Nations High Commissioner for Refugees, "Handbook and Guidelines on Procedures and Criteria for Determining Refugee Status under the 1951 Convention and the 1967 Protocol Relating to the Status of Refugees" (December 2011), online: <http://www.refworld.org/docid/4f33c8d92.html>.

30 Refworld, "Refugee Status Determination" (2018), online: <http://www.refworld.org/rsd.html>.

31 Immigration and Citizenship Canada, "Applying as an Adopted Child or Other Relative Being Sponsored" (14 February 2018), online: <http://www.cic.gc.ca/english/information/applications/3998-temp.asp>.

Under section 100(1) of the IRPA, the officer has three days to determine if the claim is eligible to be referred to the RPD. If after the eligibility hearing an officer feels that the claim is eligible, the officer will issue a notice of eligibility or notice of referral and provide the claimant with a basis of claim (BOC) form, which is an IRB-RPD document that must be filed directly with the RPD within 15 days, along with supporting documentation. The claimant will also receive a claimant's kit and notice to appear. The notice to appear will indicate the date of hearing, show the BOC needs to filed within 15 days, and list a date to appear if the BOC is not filed within 15 days. The RPD now allows documents to be filed electronically, which adds convenience.[32] If a claimant misses the 15-day deadline to file his or her basis of claim form, the claimant must attend at the IRB at 9 a.m. on the date indicated on the notice to appear, or the claimant risks a complete abandonment of his or her claim and will be precluded from filing another claim.

For inland claims, the claimant completes the basis of claim form before the eligibility interview, which is then submitted on the claimant's behalf to the RPD. If the IRCC officer decides to refer the matter, the claimant will receive a notice to appear along with a claimant's kit. The notice to appear provides the date of hearing, along with a special date of hearing in the event that the first hearing is missed. If a claimant fails to appear on the first hearing date, the claimant risks abandonment of the claim and will be precluded from filing another claim. Any further supporting documentation must be filed at least ten days before the hearing date.

Hearing Process

Immigration Division

The ID receives its authority to hold inadmissibility and detention review hearings through sections 45 and 54 of the IRPA. The IRB publishes a *Guide to Proceedings Before the Immigration Division*,[33] which is a 14-chapter comprehensive guide that will assist with understanding of hearing procedure before the ID.

ID hearings are conducted by one panel member who has control over the hearing process. Also present are the party, a public servant (hearings officer) who represents the minister, legal counsel for the party (if applicable), any witnesses who can advance claims on behalf of the party or the minister, and an

---

32 Immigration and Refugee Board of Canada, "Sign-up with the Refugee Protection Division—Online Form" (21 July 2017), online: <http://www.irb-cisr.gc.ca/Eng/contact/Pages/SendDocOnline.aspx>.

33 Immigration and Refugee Board of Canada, "Guide to Proceedings Before the Immigration Division" (23 November 2015), online: <http://www.irb-cisr.gc.ca/Eng/BoaCom/references/LegJur/Pages/GuideIdSi.aspx#table>. Note that there are 14 chapters in the guide but only 13 are available for download.

interpreter, if required. In admissibility hearings, a representative from the embassy of the country of origin for the party under review, or a representative from the UNHCR, or both may also be present.

The IRB has its own roster of approved language interpreters and provides interpretation services to those who require and request it. The interpreters are available across all four divisions of the IRB. Generally, the tribunal expects to be notified of the need for an interpreter in writing at least five days before the hearing. For matters like the 48-hour detention review, the requirement is to notify the IRB as soon as possible.

It is your role as legal representative to ensure that there are no issues regarding interpretation for your client. Sometimes, the interpreter may not speak in the same regional dialect as your client, or the person may be inaccurate in the translation. Other times, the interpreter is not saying exactly what your client has said and is paraphrasing. This is not acceptable and can be problematic because paraphrasing can remove context or important words. Translation and interpretation should be verbatim and not paraphrased in any way. Interpreters cannot offer advice or opinions and generally do a good job providing interpretation services. If your client identifies interpretation issues, or if you become aware that there are concerns regarding interpretation, it is your duty to mention this during the hearing and put your concerns on the record. It is also necessary to do so if you intend to appeal a decision. By indicating on the record that there is an interpretation issue, you reduce the belief that you only brought up issues regarding the interpreter because you were unhappy with the outcome.

IRB Hearings

IRB hearings are open to the public and are adversarial in nature. Adjudicators (or members as they are called at the IRB) are expected to be fair and impartial, and are not bound by any legal or technical rules of evidence.[34] While members are not bound by technical rules of evidence, the IRB publishes a document that explains how evidence is weighed before all tribunals under the IRB umbrella. The "Weighing Evidence"[35] guide will enhance your understanding of how evidence is assessed and weighed before IRB proceedings. As a best practice, have all documents translated by a certified translator (you provide a copy of the original and the translation to the IRB); obtain original copies of all documents (and give a reasonable explanation for not having an original to provide to the board); use your client's testimony to identify and provide a reasonable explanation for any discrepancies in your documentation, rather than hoping that discrepancies will not

34 IRPA, s 17.3.

35 Immigration and Refugee Board of Canada, "Weighing Evidence" (31 December 2003), online: <http://www.irb.gc.ca/Eng/BoaCom/references/legjur/Pages/EvidPreu.aspx>.

be identified by the member or tribunal staff at the hearing; get the best and most direct evidence possible so that the member is not asked to infer facts; and, if this is not possible, explain why you are presenting the evidence that you have provided. Think about what the adjudicator will need to make findings of fact and connect your evidence to the facts you want the adjudicator to identify. Last, think about the likely weight that an adjudicator will attribute to your evidence. Documents and testimony that hold more weight because they are deemed more credible will impact the finding of fact made by the adjudicator and ultimately affect the outcome in your matter.

Typically, a matter before the ID starts with the member providing an introduction and overview to the hearing process. If applicable, the member will also allow the interpreter and the concerned party to converse and establish that there are no issues relating to interpretation. The hearings officer (minister's counsel) presents the minister's case first, detailing the explanation and supporting evidence for a finding of inadmissibility or continued detention. The concerned person (or the person's counsel) is then given an opportunity to respond and provide submissions relating to admissibility or supporting release. Once both parties have presented their positions, the member will ask questions to clarify their positions and clear up any discrepancies. Witnesses are then presented and questioned by both sides. After all the witnesses complete their testimony, the member will render an oral decision with reasons. Matters relating to admissibility and detention rarely result in reserved decisions, given the nature and urgency of the subject matter.

When representing someone at a detention review hearing, it is important to provide a possible alternative to detention, in addition to arguments relating to discontinuing detention altogether. One common alternative to detention is to provide a bondsperson who will agree to provide supervision and either a monetary deposit or a guarantee. A bondsperson must be a Canadian citizen over the age of 18 who resides in Canada, personally knows the person of concern, offers the bond of his or her own free will, and is willing to pledge his or her own money (i.e., the funds cannot be provided by the person in detention).[36] If unsuccessful in your arguments regarding release with no terms and conditions, you may find that arguments relating to an alternative are persuasive. It is a best practice to file a bondsperson information form,[37] but it is not necessary if you provide all the information necessary for the ID to make a determination.

36 Immigration and Refugee Board of Canada, "Information for Bondspersons" (2 October 2016), online: <http://www.irb-cisr.gc.ca/Eng/NewsNouv/info/Pages/ib-ic.aspx>.

37 Immigration and Refugee Board of Canada, "Bondsperson Information" (9 August 2016), online: <http://www.irb-cisr.gc.ca/Eng/res/form/Pages/IdSi674.aspx>.

Refugee Protection Division

To prepare properly for your client's case, review his or her BOC claim form along with the eligibility interview notes so that you can identify any areas of issue or contention in advance and address them in the hearing. The IRB website has extensive resources for legal counsel specific to the RPD. Thoroughly review the NDP related to your client's country of origin/claim along with IRB RIR results to understand the IRB position about your client's issues. Obtain evidence that would refute any IRB evidence that counters your arguments. To adequately prepare your client for a hearing before the RPD, you can arrange for a "ready tour" through a coalition of refugee service agencies.[38] Tours of the IRB hearing rooms also provide an opportunity for claimants to ask questions and understand what to expect (i.e., who will be present, what the process involves, or what to do if there is a negative decision). The tours take place in Toronto, Vancouver, and Montreal.

IRB hearings are privately conducted with one panel member presiding who maintains control of the hearing process and is not bound by technical rules of evidence. Hearings tend to be informal and non-adversarial. Anyone wanting to observe (with the exception of representatives from the UNHCR) needs special permission to attend and the consent of the claimant. Also present at the hearing are the minister's counsel (from the IRCC or CBSA, if they choose to participate), the claimant, claimant's counsel (if applicable), and any witnesses. The member will start off with an introduction and will swear in the claimant (either through an oath or a solemn affirmation). The member will also ensure that the interpreter (if applicable) and claimant can understand each other and that there are no issues regarding translation or interpretation.

If the minister's counsel is participating, they will begin by questioning the claimant. Otherwise, the member will then ask questions followed by the counsel for the claimant. Any witnesses will then be called and questioned. After the witness testimony, parties are invited to make closing submissions regarding the evidence that refutes or supports their arguments. It is common for decisions to be rendered at the end of a hearing, but it is equally common to reserve more complex decisions.

38 Immigration and Refugee Board of Canada, "Refugee Claims—Claimants" (23 February 2018), online: <http://www.irb.gc.ca/Eng/RefClaDem/Pages/ClaDem.aspx>.

Decisions

ID decisions are normally rendered orally right after the parties have concluded their submissions.

Admissibility Hearings

After the admissibility hearing, the member will make one of two findings. If the member determines that there are grounds for an inadmissibility finding, he or she will issue a removal order for the person concerned. The member can issue one of three types of orders:

- Departure order: This orders the person to leave Canada within 30 days of the effective date of the order. Before leaving, the person concerned must obtain a certificate of departure from the CBSA at a POE. This provides documentation that the person intends to leave Canada. If he or she fails to leave Canada within 30 days, the departure order becomes a deportation order.
- Deportation order: This requires that the person concerned leave Canada and means he or she is unable to return without express written permission from the Canadian government. A deportation is issued for serious matters relating to security or serious infractions of the law.
- Exclusion order: This requires that the person concerned leave Canada and means he or she is unable to return for either one or two years and only with written consent of the Canadian government.

If the member believes that the allegations of the minister are unfounded or not supported by the evidence, the person concerned is found to be admissible or maintains the status currently held. If the person already held status, he or she would maintain that status, and no removal would occur.

Detention Reviews

After a detention review hearing, the member will either order the release of the person detained (with or without terms and conditions), or the member will elect to continue with detention. If an individual is released with terms and conditions, a bondsperson may supervise him or her. The person may also have to adhere to other terms, like a curfew, living with a particular person (who may or may not be the bondsperson), or avoiding alcohol and drugs.

Refugee Protection Division

After an RPD hearing, the member will either render an oral decision with reasons (sometimes a decision with reasons to follow) or reserve his or her decision and send the claimant a notice of decision in the mail. The member will either accept the claim, and determine that your client is a convention refugee or a person in need of protection, or reject the claim. The notice of decision will provide detailed reasons for the decision and will identify if an appeal should be filed with the RAD or if an application for leave and judicial review should be filed with the Federal Court. In certain circumstances, an appeal cannot be filed with the RAD:

- The claimant is a designated foreign national.
- The refugee claim was withdrawn or abandoned.
- The RPD determined that the claim has no credible basis or is manifestly unfounded.
- The claim was made at a land border with the United States, and the claim was sent to the RPD as an exception to the Safe Third Country Agreement.
- The minister applied to cease refugee protection, and the member has determined that this will occur.
- The minister applied to vacate the decision to allow the refugee protection claim, and the member has determined that this shall occur.
- The claim was sent to the IRB before the time stipulated in the amendments to the IRPA concerning appeal rights.[39]

Appeals

Immigration Appeal Division

The IAD hears five types of appeals under section 63 of the IRPA:

> 63(1) A person who has filed in the prescribed manner an application to sponsor a foreign national as a member of the family class may appeal to the Immigration Appeal Division against a decision not to issue the foreign national a permanent resident visa.
>
> (2) A foreign national who holds a permanent resident visa may appeal to the Immigration Appeal Division against a decision to make a removal order against them made under subsection 44(2) or made at an admissibility hearing.
>
> (3) A permanent resident or a protected person may appeal to the Immigration Appeal Division against a decision to make a removal order against them made under subsection 44(2) or made at an admissibility hearing.
>
> (4) A permanent resident may appeal to the Immigration Appeal Division against a decision made outside of Canada on the residency obligation under section 28.

39 Immigration and Refugee Board of Canada, “Claimant’s Guide: What Will Happen at My Hearing?” (30 November 2017), online: <http://www.irb-cisr.gc.ca/Eng/RefClaDem/Pages/ClaDemGuide.aspx#_Toc340245825>.

(5) The minister may appeal to the Immigration Appeal Division against a decision of the Immigration Division in an admissibility hearing.

The IAD hears four types of hearings:

- Sponsorship appeals: Appeals from Canadian citizens and permanent residents whose applications to sponsor a family member were denied;
- Removal order appeals: Appeals from permanent residents, foreign nationals with permanent resident status, and protected persons who have been ordered removed from Canada;
- Loss of permanent residency appeals: Appeals from permanent residents who received a negative decision overseas regarding residency obligations under section 28 of the IRPA; and
- Minister's appeal: Appeals from a decision made by the ID at an admissibility hearing.

It is the only division of the IRB that has been conferred with all the powers, rights, and privileges of a superior court.[40] IAD appeal hearings are all **de novo** hearings, meaning that they are new hearings that provide an opportunity to present new evidence.

In relation to removal order appeals, people who have been deemed inadmissible because of serious criminality carrying a punishment of six months or more, involvement in organized crime, national security concerns, or violations of human or international rights are unable to appeal matters to the IAD. Additionally, failed refugee claimants and foreign nationals who do not have a permanent resident visa are also precluded from appealing a removal order.

A matter before the IAD can be initiated by filing a notice of appeal using the form that corresponds with the jurisdictional location of the appellant (i.e., Toronto, Vancouver, or Montreal). If the appellant received the removal order at an ID admissibility hearing, the appellant has the ability to submit the Notice of Appeal by hand at the end of the ID hearing. Otherwise, the appellant must file the Notice of Appeal and a copy of the removal order with IAD within 30 days after receipt of the removal order.

The parties will first receive a notice to appear for a scheduling conference (assignment court). At the scheduling conference, the member will assess whether the matter is ready for referral to a hearing. If it is, the parties are given a date and time for hearing. The appellant must serve and file any documents along with witness information that he or she intends to rely on no later than 20 days before the hearing. The minister is also required to provide the

de novo the Latin term for "starting afresh" or "from the beginning." A de novo hearing is a new hearing that has been granted by the courts to begin anew

40 IRPA, s 174.

parties with the official record of documents from the ID hearing no later than 20 days before the hearing. The appellant is given another 10 days to provide a response (if any) to the minister's record and submissions. Any documents that are not submitted 20 days prior will not be permitted to be used in the tribunal process without consent of the member.

IAD hearings are conducted by one panel member. Also present are the appellant and the appellant's counsel, an interpreter (if needed and requested), the minister's counsel who presents evidence supporting a removal finding, and any witnesses identified by the parties. Hearings begin with the member providing an introduction and swearing in the appellant and witnesses. The appellant presents evidence first and is questioned by the minister's counsel. Witnesses are then called and questioned. After that, the appellant makes submissions supporting the case for the appellant to remain in Canada. The minister provides responding submissions supporting removal, and the appellant is given an opportunity to provide reply submissions. At the conclusion, the member either provides an oral decision or reserves the decision and will send the final determination to the parties by mail within 90 days.

Appeals are allowed if the member is of the opinion that the decision was incorrect in fact or law or that it breached fundamentals of natural justice, or when considering humanitarian and compassionate factors. If the appeal is allowed, the appellant is able to stay in Canada. If the appeal is stayed, the appellant is able to remain in Canada under terms and conditions that are determined by the member. Finally, if the appeal is dismissed, the appellant will be removed from Canada by the CBSA. The parties have the ability to appeal an IAD decision to the Federal Court by way of an application for leave and judicial review.

Refugee Appeal Division

The RAD hears appeals from the RPD and became operational with the passing of Bill C-31, *Protecting Canada's Immigration System Act*, in 2012. Bill C-31 came into effect on December 15, 2012 and amended the IRPA in many ways. In addition to other changes, the minister was able to identify a **designated country of origin** (DCO) and impose mandatory detention. The most important change, however, was the enactment of the RAD. Although the IRPA

designated country of origin (DCO) countries identified by the federal government as being unlikely to produce refugees, respecting human rights, and providing state protection. Persons who make claims from a DCO at an inland IRCC office have their first hearing within 30 days. If the claim is made at a POE, the hearing is scheduled within 45 days. Non-DCO claims are heard within 60 days. DCO claimants are also unable to apply for a work permit until after their claim has been successful

provided for an internal appeals process for refugee matters in sections 110 and 111, these sections were not proclaimed into law until they became enacted in 2012. Appeals to the RAD can only be made by claimants who initiated cases with the RPD after December 15, 2012. This is significant because the IRB still has a significant backlog of "legacy" cases that were initiated before December 15, 2012. Legacy claimants do not have access to the RAD.
In addition to legacy cases, claimants cannot appeal to the RAD if:

- they have been deemed a **designated foreign national (DFN)**.
- the claim was referred as an exception to the Safe Third Country Agreement.
- the RPD decided that the claim was unfounded or had no credible basis.
- the claim was withdrawn or declared abandoned.[41]

Neither can you appeal to RAD about:

- a decision from a rehearing of a claim that was referred to the IRB before the coming into force of the new refugee protection provisions
- a decision on a Minister's application to vacate refugee protection or on a Minister's application for cessation of refugee protection
- the deemed rejection of a claim because of an order of surrender under the *Extradition Act*
- a decision on a pre-removal risk assessment (PRRA).[42]

To initiate an appeal to the RAD, a claimant must file a notice of appeal from a RPD decision within 15 days after receipt of written reasons from the RPD.[43] The appeal must be perfected within 30 days of receipt of the written reasons by serving and filing an appellant's record. The RAD also requires that you file the appellant record checklist when submitting your record. The record consists of a written statement and memorandum not exceeding 30 pages. The RPD provides the RAD with the record of hearing from the claim, so appellants can rely on the evidence that was submitted to the RPD and do not need to provide any additional evidence. If you are presenting new

designated foreign national (DFN) in accordance with section 20.1 of IRPA, a person who is designated by the minister as an irregular arrival because, for example, the person's identity cannot be established, there is a need to determine inadmissibility, or reasonable grounds exist to believe that the person has been smuggled into Canada

41 Immigration and Refugee Board of Canada, "Refugee Appeals—Appellants" (22 December 2016), online: <http://www.irb-cisr.gc.ca/Eng/RefApp/Pages/RefApp.aspx>.

42 *Ibid.*

43 IRPR, s 159.91(1)(a).

evidence to the RAD in support of the appeal, the RAD will determine if it will be allowed by evaluating:

- if the evidence existed when the RPD issued a negative decision,
- if the evidence was not reasonably available at the time that the RPD issued a negative decision, or
- if the RPD could have expected the claimant to provide the evidence when the claim was rejected.[44]

The RAD will explain its determination regarding the new evidence in its written reasons.

If the minister is the one who initiates the appeal, the refugee claimant must file a notice of intent to respond along with a responding record within 15 days after receiving the minister's record and documents.

The RAD assigns one panel member to cases, does not normally conduct oral hearings, and generally makes determinations based on written documents. Matters before the RAD tend to rely on the evidence contained in the hearing record provided by the RPD, and decisions are mailed to the parties within 90 days of the perfecting date.

The RAD may hold an oral hearing if the appellant provides new evidence, and this evidence shows that:

- there are issues regarding credibility;
- the evidence is central to the decision in the RPD claim; or
- the evidence provides good reason to either reject or allow the appeal.[45]

If the RAD feels that it is appropriate, it may also hold a hearing with a three-member panel. The parties are notified of this change in panel structure by a notice posted on the RAD tab of the IRB website under the "What's New" heading.[46]

Hearings before the RAD follow a similar process to hearings before the IRB. The panel (whether it consists of one or three members) will deliver a brief introduction to the process and provide an opportunity for the appellant to converse with the interpreter in order to ensure that there are no issues regarding interpretation. The appellant will then provide testimony, followed by the examination of any witnesses. Parties are then invited to provide representations to explain why an appeal should be granted. The RAD rarely

44 Immigration and Refugee Board of Canada, "Appellant's Guide: Understanding the RAD Appeal Process" (April 2017), online: <http://www.irb-cisr.gc.ca/Eng/RefApp/Pages/RefAppGuide.aspx#s4.01>.

45 *Ibid.*

46 Immigration and Refugee Board of Canada, "Refugee Appeal Division" (8 January 2018), online: <http://www.irb-cisr.gc.ca/Eng/RefApp/Pages/RadSar.aspx>.

provides an oral decision and parties should expect to receive a written decision within 90 days of the hearing.

The RAD can confirm the RPD decision, set the RPD decision aside and replace it with a new decision, or send the case back for re-determination by the RPD.

Federal Court

According to section 11 of the *Federal Courts Act*[47] and section 119 of the Federal Court Rules,[48] paralegals and immigration consultants are not permitted to act as representatives in Federal Court matters. Parties can, however, be self-represented. Although the Federal Courts and related appeals processes are outside of the paralegal scope of practice, it is important for paralegals to understand the judicial review and appeal process and Federal Court jurisdiction to ensure that they provide adequate representation to clients at the tribunal level. The Federal Court jurisdiction includes the review of decisions, orders, and actions of the IRB, CBSA, and IRCC, as well as their decision-makers. In order to seek relief to the Federal Courts, you must file an application for leave and judicial review within 15 days of receipt of a decision made in Canada and within 60 days of receipt of a decision made outside of Canada (e.g., a visa office abroad). It is important to indicate the date of receipt of the decision (rather than the date of the decision itself), as that is the date from which the 15 or 60 days is calculated by the Registry Officers who receive the document.

This is a two-stage process. The first step requires the court to determine if leave should be granted. If leave is granted, then a hearing date for an oral judicial review hearing is provided. A judicial review determines whether the decision-making process was fair and reasonable. The authority to provide a review comes from section 18.1(3) of the *Federal Courts Act*, and the grounds for judicial review are set out in section 118.1(4):

> (4) The Federal Court may grant relief under subsection (3) if it is satisfied that the federal board, commission or other tribunal
>
> (a) acted without jurisdiction, acted beyond its jurisdiction or refused to exercise its jurisdiction;
>
> (b) failed to observe a principle of natural justice, procedural fairness or other procedure that it was required by law to observe;
>
> (c) erred in law in making a decision or an order, whether or not the error appears on the face of the record;

47 RSC 1985, c F-7.

48 Government of Canada, "Federal Courts Rules (SOR/98-106)" (24 April 2018), online: <http://laws-lois.justice.gc.ca/eng/regulations/SOR-98-106/>.

> (d) based its decision or order on an erroneous finding of fact that it made in a perverse or capricious manner or without regard for the material before it;
>
> (e) acted, or failed to act, by reason of fraud or perjured evidence; or
>
> (f) acted in any other way that was contrary to law.

If the court finds that one of the grounds for judicial review exists, the court can render one of three remedies:

- send the matter back to the tribunal/department/agency for re-determination by a differently constituted panel,
- quash the decision, or
- uphold the decision.

After a judicial review hearing before the Federal Court, the court will always inquire if the parties have a question that they would like certified. If no question is presented, or if the court does not certify a question posed by the parties, the decision of the Federal Court is final. Generally, the court will reserve its decision in order to properly contemplate the issues that have been argued in the judicial review hearing.

Under section 74(d) of the IRPA, leave to appeal to the Federal Court of Appeal will only be granted if the court certifies a question of general importance. If leave is granted as a result of a certifiable question, the appeal will address only the question and no other issues.

Very few matters come before the SCC. Leave to appeal to the Supreme Court is granted only if:

> the Supreme Court is of the opinion that any question involved therein is, by reason of its public importance or the importance of any issue of law or any issue of mixed law and fact involved in that question, one that ought to be decided by the Supreme Court or is, for any other reason, of such a nature or significance as to warrant decision by it, and leave to appeal from that judgment is accordingly granted by the Supreme Court.[49]

---

49 *Supreme Court Act*, RSC 1985, c S-26, s 40(1).

Case Law

Brown v Canada (Citizenship and Immigration), 2017 FC 710

Brown is a 2017 decision of the Federal Court that provided clarification of issues surrounding unlawful detention and whether the current immigration detention scheme violates the Charter. The appeal, launched in partnership with End Immigration Detention Network, argued that pre-removal detention greater than three years violates section 12 of the Charter; the fact that there is no time by which removals must occur violates sections 7, 12, and 15 of the Charter; and that a "hard cap" of 18 months for immigration detention should be instituted. The court heard extensive arguments and first-hand accounts (via affidavit) of those who have been adversely affected by immigration detention and highlighted some of the serious issues that detainees and their loved ones endure.

The court held that the length of detention depends on the facts and circumstances of each case and that the current detention scheme does not contravene sections 7 and 9 of the Charter. With regard to the section 12 argument, the SCC evaluated the four-part test that was established in *Charkaoui*[50] to make a determination and found that Brown's detention did not violate section 12. The court also conducted an analysis of section 1 of the Charter and outlined clearly the provisions in the IRPA and regulations regarding the minimum legal requirements for lawful detention. This is useful to have as a checklist to ensure that your client has been handled in compliance with the law. Despite Mr Brown's unsuccessful appeal, the court provided a very useful decision that gave clarity regarding a controversial and difficult subject. The court also certified a question that will now go forward for consideration:

> Does the *Canadian Charter of Rights and Freedoms*, Part I of the *Constitution Act, 1982*, being Schedule B to the *Canada Act, 1982* (UK), 1982, c 11 impose a requirement that detention for immigration purposes not exceed a prescribed period of time, after which it is presumptively unconstitutional, or a maximum period, after which release is mandatory?[51]

Singh v Minister of Employment and Immigration, [1985] 1 SCR 177

Singh is an important SCC case that actually led to the creation of the IRB and dismantled the previous refugee determination scheme. It is also important because the court clarified who is protected under section 7 of the Charter and further clarified procedural fairness for refugee claimants. In *Singh* the court extended section 7 protection to any person in Canada, regardless of the

50 *Charkaoui v Canada (Citizenship and Immigration)*, 2007 SCC 9, [2007] 1 SCR 350.

51 *Brown v Canada (Citizenship and Immigration)*, 2017 FC 710 at para 162.

person's status in the country, holding that removal to a country where there is a threat to life, liberty, and security of the person was a violation of section 7. Furthermore, the court determined that where credibility is a serious concern, hearings based solely on written submissions are also a violation of the meaning of fundamental justice as outlined in section 7. Failure to provide an oral hearing in such circumstances is not saved by section 1, which provides for exceptions to Charter provisions. As such, the federal government created the IRB and overhauled the refugee determination system to hold quasi-judicial oral hearings for matters originating in Canada.

YZ v Canada (Citizenship and Immigration), 2015 FC 892, [2016] 1 FCR 575

In 2009, an auditor's report was published indicating widespread abuse of the refugee protection system, especially with regard to refugee claims made by individuals who come from countries not traditionally associated with persecution. Additionally, Canada received significant criticism for not instituting the internal appeals process component of the IRPA. In response to this report and to address concerns regarding the fairness of the refugee appeals process, the federal government announced a number of reforms in 2012 through Bill C-31. Among other reforms, change included the creation of the RAD, the designation of certain countries as DCOs, and limitations placed on claimant rights for individuals from DCOs. Claims associated with DCOs have shorter timelines for first hearings at the IRB. DCO claims initiated at IRCC inland offices are heard in 30 days; DCO claims initiated at the POE are heard within 45 days; and non-DCO claims are heard within 60 days. Additionally, DCO claimants were not allowed to appeal to the RAD when Bill C-31 was first instituted. The government position is that DCOs (e.g., the US, UK, Australia, France, Germany, and Israel) are "countries that do not normally produce refugees and respect human rights and offer state protection,"[52] and "the Designated Countries of Origin policy is meant to deter abuse of the refugee system by people who come from countries generally considered safe."[53] Given this position, the government had determined that if a DCO claim were unsuccessful before the RPD and already carried with it a belief that the country of origin was unlikely to be associated with legitimate refugee claims, the claim should therefore not have an appeal option available.

The appeal in YZ dealt with the timeline issue and the right to appeal issue. The applicant claimed that differential timelines for DCO claimants were discriminatory and that the inability to appeal to the RAD for unsuccessful DCO

52 Immigration and Citizenship Canada, "Designated Countries of Origin Policy" (3 April 2017), online: <http://www.cic.gc.ca/english/refugees/reform-safe.asp>.

53 *Ibid.*

claimants was a violation of section 15 of the Charter. After significant analysis in a 118-page decision, the court certified the following two questions:

> Does paragraph 110(2)(d.1) of the *Immigration and Refugee Protection Act* ("IRPA") comply with subsection 15(1) of the *Charter?*
>
> If not, is paragraph 110(2)(d.1) of the *IRPA* a reasonable limit on *Charter* rights that is prescribed by law and can be demonstrably justified under section 1 of the *Charter?*[54]

The court also held that the timeline issues were irrelevant, but denying DCO claimants the right to appeal to the RAD violated the Charter. DCO claimants can now appeal decisions to the RAD.

KEY LEGISLATION

Immigration and Refugee Protection Act

Immigration and Refugee Protection Regulation, SOR/2002-227

Bill C-31, *Protecting Canada's Immigration System Act*

Safe Third Country Agreement

1951 and 1967 Convention Relating to the status of Refugees (signed in 1969)

1966 International Covenant on Civil and Political Rights (ICCPR) (signed in 1976)

1984 Convention Against Torture and Other Cruel, Inhuman, or Degrading Treatment or Punishment (signed in 1969)

Second Optional Protocol to the ICCPR, Aiming at the Abolition of the Death Penalty (signed in 2005)

Federal Court Rules, SOR/98-106

Federal Courts Immigration and Refugee Protection Rules, SOR/93-22

54 *YZ v Canada (Citizenship and Immigration)*, 2015 FC 892, [2016] 1 FCR 575 at para 183.

KEY TERMS

alienage, 328
convention refugees, 318
de novo, 336
designated country of origin (DCO), 337
designated foreign national (DFN), 338
foreign national, 324
in status, 324
nexus, 328
non-refoulement, 318
permanent resident, 324
safe third country, 321

REVIEW QUESTIONS

1. What is a convention refugee?
2. What is a person in need of protection?
3. How did the decision in *Singh v Minister of Employment and Immigration* impact Canada's refugee determination system?
4. What were the changes to Canada's refugee determination system that came into effect with the passing of Bill C-31, *Protecting Canada's Immigration System Act*?
5. What changes were made to the refugee determination process in Canada as a result of the decision in *YZ v Canada*?
6. How are members of the IRB appointed?
7. What are the five types of appeals that the IAD hears?
8. Explain what a de novo hearing is.
9. What are the jurisdictions of the RPD, RAD, ID, and IAD?
10. What are the four elements that must be established for a person to be deemed a convention refugee?

SCENARIOS

Scenario 1: The RPD

Maude is a 21-year-old student who comes from Denlandia.[55] Denlandia is known for abuse and persecution of those who speak out against the government. In recent years, accusations have been made against the government related to a number of incarcerations and reports of torture associated with activism. Maude was raised in a relatively affluent area of the country and was not politically involved while she was a teen. In fact, her father is a well-known businessperson who has received many government contracts. When Maude began her university studies, she was part of a student group that was involved in activism related to social issues. At first, the issues were related to homelessness and poverty. As time progressed, the students examined oppressive government policies and legislation, and they organized student rallies to bring attention to these matters.

Maude was sure that this was her life's work and changed her major to include studies in international development. After one particular rally on campus, Maude and her colleagues were identified as the organizers. They were arrested, questioned for four hours, and threatened with further consequences if they did not stop their behaviour. They began to organize another rally that would take place within two months. Within a month of Maude being arrested and detained, her father lost a very important contract with the government. He was told that until he could control his daughter, he did not deserve to receive any benefit from the government. Maude started to notice that she was being followed by men that she did not know. Some of her friends in the group had stopped coming to school, and she was unable to reach them. Maude also began to receive phone calls where someone would yell obscenities into the phone and hang up. Scared, Maude's family sent her to live with an aunt on the other side of the country. Within one month of moving, the phone calls started, and Maude was being followed again. Concerned for her safety, Maude travelled to Canada and made a refugee claim at the Toronto International Airport.

What are Maude's prospects of being deemed a convention refugee or person in need of protection?

55 This is a fictitious country.

Scenario 2: The ID

Frankie came to Canada in 2001 from Rossland on a six-month visitor's visa. He decided that he did not want to go back to Rossland because his employment prospects there were poor, and life was very difficult. Although his status in Canada has been precarious, he has been able to work on a cash-only basis, find long-term companionship, start a family, develop community ties, and send money home to help his family. They rely on the remittances that he sends on a biweekly basis.

One day, Frankie was picked up by the CBSA at his place of employment. It had been reported that his employer hired many individuals who were not authorized to work in Canada, and Frankie was detained. An immigration officer has completed a section 44 report. The immigration officer has determined that Frankie should be removed, and the matter has been referred to the ID for a detention hearing. Frankie is currently in immigration detention, pending the outcome of the hearing before the ID.

What arguments should you make to increase the likelihood that Frankie will be released?

GLOSSARY

abatement: a reduction in the amount of rent due awarded by the Landlord and Tenant Board when landlords fail to fulfill their maintenance obligations

adjournment: the postponement of a case conference or hearing until some future date (the LAT Rules describe how to request an adjournment and the circumstances when an adjournment may be granted by the tribunal)

adjudicator: a decision-maker who presides over (or hears) formal disputes between parties and makes a decision

adversarial: two parties arguing their case before an independent trier of fact

alienage: one of the four components of refugee determination: refugee claimants must be outside their country of nationality or country of former habitual residence and unwilling or unable to return to said country because of a fear of persecution and the belief that they are unable to avail themselves of state protection

ancestry: family descent or genealogy

arbitration: one of the four components of alternative dispute resolution (negotiation, mediation, and collaborative law being the other three) meant to attain a legal settlement outside of the court room; arbitrator hears legal arguments from both sides and determines an award for one party; result is legally binding (although some exceptions exist)

benchers: elected licensees or appointed officials who sit on convocation and govern the LSO; some sit as LST members

benefit unit: a person and all dependants on behalf of whom the person receives or applies for income support

bona fide: a Latin term that when translated means "good faith." In the context of the CHRT, this term is usually used in relation to exceptions. Actions that are sincere, honest, and without deceit are considered bona fide

Book of Authorities: a bound book of case law and/or references to legislation that you will be using to support your client's case in your closing at the hearing before the CHRT

case conference: the first meeting between the parties in a dispute and an adjudicator. This is an opportunity for the parties to discuss the dispute with an adjudicator and attempt to settle the claim; if the case does not settle, the adjudicator will assist the parties in preparing for and scheduling a hearing date

case conference report and order: issued after a case conference by the adjudicator and sets out any orders made, such as the date and format of the hearing, the specific witnesses who will give evidence, and any documents that must be exchanged or produced

certification: a trade union's status to negotiate on behalf of a group of workers

citizenship: membership in a state or nation

collective agreements: shared contracts among members of trade unions vis-à-vis their employers

collective bargaining: the process when a trade union negotiates new contract terms with an employer as the basis of a new collective agreement

colour: the hue of a person's skin; associated with race

commencement days: the date assigned by the ARB as the start date of the appeal and from which all further events are scheduled in accordance with the schedule of events

Common Rules of Practice and Procedure: Effective October 2, 2017, the Licence Appeal Tribunal, Animal Care Review Board, and the Fire Safety Commission adopted the Common Rules of Practice and Procedure, which will apply to all tribunal proceedings filed on or after October 2, 2017; previous versions of the Rules will continue to apply to matters filed before October 2, 2017

compensation: consideration paid from one party to another for damages caused

computation of time: the act of computing, counting, or numbering for the purpose of serving legal documents, providing notification to parties, or filing documents with the tribunal; errors may lead to the legal action being invalidated

convention refugees: persons who are outside of their country of birth or habitual residence who are unwilling or unable to return to their country of birth or habitual residence because of a well-founded fear of persecution based on race, religion, political opinion, nationality, or membership in a particular social group

costs: expenses that can be claimed by either party after a legal proceeding (allowable costs and test for awarding costs are set out in the Rules)

country or place of origin: country or region a person is from

creed: a set of beliefs or aims that guides one's actions; sometimes connected to religion or faith

cross-appeal: a new appeal launched by the original respondent to an application against the original applicant; the original respondent becomes the appellant in the cross-appeal, and the original applicant or appellant becomes the respondent for the purposes of the cross-appeal only

date of loss: date the accident occured

de novo: the Latin term for "starting afresh" or "from the beginning." A de novo hearing is a new hearing that has been granted by the courts to begin anew

designated country of origin (DCO): countries identified as by the federal government as being unlikely to produce refugees, respecting human rights, and providing state protection. Persons who make claims from a DCO at an inland IRCC office have their first hearing within 30 days. If the claim is made at a POE, the hearing is scheduled within 45 days. Non-DCO claims are heard within 60 days. DCO claimants are also unable to apply for a work permit until after their claim has been successful

designated foreign national (DFN): in accordance with section 20.1 of IRPA, a person who is designated by the minister as an irregular arrival because, for example, the person's identity cannot be established, there is a need to determine inadmissibility, or reasonable grounds exist to believe that the person has been smuggled into Canada

disability: (1) a medical condition that a person has; from this perspective, disability covers a broad range and degree of conditions, some visible and some not visible; (2) a problem that occurs when people's environments are not designed to suit their abilities

disclosure: providing to the other party a copy of the evidence that one party plans to use during a hearing

discrimination: subjecting another person to differential treatment by either imposing a burden on them or denying them a privilege, benefit, or opportunity enjoyed by others because of their characteristics

employers: defined under the WSIA as persons having in their service under a contract of service or apprenticeship another person engaged in work in or about an industry, including (1) trustees, receivers, liquidators, executors, or administrators who carry on an industry; (2) persons who authorize or permit a learner to be in or about an industry for the purpose of undergoing training or probationary work; or (3) deemed employers

ethnic origin/ethnicity: sharing a distinctive cultural and historical tradition; often connected to race, place of origin, ancestry, religion, or creed

evaluative mediation: a mediation in which the mediator provides their opinion and assessment of the merits of the case

evidence: testimony and presentation of documents, records, objects, and other such items relating to the existence or non-existence of alleged or disputed facts being decided by a court or tribunal

exemption: not bound to fulfill an obligation or a requirement that others must observe

expedited proceedings: an internal process through which applications can be fast-tracked through the standard hearing process

expert witnesses: specialists in a subject, often technical, who may present an expert opinion in a legal proceeding (procedures for using expert witnesses are set out in the Rules)

expropriation: the act of a municipal, regional, provincial, or federal government to reclaim private property for government use

family status: according to the OHRC, "the status of being in a parent and child relationship. This can also mean a parent and child 'type' of relationship, embracing a range of circumstances without blood or adoptive ties but with similar relationships of care, responsibility and commitment"

Financial Services Commission of Ontario (FSCO): a regulatory agency of the Ministry of Finance that regulates insurance, pension plans, loan and trust companies, credit unions, caisses populaires, mortgage brokering, and co-operative corporations in Ontario

foreign national: according to section 2(1) of the IRPA, a person who is not a Canadian citizen or a permanent resident, including a person who is stateless

gender: societally attributed characteristics of masculinity and femininity

gender expression: the external attributes, behaviour, appearance, dress, etc., by which people express themselves and through which others perceive those people's gender

gender identity: a person's conscious sense of maleness and/or femaleness; this sense of self is separate and distinct from biological sex

Governor-in-Council: the Governor General acting on the advice of the members of Cabinet, also known as the Privy Council

greenbelt: 7,200 square kilometres of protected green space, such as forests, farmland, and watersheds, surrounding the Golden Horseshoe region of Ontario; created by the Ontario government through legislation in 2005

harassment: engaging in a course of comments or actions that are known, or ought reasonably to be known, to be unwelcome. It can involve words or actions that are known or should be known to be offensive, embarrassing, humiliating, demeaning or unwelcome

hearing de novo: a hearing in which the adjudicator deals completely afresh with a matter that has already been heard once before

hearing on the merits: proceedings in which the panel will entertain the final question of law or fact to be determined and conclude the matter by providing a decision that will dispose of the legal issue up for determination; not an interim proceeding

in status: legally entitled to remain in Canada; to maintain status means to renew visitor's visas, student visas, work permits, etc., and to not stay in Canada beyond the time limits or dates indicated on immigration documents

infrastructure: the physical assets, such as roads, bridges, and utility power lines, owned by governments or corporations for the benefit of an organized society

interim compensation: assistance awarded before the final determination of the issue

interlocutory orders: interim orders; do not dispose of the matter

intervenors: interested parties in the outcome of a case, but neither the applicant nor the respondent, who are granted status by the tribunal to give limited submissions to a hearing panel

joint document brief: a collection of documentary evidence that both parties agree is relevant and should be put before the decision-maker for the hearing, the organization of which keeps the hearing more organized and focused and the volume of paper down

judicial independence: a cornerstone of the Canadian judicial system that ensures security of tenure, financial security, and administrative independence

judicial review: a process that allows courts to review the decisions of administrative tribunals and supervise how they exercise their statutory powers. Individuals can challenge the decisions made by public bodies, such as agencies, boards, and tribunals, to ensure they have stayed within the powers delegated to them by the government and the law has not been misapplied. It is important to note that bringing an application for judicial review is meant to be a last resort and parties should generally exhaust any internal appeal or reconsideration options that may exist within the tribunal first

land use planning: an assessment process intended to provide guidance in the inherent conflict between rural land use, urban development, and industrial expansion by selecting the land uses that will best serve the needs of the people while protecting scarce resources

landlord: an individual or a corporation that owns real estate and, in turn, leases use of the owned premises to another entity (individual or corporation) for a specified term

Law Society of Ontario: the licensing and regulatory body in Ontario for lawyers and paralegals

leave to appeal: permission for an appeal to be heard; not an automatic right of appeal

loss-of-earnings (LOE) benefits: payments from the WSIB intended to replace some of the future wages the worker lost as a result of the work-related injury or illness

marital status: section 10 of the Code defines marital status as "the status of being married, single, widowed, divorced or separated and includes the status of living with a person in a conjugal relationship outside marriage," including both same-sex and opposite sex relationships

mediation: a way of settling an issue without going to a hearing by the parties discussing possible settlements with a mediator; if a settlement is reached it goes to a vice-chair for approval, after which the case can be closed

mediation brief: a bound book of documents filed in advance of a mediation, which may include things such as the facts, evidence, case law, legal principles, assessment of costs or damages, etc.

mediation-adjudication (med-adj): an option available at the CHRT to resolve the complaint in which the member who conducts the mediation would hear and adjudicate the matter if mediation was unsuccessful

minor variances: procedural requests made by individuals or corporations to be exempt from a specific zoning by-law because of hardship or circumstance

municipalities: legal entities incorporated as boroughs, villages, towns, or cities

nexus: a connection between, or intersection with, more than one thing. To be deemed a convention refugee, the person must show that the well-founded fear of persecution is connected (or has a nexus) to race, religion, political opinion, nationality, or membership in a particular social group (see convention refugee)

non-binding: materials or case law that the decision-maker is not required to follow; items are persuasive but no requirement to abide by them

non-economic loss (NEL) benefits: an award from the WSIB for workers who have a work-related permanent impairment that recognizes the permanent effects of a workplace injury on a worker's life outside work

non-refoulement: a fundamental principle of refugee law which in essence states that we should not be returning a refugee claimant to a country where they will face persecution. Signatories to international refugee conventions agree that they will not remove someone to a country where they will face persecution and irreparable harm

notice of contravention: issued pursuant to the *Ontario College of Trades and Apprenticeship Act, 2009* against an uncertified person practising a trade

notice period: the timeframe within which a landlord or tenant is required to provide an opportunity to remedy or resolve an issue

oral hearing: the proceeding whereby the applicant/appellant is provided the opportunity to verbally tell the WSIB/WSIAT why he or she is entitled to the benefits and the respondent is allowed to respond to the claims

overpayment: money paid to a recipient that is in excess of the correct amount the person should have received, thus creating a debt to the Crown

pecuniary: a cost award that is given as compensation for something that is measurable or quantifiable

permanent resident: according to section 2(1) of the IRPA, "a person who has acquired permanent residency status and has not subsequently lost that status under section 46." Permanent residents have the right to live, work, and study anywhere in Canada; apply for citizenship; receive most of the social benefits that Canadian citizens receive, including health care coverage; and are protected under Canadian law and the Charter

privative clause: a statutory provision that limits the availability of appeal or review of the decision of an administrative body (e.g., s 123 of the WSIA)

prohibited or discriminatory grounds: personal characteristics outlined in the Ontario Human Rights Code upon which discrimination is prohibited

property classification: the categories into which properties may be placed, for the purposes of assessment, such as farm or residential

public utilities: providers of public services, such as energy, gas, telecommunications, waste disposal, or water

quantum of benefits: the monetary amount of the benefit

quorum: the base number or minimum number of people required to be present to proceed

race: "There is no such thing as race—instead, it is a 'social construct.' This means that society forms ideas of race based on geographic, historical, political, economic, social and cultural factors, as well as physical traits, even though none of these can legitimately be used to classify groups of people"

reconsideration: a party can request that the tribunal reconsider a decision made by the tribunal and issue a new or different decision in light of that review (procedures and test for a reconsideration of a LAT AABS decision are set out in the Rules)

registrar: an officer of the court who is responsible for the registry or register of the Ontario courts

rent control: legislation and regulations that govern residential rents and provides a price ceiling on residential rents in Ontario

reprisal: actions or threats that are intended to retaliate against an individual who has exercised his or her rights under the Code or has refused to violate someone else's rights under the Code

return-to-work plan: a proactive, formal plan that helps injured workers remain at work or safely return to suitable work and outlines the steps that workers, supervisors, and others within the organization need to take if an injury occurs

review: a request to the ARB to internally review a decision of the ARB

Rules of Conduct: mandatory ethical guidelines for licensed paralegals in Ontario

safe third country: a country from which a claim for refugee protection should have been made, when a refugee claimant was passing through it. If someone faces persecution in one country and, while headed to another country to seek asylum, he or she passes through a third country where a claim can be made, he or she must do so. So far, Canada only has a Safe Third Country Agreement with the United States

schedule of events: a timeline of how proceedings will flow from the commencement day, highlighting events such as disclosure

sex: a person's biological characteristics; discrimination under this Code ground is closely related to gender and includes pregnancy and breastfeeding

sexual harassment: similar to harassment, sexual harassment is any conduct or commentary that is unwanted or unwelcome.

sexual orientation: a personal characteristic that traverses the range of human sexuality; distinct from gender identity

sheriff: the person who manages and transports court prisoners and serves and enforces orders that have been filed with the court

statutory accident benefits: benefits provided to persons in Ontario injured by the use or operation of a motor vehicle; governed by the Statutory Accident Benefits Schedule, which is a regulation made under the Insurance Act of Ontario (also called no fault benefits)

stay: when proceedings are placed on hold or paused

stereotypes: incorrect assumptions about an individual or members of a group that are often based on misconceptions and false information

submissions: legal documents or closing oral remarks that summarize the arguments in a legal dispute

summarily dismiss: dismiss an application before a hearing on the merits, if the tribunal is satisfied that the application has no reasonable chance of success

systemic discrimination: patterns of behaviour, policies, or practices that are part of the social or administrative structures of an organization, and which create or perpetuate a position of relative disadvantage for groups identified under the Human Rights Code

tax assessment: the value of a property as determined by the Municipal Property Assessment Corporation for the purposes of paying taxes to the municipality

tenant: an individual or a corporation that possesses real estate for a set term under a lease that stipulates the amount of rent to be paid for the term

termination date: an expiration date; the date on which a leasing agreement is no longer active

terms of settlement: the details of an agreement made between parties by way of negotiation or mediation

trade unions: collections of workers who unite to promote favourable working conditions, including negotiation of fair employment contracts (collective agreements)

tribunal: a quasi-judicial body with limited jurisdiction that determines questions of fact or law

without prejudice: communications that are precluded from being disclosed or referred to in any subsequent proceedings, such as communications made between the applicant and respondent during a WSIAT mediation; they are therefore inadmissible as evidence at any subsequent proceeding, such as the hearing

work-transition plan: a plan to assist an injured worker's transition back into work and outlines the assistance and services required to enable the worker to return to the previous employer in the identified suitable and available work or, if required, to re-enter the labour market in the identified suitable occupation

workers: defined under the WSIA as persons who have entered into or are employed under a contract of service or apprenticeship, including (1) a learner, (2) a student, or (3) an auxiliary member of a police force

Writ of Possession: a writ of execution used to enforce a judgment to recover property; this authorizes the sheriff to enter premises and give possession back to the landlord when there has been a finding against a tenant

zoning by-laws: regulations established by a government on the acceptable use of an area of land

INDEX

A

abatement, defined, 62
accountability principle, 10-12
adjournment, defined, 170
adjudicator
  appointment of, 15
  defined, 173
  roles of, 15-17
adversarial, defined, 82
alienage, defined, 328
ancestry, defined, 34
arbitration, defined, 127
Assessment Review Board
  appeals, 137, 143-45, 150
    assessment appeals, 143-45
    tax appeals, 143-45
  Appeals Management Advisory Committee, 137
  application process, 142-45
  Assessment Act, 136, 138
  Assessment Review Board Act, 136, 137
  case law, 151
  City of Toronto Act, 2006, 137, 140
  commencement days, 142
  Condominium Act, 137, 140
  decisions, 150
  Education Act, 137, 141
  generally, 136
  hearing process, 145-50
    adjournments, 146
    general proceedings, 145
    mandatory meetings, 146-47
    mediation, 150
    settlement conferences, 148
    streaming, 147
    summary proceedings, 146-47
  history of, 136
  key legislation, 153
  legislation and regulations, 137-42
  Municipal Act, 137, 139
  Municipal Property Assessment Corporation, 136, 141
  Municipal Property Assessment Corporation Act, 1997, 136
  property classification, 136
  Provincial Land Tax Act, 2006, 137, 140
  quorum, 138
  reconsiderations, 150
  review, 150
  Rules of Practice and Procedure, 141
  schedule of events, 142
  Statutory Powers Procedure Act, 137
  tax assessment, 136
Automobile Accident Benefits Service, *see* Licence Appeal Tribunal

B

benchers, defined, 256
benefit unit, defined, 71
bona fide, defined, 281
Book of Authorities, defined, 287

C

Canadian Human Rights Tribunal, *see also* Human Rights Tribunal of Ontario
  appeals, 288
  application to, initiating, 283
  Book of Authorities, 287
  Canadian Bill of Rights, 279

Canadian Human Rights Tribunal (cont.)
- *Canadian Charter of Rights and Freedoms*, 279
- *Canadian Human Rights Act*, 278
- case law, 288-91
- Charter values, 279
- costs, 288
- decisions, 287
  - review by Federal Court, 287
- *Employment Equity Act*, 279, 282, 283
- Employment Equity Tribunal, 280
- *Genetic Non-Discrimination Act*, 280
- grounds of prohibited discrimination, 280-82
  - accommodation, 281
  - bona fide justification, 281
  - good faith exceptions, 281
- guidelines and regulations, 282
- hearing process, 286
- history of, 278-80
- Jordan's Principle, 289
- mediation, 284-86
  - described, 284-86
  - evaluative mediation, 284
  - mediation brief, 284
  - mediation-adjudication (med-adj), 285
- remedy orders, 287
- Rules of Procedure, 283
- *Universal Declaration of Human Rights*, 280

case conference, defined, 167
case conference report and order, defined, 170
certification, defined, 194
citizenship, defined, 34
clusters, *see* tribunal practice
collective agreements, defined, 194
collective bargaining, defined, 192
colour, defined, 34
commencement days, defined, 142
Common Rules of Practice and Procedure, defined, 162
compensation, defined, 116
computation of time, defined, 56
convention refugees, defined, 318
costs, defined, 175
country/place of origin, defined, 29
creed, defined, 34
Criminal Injuries Compensation Board
- appeals, 106
- application process, 104
- *Compensation for Victims of Crime Act*, 100-4
- *Criminal Code*, 104
- case law, 107-11
- decisions, 106
- factors considered, 102
- government assistance programs, 103
- hearing process, 105
- key legislation, 111
- history of, 100
- interim compensation, 102
- pecuniary awards, 101
- reconsiderations, 106
- rules of procedure 104-7
- *Statutory Powers Procedure Act*, 105
- stay pending criminal trial, 102
- *Victims' Bill of Rights*, 103

cross-appeal, defined, 271

D

date of loss, defined, 161
de novo, defined, 336
designated country of origin (DCO), defined, 337
designated foreign national (DFN), defined, 338
disclosure, defined, 168

E

employers, defined, 231
Environment and Land Tribunals Ontario, *see* Assessment Review Board, Local Planning Appeal Tribunal
ethnic origin/ethnicity, 32
evaluative mediation, defined, 284
evidence, defined, 173
exemption, defined, 36
expedited proceedings, defined, 194
expert witnesses, defined, 174
expropriation, defined, 120

F

family status, defined, 34
federal tribunals, *see* Canadian Human Rights Tribunal; Immigration and Refugee Board; Social Security Tribunal; tribunal practice
Financial Services Commission of Ontario (FSCO), 158-59, 163-64
foreign national, defined, 324

G

gender, defined, 29
gender expression, defined, 34
gender identity, defined, 34
Governor-in-Council, defined, 18, 300
greenbelt, defined, 117

H

hearing de novo, defined, 243
hearing on the merits, defined, 267
Human Rights Tribunal of Ontario, *see also* Canadian Human Rights Tribunal
  additional discriminatory grounds, 34-35
  adjudicators, 33
  ancestry, 35
  application, consideration of, 35
  application process, 37-40
    considerations, 38
    defer consideration request, 37
    Form 1, use of, 37
    response to application, 38-39
  case law, 44-46
  citizenship, 35
  colour, 35
  country/place of origin, 29, 31
  creed, 35
  decision, 42-43
    judicial review application, 43
  described, 28-34
  disability, 28, 30
  discrimination, 28, 30
  enforcement, 33
  ethnicity, 32, 33
  exemption for discriminatory practice, 36
  Fair Accommodation Practices Act, 31
  Fair Employment Practices Act, 31
  family status, 35
  Female Employees' Fair Remuneration Act, 31
  gender, 29, 31
  gender expression, 35
  gender identity, 35
  harassment, 28, 30
  hearing process, 40-42
    hearing/case resolution conference, 42
    mediation, 40
    mediation-adjudication (med-adj), 42
    preliminary hearings, 41
  Human Rights Code, 28, 32, 34
  Human Rights Legal Support Centre, 39
  key legislation, 46
  Labour Relations Act, 1950, 31
  marital status, 35
  Ontario Anti-Discrimination Commission Act, 31
  orders, non-compliance, 43
  prohibited/discriminatory grounds, 28-30, 34-35
  race, 28, 30
  Racial Discrimination Act, 1944, 29
  reforms, 33
  remedies, 42
  reprisal, 28, 30, 35
  sex, 30
  sexual harassment, 29, 30
  sexual orientation, 29, 31
  social areas of discrimination, 28, 34
  stereotypes, 29, 31
  Statutory Powers Procedure Act, 36
  systemic discrimination, 32, 33

I

Immigration and Refugee Board
  admissibility hearings, 325, 334
  alienage, 328
  appeals, 335-41
    Federal Court proceedings, 340
    Immigration Appeal Division proceedings, 335-37

Immigration and Refugee Board (cont.)
leave to appeal, 341
Refugee Appeal Division proceedings, 337-40
applications
Immigration Division, to, 324-27
Refugee Protection Division, to, 327-30
Bill C-31, *Protecting Canada's Immigration System Act*, 321, 337, 343
case law, 342-44
convention refugees, 318
decisions
admissibility hearings, 334
detention reviews, 334
Refugee Protection Division, 334
de novo, 336
described, 318-20
designated country of origin (DCO), 337
designated foreign national (DFN), 338
detention reviews, 326, 334
Federal Court, appeals to, 340
Federal Court Rules, 340
foreign national, 324
hearing process
Immigration Division, 330-32
IRB hearings, 331
Refugee Protection Division, 333
history of, 318
Immigration and Refuge Protection Act, 320-24
Immigration Appeal Division, 318-19, 322-23, 335-37
Immigration Division, 318-19, 322, 324-27, 330-35
in status, 324
international conventions
1984 Convention Against Torture and Other Cruel, Inhuman, or Degrading Treatment or Punishment, 320
1951 and 1967 Convention Relating to the Status of Refugees, 320
1966 International Convention on Civil and Political Rights, 320
key legislation, 344
nexus, 328
non-refoulement, 318
permanent resident, 324
Refugee Appeal Division, 319, 337-40
refugee determination systems, 319
Refugee Protection Division, 318-19, 322-23, 329-30, 334, 337-40
Safe Third Country Agreement, 321
Second Optional Protocol to the ICCPR, Aiming at the Abolition of the Death Penalty, 320-21
in status, defined, 324
infrastructure, defined, 116
interim compensation, defined, 102
interlocutory orders, defined, 259
intervenors, defined, 261

J

joint document brief, defined, 172
judicial independence, defined, 7
judicial review, defined, 177, 246

L

land use planning, defined, 120
Landlord and Tenant Board
abatement, 62
appeals, 63
application process, 53-60
applications and fees chart, 57-59
case law, 64-66
decisions, 62-64
enforcement of orders, 64
hearing process, 61
history of, 50
Human Rights Code, 52
key legislation, 66
landlord, defined, 50
non-binding interpretation guidelines, 53
notice periods, 54-57
computation of time, 56
notice requirements chart, 54-55
Ombudsman Act, 51
reconsideration/review of decision, 63
registrar, 64
rent control, 51, 50

Rental Fairness Act, 2017, 52
Residential Premises Rent Review Act, 50
Residential Tenancies Act, 2006, 50
sheriff, 64
Statutory Powers Procedures Act, 52
stay, 64
tenant, defined, 50
termination date, 57
terms of settlement, 60
writ of possession, 64
landlord, defined, 50
Law Society of Ontario, defined, 3
Law Society Tribunal
Adjudicator Code of Conduct, 256-57
appeal division, 260, 270-72
appeals, 270-72
application process, 265-67
benchers, 256
case law, 273
cross-appeal, 271
decisions, 270
described, 256-58
Guides to the Tribunal Process, topics covered, 262-65
hearing on the merits, 267
hearing division, 259, 265-70
hearing process, 267-70
adjournments, 268-69
disclosure, 269
evidence, 270
history of, 256
interlocutory orders, 259
intervenors, 261
Law Society Act, 256, 259
mission statement, 257
Modernizing Regulation of the Legal Profession Act, 2013, 256, 258-59
pre-hearing conferences, 266-67
Rules of Practice and Procedure, 261-62, 265-72
Solicitors Act, 259
Statutory Powers Procedure Act, 258
Tribunal Book of Authorities, 262
leave to appeal, defined, 300
Licence Appeal Tribunal
AABS application
adjournment, 170
case conference, 167-70
case conference report and order, 170
completing, 165
disclosure, 168, 169
e-filing, 165
filing, 164
motions, 171
preliminary issues, 166
process, 165
AABS hearing
adjudicator, role of, 173
costs, 175
decision following, 176
described, 172
disclosure, 172
evidence vs. submissions, 173
expert witnesses, 174
joint document brief, 172
orders, 176
participants, 173
preparation, 171
presentation of case, 173
procedure, 171, 172
reconsideration of decision, 176
witnesses, 174
written hearings, 178
AABS response, 166
appeal of AABS decision, 177
Automobile Accident Benefits Service (AABS)
application, *see* AABS application
benefits available, 159
case law, 163, 179-84
date of loss, 161
described, 158
dispute resolution process, 164
eligibility for benefits, 160
hearing, *see* AABS hearing
Insurance Act, 161
limitation period, 164
statutory accident benefits, 159

Licence Appeal Tribunal (cont.)
- Statutory Accident Benefits Schedule, 161
- Superintendent's and Commissioner's Guidelines, 163
- case law
  - exclusion defences, 181
  - insured person, defined, 181
  - insurer delay, 184
  - insurer examinations, 180
  - interest, 184
  - IRB disability test, 182
  - limitation periods, 179
  - NEB disability test, 183
  - minor injury issues, 181, 182
  - reasonable and necessary test, 183
  - repayment, 181
  - technical non-compliance, 180
- Common Rules of Practice and Procedure, 162
- described, 158
- judicial review, 177
- *Judicial Review Procedure Act*, 161
- key legislation, 185
- *Licence Appeal Tribunal Act, 1999*, 158
- *Statutory Powers Procedure Act*, 161

Local Planning Appeal Tribunal
- *Aggregate Resources Act*, 121
- Appeal Guides, 121-23
- appeals, 124, 125, 129
- application process, 119, 123-27
- arbitration, 127
- *Building Better Communities and Conserving Watersheds Act*, 118
- case conferences, 124
- case law, 130
- compensation, 116
- *Conservation Authorities Act*, 118
- *Consolidated Hearings Act*, 121
- decisions, 129
- described, 116
- *Development Charges Act, 1997*, 120
- *Environmental Assessment Act*, 121
- expropriation proceedings, 120, 126
- *Expropriations Act*, 122
- greenbelt, 117
- hearing process, 127
- history of, 116-19
- infrastructure, 116
- *Local Planning Appeal Tribunal Act, 2017*, 116, 118
- *Local Planning Support Centre Act, 2017*, 118
- minor variances, 120, 122
- *Municipal Act, 2001*, 122
- municipalities, 116
- Rules of Practice and Procedure, 121
- *Ontario Heritage Act*, 120
- Ontario Municipal Board, responsibilities of, 117
- *Ontario Municipal Board Act*, 117
- *Planning Act*, 116
- public utilities, 117
- *Smart Growth for Our Communities Act, 2015*, 118
- *Statutory Powers Procedure Act*, 121
- Toronto, City of, 122, 123
- zoning by-laws, 116

loss-of-earnings (LOE) benefits, defined, 237

M

marital status, defined, 34
mediation, defined, 242
mediation-adjudication (med-adj), defined, 42, 285
mediation brief, defined, 284
minor variances, defined 120
municipalities, defined, 116

N

nexus, defined, 328
non-binding, defined, 53
non-economic loss (NEL) benefits, defined, 237
non-refoulement, defined, 318
notice of contravention, defined, 191
notice period, defined, 56

O

Ontario Labour Relations Board
- *Agricultural Employees Protection Act, 2002*, 196
- anti-discrimination principles, 192
- appeals, 203
- application process, 198-201
- *Canadian Charter of Rights and Freedoms*, 192, 194
- case law, 204-6
- certification, 194
  - application for certification, Form A-1, 210-20
- collective agreements, 194
- collective bargaining, 192
- *Collective Bargaining Act*, 192
- *Colleges Collective Bargaining Act, 2008*, 196
- *Crown Employees Collective Bargaining Act, 1993*, 197
- decisions, 203
- described, 190-93
- *Employment Standards Act*, 193
- *Environmental Bill of Rights Act, 1993*, 197
- *Environmental Protection Act*, 196
- expedited proceedings, 194
- *Freedom of Information and Protection of Privacy Act*, 201
- hearing process, 201-3
- history of, 190
- *Human Rights Code*, 194
- interim order, application for (Form A-14), 199, 221-28
- *Judicial Review Procedure Act*, 203
- key legislation, 207
- *Labour Relations Act, 1995*, 190, 193-96
  - key features of, 193-96
  - regulations, 196
- notice of contravention, 191
- *Occupational Health and Safety Act*, 201
- *Ontario College of Trades and Apprenticeship Act, 2009*, 191
- *Police Services Act*, 196
- *Public Service Act*, 190
- *Public Service Labour Relations Transition Act, 1997*, 197
- reprisal, 201
- response to application, 199
- *Rules of Civil Procedure*, 191
- Rules of Procedure, 197
- *Smoke-Free Ontario Act*, 196
- *Statutory Powers Procedure Act*, 191
- trade unions, 190

Ontario Municipal Board, *see* Local Planning Appeal Tribunal

oral hearing, defined, 243

overpayment, defined, 79

P

pecuniary, defined, 101

permanent resident, defined, 324

privative clause, defined, 246

property classification, defined, 136

public utilities, defined, 117

Q

quantum of benefits, defined, 233

quorum, defined, 138

R

reconsideration, defined, 83, 176, 245

registrar, defined, 64

rent control, defined, 50

reprisal, defined, 201

return-to-work plan, defined, 233

review, defined, 150

Rules of Conduct
- defined, 3
- key rules, list of, 4-7
- *Paralegal Rules of Conduct*, 3-7

S

safe third country, defined, 321

Safety, Licensing Appeals and Standards Tribunals Ontario, *see* Licence Appeal Tribunal

schedule of events, defined, 142

sexual orientation, defined, 29

sheriff, defined, 64

Social Benefits Tribunal
- appeals, 79, 83, 84-88
- application process, 78
  - Ontario Disability Support Program, 78
  - Ontario Works, 78
- benefit unit, defined, 71
- case law, 91-96
- decisions, 83
  - reconsideration of, 83, 89-90
- director's decisions, 79
- forms, 83-90
  - application for reconsideration (Form 2), 89-90
  - instructions for filing an appeal (Form 1), 84-88
- hearing process, 80
  - adversarial approach, 82
  - generally, 80-81
  - oral hearings, 82
  - written submissions, 82
- history of, 70
- internal reviews, 79
- key legislation, 96
- *Ontario Disability Support Program Act, 1997*, 70, 71-73
  - judicial consideration of, 73-76
  - provisions of, 72
- *Ontario Works Act, 1997*, 70-71
- overpayments, 79
- procedural rules, 76-77
- SBT Rules of Procedure, 76
- Social Justice Ontario Common Rules, 76-77
- *Statutory Powers Procedure Act*, 70
- *Tranchemontagne v Ontario (Director, Disability Support Program)*, 73-76

Social Justice Tribunals Ontario, see Criminal Injuries Compensation Board, Human Rights Tribunal of Ontario, Landlord and Tenant Board, Social Benefits Tribunal

Social Security Tribunal
- adjournments, 301
- Appeal Division, 300, 310
- application process, 305-9
  - decision, 308
  - leave to appeal, 308-9
  - method of hearing, 307
  - Notice of Readiness, 306
  - procedures, 305
  - summary dismissal of appeal, 306
- Canada Pension Plan, 296, 301, 302
- Canada Pension Plan Regulations, 302
- case law, 311-14
- decisions, 308, 310
- *Department of Employment and Social Development Act*, 300
- described, 296-300
- divisions of, 297
- Employment Insurance, 296
- *Employment Insurance Act*, 301
- Employment Insurance Regulations, 301-2
- employment insurance section, 297, 299, 300, 303, 305-8
- *Federal Courts Act*, 301
- General Division, 300, 310
- Governor-in-Council, appointments by, 300
- history of, 296-300
- income security section, 297, 299, 300, 303, 305-8
- key legislation, 314
- legislation and regulations, 300-5
- members of, efficiency and effectiveness, 297-300
- Old Age Security, 297, 301, 302
- Old Age Security Regulations, 303
- Practice Directions, 303-5
- Reconsideration Request Regulations, 302
- Social Security Tribunal Regulations, 301

statutory accident benefits, defined, 159

stay, defined, 64, 102

stereotypes, defined, 29

submissions, defined, 174

summarily dismiss, defined, 306

systemic discrimination, defined, 32

T

tax assessment, defined, 136

tenant, defined, 50

termination date, defined, 57

terms of settlement, defined, 60
trade unions, defined, 190
tribunal, defined, 2
tribunal practice
- access to justice and, 2-3
- accountability principle, 10-12
- *Adjudicative Tribunals Accountability, Governance and Appointments Act, 2009*, 7-11
- adjudicators
  - appointment of, 15
  - roles of, 15-17
- case law, 20-24
- described, 2, 19
- federal tribunals
  - *Administrative Tribunals Support Service of Canada Act*, 18
  - appointment of adjudicators, 18
  - described, 17
  - governance and accountability, 18
- judicial independence, defined, 7
- key legislation, 24
- Law Society of Ontario and, 3
- non-clustered tribunals, independence and accountability in, 11-12
- Ontario clusters approach, 7-11
  - Environmental Land Tribunals Ontario cluster, 9-11
  - Safety Licensing Appeals and Standards Tribunals Ontario cluster, 9
  - Social Justice Tribunals Ontario cluster, 9-11
- *Paralegal Rules of Conduct*, 3-7
- ombudsman, role of, 12
- *Statutory Powers Procedure Act*, 13-15
- transparency issues, 13
- tribunal independence, 8, 11-12

W

without prejudice, defined, 242
workers, defined, 231
workplace law, 230
Workplace Safety and Insurance Appeal Tribunal
- case law, 247-51
- commencing appeal, 241
- confirmation of appeal, 241
- decisions, 244-46
- described, 234
- expert evidence, 244
- hearing de novo, 243
- history of, 234
- jurisdiction of, 235
- mediation, 242
- oral hearing, 243
- Practice Direction and Guidelines, 237
- pre-hearing, 243
- privative clause in WSIA, 246
- reconsiderations, 244-46
- without prejudice, 242
- WSIAT Medical Discussion Papers, 237

Workplace Safety and Insurance Board
- administration and adjudication by, 232
- appeal of decision, 233-34
- appeals, *see* Workplace Safety and Insurance Appeal Tribunal
- benefits and services
  - health care, 238
  - independent allowance, 239
  - loss of earnings, 238
  - non-economic loss, 238
  - personal care allowance, 239
  - qualifying for, 231
  - quantum of, 233
  - survivor benefits, 240
  - work reintegration and transition, 239
- coverage, 231
- employers, classification of, 231
- generally, 230
- history of, 230
- jurisdiction of, 231
- return-to-work plan, 233
- right to sue, 235
- work-transition plan, 233
- workers, defined, 231
- workers' compensation, 230

Workplace Safety and Insurance Act, 1997, 230
recent amendments to, 236
WSIB Operational Policy Manual, 237
work-transition plan, defined, 233
Writ of Possession, defined, 64

Z

zoning by-laws, defined, 116

CREDITS

Chapter 2

Opening quotation: Permission to reproduce content from Canada's Human Rights History website www.HistoryOfRights.ca.

Quotation (page 34, "The Code identifies…"): © Queen's Printer for Ontario, 2015.

Quotation (page 38, "When initiating…"): © Queen's Printer for Ontario, 2015.

Chapter 3

Table 3.2: © Queen's Printer for Ontario, 2015. http://www.sjto.gov.on.ca/ltb/filing-and-fees

Chapter 4

Form 1 Instructions for Filing an Appeal and Form 2 Application for Reconsideration: © Queen's Printer for Ontario, 2017

Chapter 9

Quotation (page 200, "The Procedural Guide is an all-in-one document that offers guidance for any type of application …"): © Queen's Printer for Ontario, 2003.

Quotation (page 202, "Consultations are presided over by the vice-chair, or by a panel …"): © Queen's Printer for Ontario, 2003

Quotation (page 203, "There is also an Information Bulletin 19 – Requests for Reconsideration …"): © Queen's Printer for Ontario, 2003.

Quotation (page 203, "The Information Bulletin also highlights …"): © Queen's Printer for Ontario, 2003.

Appendix 9.1, Form A-1, Application for Certification: Labour Relations Act, © Queen's Printer for Ontario, 2014.

Appendix 9.2, Form A-14, Application for Interim Order: Labour Relations Act, © Queen's Printer for Ontario, 2014.

Chapter 12

Quotation (page 289, Jordan's Principle): Government of Canada, Department of Indigenous and Northern Affairs Canada,"Definition of Jordan's Principle from the Canadian Human Rights Tribunal," 14 May 2018, online: https://www.canada.ca/en/indigenous-services-canada/services/jordans-principle/definition-jordans-principle-canadian-human-rightstribunal.html.